Visual Genders
Visual Histories

A Special Issue of *Gender & History*

EDITED BY
PATRICIA HAYES

Blackwell
Publishing

© 2006 by Blackwell Publishing Ltd

First published as a special issue of 'Gender & History'

BLACKWELL PUBLISHING
350 Main Street, Malden, MA 02148-5020, USA
9600 Garsington Road, Oxford OX4 2DQ, UK
550 Swanston Street, Carlton, Victoria 3053, Australia

The right of Patricia Hayes to be identified as the Author of the Editorial Material in this Work has been asserted in accordance with the UK Copyright, Designs, and Patents Act 1988.

All rights reserved. No part of this publication may be reproduced, stored in a retrieval system, or transmitted, in any form or by any means, electronic, mechanical, photocopying, recording or otherwise, except as permitted by the UK Copyright, Designs, and Patents Act 1988, without the prior permission of the publisher.

First published 2006 by Blackwell Publishing Ltd

Library of Congress Cataloging-in-Publication Data has been applied for

ISBN 1-4051-4665-6 (paperback)
ISBN 13: 978-1-4051-4665-4

A catalogue record for this title is available from the British Library

Set in 10.5/12.5pt Times NR Monotype
by Graphicraft Limited, Hong Kong
Printed and bound in the United Kingdom
by TJ International, Padstow, Cornwall

The publisher's policy is to use permanent paper from mills that operate a sustainable forestry policy, and which has been manufactured from pulp processed using acid-free and elementary chlorine-free practices. Furthermore, the publisher ensures that the text paper and cover board used have met acceptable environmental accreditation standards.

For further information on
Blackwell Publishing, visit our website:
www.blackwellpublishing.com

CONTENTS

Notes on Contributors vii

Introduction

1 Introduction: Visual Genders
PATRICIA HAYES 1

Documenting

2 Does Gender Matter? Filmic Representations of the Liberated Nazi Concentration Camps, 1945–46
ULRIKE WECKEL 20

3 Images of Virtuous Women: Morality, Gender and Power in Argentina between the World Wars
MARÍA FERNANDA LORENZO, ANA LÍA REY and CECILIA TOSSOUNIAN 49

4 The General View and Beyond: From Slum-yard to Township in Ellen Hellmann's Photographs of Women and the African Familial in the 1930s
MARIJKE DU TOIT 75

5 Racialising the Virile Body: Eadweard Muybridge's Locomotion Studies 1883–1887
ELSPETH H. BROWN 109

Trafficking

6 History, Memory and Trauma in Photography of the *Tondues*: Visuality of the Vichy Past through the Silent Image of Women
ALISON M. MOORE 139

7 A Glance into the Camera: Gendered Visions of Historical Photographs in Kaoko (North-Western Namibia)
LORENA RIZZO 164

8 Decoration and Desire in the Watts Chapel, Compton:
   Narratives of Gender, Class and Colonialism
   ELAINE CHEASLEY PATERSON   196

Experimenting

9 Faces and Bodies: Gendered Modernity and Fashion
   Photography in Tehran
   ALEC H. BALASESCU   219

10 Arne Svenson's Queer Taxonomy
   ELIZABETH C. BIRDSALL   251

11 The Temperance Temple and Architectural Representation
   in Late-Nineteenth-Century Chicago
   PAULA YOUNG LEE   275

12 There's Something about Mary Wigman: The Woman
   Dancer as Subject in German Expressionist Art
   SUSAN LAIKIN FUNKENSTEIN   308

   Index   342

NOTES ON CONTRIBUTORS

Alexandru Balasescu holds a DEA in ethnology from the Université Lumière, Lyon 2, and a PhD in Anthropology from the University of California, Irvine (September 2004). After teaching at the University of California centre in Paris, and at the American University in Paris, Alexandru Balasescu is now BA Fashion Programme Leader at the Royal University for Women in Bahrain.

Elizabeth C. Birdsall is a PhD student in art history at the University of Virginia's McIntire Department of Art. She works primarily on the history of photography and is a former director of the SK Josefsberg Gallery in Portland, Oregon.

Elspeth H. Brown is an Associate Professor at the University of Toronto Centre for Visual and Media Culture. She is the author of *The Corporate Eye: Photography and the Rationalization of American Culture, 1884–1929* (Johns Hopkins University Press, 2005). Her current research on Eadweard Muybridge forms part of a larger research project on the history of commercial modelling in the United States.

Alison M. Moore is postdoctoral research fellow at the Centre for the History of European Discourses, University of Queensland. She has lectured in French at Wollongong University and in the Department of History at the University of Sydney. She has published articles on the history of sexuality in France and Europe and is currently finishing a book manuscript called *Sexualised Memories of World War Two*. Her ongoing project is about the history of attitudes to excretion in modern Europe.

Marijke du Toit lectures in Historical Studies at the University of KwaZulu-Natal, Durban, South Africa. She has published papers in the field of gender and nationalism, including 'Framing Volksmoeders: The Politics of Female Afrikaner Nationalists, 1904–c.1930', in Paola Bacchetta and Margaret Power (eds), *Right-wing Women: From Conservatives to Extremists Around the World* (New York and London: Routledge, 2002). Her recent research is on the early twentieth-century visual economy in South Africa and includes 'Blank Verbeeld, or the Incredible Whiteness of Being: Amateur Photography and Afrikaner Nationalist Historical Narrative', *Kronos* (2001). She also works with social documentary photographer Jenny Gordon as co-director of the Durban South Photography project, which combines research into popular local visual cultures with the production of documentary photography

Patricia Hayes studied in Zimbabwe and the UK, and has worked at the University of the Western Cape since 1995. She teaches African history, gender history and visual history. Jointly edited publications include *Namibia under South African Rule, The Colonising Camera: Photographs in the Making of Namibian History* and *Deep* hiStories*: Gender & Colonialism in Southern Africa*. She is currently investigating photographic practices in recent southern African history.

Susan Laikin Funkenstein is an Assistant Professor of Art History at the University of Wisconsin-Parkside. She researches depictions of dancers in Weimar German visual culture and has published on Otto Dix and dance in *German Studies Review* and *Woman's Art Journal*. In 2005–6 she will be a UW-System Fellow at the Center for 21st Century Studies at UW-Milwaukee.

Paula Lee holds a doctorate in architectural history from the University of Chicago. Her essays on the architecture of display have appeared in the *Art Bulletin, Journal of the Society of Architectural Historians, Journal of Architecture* and elsewhere. Her research has been supported by numerous grants, including fellowships from the National Endowment for the Humanities and the Graham Foundation for Advanced Studies in the Fine Arts. She is the editor of an interdisciplinary collection of papers on nineteenth-century slaughterhouses (*Making Meat: Animal Slaughter and Modern Sensibilities*, forthcoming) and is completing a socio-spatial study of animal exhibition in nineteenth-century Paris.

María Fernanda Lorenzo is Professor of History at the University of Buenos Aires. She is a researcher in the project *Archivo Palabras e Imágenes de Mujeres* (APIM, Women Words and Images Archive Project), Instituto Interdisciplinario de Estudios de Género (IIEGE, Interdisciplinary Gender Studies Institute) at the University of Buenos Aires.

Elaine Cheasley Paterson is Assistant Professor of Craft and Decorative Art History at Concordia University, Montreal, Canada. Her current research concerns women's cultural philanthropy in late nineteenth-century British, Irish and Canadian home arts and industries. She is the author of 'Crafting a National Identity: The Dun Emer Guild, 1902–1908' in *The Irish Revival Reappraised* (Dublin: Four Courts Press, 2004), and is co-curating the exhibition *Re-Crafting Tradition* at the Musée des maîtres et artisans du Québec (January–March 2006).

Ana Lía Rey is Professor of History and Researcher in the Programa de Estudios de Historia Económica y Social Argentina (PEHESA, Argentine Economic and Social History Studies Program) at the University of Buenos Aires. She is a researcher in the project *Archivo Palabras e Imáagenes de Mujeres* (APIM, Women Words and Images Archive Project), Instituto Interdisciplinario de Estudios de Género (IIEGE, Interdisciplinary Gender Studies Institute) at the University of Buenos Aires.

Lorena Rizzo is assistant in the History Department, University of Zurich. She is at work on a PhD project at the University of Basel on the history of Kaoko, North Western Namibia, in the first half of the twentieth century. She is also a participant, with Patrick Harries, Patricia Hayes and Giorgio Miescher, in a research project titled 'The Borders of Empire – New Perspectives on Southern African Frontiers and Border Sites'. Her many publications in German, Italian and English include 'N. J. van Warmelo: Anthropology and the Making of a Reserve' in Giorgio Miescher and Dag Henrichsen (eds), *New Notes on Kaoko: The Northern Kunene Region (Namibia) in Texts and Photographs* (Basel: Basler Afrika Bibliographien, 2000).

Cecilia Tossounian is working on a doctorate entitled: 'Feminine Organisations, "Women's Issues", and the Emergence of a Social State: Buenos Aires in the Years between the Wars', at the University of San Andrés. She is a researcher in the project *Archivo Palabras e Imágenes de Mujeres* (APIM, Women Words and Images Archive Project), Instituto Interdisciplinario de Estudios de Género (IIEGE, Interdisciplinary Gender Studies Institute) at the University of Buenos Aires.

Ulrike Weckel DPhil, is a historian affiliated with the European University Institute, Florence. Her current research project is entitled 'The Ambiguous Past: Cultural Representations of Nazism and Their Reception by Postwar Audiences'. Her many publications include *Zwischen Häuslichkeitund Öffentlichkeit: Die ersten deutschen Frauenzeitschriften im späten 18. Jahrhundert und ihr Publikum* (Tübingen: M. Niemeyer, 1998) and 'The *Mitläufer* in Two German Postwar Films: Representation and Critical Reception', *History& Memory* 15 (2003). She co-edited *'Bestien' und 'Befehlsempfänger': Frauen und Männer in NS-Prozessen nach 1945* (Göttingen: Vandenhoeck and Ruprecht, 2003) and *Zwischen Karriere und Verfolgung: Handlungsräume von Frauen im nationalsozialistischen Deutschland* (Frankfurt/Main and New York: Campus, 1997).

1 Introduction: Visual Genders
Patricia Hayes

I

The photograph on the cover of this book was taken in the early 1960s by Daniel Morolong, at an East London beach in South Africa. Morolong was a press photographer covering popular leisure and social events in the city during the period before apartheid policies led to the forced removal of these residents to Mdantsane, a township later incorporated into the Ciskei bantustan. In the photograph, Morolong's mother and her two sisters are seated on the rocks by the sea. Aesthetically the image slides between two worlds, that of the black and white documentary photograph and that of the family seaside snap. Historically it also slides between a past and present denoting the inclusion and exclusion of African people in urban South Africa. On the right, the indeterminate space of the sea suggests a further slide, opening up another thinking space and rescuing the photograph from a single or dual history and genre. This openness is accentuated by the dispersed gazes of the three women, with the first looking back at the camera and the others at different points of the horizon, their bodies gradually inclining towards the sea. The photograph formed part of Morolong's extensive body of work, which has only recently drawn the attention of historians.[1] Then in 2004, a remarkable thing happened. The photograph was printed on a large conference poster. When numerous copies of it were pasted up around a busy South African university campus, it disappeared. More copies were put up, only to disappear again very quickly. The repeated theft of the image, which happened largely in silence, suggested some kind of connection. It revealed a relationship. It was not vandalism, but appropriation. The image belonged to the category of 'the ones that are wanted'.[2]

In '*Photos of the Gods*', Chris Pinney proposes that 'a new kind of history needs to be written' against a backdrop of practices that privilege precisely what we have outlined above: 'the power of the image and visually intense encounters'.[3] In arguing for a visual history, he suggests that pictures have a different story to tell from words. What if we allowed them to do so, at least partly, on their own terms? Is it possible, Pinney asks, to 'envisage history as in part determined by struggles occurring at the level of the visual?'. Not so much a history of the visual, but a history made by visuals?[4]

In a way there is nothing new about this proposal, given that certain disciplines have long dealt with visuality. David Freedberg challenged art history long ago to shift away from a history of art towards something else, namely 'the relations between images and people in history'.[5] This converges with the push to study audience reception, advocated strongly by race and gender critiques of art history. These critiques questioned art history's construction of an 'emotionally detached, objectively accurate vision' of the (masculinist) connoisseur or trained expert and of the adherence to theories of innate aesthetic value.[6] New scholarship extends the call for the study of reception to mediation, transmission, circulation, to the inter-textual or inter-ocular receptivities and creativities that are generated in the course of this interaction, and to their effects on viewers and agency. But central to it all is the need, in social, historical and political analysis, to 'reflect on the significance of seeing itself'.[7] According to W. J. T. Mitchell, this involves the effort to 'overcome the veil of familiarity and self-evidence that surrounds the experience of seeing, and to turn it into a problem for analysis, a mystery to be unraveled'.[8]

Historians and other scholars have been waking up to the unacknowledged visual dimensions of gender.[9] The phrase 'unacknowledged visuality' comes from Alison Moore's study of the *tondues* images in liberation France, included in this volume, where photographs of women scapegoated for collusion with Germans during the Occupation keep coming back to the surface. She argues that it is precisely within this unacknowledged visuality that gender features, voicelessly and implicitly. Indeed, the processes through which *gender* history is made by visuals is the direct concern of this work.

The explicit visual focus of this volume elicited the record-breaking number of responses from potential contributors to *Gender & History* Special Issue, on which this book is based. In bringing gender, history and visuality together, the range of abstracts submitted to the journal appears to suggest a new readiness to bring gender history within the scope of the recent interdisciplinary field of visual studies. But contributors are not drawn so much by the allure of visual culture *per se*.[10] Rather, we are witnessing a specific urgency about gender in relation to the visual or 'pictorial' turn that the disciplines are taking in a much broader sense.[11]

In his key article 'Showing Seeing', W. J. T. Mitchell argues that a common core of scholarly interest has emerged with regard to the visual, though methods and reading lists may vary widely across disciplines. It begins with the hypothesis that vision is culturally constructed, that it is 'learned and cultivated, not simply given by nature'. Vision has a history related (in ways yet to be determined) to 'the history of arts, technologies, media, and social practices of display and spectatorship'. It is 'deeply involved with human societies, with the ethics and politics, aesthetics, and epistemology of seeing and being seen'.[12] Moreover, there are different ways of seeing, different histories of vision – again, most of these genealogies are yet to be determined. We shall return to this point later.

In total, we might refer to the above as the social construction of vision. But Mitchell goes further, to propose that we think directly about the visual construction of the social.[13] In a sense, this volume takes its departure from that point, for the direction we are pushing now is gender. Thus we do not confine ourselves to the social or cultural construction of gender. Instead, if the visual can take us more deeply into the cultural and historical configurations of society, as it seems able to do, then we are beginning to ask new questions – across history – about the visual construction of gender.

II

Acknowledging the visual immediately poses a number of questions. To begin with, the terminology of gender scholarship is loaded with visual metaphors, especially around visibility. Some distinction needs to be made between visibility and visuality. The term visibility often conflates 'seeing' with audibility, which in turn implies a transcription into textuality. The question of power is implicit in these formulations. In older feminist historical discourses of the 'recovery' of lost histories, the oft-stated problem of the invisibility of women begins to take on a different slant when visuality itself becomes the central focus.[14] This helps us to move beyond the positivist mandate to 'make visible' as the panacea for all gender ills, because it questions *how things are made visible* and asks on what terms this takes place. We immediately engage in a problematic zone, for the act of 'making visible' can silence women further. Visibility does not necessarily mean 'voice', or empowerment. For example, how can notions of 'recovery' and 'visibility' work when it comes to the *burqah*? In certain societies, as Alec Balasescu's essay on Iran suggests, women's public visibility has functioned in inverse proportion to social mobility. To push uncritically for all-out visibility is perilous: at its extreme, compulsory visibility comes from a certain historical-cultural space and could be construed as a repressive and indeed an imperialist practice. There are contexts in which being invisible, unseen and even unknown have been and continue to be preferred options, giving scope and time to negotiate the difficult conditions of social and gendered existence.

In order to highlight the distinction between visibility itself, which is often used in an empirical sense, and visuality, which carries more discursive and rhetorical connotations, it is helpful to peel away the self-evidentiary language of seeing. There is something ironic in the fact that engaging with the visual demands a much greater precision with language itself, calling into question the appropriateness of visual metaphors in gender studies. In addition, when putting into language the frequently sensitive and power-laden issues around gender, race and class that emerge from visual material, we need to attend closely to what Michelle Rowley has called the ethics of articulation.[15] These ethics are connected with the more obvious problem of reproducing actual visual materials during research and publication, where great care must be taken to avoid replicating and re-circulating the power relations and gestures that went into their making. Contributors and editors have had to confront this problem directly, especially with regard to difficult photographic and film material of women during World War Two studied by Ulrike Weckel and Alison Moore in this volume, and Elspeth Brown's work on human locomotion. To historicise and problematise each frame is the method we have tried to sustain, acknowledging that neither can foreclose any debate about showing and seeing pictures for the reader-viewer.

In the essay about the Beneficent Society of Argentina in this volume, there is plainly a class politics involved in making visible those poor women selected for its 'Virtue Awards'. The authors depict society ladies poking their noses into working-class homes in Buenos Aires, their photographers making the 'popular classes hand their intimacy over'. In Iran, as Balasescu argues, the historical phase of unveiling under Reza Shah in the 1920s worked comprehensively to exclude working-class women from the public domain. The veil in fact facilitated women's mobility, their access to education and employment, which was disastrously curtailed with the increased forms of bodily visibility and changes in dress code introduced by the ostensibly modernising Shah.

Asking *how* things are made visible (or not) shifts 'gender' as an unmediated category of historical analysis to gender as a vehicle of specific representations. For historians of Africa, the study of nineteenth- and early twentieth-century photographic collections reveals the extent to which women were 'pushed into visibility' by the camera.[16] This is in striking contrast to the frequently stated problem of a lack of women's 'voice' to be found in the archive of texts. The African woman visually fills the frame, unlike the way she subsists on the edges in the official report.

In her very objectification she is constructed as a subject. If photographs are granted the status of 'record' and placed alongside textual documentation, it appears overwhelmingly that African women were seen and not heard. What then is this culture of visual documentation? Does it arise from the brutal simplification of photography? Were their stories too difficult? Or was it too cumbersome to produce the texts through a local male go-between? Were colonial photographers such as Heinz Roth in Namibia, featured in the essay by Lorena Rizzo, producing visual knowledge and therefore taken up with bodily appearances?[17] Photographing the latter – especially if it was 'thievish' as Rizzo suggests – may have required less mediation than a verbal relationship. In some cases the camera was invasive and immediate, effecting a gendered extraction.

As we broach the visual construction of gender, it often seems that sexualisation is the predictable lot of women. Yet Alison Moore's work on France during the Liberation shows it is not a simple matter. Frenchwomen accused of having relations with Occupation forces during World War Two were cast as the passive sexual recipients of 'German penetrative masculinity'. In a convulsive and compulsive sequence repeated in numerous French towns, there was a public spectacle of outing, shaving and shaming of these women in the street. An important ingredient seems to have been the presence of photographers. Significantly, Robert Capa's photograph includes the national flag in the frame. The phenomenon appeared to juxtapose an explosive and cathartic conjuncture of sexualisation (the feminisation of collaborative guilt) and desexualisation (the shearing of hair to remove the source of physical attraction). The symbolic mutilation of femininity offered a fast-track exorcism of the complicit humiliation and ambiguity concerning the German Occupation. But as Moore argues, the cultural and historical recurrence of the image of the *tondues* points to it being a traumatic fixed symptom of the Vichy syndrome which does not go away.

Moore's essay highlights what visuality brings to gender history as opposed to textualities alone. Its pathway is more immediate and affective, even visceral. The ambiguities of becoming or being made visible emerge particularly strongly in relation to sexuality and desire. Many of the essays work with this problem. It is notable for example that in Weimar Germany the dancer Mary Wigman, as interpreted by Susan Funkenstein in her essay, made spirituality visible rather than sexuality; that Argentine women written about by María Fernanda Lorenzo, Ana Lía Rey and Cecilia Tossounian likewise foregrounded respectability. Elizabeth Birdsall explores this troubling question in relation to queer sexuality in the exhibition *Faggots*, and concludes that without the text accompanying the photographed men, 'the simple question of visibility resists an answer'.

This Introduction has already touched on the existence of different histories of vision across the world. Gender is a cross-cultural issue, but so is seeing itself. There is an urgent need to address 'different ways of seeing'. This volume is intended as the first step in a longer and more sustained process,[18] given the importance of interrogating the alleged primacy and naturalisation of models of Western vision. Part of this relates to arguments that the eye tended to become privileged over other human senses;[19] that it became increasingly separated from the rest of the body, especially with the development of Cartesian perspectivalism and nineteenth-century industrial technology. Jonathan Crary for example speaks of the 'increasing abstraction of vision' in Western European history.[20] By contrast, a growing scholarship on India poses alternatives to this narrative of the disembodied, secularised eye. Pinney's work on popular Hindi visual production and consumption for example emphasises what he calls 'corpothetics', 'embodied, corporeal aesthetics'. The concept of *darshan*, whereby devotees experience 'seeing and being seen' in relation to the image of the deity, can be understood as the mobilisation of vision 'as part of a unified human sensorium'.[21] This is quite apart from Islamic visual cultures, which constitute a multitude of challenges to any notional Eurocentric model that historically privileges disembodied vision. We are also a very long way from understanding the histories of different ways of seeing on the African continent. In the making of this work, discussions have highlighted how any putative Eurocentric model should itself be provincialised and vernacularised into a thousand specific practices and histories.[22] Europeans may have invented the gun and the camera, but they have had little hope of monopolising the deployment and proliferation of either technology ever since. Nor should dominant Euro-American interpretations dictate what norm global photographic artefacts should be read against, though the tendency remains very strong.

This volume in fact offers a number of peculiar provincialities when it comes to 'Western' visual histories. In a sense these episodes highlight Walter Benjamin's concern with the 'central problematic of the effect of industrial production on traditional cultural forms'.[23] Eadweard Muybridge's photographs of human locomotion in Elspeth Brown's essay show how technology penetrated highly particular recesses of cultural-scientific practice in the United States. This concerted attempt to freeze motion and demonstrate what the eye could not see was all in the cause of a higher form of masculinity. At one level the University of Pennsylvania case is a welcome addition to the vast research on physical and racial typologising that normally focuses on colonial territories (to which Marijke du Toit's essay briefly alludes), for in case we had forgotten about Hillary Rodham Clinton's experience with posture photographs at Wellesley.[24] Brown reminds us that those entering elite universities were also targeted in the USA. The dissemination of photographic methods of racial, gendered and ethnographic research across the globe are therefore not so much evidence of a single dominant source from which everything emanates, but rather signs of dispersed trafficking in the visual technologies of control that were being opened up internally and externally through specific scientific projects and collaborations.

In thinking about cross-cultural ways of seeing, and reiterating Mitchell's point that histories of vision are related to 'arts, technologies, media' and the social practices around these and other forms of display,[25] it is striking how many contributions here have honed in on photography, though we do include here film, dance, decorative arts, architecture and more. It has been a criticism of visual studies that it tends to focus on a very small subset, 'popular Western images from the invention of photography, but mostly objects of mass culture of the last 50 or so years',[26] the so-called visual media like television, film, video and the Internet. Mitchell calls this the 'fallacy of technical modernity', and rightly disputes the assumption of a Western monopoly of visuality or the pictorial turn, specific to the rise of new media technologies. He argues for a 'study of all the social practices of human visuality, and not confined to modernity or the West'.[27] Thus there should also be space for the more embodied, haptic or devotional kinds of seeing rooted in earlier histories of vision in the so-called West, let alone everywhere else.

The essays here do allow for the global flows and local dynamics of the photographic medium, its malleability and slipperiness, its capacity for alleged 'truth-telling' as well as audience 'misrecognition' and recoding.[28] They also explore its contagious effects on other visual and textual media, in closely historicised ways. Such bleeding between genres, media and visualities has already been highlighted elsewhere, for example in Nancy Rose Hunt's work on comics and painting in the Congo, and more generally in the useful collection entitled *Images and Empires*.[29] But while this volume (like so many others) concentrates on late nineteenth- and twentieth-century visual cultures and histories, its main contribution lies in making gender the centrepiece of its writing on the visual.

III

In order to allow the media and their gender issues to speak to each other more productively, we have arranged the papers on visual genders under three subheadings: documenting, trafficking and experimenting. These subheadings highlight the ongoing nature and open-endedness of visual meaning and movement. While they allude to three powerful characteristics in visual representation, namely the positivist, the mobile and the subversive, the sections are by no means self-contained.

Documenting

The idea of documentary with its evidentiary underpinnings is a useful starting point, given the associations with empirical observation, recording of existing phenomena, realist discourses, sobriety, seriousness and truth-telling. Scholars have highlighted its Latin root in the verb *docere*, to teach, which was then transposed to legal settings and took on the persuasiveness of proof. The notion of a documentary genre emerged in the 1920s in the specific context of film,[30] where the proliferation and growing complexity of visual fields and specialisations meant it was taken up more broadly.

What does the notion of documentary conceal, and even more so, what does it congeal? In the history of photography and film, modes of empirical documentation can have repressive functions, though they may also 'spring leaks', in part as a result of their 'messy contingencies'.[31] This section deals mainly with photography, but begins appropriately with film. Bill Nichols speaks of film's ability to 'document pre-existing phenomena' and the 'uncanny capacity of the photographic image (and later of the recorded soundtrack) to generate precise replicas of certain aspects of their source material'. He adds that 'these modes rely heavily on the indexical quality of the photographic image'.[32] The 'index' here refers to the physical connection between photograph and subject, what Roland Barthes calls the 'certificate of presence'.[33] In the case of film, this indexicality creates trust in the audience, helping to suspend doubt, 'rendering an *impression* of reality, and hence truthfulness'. This impression does not necessarily 'guarantee full-blown authenticity in every case', though it fulfils the needs of rhetoric.[34]

In Ulrike Weckel's essay on documentary film, the footage of conditions in concentration camps was framed and shaped explicitly as visual evidence. This was aimed at two audiences: Allied and German. The 'visual confrontation' with evidence of genocide and inhuman treatment of prisoners was intended to justify the losses and sacrifices made by the allied powers, but also to force Germans themselves to look. Weckel reveals that because of the prioritisation given to filmic evidence by the Allies on the Western Front and the chaos surrounding the Western camps as opposed to the eastern camps, a few select places came to symbolise the Nazi genocide, 'which had largely been carried out elsewhere and by other means'. She concludes that certain scenes in the finished films – such as the arrival of the liberators with ceremonial soundtrack – must have been recreations, thus unsettling their relationship to 'the real'.

More powerfully, the article reveals the immense difficulties of seeing itself. Margaret Bourke White recalled having to 'work with a veil over my mind' as she photographed. Witnesses confronting the human remains and survivors of the extermination and labour camps often expressed the view that what they saw, even on film, defied all understanding. Affect was difficult, cognition even more so. Weckel here touches on the troubling way that well-intentioned documentation might overlap with voyeurism. Her central question is whether gender matters; she charts the processes of stripping down of gender markers in the camps through the 'radical eradication of individuality and intimacy', including the execution of pregnant women and mothers with small children, the shaving of women's heads, the loss of clothing and the general extreme emaciation, so that arriving allied forces often found it difficult to distinguish men and women amidst these seemingly genderless beings. Weckel discusses gestures within the camps towards recovery of femininity, and the problematic, gendered filmic and textual responses by male cameramen.

The chapter by María Fernanda Lorenzo, Ana Lía Rey and Cecilia Tossounian concerns the establishment of the Virtue Prizes for poor women in Argentina at a time of threatening social change in the interwar years. Part of the visual construction of these working-class women in Argentina was to portray them covered in long dark coats, a presence in which the body itself is diminished, thus making respectability visible, rather than sexuality. At the annual public performance, which was recorded photographically, they were positioned strategically within a hierarchical class panorama, in a setting that was ostensibly secular but figuratively very liturgical, resembling a 'polyphonic choir'. Close reading of the photographs here suggests how the Virtue prize-winners were usually represented through the 'long shot', not featured at centre stage. Even as they were brought into the public view, the positionings and tonalities of their subordination were evident. The ceremony and its photography presented the prize-winners as women who would not challenge the social and gender order. The authors liken the visual arrangement to a female family tree with the elite society ladies posing as the 'lineage heads'. This value system however was turned on its head by popular theatre in Buenos Aires. The authors conclude the essay with the case of a *sainete* (play) which presented two sisters, one 'virtuous' and eligible for an award, the other a prostitute financially supporting her family. The play slyly argues that the latter represents genuine self-denying virtue; she is in fact mistakenly addressed by the ladies as involved in charity. The parody of the official award process – with accompanying photo ceremony – deconstructs the original 'document' as it were, suggesting how the event itself was 'unnatural', choreographed and self-legitimising.

Ellen Hellmann's photographs, featured in the essay by Marijke du Toit, also deal with 'the poor', in this case urban African women in the city of Johannesburg. Hellmann likewise inscribed women into respectability, though Du Toit points out that many women survived in the alcohol-based economy of beer-brewing. The article is an exploration of a particular moment in South African documentary photography in the 1930s, where it intersected with the emergence of social anthropology as a discipline and a new focus on the urban. Photographic theorists such as Abigail Solomon-Godeau have pointed to the consistent purpose of documentary photography in seeking to trigger social change,[35] to 'reconfigure its referent';[36] Hellmann's liberal networks outside the academy would support this argument. As in several other contributions, however, the woman photographer or artist occupied a privileged social position, in Hellmann's case inflected with both class and race. Not all of Hellmann's 'visual note-taking' translated into publication. Du Toit discusses both published and unpublished work in detail, exploring their possibilities as historical documents. An explicit methodological question she raises is how we can write photographs into feminist history.

The 'general view' signifies not only the encapsulation of the environment, thus shifting anthropology away from its prior emphasis on racial typologies and the body, but also speaks to the theoretical notion of photographic excess. Pinney refers to this as the 'ineradicable surfeit'. The alleged inability of the camera lens to discriminate, he argues, 'will ensure a substrate or margin of excess, a subversive code present in every photographic image that makes it open and available to other readings and uses'.[37] These are the opportunities to escape predictable or generic readings, with implications not only for gender but for revisiting the social history of urban South Africa more generally.

Attention shifts from the environment in which people function, to the empirical edifice of the body in the essay by Elspeth Brown. As mentioned earlier, this contribution examines the work of Eadweard Muybridge at the University of Pennsylvania, a project deeply embedded in late-nineteenth-century race and gender politics. The fascination with human movement as a means of indexing racial types drew Muybridge and his photography into a complex scientific institutional landscape. Brown explores the project of mapping somatic differences and pathologies through the conjunction of multiple cameras and freezing bodily action through separate frames. White male students destined to become leading professionals were the object of concern about 'feeble bodies' and 'enervation'. The photographic 'grid' in this institutional space highlighted the gendered nature of ideas about racial progress. Brown also alludes to the important visual correspondences between Muybridge's photographic sequences and filmic narrative, with film history having claimed the photographer as a foundational figure.

Trafficking

The evidentiary and often repressive functions of photography in particular have a fixing, or immobilising, effect. In relation to gender this is especially germane. But if there is a question of visibility affecting mobility, there is equally a set of questions around the mobility of visuality itself: through reproducibility, transportability and circulation. These relate to how pictures or visual motifs are set in motion – they become unfixed – and lead to wider reactions, which often translate into further interpretations within the genre or medium, more pictures in different media, texts that describe the pictorial, and in some cases, actions that are highly visible. Mitsuhiro Yoshimoto uses the term 'intertextual fermentation' in the context of film; Pinney speaks suggestively of 'inter-ocularities'.[38] Others rightly point out that images may resurface across both texts and visuals, with the latter very broadly defined. Here we refer to this simply as trafficking. The essays explore traffic across public spectacle, photography, the decorative arts and crafts and more.

In Alison Moore's article, the spectacle and performance of the shaming of the *tondues*, followed by its visual representation, presented French publics (and historians) after the Liberation with both the event (out in the street) and its simulacrum (in the photograph). While the traffic or circulation of photographs of *tondues* in relation to actual episodes is not the central issue here, the essay raises questions of how visibility and visuality work in conjunction. It brings to mind the specular relationship between the public act of lynching and the production and circulation of postcards in the United States, which was a distinctive but also deeply gendered and visual phenomenon.[39] In Moore's essay, the women who became *tondues* came to stand in for the French nation. As argued earlier, the assertion of blame, and its sexualisation and feminisation, provided an outlet for the ambivalent sentiments of a population who had for years lived with its occupiers. Moore's emphasis on the unacknowledged visuality in the 'traumatic fixing' of the *tondues* offers a powerful new route into the Vichy syndrome and questions the way recent historiography treats the issue.

Lorena Rizzo's contribution follows expeditionary photographs of Kaoko out of the archive and back into local circulation in northern Namibia, in the same places where they were taken over fifty years earlier in 1951. The author refers to the state of the normal photographic archive or collection as decontextualised, unsystematic and ephemeral. Certain archival constraints, such as the separation between photographs and accompanying documents, can be overcome through reconnection with local subjects. Rizzo brings a number of concepts related to visuality to bear on a marginal colonial history, where German control had given way to South African mandatory rule after World War One. She analyses the practice of chiefly portraiture as a symptom of the successful occupation of 'the visual field', where insignia and status were mobilised and enhanced through photographs. The expedition photographer Heinz Roth could not resist the popular settler trope of the empty land, but the involvement of museums in the organisation of this expedition signalled a new visual economy linked to colonial consumption outside the region. Masculinities feature in what Rizzo calls the parallel economy of guns and cameras, and we have already alluded to the photography of African women in this extractive economy. Rizzo also highlights what she calls the inter-visualities between colonial images, including paintings and maps, which anchor Roth in a genealogical line. While repetitious and generic photographs worked to reduce the individuality of African subjects, the post-colonial encounter with Kaoko residents re-opened identifications, as well as long-standing debates over the social mobility of women.

The reference to colonialism continues in Elaine Cheasley Paterson's article, where 'trafficking' encompasses Celtic, Asian and North African design motifs that were incorporated into the Watts Mortuary Chapel in Surrey. Inspired by the Home Arts Movement started by women in late-nineteenth-century Britain, Mary Seton Watts pushed the goal of self-realisation for women through arts and crafts. With the inclusion of local craft training and work on the chapel across social class, she attempted to reshape the 'interior and exterior landscapes' of workers through the transformative effects of art. The essay explores the divide between the masculinised (public) art and feminised (domestic) craft worlds of the time, and the ways in which Seton Watts sometimes blurred the boundaries. Born in India, raised in Scotland, then travelling in Egypt, Greece and Turkey with her artist husband on honeymoon, Seton Watts recorded decorative details which were later incorporated or 'translated' into the chapel and its design objects. While grounded in colonial assumptions and drawing on a 'pervasive orientalism', Paterson argues that Seton Watts intended the chapel as a site of symbolic interchange linking different cultures. This of course takes on new dimensions and translations in a contemporary context of global tourism.

Experimenting

The essays here focus on strategies to unsettle or challenge dominant visual discourses and expectations around gender. We have already touched on the difficult relationship between mobility and visibility in Iran's history, but Balasescu's work also offers insight into wider debates on multiple or vernacular modernities. From the 1920s it seems that the lines of modernisation did not necessarily go with new secular dress for men, let alone women. Behaviour, body mobility and gestures are incorporated into the analysis of social compliance and experimentation across public and private domains, into those contemporary interstitial spaces where fashion photography can be found. This rather fragmented field is the site of much contest, Balasescu argues, because of its immediate reference to 'modernity'. The lack of physical movement and use of headscarves in acceptable fashion photography of women leads one photographer in Tehran to complain, for example, of the difficulty in visually constructing femininity, but other photographers do not necessarily agree. A crucial feature of this experimentation with fashion photography and gendered subjectivities is the way it is facilitated by the vibrant film industry and its public posters, which generate considerable visual traffic 'from the screen to everyday life'.

Elizabeth Birdsall's analysis of Arne Svenson's exhibition entitled *Faggots* studies the artist's adoption of a very dense tradition of documentation, the serial or archival method of photographic recording. Svenson uses an 'archival aesthetic', reminiscent of nineteenth century policing and pathologising methods in the tradition of Alphonse Bertillon and Francis Galton.[40] The implicit references to visual classification, archival method, repetitive photographic technique and near-uniformity also evoke the Muybridge *oeuvre*. Svenson is quoted as saying that he photographs taxonomically in order to understand that which is otherwise opaque. The point is to pose questions about what can be revealed about a person photographically. The exhibition unsettles taxonomic practices by their very deployment, through repetitious portraits of different men in an identical setting. Birdsall calls it 'creative documentation', the effect one of 'riffed taxonomy'. By repositioning this body of work within the art gallery, Svenson distances the exhibition from its origins in the 'social sciences'. As elsewhere, we find troubling consequences for the visibility of sexuality. According to Birdsall, this makes Svenson's subjects a possible target for homophobia, even as it means that the 'desiring eye knows where to look'.

The Women's Temperance Temple in Chicago was a unique effort by a sector of the American women's association to appropriate the medium of architecture and put it to work for a bigger cause. The feminisation of public space through urging middle-class women to go out and rescue drunken men in the streets was eclipsed by this ambition to erect a skyscraper in the 1890s, with funds raised by the Women's Temperance Movement. Paula Lee's article focuses on the critical reception of the building and the politics of architectural representation, rather than the ultimate failure of the experiment. According to Lee, the Temple represented a 'site of convergence' that could transform business into a worthy, even spiritual practice. Aesthetic properties were argued to give rise to social responsibility. Briefly the tallest building in the world, the technologically advanced skyscraper offered a prominent urban location, increased verticality, and more light, which was integral to the architectural 'vernacular of capitalism'. The increased interior space was an environment where 'quiet, repetitive work could operate as a bourgeois expression of virtue'. But as Lee puts it, wealth remained 'coded through gender', and the heyday of this skyscraper founded and funded by women was short-lived. The Temple was soon outstripped, and within forty years, demolished.

The volume ends fittingly with dance, and the expressionist performance and choreography of Mary Wigman in Weimar Germany (1918–33). According to Susan Laikin Funkenstein, the artist challenged the seemingly fixed dynamics of spectatorship. Wigman's use of African masks complicated the audience's gaze and allowed her to 'stare back'. The incorporation of African and Asian visual forms in her dance did not lead to exotic or erotic gestures and movement. Wigman in fact avoided the objectification and sexualisation of the female body by a variety of strategies, including the obscuring of physical outlines. Her dance work became the subject of two male painters, Emil Nolde and Ernest Ludwig Kirchner, who in their specific ways both reduced the totality of Wigman's art. Movement in particular was lost on the canvas or paper. But in the specific visualisations of the body represented through dance, Wigman emphasised spirituality, individuality and androgyny, producing a highly distinctive choreography of gender.

IV

The challenge, as Patricia Mohamed has argued from the perspective of the Caribbean, is to reach the point where research on the visual can give us new theoretical insights into gender.[41] Some of the historical routes taken by 'visual genders' have been mapped out by Griselda

Pollock, writing about the period the 1970s to the present: 'Feminist cultural theories of the image have moved along a trajectory from an initial denunciation of stereotyped images of women to a more exacting assessment of the productive role of representation in the construction of subjectivity, femininity, and sexuality'.[42] The problematic that Pollock identifies around 'images of women' results in a greater emphasis on process over product, and reminds us that 'images are densely rhetorical products of material, social and aesthetic practices'.[43] Many of the current articles here follow Pollock's recommendation for 'careful analysis of the specific constructions' of the gendered body, 'as well as of specific modes and sites of representation and discussion of address and the imagined spectator'.[44]

If we draw out some of the recurrent issues emerging from this volume however, something very striking about movement and mobility materialises in relation to a number of chapters. This something ties in with travel, urban life, colonialism and modernities. Zones of experimentation and desire exist in the dialectic and tension between visibility and invisibility. A double possibility exists of fixing and unfixing. The terms on which subjects move between visibility and invisibility relate directly not only to mobility, but to power. This volume suggests there are several levels to this relation between seeing and power, which brings us back to the subtle but important distinction between the visible and the visual. Visibility implies that one can be seen, that there is an empirical presence. But visuality is the condition of being mediated specifically through sight, which does something specific as opposed to other kinds of mediation. It lends itself to certain rhetorical effects and genealogies which can be very persuasive over time. Several essays here suggest that making women visible, as in the ethnographic photograph from the Kaoko, the framing of Virtuous Poor women in Buenos Aires, or the standard female fashion photo in present-day Tehran, may have immobilising effects. These examples point to complex dynamics around both the attempts to control mobility, and to escape that control. Visuality then flickers across these scenarios, opening endless new possibilities through the malleability, mobility and inter-visual contagion of image forms themselves.

This brings me back to the photo on the cover. For South Africa, in terms of images that have made their way into the public domain, Morolong's photograph is very unusual.[45] The photographs discussed by Marijke du Toit in this volume come closer to the generality of official archives on black women. The conviviality and companionship, the way the women comfortably inhabit this leisure space, are portrayals not often seen from that era. But there is a tension, a tautness, about this photograph of Morolong's mother and her sisters at the beach. Not only are they caught between the splintering genres of the documentary that is evidential and the family shot that is personal, but they occupy a series of further liminalities. One is the beach, the boundary between elements. Beaches are made of 'sensible things, raucous laughter' and intimacies, as Elizabeth Edwards remarks.[46] In hindsight these women were on the brink of losing access to these spaces through forced removals from East London. The photograph has the capacity to pull us into their history. On the rocks next to the waves, they are on the verge of being pushed out of their homes and out of urban visibility in apartheid South Africa. Despite the transfixed pleasures of the shot, their fate is mutable, like photographic meaning. In their case, they are poised on the knife-edge of history; in the harsh terms dealt out by apartheid, facing a loss of modernity.

But four decades later, when they appear on posters in a post-apartheid university, Nomakhosazana Morolong and her sisters immediately become 'the ones that are wanted'. With their quality of familiarity, and a lost feminine modernity spreading into the bigger horizon of the sea, they find their way on to many student walls. If not themselves, their image is finally taken home.

Figure 1: 'Sunday Beach Outing'. Mrs Morolong and her sisters. From left to right, Nomakhosazana, Lulu and Nompueuko Morolong. Eastern Beach, East London. Photo by Daniel Morolong. Source: Fort Hare Institute of Social and Economic Research, University of Fort Hare, East London, South Africa.

Notes

This book is the product of many collaborations. The Editor thanks Nancy Rose Hunt and Helmut Puff of the journal *Gender & History* in Michigan for their unmatched intellectual and editorial support, Marti Lybeck for dedicated reading and correspondence and Michele Mitchell and Erik Huneke for their contributions in the final stages. Karen Adler also gave crucial input. More widely, the participants at the International Workshop on Gender & Visuality in Cape Town in August 2004 and at the Training Workshop on Visual Sources as Alternative Histories in Maputo in September 2004, helped to open and shape ideas in ways they cannot imagine. Colleagues and students working in visual and public history at the University of the Western Cape provided a steady source of critique and stimulation. Lastly, the Editor thanks all contributors, readers and producers of images (and their archives or copyright-holders) who made this volume possible.

1. A selection of Daniel Morolong's work was curated for exhibition by Gary Minkley in East London in July 2003. The collection is now located at the Fort Hare Institute for Social and Economic Research, University of Fort Hare, East London. We are grateful to Daniel Morolong for his permission to publish the cover photograph and to Gary Minkley and Anne King for facilitating the process.
2. The phrase comes from Corinne A. Kratz, *The Ones that Are Wanted: Communication and the Politics of Representation in a Photographic Exhibition* (Berkeley: University of California Press, 2002). One of the few comments explaining the popularity of this poster stated that the photograph reminded students of their mothers. Anonymous personal communication to Thandiwe Chihana, University of the Western Cape, August 2004.
3. Christopher Pinney, *'Photos of the Gods': The Printed Image and Political Struggle in India* (London: Reaktion, 2004), p. 9.
4. Pinney, *'Photos of the Gods'*, p. 8.
5. David Freedberg, *The Power of Images: Studies in the History and Theory of Response* (Chicago: University of Chicago Press, 1989), p. xix.
6. See Lisa Bloom, 'Introducing *With Other Eyes: Looking at Race and Gender in Visual Culture*', in Lisa Bloom (ed.), *With Other Eyes: Looking at Race and Gender in Visual Culture* (Minneapolis: University of Minnesota Press, 1999), pp. 1–17, here pp. 4–5.
7. John Berger, *Selected Essays*, ed. Geoff Dyer (New York: Vintage International, 2003), p. 282.
8. W. J. T. Mitchell, 'Showing Seeing: A Critique of Visual Culture', in Michael Ann Holly and Keith Moxey (eds), *Art History, Aesthetics, and Visual Studies* (Williamstown, MA: Clark Institute of Art, 2002), pp. 231–50, here p. 231.
9. On the tendency of the historical discipline more generally to subordinate images to text – History's scopophobia – and the critique of pictures as mere 'illustration' to the text, see Patricia Hayes, Jeremy Silvester and Wolfram Hartmann, 'Photography, History and Memory', in Wolfram Hartmann, Jeremy Silvester and Patricia Hayes (eds), *The Colonising Camera. Photographs in the Making of Namibian History* (Cape Town: University of Cape Town Press, 1998), pp. 2–9.
10. Mitchell, 'Showing Seeing', p. 231, distinguishes between visual studies and visual culture by stating that they are the field of study and the object or target of study respectively.
11. On the pictorial turn in the human sciences and public culture see W. J. T. Mitchell, *Picture Theory* (Chicago: University of Chicago Press, 1994), especially ch. 1.
12. Mitchell, 'Showing Seeing', p. 232.
13. Mitchell, 'Showing Seeing', p. 237.
14. See e.g., Ciraj Rassool and Patricia Hayes, 'Science and the Spectacle: Khanako's South Africa, 1936–37', in Wendy Woodward, Patricia Hayes and Gary Minkley (eds), *Deep hiStories: Gender and Colonialism in Southern Africa* (Amsterdam: Rodopi, 2002), pp. 117–61.
15. Michelle Rowley, plenary discussion, International Workshop on Gender & Visuality, University of the Western Cape, 26–29 August 2004.

16. The phrase comes from Elizabeth Edwards, 'Photography and the Performance of History', *Kronos*, Special Issue: Visual History 27 (2001), pp. 15–29, here p. 19.
17. By visual knowledge I refer mainly to the photographic agendas of physical anthropology, which remained in vogue in southern Africa longer than in the metropoles. See Rassool and Hayes, 'Science and the Spectacle'. There is a vast literature on photography and the racial and ethnographic sciences. See *inter alia* Elizabeth Edwards, *Raw Histories: Photographs, Anthropology and Museums* (Oxford: Berg, 2001), esp. pp. 131–55; Andrew Bank, 'Anthropology and Portrait Photography: Gustav Fritsch's "Natives of South Africa", 1863–1872', *Kronos*, Special Issue: Visual History 27 (2001), pp. 43–76. One of the few recent studies to analyse gender more seriously in this field is Christopher Wright, 'Supple Bodies: The Papua New Guinea Photographs of Captain Francis R. Barton, 1899–1907' in Christopher Pinney and Nicolas Peterson (eds), *Photography's Other Histories* (Durham: Duke University Press, 2003), pp. 146–69.
18. This coincides with *Gender & History's* own push towards a more 'global turn'. A South-South workshop on Gender & Visuality was held in Cape Town in August 2004 as a preliminary step.
19. See Martin Jay, *Downcast Eyes: The Denigration of Vision in Twentieth-Century French Thought* (Berkeley: University of California Press, 1994); Oyèrónké Oyěwùmi, 'Visualizing the Body', in P. H. Coetzee and A. J. P. Roux (eds), *Philosophy from Africa* (Oxford: Oxford University Press Southern Africa, 2002), pp. 391–415.
20. Jonathan Crary, *Techniques of the Observer: On Vision and Modernity in the Nineteenth Century* (Cambridge: MIT Press, 1990).
21. Pinney, '*Photos of the Gods*', pp. 8–9. See also Diana L. Eck, *Darśán: Seeing the Divine Image in India* (Chambersburg, PA: Anima Books, 1981). I am grateful to participants at the CODESRIA-Sephis Workshop entitled *Visual South: Visual Sources as Alternative Histories* held in Maputo, Mozambique, September 2004 for their many insights and arguments about different ways of seeing in South Asia, Africa, Latin America and the Caribbean.
22. A problem hangs over the title of a recent edited collection, the otherwise excellent (and at times superb) *Photography's Other Histories*. While the book deals with previously neglected aspects of photographic theory and history, by default the title suggests that the former colonial world orbits around a single foundational history, constituting plural negatives to one positive.
23. Susan Buck-Morss, *The Dialectics of Seeing: Walter Benjamin and the Arcades Project* (Cambridge: MIT Press, 1995), p. 53.
24. Students entering Ivy League institutions were subjected to the rigours of anthropometric photography until the late 1960s. These so-called 'Posture Photos' were stored in university archives. See Ron Rosenbaum, 'Even the Wife of the President of the United States Sometimes Had to Stand Naked', *Independent*, 21 January 1995, pp. 25–6, originally published in the *New York Times*. Thanks to Ciraj Rassool for this reference.
25. Mitchell, 'Showing Seeing', p. 232.
26. Howard S. Becker, review of James Elkins, *Visual Studies: A Skeptical Introduction* (New York: Routledge, 2003), *Visual Studies* 20 (2005), p. 86.
27. Mitchell, 'Showing Seeing', p. 241.
28. Christopher Pinney, 'Introduction: How the Other Half . . .', in Pinney and Peterson (eds), *Photography's Other Histories*, pp. 1–14, here p. 7.
29. Nancy Rose Hunt, 'Tintin and the Interruptions of Congolese Comics', in Paul Landau and Deborah Kaspin (eds), *Images and Empires: Visuality in Colonial and Postcolonial Africa* (Berkeley: University of California Press, 2002), pp. 90–123.
30. On Grierson's consolidation of the category, see Bill Nichols, *Introduction to Documentary* (Bloomington: Indiana University Press, 2001), p. 84. On the importance of the notion of the document to historians, and its relationship with the archive, see Ann Laura Stoler, 'Colonial Archives and the Arts of Governance: On the Content in the Form', in Carolyn

Hamilton, Verne Harris, Jane Taylor, Michèle Pickover, Graeme Reid and Razia Saleh (eds), *Refiguring the Archive* (Cape Town: David Philip, 2002), pp. 83–100, here p. 83.
31. See Allan Sekula, 'The Body and the Archive', in Richard Bolton (ed.), *The Contest of Meaning: Critical Histories of Photography* (Cambridge: MIT Press, 1989), pp. 343–79.
32. Nichols, *Introduction to Documentary*, pp. 84–5.
33. Roland Barthes, *Camera Lucida*, tr. Richard Howard (London: Vintage, 1993), p. 87. A useful discussion of indexicality appears in Geoffrey Batchen, 'Ere the Substance Fade', in Elizabeth Edwards and Janice Hart (eds), *Photographs Objects Histories: On the Materiality of Images* (London: Routledge, 2004), pp. 32–46.
34. Nichols, *Introduction to Documentary*, p. 86.
35. Abigail Solomon-Godeau, *Photography in the Dock* (Minneapolis: University of Minnesota Press, 1996), pp. 169–83.
36. Pinney, 'Introduction', p. 1.
37. Pinney, 'Introduction', p. 6.
38. Mitsuhiro Yoshimoto, *Kurosawa: Film Studies and Japanese Cinema* (Durham: Duke University Press, 2000), p. 218; Pinney, '*Photos of the Gods*'.
39. Lynching postcards were the subject of *Without Sanctuary*, an exhibition mounted in New York (2000) and Atlanta (2002). For the more problematic catalogue, see James Allen, Hilton Als, Congressman John Lewis and Leon F. Litwack, *Without Sanctuary: Lynching Photography in America* (Sante Fe, NM: Twin Palms, 2000).
40. See Sekula, 'The Body and the Archive'.
41. Patricia Mohamed, closing remarks, International Workshop on Gender & Visuality, University of the Western Cape, 29 August 2004.
42. Griselda Pollock, 'Missing Women: Rethinking Early Thoughts on Images of Women', in Carol Squiers (ed.), *OverExposed: Essays on Contemporary Photography* (New York: The New Press, 1999), pp. 229–46, here p. 229.
43. Pollock, 'Missing Women', p. 231.
44. Pollock, 'Missing Women', p. 233.
45. Apart from their obvious difference from official or documentary photographs of Africans in the Eastern Cape, Morolong's photographs are not as stylised as the highly publicised *Drum* images of a similar era, which cover urban life in Johannesburg.
46. Edwards, 'Photography and the Performance of History', p. 20, citing Greg Dening, *Islands and Beaches: Discourse on a Silent Land: Marquesas 1774–1880* (Honolulu: University Press of Hawaii, 1980), pp. 31–2.

Does Gender Matter?
Filmic Representations of the Liberated Nazi Concentration Camps, 1945–46

Ulrike Weckel

The question posed in the title of this essay is meant genuinely, not rhetorically. It is certainly conceivable that at their first visual confrontation with Nazi crimes, camera operators, film editors and viewers of the subsequent compilation films were concerned with issues that had little to do with the sexual identity of victims and perpetrators. Few people had imagined it possible that there had been hundreds of work camps, concentration camps and extermination camps and that – in the latter venue in particular – murder had been carried out in such a modern, almost industrial fashion: meticulously organised, conceived not only to kill the victims but even to plunder their bodies and former possessions. Since 1942, rumours as well as reliable reports about systematic deportations and killings in the Third Reich had reached the Western Allies. But most people had dismissed the disturbing news as war propaganda. When in the spring of 1945 American and British troops discovered more and more camps and remnants of Nazi Germany's forced labour system, full of starving prisoners and corpses, disbelief was no longer possible. Military film units received orders to carefully document the sites, official delegations were invited to visit them and at many places occupation commanders forced the inhabitants of nearby towns and villages to view them.[1] Still, that which met the eyes, though evident, defied understanding. This was true not only for most eyewitnesses but also for many viewers of the resulting documentaries. To a certain extent filmgoers and eyewitnesses shared complicated, sometimes paralysing reactions and contradictory feelings of pity, rage, shame, fear and disgust when confronted with visual evidence of incomprehensible crimes. Was it not of comparatively minor importance, then, whether the dead and the tortured were women or men and to which sex those who had organised and supervised their imprisonment belonged?

In the field of Holocaust studies, a similarly sceptical attitude has put theorists of gender on the defensive, ensuring that gender analyses have continued to exert little influence on mainstream research. As Holocaust studies emphasise the unique nature of the destruction of European Jewry, comparative approaches are often suspected of leading to one or another form of relativism. The question of gender-specific experiences of suffering or gender-based harm during the Holocaust is considered even more out of place than comparisons of the Holocaust to other genocides or comparative analyses of the persecution of different groups by the Nazi regime. When women's studies scholars talk about the 'double jeopardy' of Jewish women as Jews and women, many Holocaust researchers fear the emergence of a hierarchy of victimisation. In a broader public circle, it has been charged that feminist hairsplitting or political correctness has reached a new level of tastelessness in which the mass murder of the Jews has become one of many arenas for political debate, and hence trivialised.[2] In rejecting such reproaches, Atina Grossmann points out their unspoken premise: 'If the Holocaust is available for historical analysis, rather than occupying a sacred dark void in which awed silence must reign, then gender analysis of the Holocaust is as legitimate as it is for any other historical inquiry'.[3]

Paradoxically, however, taking gender into account highlights that aspect of the Holocaust distinguishing it from 'ordinary' wartime massacres – its attempted extermination of all European Jews, including women and children. But if this invocation of women and children is to do more than merely induce pathos,[4] then further investigation into the motivations of the perpetrators and the consequences for the victims is necessary. Joan Ringelheim summarises the Nazis' motives in the following terms: 'Jewish women were to be killed as Jewish women, not simply as Jews – women who may carry and give birth to the next generation of Jews'.[5] The upshot for deported pregnant women and mothers with small children was that they were murdered on arrival at the extermination camps. In addition to the worries and dangers of pregnancy and maternity, women's and gender studies have shed light on several differences between the experiences and survival strategies of Jewish women and men. Although selection for persecution was based upon their Jewishness, women and men were still victimised in particular ways. Research on gender within Holocaust studies, I would argue, has thus long since affirmatively answered the question raised in my title and has done so convincingly – and has proceeded from that point to investigate the problem of *how* gender mattered.

That problem has not yet been satisfactorily explored in historical literature on the perpetrators. Official Nazi Germany cultivated a militaristic, clearly male demeanour and most perpetrators – both murderers and administrators – were men, often acting in exclusively male organisations and circles. When, after the war, women who had also committed crimes against humanity were brought to trial, their gender often heightened public attention and stimulated sensationalistic news coverage. Academic research, however, has shown hardly any interest in female perpetrators.[6] For example, the fact that women could become members or employees of the SS is either not mentioned in mainstream historiography or not addressed analytically.[7] During the last decade, research on male perpetrators has developed more refined analytical questions, taking into consideration factors such as shared biographical backgrounds within members of certain generations, group dynamics and the effects of the ideology of comradeship. It comes as a surprise, then, that very little of this work systematically enquires into the way these men understood masculinity or manliness; how they reinforced each other's ideas in this respect and put them into practice; and how they managed both to extend the boundaries of what was acceptable (if any such boundaries still existed) and to minimise their sense of shame. Thus, for example, citing Himmler's October 1943 remarks to SS leaders in Posen, in which he bragged about the murder of the Jews as a deed that would go down in the annals of world history, expressing the highest praise to the assembled mass murderers for having 'remained decent' in the light of their bloody business, will inevitably elicit horror.[8] But feeling such horror at a perversion of decency is no substitute for analysing how the organiser of the extermination defined manly virtues.

Much about how gender mattered in the process of Nazi persecution and extermination can still be discovered. This article, however, is not meant as a contribution to research on victims and perpetrators in a narrow sense. Rather, it is associated with the various studies on the role of gender in Holocaust representations, drawing attention to a field that has been explored less often than literature, feature films and the fine arts: the visual evidence of Nazi crimes in the recently liberated concentration camps.[9] High hopes rested on these shocking images and their quick publication. Seeing scenes of the unprecedented crimes was supposed to be more convincing than hearing or reading about what had happened there. For the Allied nations, the filmic documentation of Nazi atrocities served as reconfirmation that they had fought a just war and that their losses had not been in vain. The same filmic evidence should have forced the Germans, however – most of whom claimed not to have known anything about such crimes – to look at what had been going on in their midst. Through considering early documentary films and in one case photographs, I wish to explore how gender did and did not matter in liberators' perceptions of victims and perpetrators, their post-war representations and the reception of these representations. I approach the question from three directions: (1) photographers' attitudes toward freed inmates; (2) the films' presentations of corpses and survivors, especially their nakedness; and (3) the filmic commentaries on perpetrators. First though, I will give some brief background information about the Nazi camps and their liberation.

Immediately after coming to power in 1933, the Nazi government had begun opening concentration camps (*Konzentrationslager*, abbreviated as KL or KZ) to lock up first political opponents and later also other groups it wanted to exclude from the German *Volksgemeinschaft* (national community). Most of these camps kept only men prisoners; the much smaller numbers of women were interned in a female-only camp. With Nazi Germany's expansion, camps were set up in the occupied countries as well, primarily in the East, serving to exploit and finally murder deported European Jews, Gypsies and foreign political opponents of German occupation. Except where victims were killed upon arrival, men and women would be imprisoned in different camp sections. Towards the end of the war, however, the bureaucratic organisation of exploitation and extermination became more and more chaotic, and separating the various groups of internees could no longer be accomplished as strictly. Because of the German war economy's increased need for human labour, the Nazis abandoned their policy of keeping Jewish prisoners outside the Reich. They transported thousands of them, as well as foreign forced labourers, to both concentration camps and a growing number of satellite labour camps in Germany itself. Moreover, as Allied troops advanced, the SS started to cover up the traces of their crimes. After the Red Army overran Majdanek in July 1944 and pictures of its gas chamber and crematorium appeared in the international press, word was given out that no intact camp or living prisoners should fall into the Allies' hands. By the end of the year, most of the killing centres in Poland were levelled. Their inmates were murdered, forced to undergo death transports westwards, or left behind without any food. Therefore the Soviet army met no more than 7,000 abandoned sick and weak prisoners when they reached Auschwitz, the largest extermination camp, in late January 1945. US and British divisions entering Germany and Austria from the west in April and May came across numerous smaller camps, either overcrowded with exhausted, starving and ill prisoners or filled with corpses that the hastily fleeing SS guards had left unburied. Because people in the West more willingly believed their own troops' filmic evidence, and because the conditions in the camps on

German and Austrian soil had grown even more appalling than those in the remains of the eastern death camps, images from the liberation of Buchenwald, Bergen-Belsen, Dachau and Mauthausen became symbols of a Nazi genocide that had largely been carried out elsewhere and by other means.

Photographers' attitudes towards freed camp inmates

Those who operated the cameras during the Western Allies' advance were predominantly semi-skilled soldiers, but there were also some professional camera operators and photojournalists, including a few women.[10] One of their tasks for the Departments of Information and Psychological Warfare at SHAEF (Supreme Headquarters, Allied Expeditionary Forces) was to document Nazi crimes. The footage was to be compiled into newsreel sequences and documentary films presenting irrefutable evidence to the British and American public, and to the Germans, most of whom had apparently accepted the inhumanity perpetrated in their vicinity without much concern. After the first pictures from liberated camps were sent back, intelligence officers formulated detailed directives on what kind of shots were needed for the 'atrocity films' they had in mind: camera operators were to set up panning shots of the region, preferably including some recognisable local landmarks, to show how closely the camp bordered residential areas and to emphasise the contrast between the sordidness inside the camp and the attractiveness outside. The internees' huts were to be filmed, as well as where they had to work and where they were tortured, killed and cremated. Victims of both sexes and all ages were to appear in various stages of malnutrition and disease, both those alive and receiving medical treatment from Allied doctors and nurses and those who were already dead. Camera operators were required to ascertain an individual photograph subject's name, nationality, religion, and reason for and length of imprisonment whenever possible, especially if a particular internee was a well-known politician or intellectual. The warders were to be exposed to the cameras and special personnel indicated by name and rank. In order to make it difficult to discredit the photographic evidence, members of international delegations and forced German visitors to the sites were to be covered prominently and filmed against the background of the camp.[11]

Many such instructions came too late or proved impractical in the field. British and American troops encountered an unexpectedly high number of camps and satellite camps of various sorts, as well as sites of massacres, mass graves and dead prisoners who had died or been shot during forced transports on the road or in the freight cars of evacuation trains. With no clear plan as the chain of command disintegrated, the SS had fled most of these sites, eager to save their own necks. The barracks in the main camps where thousands of evacuated prisoners had been dumped were overflowing with starving inmates. Epidemics were rampant. In only a few camps were some survivors still able to greet Allied soldiers and celebrate their own liberation. Mounds of corpses had to be interred as quickly as possible; more former prisoners died daily. The remaining survivors urgently needed food and medical help. Barracks that had been cleared of their occupants had to be burnt to stop the spread of epidemics. Notwithstanding the excessive demands thus imposed on the emotional, rational and professional capacities of the camera operators, a race against time would appear to have taken place in order to document the most horrifying sights.

The renowned *Life* photojournalist Margaret Bourke-White said people often asked her how it was possible to photograph such atrocities. She had visited the recently liberated concentration camp Buchenwald and come across a factory near Leipzig where the guards, before escaping the approaching American troops, had burnt the forced labourers alive. In her memoirs, she responded:

> I have to work with a veil over my mind. In photographing the murder camps, the protective veil was so tightly drawn that I hardly knew what I had taken until I saw prints of my own photographs. It was as though I was seeing these horrors for the first time. I believe many correspondents worked in the same self-imposed stupor. One has to, or it is impossible to stand it.[12]

Soon after her assignment in defeated Germany, the experienced journalist published a report about her experiences, together with a selection of her photographs, expressing disdain for the German bystanders.[13] Less-professional eyewitnesses sought other outlets for their troubled state of mind. Peter Tanner, responsible in the British Ministry of Information for reviewing the armies' footage, was struck by the fact that shots from the camps were accompanied by far more detailed notes than usual. Normally the notes were limited to matter-of-fact explanations: when and where the film had been shot and what it showed. Here, he recalled, most of the cameramen had been unable to resist recording their personal feelings. And he found these feelings almost as upsetting as the pictures.[14]

Another challenge to both liberators and camera operators was that many survivors did not look like suffering yet ennobled victims. The tone of many of these first eyewitnesses signals at least as much disgust as shock concerning the internees' 'animal-like' appearance and behaviour; there is mention of 'huge, lethargic spiders', 'monkeys' or 'absent-minded apes in their striped prison suits'.[15] Extreme emaciation and long-term inhuman treatment had distorted human proportions: the liberators encountered sunken eyes staring from hollow, shaven skulls, skinny arms and legs that appeared excessively long. Hunger, disease and hopelessness had slowed down movement and limited the normal potentials of body language. With characteristic appearances diminished, it became difficult for eyewitnesses to perceive the survivors as individuals. Reporter Martha Gellhorn told her readers, 'They have no age and no faces; they all look alike and like nothing you will ever see if you are lucky'.[16] At the same time, in a rebuke to sentimental fantasies, the struggle for survival had not fostered inter-subjective decency and solidarity: there was greed for food, theft, rivalry and resentment towards inmates of other nationalities. In memoirs and novels, some survivors have delineated a border-region between maintaining human feelings and abandoning oneself to another state, sometimes directly described as animal-like.[17] These individuals were often fully aware that dehumanisation was one goal of the SS, achievement of which would confirm the Nazi definition of their enemy's essential nature. In Primo Levi's 'If this is a Man', for example, a co-inmate explains to the narrator why they must continue to polish their shoes, walk erect and wash their faces even in dirty water: 'precisely because the Lager was a great machine to reduce us to beasts, we must not become beasts'.[18] In any case, for the liberators, the perception of those they had just freed as non-human appears to have expressed an instinctive need for distance, in part to evade the disturbing insight that any human being could be destroyed in such a manner.[19] On rare occasions, liberators recognised the deep irony of their response: in their 'Preliminary Report', psychological warfare experts Egon Fleck and Edward Tenenbaum indicated that the neglected inmates of Buchenwald's 'Little Camp' were 'brutalised, unpleasant to look on ... It is easy to adopt the Nazi theory that they are subhuman, for many have in fact been deprived of their humanity'.[20]

Eyewitnesses' feeling of having entered 'another planet' did not necessarily lead them to insight into a separate logic reigning in the camps that was drastically different from ordinary civilised life. Rather, the alienation seems to have been so strong that empathy and understanding often simply failed. I now want to look at two cases in which the responses of a British cameraman to two different occurrences in Bergen-Belsen appear to have resulted from a presumption of omnipresent gender differences, an idea of prototypical female behaviour that ruled out other possible interpretations of the situations he was confronting.

After the forced transports of internees at the end of the war, many more concentration camps within Germany held both sexes prisoner. Bergen-Belsen was different from all others in that female inmates were clearly in the majority among the 60,000 still alive when British troops entered it on 15 April 1945. Women figure prominently in the images from this camp, which confronted the liberators perhaps with the most horrendous impressions and whose footage caused general dismay. Typhus, tuberculosis, dysentery and other infectious diseases were rife. Thousands of corpses lay unburied as survivors crouched among the dead. More than half of the survivors required urgent hospital treatment. Most had no food or water and the sanitary situation was catastrophic. Brutal neglect and indifference, rather than shootings or other methods of systematic mass murder, had produced a tremendous mortality rate, which could be reduced only slowly in the weeks following the liberation.[21]

Reading through summaries of this footage, I came across an account whose playfulness appears confusing, presumably written by the cameraman. The dope sheet, like the film sequence it describes is entitled 'Harrods' and gives background information and commentary on a distribution of clothes and shoes to freed female prisoners in mid-May. It centres around a familiar cliché: 'It is interesting to note', the description of the images explains, 'that as soon as the first primitive necessities of food and rest and warmth had been met, the patients, particularly the women, were immediately crying out for clothes'. It came as a surprise to me that the scene suggested to the author a specifically female interest in outer appearance, since new clothes were essential to all Bergen-Belsen inmates. In order to prevent the further spread of typhus, which is communicated by lice, all internees were shaved, washed, dusted with DDT and their prisoners' clothing burnt before they left the camp or were evacuated to a hospital. The text did indeed mention that the freed women had been 'stripped of their foul and vermin-ridden rags' and that they had 'entered their new life of freedom and care clothed only in a British army blanket'. It further explained that clothes were not only a 'medical necessity' but also a 'powerful tonic against the dangerous apathy of the very weak'. Still, it apparently did not occur to the author that the staging of a shopping trip might have constituted a dubious joke. As can be seen in the film sequence, the British army and relief personnel had, with some expenditure, produced signs with the name of the famous London department store and icons of a blouse, jacket, skirt and pair of trousers 'dancing' around the letters.[22] One sign served as a signpost for the ambulance drivers transporting the recipients of new clothing (Figure 1). Another was put on the door of the hut in which relief workers laid out women's clothes and shoes they had collected from local German families and received in parcels sent from the United Nations Relief and Rehabilitation Administration. (Whether the same staging was organised for men – which the sign with its clearly gendered icons suggests – I could not find out.) The 'Harrods' sign is

Figure 1: Clothing distribution signpost inside Bergen-Belsen. Photograph courtesy of the Imperial War Museum, London.

reminiscent of British soldiers in World War I who, in a mixture of military gallows humour and patriotic sentimentality, often named trenches after famous London places or streets in their home towns. But the question here arises who was meant as the target audience for this joke.

While the intentions remain unclear and were perhaps not fully realised by the initiators themselves, we can see that the sign at least inspired the author of the dope sheet and guided his perceptions. He seems to have taken a certain pleasure in interpreting the shots as a harmless scene of fashion-conscious women in a department store. On the one hand, he acknowledged soberly enough that the women, many of whom had to be brought to the distribution point by ambulance and were too weak to dress themselves, were about to get their first clothing – indeed their first individual possessions – in a long time. He also noted that through this action the liberators hoped to speed up the recovery of those they had freed, itself an acknowledgement of the profound role played by the possession of clothing in one's very sense of being human. Nevertheless, the author commented on the shots he listed in the following way:

(a) Interior of the stable, the blouse and jumper department.
(b) Mrs. H Tanner, of Stoke Rectory, Grantham, Lincs, helps an undecided customer to make up her mind over the important problem of whether green is more becoming than speckled brown.

(c) The deal is clinched and another satisfied customer passes on to the boot and shoe department.[23]

The persistence with which a stereotype of female vanity was brought into play appears striking, although the reality in front of the camera gave few grounds for it. The shots, which the author had either taken himself or, if he was an army censor, had watched before he wrote this description, show no indecision on the part of the inmates or advice on the part of the relief workers. Instead, inmates hold up some tops in order to estimate whether the size is about right for them.

Presumably, the attempt at playful normalisation through the sign, leading to a corresponding phrasing of the filming notes for this episode, reflects a desire or need to diminish the gravity of the situation. But to what extent was this staging meant to give a little pleasure and diversion to the liberated women themselves? Whether or not the women noticed, understood and appreciated the joke, it appears to have primarily served to diminish the liberators' distress. Significantly, the only brief mention of the Harrods staging I have found in the literature appears among measures taken to help British relief personnel perform their most difficult duties, which included: increased alcohol and cigarette rations, theatre and film performances, a dartboard and a radio for the mess, and a night club called 'Coconut Grove' with room for twenty-five men and their female companions and a band playing for dancing. A medical student is quoted with the words 'we needed that type of thing to give us a feeling maybe that we were still in the world of the sane'.[24] While this aspect of the liberation should not be forgotten in retrospect, it seems doubtful whether a joke could work for both liberators and liberated. While the cameraman's cheerful reference to an allegedly typical female predilection for fashion and shopping tried to 'normalise' a hardly bearable situation, it obscured the deeper meaning of what receiving their own clothing must have meant to former prisoners in general, but in fact more so to women. During their socialisation most girls would have learnt to remain modest and chaste by dressing appropriately. In interviews and memoirs, female survivors, much more often than men, recalled the shame they felt when stripped naked and shaven upon arrival at the camps. The liberators certainly had opposite intentions from those who had imprisoned the women years before. But since most of the liberators were men, female survivors during the liberation once again were exposed to men's gazes.[25]

My second example is a series of three photographs taken in Bergen-Belsen on the same day and by the same photographer.[26] His attitude towards the female subject in his shots, as recorded in his written commentary, signals a failure of communication between the photographer and subject to which unarticulated norms regarding proper female behaviour appear to have contributed significantly. At the same time, the occurrence illustrates that the idea of what a picture shows can differ considerably between the photographer and the person being photographed, not to mention the various viewers who look at a picture from their own perspectives, with personal associations, in different times and varying circumstances.[27]

The first shot is that of another photograph, which is fixed to a wooden beam with sticking plaster and shows a couple in bathing costumes standing on a lawn, holding a little girl by the hands between them, with palm trees in the background. It is a typical and clearly staged holiday memento, not a snapshot but presumably taken by a commercial photographer on the promenade of some seaside resort. Because of the motif's conventionality, the viewer assumes that spouses and daughter are shown posing in front of the camera in order to bring home a document of happy family life for the family's photo album. The other two pictures show the woman in the first photograph – which she had somehow managed to keep with her throughout her imprisonment – after the liberation. In one picture she is lying on a hospital bed in a striped shirt, her right lower leg and left hand bandaged; in the other we see her naked, propping herself up between two bedsteads. We learn only from the captions that she was the young woman in the two-piece bathing suit in the first photograph. Once a little on the plump side, shyly smiling into the camera, she is now only skin and bones, her hair short and tousled. She bows her head and looks at the floor.

The sharp contrast between the photographs induces viewers to fill in the missing story. Being called upon to translate historical knowledge into imagination makes the effect of the series all the more powerful. Those at SHAEF who were working on an 'atrocity film' pointed to another function when in their instructions they asked camera operators on site to trace 'stills or moving film of victims before their imprisonment'. By showing what internees were like before entering the camp, it would avoid the impression that they were 'sub-human beings'.[28] Perhaps these instructions never reached the photographer at Bergen-Belsen. The captions for his shots, in any case, indicate that he was not thinking about effective documentation so much as struggling with strong emotions. First, he noted what the viewer of the series already suspected. The summer-vacation photograph had been taken shortly before the woman was arrested by the Gestapo. On his two photographs of the liberated prisoner he commented:

> This wretched festering body and unhinged mind is all that is left of Margit Schwartz, thirty-one years old, born of Jewish parents in Budapest. That she is

still alive is both incredible and unfortunate. She is almost completely mad and one of the few things that makes any impression upon her mind is the photograph of herself and this is obviously her choisest [sic] possession. When he produced a camera before her, she did a most incredible thing. Although she has been unable to move and has to be fed and even turned in her bed by the nursing sister, Margit Schwartz not only climbed out of the bed unaided, but managed to stand in a position approximating that taken formerly in the old photograph, while the revolted cameraman took two stills.[29]

Nothing approximates the old photograph any more and – given what we find out about the genesis of the series – it appears likely that Margit Schwartz was conscious of this fact.[30] She was then not only emaciated and unable to stand without support, she also was alone, separated from her husband and daughter, most probably without any news of them. The picture of the young family had presumably been taken to remind them of past happy holidays. With Margit Schwartz's deportation and imprisonment it must have become a reminder of their past in general, of a life that had been destroyed. Annette Kuhn has characterised family photographs as 'a prop, a prompt, a pre-text', setting the scene for changing recollections in a 'never-ending process of making, remaking, making sense of, our selves' in the particular present.[31] We can only guess what the photograph meant to Margit Schwartz and why she wanted to be photographed after the liberation. Perhaps she wanted to demonstrate, not least to herself, that she was still alive; perhaps she thought of showing a sign of survival to her family; maybe her effort was an act of defiance or even protest, aimed at a public that would hopefully be appalled at the sight of her.[32]

The photographer, however, did not articulate compassion but disgust. How can that be understood? Many liberators told of a numbing effect. Especially in Bergen-Belsen, where more than 10,000 corpses had to be buried and hundreds of inmates were still dying every day, many reported that they had stopped perceiving the victims as individuals or even that one had to get used to seeing inmates collapse 'and to restrain oneself from going to their assistance'.[33] The photographer expected Margit Schwartz to die.[34] But besides conserving his empathy, the photographer seems to have struggled with concepts of female modesty and beauty, not fully comprehending that the camps had annulled them. In my reading of his comment, he was shocked that a woman in the most miserable condition took the initiative, got undressed and 'posed' naked in front of his camera. In view of the convention of handsome women posing in such a way, often upon (male) request, he could only recognise inappropriateness in her action. The fact that Margit Schwartz was a woman seems to have triggered gender-specific associations that limited the photographer's interpretation of his subject's motivations. Perhaps he was simply overwhelmed by the contrast of the woman in the old photograph and the woman in front of his lens. But I wonder whether he would also have diagnosed madness if the victim involved had been a man.

Filmic representations of victims

Neither the film sequence of 'Harrods' at Bergen-Belsen nor the photographs showing Margit Schwartz before her deportation and a month after she was freed made it into any of the 'atrocity films' that were screened in the immediate post-war period.[35] These compilation films were intended, as indicated, for public viewing in the Allied countries but also – above all – as a re-education measure imposed on German civilians and German prisoners of war. (Some would also be used in trials against German war criminals and concentration camp personnel.)[36] Outraged by the atrocities they discovered, many Allied observers felt that the Germans should be forced to look at what they had refused to see or care about during Nazi rule. Film screenings replaced compulsory inspections of corpse-filled camps as such visits were only possible for a short time and for relatively few people.

Great hope rested on visual confrontation with Nazi crimes. Since these new sorts of crimes defied imagination, pictures were expected to be more effective than written or oral accounts in convincing the general public that all of this had really happened. Once and for all, filmic evidence should make disbelief and denial impossible. Furthermore, the images were to compel German viewers to recognise the Nazi regime's criminal character, to renounce their last faith in Nazi ideology, to accept their guilt as perpetrators or their responsibility as accomplices or at least make them feel ashamed of having accepted such crimes without much concern. These ambitious cognitive and emotional goals were founded on the liberators' own on-site visual confrontation with the camps, experiences which had both mobilised their moral emotions and abruptly erased the doubts that many of them had still harboured after hearing or reading of political persecution and genocide in Nazi-occupied Europe. They therefore hoped that images on the big screen could have the same potency. Film theory confirms such beliefs. Motion picture images provoke kinaesthetic responses, like muscle reflexes and motor impulses, even before a viewer processes them intellectually. They catch and hold the viewer's eyes, so that in the dark, anonymous movie theatre one can hardly escape their sensory and emotional appeal.[37] Hence, horrifying images like those in the concentration camp films can induce psychological responses in viewers, even though – or rather, all the more so because – their intellects are still overtaxed. Another reason for the Allies' hopes for the films' persuasiveness was that documentary footage could not be manipulated easily at that time; therefore its veracity was hardly questioned. Furthermore, audiences were not yet inured to shocking screen images.

In spring 1945, newsreel production companies and commanders of POW camps and of the occupying forces in Germany seem to have shown whatever was at their disposal. The earlier the pictures were shown, the more sensational they were. Soon, however, several directors, authors and cutters started working on more carefully edited compilation films. Instead of relying on the images to speak for themselves, deliberate montage and specific commentaries for different target groups steered audience reaction. Some of these films were screened later in 1945 or in 1946, their distribution often planned and organised and their effects on viewers monitored. Other films were completed too late – after the occupation powers had changed their policy towards Germany, after many POWs had been released and when most Germans demanded to draw a line under debates about Nazism and its crimes.

Copies of several, though not all, of these films can still be found in the archives. The following remarks will not focus on any of the films in detail, but will draw on a repertoire of images from the various films I have seen.[38] Points of departure for my arguments will be the spectrum of images; their selection; which images were chosen regularly and thus were considered particularly telling and which appeared in only one or a few of the films; and lastly, questions of montage and commentary.

If, in studying these documentaries, one anticipates and looks for gender differences in the representations of victims, one risks missing their most distressing aspects. What feminist scholars are prepared to find in filmic depictions of femininity – women turned into mere objects of the camera's gaze – here applies to all internees, female and male alike, dead or alive. In fact, one aspect of this lack of gender distinction is perhaps the most disturbing: mutilation and emaciation have erased any sex and gender significance from some of the bodies. Since we are used to distinguishing male and female bodies at first sight, the shock if we cannot is all the more powerful.

The breadth of motifs suggests that camera operators and film editors felt no taboos regarding their work, or that if they did, they decided to overcome them. Joseph Kushlis, who as an amateur took pictures at Ohrdruf, the first camp the American troops came across, later remembered his initial hesitation: 'It did occur to me that there was probably a question of morality or decency in even photographing these unfortunate people but then I quickly resolved the question to my own satisfaction in realising that here was history that should be recorded'.[39] With unrestrained brutality needing documentation, there appears to have been little room for tact towards any subject, without discrimination. In our context, it is important to keep in mind that the photographers often did not have the opportunity to choose whether to take pictures of men or women, because the camp or camp section they visited had held either exclusively men or, more seldom, women captive. If anybody involved in the production of the documentaries had wished to pay some attention to the sexual identity of the victims, it would have been the film editors, who made decisions about the selection of images and the authors, who wrote the commentaries on them.

There is hardly any evidence that they paid much attention to gender. All the documentaries contain images of fields and mounds of corpses, corpses in open mass graves and on trucks. Often it is quite impossible to make out which parts of the body belonged to which contorted corpse. The takes regularly change between panning shots to stress the huge number of corpses and medium close-ups that show most of them as mutilated. Sometimes the camera captures individuals in close-up, generally of the head, lingering briefly in a 'frozen image'. Most of the dead bodies are naked, which is a distressing sight *per se* since in most societies the deceased are covered and their eyes closed as soon as possible.[40] Still, it is relatively seldom that genitalia are included in the picture; one assumes that this sight (at the time still unusual on screen) was deliberately limited.[41] In any event, after torture and the ways in which they had been murdered, only a few individuals could be still clearly identified as either male or female. Film viewers would have had to know about the sex segregation of the camp system and would have needed background information about each site mentioned in a film to realise that most corpses they saw were indeed male.

The voice-over marks a few shots of the dead explicitly in gender terms. In a sequence from Hadamar, which appears in at least two films, we see a body with long hair being exhumed by Allied soldiers. As most prisoners' heads were shaven as soon as they entered a camp this is an unusual sight, the hint of femininity allowing the corpse to appear perhaps a bit less alien than the others. The commentaries indicated as much. In the official Anglo-American newsreel for the British and American Zones, *Welt im Film* No. 5, a male off-screen voice[42] reproachfully exclaims: 'This was a woman!' And in the more carefully directed American compilation film *Die Todesmühlen*, which was screened in the American Zone in early 1946,[43] the viewer is told: 'Once this was a strong woman with a zest for life, before she fell into the hands of the Nazi executioners'.[44] In another sequence in this latter film, the camera captures a dead newborn whose umbilical cord has not yet been severed, the narrator commenting: 'Next to the murdered mothers, the corpses of newborn children'. The plural is misleading here, however, as female inmates hardly ever gave birth in concentration camps. A discovered pregnancy usually was a death sentence for a woman, at least in the extermination camps, as was arriving there with a young child.[45] In one film, a male corpse is singled out and even identified: 'This man once was a well-known Polish engineer'.[46] It had been possible to provide such information in this case because the few survivors of a very recent massacre at a work camp near Leipzig had returned to the site and told the American photographers what had happened.[47] Such commentaries, however, are the exception. Generally the narrations offer sweeping references to the millions of murder victims, sometimes stressing their natural equality in particular: 'Once these were people – God's children'.[48] In this manner, emphasis was placed on the limitless and universal nature of these crimes against humanity rather than on anything unique about the victims such as their ethnicity or nationality,[49] their sex[50] or their age.

The problem of objectification of the victims through the camera's gaze becomes more acute in regard to representations of survivors. Most films concentrate on terribly maltreated, physically extremely fragile internees of both sexes who are either utterly unaware of the camera or stare apathetically into the lens without being able to really make contact with their liberators. Rarely does one of these liberated people smile. If he or she does, it is apparently a photo-studio reflex learned in an earlier time, a reflex with an oppressive effect in this situation.[51] The British hour-long documentary, which was not screened to the public until after its rediscovery in 1983, when various television channels broadcast it under the title *Memory of the Camps*,[52] demonstrates that other images would have been available too. In addition to pictures of survivors in relatively good health who cook, eat, drink or laugh, we can for example see a female inmate gratefully grabbing the hand of one of the liberators. In their endeavours to drive home the message of the unimaginable cruelty of the Nazis, the 1945 short films, however, selected some of the most horrifying shots.[53] Cheerfulness was more or less reserved for crowds of male survivors who celebrate their liberation by waving their caps, holding up banners and hoisting flags. Frequently the documentaries introduce such sequences, which must have been recreated[54] or filmed during ceremonies several days after Allied troops had entered the camp, with a shot of a camp gate being pushed open, accompanied by a ceremonial sound track. The images thereby become a symbol of liberation and constitute the only brief triumphant moments in the early documentaries. That almost exclusively male survivors appear in these scenes probably results from the fact that the most impressive liberation festivities took place in the main concentration camps like Dachau and Buchenwald, which had been built for male political prisoners. It is conceivable, though, that such images of active, apparently unbroken men gave cameramen the reassuring feeling that, at least for some of the survivors, a return to 'normality' was possible, a normality that for women was imagined as a return to an interest in fashion and beauty.[55]

Cameramen were also present while former prisoners underwent medical examination. These are the film sequences in which living internees can occasionally be seen naked. But in contrast to the photographic encounter with Margit Schwartz, it seems that here the victims had not requested that their wretched condition be documented. Rather the cameramen seem to have asked the patients to present their injuries. Particularly awful injuries were chosen for filming. Some inmates on the verge of starvation are shown being helped to walk a few stumbling steps, the camera recording their pitiful movements. They have been stripped naked for demonstration purposes, while the helpers supporting them remain clothed: a situation that, however self-evident, intensifies an impression of the survivors as objects entirely lacking in autonomy, unable to protest treatment beyond their control. Their nakedness, however, reveals more than catastrophic malnutrition. These bodies, to which the term 'walking skeletons' has often been applied, hardly show any distinguishing characteristics: their heads have all been shaved; their age cannot be estimated; their genitals are so withered that their sex cannot be classified; their body gestures express only weakness; their emaciation is far too pronounced to make out individual facial features.[56] The viewers see people literally caught between life and death. They become witnesses to a dying which neither they nor the doctors on the scene can halt.

According to Susan Sontag's reflections in *Regarding the Pain of Others*, the inability to alleviate photographically reproduced suffering or to learn something from the sight of it turns viewers of the photos into voyeurs.[57] If we follow her argument, the decisive question for us would be: how many and what sorts of images were necessary to mobilise viewers to support survivors actively or to teach viewers a lesson? Or indeed: is there any lesson that can in fact be learned in this way beyond that of the mass torture and murder really having occurred? I, at least, am uncertain whether an inability to alter or prevent suffering truly marks the border between well-intentioned documentation and exploitative voyeurism. It may be the case that images of the 'walking skeletons' were among those most likely to arouse pity among viewers. Any sense of being a voyeur while viewing these images may have less to do with one's own helplessness than with the helplessness of the photographic subjects. One doubts whether these survivors had a chance to demur on being photographed in such a state: with the radical eradication of individuality and intimacy in the concentration camps, an absence of explicit protest could not have been taken as approval. Some shots demonstrate that attentiveness and sensitivity in this respect were often missing. In a sequence from the French production *Les Camps de la Mort*, male prisoners in Mittelgladsbach are disinfected by use of a spray gun. One of the men clearly tries to cover his nakedness, at least before the camera. Although he turns away from the lens, the filming continues. Such lack of respect for the survivors' sense of shame would appear to break the bounds of decency inherent in committed documentation. The photographers seem to have shown such lack of respect to male and female survivors alike. To women though, it might have made a difference that most of those watching and filming them were men.

From today's perspective and from our experience with documentaries on the Holocaust that were produced later, what appears equally problematic is the fact that the survivors were almost never given an opportunity to speak for themselves. This may appear self-evident, since normally filming during the war was done without a soundtrack. But little effort to compensate for the inmates' muteness was manifest in the early documentaries. By focusing to a great extent on the very weak, the films seldom showed survivors addressing the liberators or reporting what had happened in the camp to members of official delegations. Even their perspective hardly ever made it into the commentaries. Most documentaries thus undoubtedly told the liberators' story about the victims, not the victims' story about themselves.

There were, however, a few exceptions. The hour-long American documentary *Nazi Concentration Camps*, screened in the Nuremberg courtroom in November 1945 during the second week of the trial against the major war criminals, included three witness accounts filmed in front of microphones and recorded in original sound: an American prisoner-of-war at Mauthausen testified that he and his fellow prisoners had not been treated according to the Geneva Convention; a British officer at Bergen-Belsen indicated that they had found 'unbelievable conditions' in the camp but that things would go 'fairly well' now; and a freed prisoner-doctor in the women's ward at the Bergen-Belsen 'infirmary' gave graphic descriptions of these unbelievable conditions before the liberation: events of cannibalism, poisonous injections and forced sterilisations – descriptions that possibly managed to exceed the horrors filmed in the freed camps.[58] The other one-hour documentary, *Memory of the Camps*, also contains a few brief testimonies and, in addition, a sound filming of a British officer in Bergen-Belsen making an accusatory speech in front of SS guards and local Nazi officials whom the military police had assembled around an open mass grave. Perhaps initially recorded as an unintended side-effect, we can hear loud grumbling in the background. The camera pans and captures angry freed female prisoners cursing their torturers and making threatening gestures in their direction. By selecting this sequence, the British documentary carried out an idea that appeared in the instructions for cameramen. 'An especially dramatic scene would be one', it says, 'in which victims accuse an SS officer or guard with whom they are brought face to face'.[59] None of the other documentaries included such images. They did not even mention the fact that former inmates were sometimes able to observe Germans being forced to visit the camp or to bury the dead – a confrontation that probably furnished some of them with a modicum of satisfaction. *Deutschland Erwache*, a US War Department production that explicitly addressed German POWs, borrowed an excerpt from the British officer's speech but omitted the background curses. Pictorial material from Dachau that showed liberated prisoners attacking guards and stabbing one of them was not released by the censors; nor would they allow the screening of an Allied soldier kicking an SS man.[60] Political considerations seem not to have given rise to an idea of presenting the liberated in all their variety, their contradictory emotions and various activities.

Filmic commentaries on perpetrators

Perpetrators appear in all the documentaries as Allied prisoners. Since command-level SS personnel and the SS warders of most camps had fled shortly before the Allied soldiers' arrival, these soldiers rarely had the opportunity to capture the men and women responsible for the horrors confronting them. The dismay at the insight that human beings had been capable of doing this to other human beings is frequently reflected in a questioning of the perpetrators' basic human nature. Josef Kramer, the last commandant of Bergen-Belsen, is introduced in the British *Movietone News* as 'a thing called Kramer – you may have seen his photograph in the papers', in part a reference to the prototypically coarse, hence memorable, nature of Kramer's facial features and to the brutal and dumb expression he had upon his arrest. The physicians of the so-called 'T4 action' or 'euthanasia programme' whom the Allies caught at Hadamar were clearly from another social background and were pursuing a different sort of career in the Nazi state. To demonstrate the deviation of these educated men from both ethical medicine and common human decency, *Death Mills*, the American version of *Todesmühlen*, paraphrases the answers of the interrogated doctors with bitter sarcasm: 'The camp commander and chief physician are brought into the room.

They can explain everything: Of course, the prisoners were used as guinea pigs, of course poison was injected into their bloodstream and they died. Herr Doktor seems surprised that anyone should find anything wrong with this'.[61] The fact that many of those arrested displayed a complete lack of awareness of wrongdoing was an additional provocation. Many commentators felt invited to pronounce their own crushing judgements: 'What subhumans did these things?' *Death Mills* rhetorically asks when a Mauthausen warder appears on screen, the barrel of a rifle pointing at him. The same film refers to Kramer as 'the beast of Belsen'.

Such strategies of dehumanising or demonising the originators of the incomprehensible horrors seem to have appeared even more convincing when the films presented pictures of a relatively large group of female SS personnel arrested at Bergen-Belsen. The women, in fact, appear in almost all early documentaries. One can assume that for those liberators, film editors and film viewers who were unaware that the SS recruited women, the sight of these women in uniform and boots would have been all the more scandalous. For not only had these female warders broken the basic prohibition on intentional murder and torture; they had violated the norms of femininity, grounded in a belief that 'by nature' women are the peaceable and caring sex. Instead of 'civilising' their men, who were supposedly innately violent, or at the very least shrinking from the sites of mass murder and torture, they had been willing participants in the process. *Memory of the Camps* stresses this idea by calling them 'volunteers who came of their own free will to do their bit'. Contrasting the SS women with the inmates, the commentary goes on to describe them as 'not sickly pale with hollow faces and hungry eyes, but well-fed and well-kept with a strutting arrogance'. Criticism of the SS men takes the opposite tack. An imposing appearance is not the target, as in the case of the women in uniform, but the men's loss of it. With undisguised *Schadenfreude*, the narrator 'watches' male warders carrying the dead to a huge pit: 'The SS men are not so spick and span now. Seven days of being shouted and cursed at and handling corpses by the hundred are beginning to tell'.

In its evenly distributed malice toward both groups of arrested warders, men and women, *Memory of the Camps* once again constitutes an exception. All other documentaries focus particularly on the female warders. Two provide relatively matter-of-fact commentary on the sequence in which the women were taken away. It may be that the film producers anticipated a special indignation on the part of viewers at the sight of female perpetrators, but the commentaries are nevertheless restrained. *Movietone News* follows the thesis that ascribed a violent national character to all Germans, irrespective of gender. Its commentary on the arrested women speaks of freed prisoners reporting many atrocities by female warders against women and children. If such accounts were meant to imply actions worse than the usual crimes, the intensified wickedness would have involved the fact that the Germans even used a gender-specific division of labour in carrying out torture. The American documentary screened at Nuremberg, however, merely mentioned that the liberators had ordered SS women to bury the dead.

In contrast, the commentaries of other two films underscore the special dismay provoked by female cruelty, making use of what we can today decipher as sexualised (male) fantasies.[62] *Welt im Film: KZ* offers a meaningful clue: 'Their equipment includes whips of untanned leather'. The original German-language version of *Todesmühlen* draws a comparison between male and female camp personnel, emphasising that these women were no less brutal than men. The commentary provides a succinct, graphic depiction, indirectly evoking traditional assumptions that women should behave according to their 'nature': 'These women used their whips just as brutally, torturing and tormenting and killing without conscience, just like their male colleagues'. Particularly given the hard faces of the uniformed women on the screen, viewers could conclude from this passage that these female warders surely had to be 'mannish women'. Interestingly, the passage was changed markedly in the English-language version. Judging by the modifications in the narration, *Death Mills* was meant to be shown to occupation troops before they left for Germany. As those young American men had not themselves taken part in the war in Europe, a clear warning was added against 'fraternising'. The Germans who would soon appeal to their sympathies were perpetrators and bystanders just like the Germans on the screen, the narrator explained. His commentary on the SS women was nothing short of sensational: 'Amazons, turned Nazi killers, were merciless in the use of the whip, practised in torture and murder, deadlier than the male'. Without referring to any witnesses, the linguistic image used classic ingredients such as 'amazons', 'merciless' and 'whip' to evoke the cliché that women, once they cross the line of their sex and turn to violence, become out-and-out Furies who develop a wild desire to undertake appalling actions. Therefore they were even worse than men.[63] The American press had already worked on this theme. For example, the *Boston Globe* captioned the first photographs from Bergen-Belsen, 'Brutal Nazi Girls Danced as Victims Were Burned'.[64]

Interestingly enough, one account describes how German prisoners-of-war held in the UK responded to the images of SS women in *KZ*, shown to them in summer 1945. Summarising reports from various camps, Lt Col Frazer made out 'varying reactions':

In many cases they are cited as evidence of the degradation to which Nazi rule has submitted the German people; in some cases they are seized upon as reasons why the film may be faked, on the grounds that obviously no German woman would fall to this level; in another case their appearance was regarded in the light of nothing so much as a mannequin parade. Probably the soundest view on them is that expressed by camp 69, where the British Interpreter Officer wrote:

> 'The general opinion concerning the K.Z. staff personnel is that they were selected at first as being 100% Nazis and then by the nature of their work became "*vertiert*" [brutish]. The women are described by some prisoners as very low types and probably harlots, Nazis who "preferred that type of work to the hard manual labour in factories" '.[65]

After the end of the war, most German POWs distanced themselves from the SS. If Germans had committed crimes it must have been them – fanatics from the very beginning, further brutalised through their bloody business. While the male SS served as a convenient explanation of alleged excess carried out by a National Socialist elite organisation, the participation of women in the daily routine of torture and murder burdened apologetic arguments with the question how *they* had become involved. Some POWs believed that this just could not be true (or at least said so); others suspected that only particularly thoughtless, slovenly, frivolous or lazy women and not ordinary petty bourgeois women, no matter how ambitious, could have chosen such a job.

Conclusions

Unimaginable crimes had been perpetrated in Nazi-occupied Europe. The world appeared to be out of joint. Among the shaken certainties was the familiar gender order: the Nazis had persecuted and killed political opponents and declared 'racial enemies' without sparing anybody – not women, not children, not sick or old people. When the liberators entered the concentration camps they could not identify some of the inmates as men or women; most of them looked much alike and at the same time extremely different from both male and female eyewitnesses. The films shot by Allied cameramen document their inability to perceive the victims as individuals. At the same time, the perpetrators seemed to have eradicated the allegedly 'natural' gender order of difference among themselves as well, in some odd way: men had planned and executed a genocidal project and women had actively participated in it. Even more shocking than the traditional gender-specific division of labour prevailing in the Nazi camp system – men guarding men, women guarding women – was the idea that women might have ruled over men. There was not much evidence of that in Nazi Germany, which might account for the eagerness with which the ghastly rumours about 'the witch of Buchenwald', Ilse Koch, a commandant's wife, were circulated – it was assumed that the pieces of flayed, tattooed skin found in the camp's pathological collection had been preserved for her after she had selected the motifs while the bearers of the tattoos were still alive.[66] Several documentaries mentioned her name when showing citizens from the nearby town of Weimar being forced to look at these atavistic SS trophies.[67]

Was the confusion by cameramen and film makers regarding an invalidated gender order simply the indicator of a general inability to grasp what had happened? Or was the disturbance of that order one of the reasons for the confusion? The sources cited in this article do not offer an easy answer. All we can say is that some photographers appear to have maintained expectations of gender-appropriate behaviour on the part of inmates, although their pictures showed people who had lost virtually all markers of gender and sex significance. Violations of such norms by the freed inmates did not necessarily mobilise the eye-witnesses' pity, but could also arouse aversion or disgust. On the other hand, liberators' adherence to a gender-specific perspective can also be read as an effort to re-establish a familiar pattern in a situation of overwhelming chaos. The gendering of relief measures might well have served two different motivations: to reassure the liberators' own sense of 'normality' and to allow survivors to retransform themselves into gendered beings, women and men, mothers and fathers. Neither possibility – either reassuring the liberators' sense of normality or allowing survivors to reclaim gender – makes it less likely that other thoughts than those about gender dominated their response to the situation. This marks a difference from their perception of the perpetrators they encountered. The fact that both sexes had been involved in the crimes appears to have escaped nobody. Clearly distinguishable in their outer appearance, male and female SS warders nevertheless had committed the same deeds. In the eyes of some observers, the surprising indications of gender 'equality' within the camp personnel confirmed a sense that the Nazis had set normality aside. This sense was reinforced by fantasies about particularly evil Nazi women – women so wicked that they turned the gender order upside down. Far from today's studies of 'ordinary men', 'ordinary women' and 'ordinary Germans',[68] most contemporaries preferred to imagine the executioners of such extraordinary crimes as themselves extraordinary, hence categorically different from the rest of mankind.

The question of visuality adds a new twist to the debate over the significance of gender for Holocaust studies. It leads us to focus on observers' perceptions of the events that now have become summarised as the Holocaust. Independent of how male and female victims were persecuted, how they experienced and responded to terror, torture and mortal fear, their filmic representations become the subject of investigation. While the persecuted themselves presumably never forgot whether they were women or men, those who looked at them and took their pictures were confronted with the results of dehumanisation and 'de-gendering' in the process of persecution and extermination.[69] And so are the viewers of these images. Since viewers are used to identifying a represented person not least by his or her sex, damage and destruction of sex characteristics have a distressing impact. Not surprisingly for scholars of visual representations, the images of victims of the Holocaust are – like all images – far from unambiguous. The Allies' hope that their documentaries from the recently liberated concentration camps would speak for themselves and teach the world one clear message turned out to be unrealistic. To be sure, few people questioned the authenticity of the images. But responses to such visual evidence are much more complex. With regard to representations of perpetrators, the Allies seem to have been much more aware of the fact that different readings were possible. Commentaries on films and captions for photographs were to guide the viewers' interpretation, mostly assuring them that these people might look ordinary but were indeed extraordinarily cruel and evil. To arouse viewers' distrust in their often unspectacular appearances seemed to be easier when the pictures showed female perpetrators. The sight of them was relatively unusual and for many, unexpected. What is more, comments could hint at the suspicion that women are accomplished in the art of pretence and therefore their visual representation cannot be trusted. As viewers read against the backdrop of their certainties about visual genders, images cannot be gender-neutral.

Notes

This paper was written while in receipt of a grant from the *Berliner Programm zur Förderung der Chancengleichheit für Frauen in Forschung und Lehre* and reworked during a research fellowship at the International Research Center for Cultural Studies (IFK) in Vienna. I am also grateful to Christina von Braun and Cornelie Usborne for the opportunity to present earlier versions at the Van Leer Jerusalem Institute and the Women's History Seminar at the Institute for Historical Research in London. In addition to the participants in these discussions, Krisztina Robert, Stefanie Schüler-Springorum, Greg Sax, Joel Golb, Lesley McBain and Marti Lybeck offered stimulating comments and the necessary linguistic assistance. In particular, I would like to thank Patricia Hayes and the two anonymous readers for *Gender & History* for their constructive criticism.

1. Though the Soviets also sent cameramen to the camps that the Red Army discovered in the East, this article focuses on the Western Allies' liberation of camps in the West and on documentary films produced by the Americans, British and French. An examination of

whether gender played a different role in the more explicitly accusatory and triumphant Soviet films could be worthwhile.

2. For the heated public debate, see Gabriel Schoenfeld, 'Auschwitz and the Professors', *Commentary* 105/6 (June 1998), pp. 42–6 and numerous letters written in response in *Commentary* 106/2 (August 1998), pp. 14–25.

3. Atina Grossmann, 'Women and the Holocaust: Four Recent Titles', *Holocaust and Genocide Studies* 16 (2002), pp. 94–108, here p. 94.

4. The scandalousness of killing women and children originates in an idea of warfare that defines war as armed men fighting each other. Although purposeful killing of civilians has occurred in most wars – often used systematically to humiliate the enemy – soldiers prefer to think of themselves as brave warriors. Even members of firing squads showed more scruples when ordered to shoot women and children. See Christopher Browning, *Ordinary Men: Reserve Police Battalion 101 and the Final Solution in Poland* (New York: HarperCollins, 1992), pp. 66, 67, 69, 73, 75, 185, 187. International law defines violent acts that are unnecessary to win a battle as war crimes. What I mean to criticise here, however, is the thoughtless convention of the media today to count the casualty figures for women and children separately, involuntarily implying that the death of men is less unjustifiable or 'tragic'.

5. She bases her analysis on Himmler's speeches in front of SS men, in which he called his order to kill women and children as well 'not so easy to give or so simple to carry out' and justified this order by the consideration that it would not make sense to exterminate the men 'while letting avengers in shape of children ... grow up'. Joan Ringelheim, 'Women and the Holocaust: A Reconsideration of Research', in Carol Rittner and John Roth (eds), *Different Voices: Women and the Holocaust* (New York: Paragon House, 1993), pp. 373–405, here p. 392. In the field of women's studies, scholars like Gisela Bock have stressed repeatedly that during the Third Reich race was a more basic category than gender: Jewish women were targeted for persecution and death together with Jewish men. Although Nazism was male-dominated in political practice and ideology, so-called 'Aryan' women, loyal to the regime, could pursue careers and receive promotion and various benefits. Feminist research thus goes astray when it assumes that all women were victims in Nazi Germany. See, e.g., Gisela Bock, 'Nazi Gender Policies and Women's History', in Georges Duby and Michelle Perrot (eds), *A History of Women in the West*, vol. 5: *Toward a Cultural Identity in the Twentieth Century* (Cambridge: Belknap Press of Harvard University Press, 1994), pp. 149–76.

6. For an exception to this rule, see Ulrike Weckel and Edgar Wolfrum (eds), *'Bestien' und 'Befehlsempfänger': Frauen und Männer in NS-Prozessen nach 1945* (Göttingen: Vandenhoeck & Ruprecht, 2003).

7. The basic work on SS women is by Gudrun Schwarz. See, for example, her English article, 'During Total War, We Girls Want to be Where We Can Really Accomplish Something: What Women Do in Wartime', in Omer Bartov, Atina Grossmann and Mary Nolan (eds), *Crimes of War: Guilt and Denial in the Twentieth Century* (New York: New Press, 2002), pp. 121–37.

8. The speech is reproduced in *Internationaler Militärgerichtshof: Prozess gegen die Hauptkriegsverbrecher (International Military Tribunal for the Trial of German Major War Criminals)*, Document 1919-PS, vol. 29 (Nuremberg, 1948), pp. 110–73, here p. 145.

9. There is hardly any literature on the early documentary films I analyse here. Several studies, however, deal with photographs taken during the camps' liberation. Except for the work of Barbie Zelizer, which I discuss below, these books do not systematically take questions of gender into account.

10. Barbara Johr, 'Die alliierte Kamera – Das US-Army Signal Corps', in Barbara Johr, *Reisen ins Leben – Weiterleben nach einer Kindheit in Auschwitz* (Bremen: Donat, 1997), pp. 179–206. On the British Army Film and Photographic Unit (AFPU), see Martin Caiger-Smith (ed.), *The Face of the Enemy: British Photographers in Germany 1944–1952* (London: Nishen, 1988), pp. 5–26.

11. 'General Directive for Cameramen in the Field' and 'Material Needed for Proposed Motion Picture on German Atrocities', undated, the first presumably written shortly before, the latter shortly after the end of the war. National Archives and Records Administration, College Park, Maryland (NARA), RG 260/OMGUS, ICD, MPB, Box 290, Folder: Film Atrocity.
12. Margaret Bourke-White, *Portrait of Myself* (New York: Simon and Schuster, 1963), pp. 259–60.
13. Margaret Bourke-White, *'Dear Fatherland, Rest Quietly': A Report on the Collapse of Hitler's 'Thousand Years'* (New York: Simon & Schuster, 1946).
14. Elizabeth Sussex, 'The Fate of F3080', *Sight and Sound* 53 (1984), pp. 92–7, esp. p. 93.
15. In Robert Abzug, *Inside the Vicious Heart: Americans and the Liberation of Nazi Concentration Camps* (New York: Oxford University Press, 1985), pp. 56, 86, 132. The commentator in the last quotation was surprised to discover professors, doctors, writers and generals among them, some of whom spoke English.
16. Martha Gellhorn, *The Face of War* (New York: Simon & Schuster, 1959), p. 235.
17. See as one of the most intriguing examples Imre Kertész's novel *Fateless*, trans. Christopher C. Wilson and Katharina M. Wilson (Evanston: Northwestern University Press, 1992), pp. 91–8.
18. Primo Levi, *Survival in Auschwitz: The Nazi Assault on Humanity*, trans. Stuart Woolf (New York: Collier Books, 1959), p. 36. The literal translation of the Italian title *Se questo è un uomo* is 'If this is a man'.
19. See also reminiscence of former intelligence officer Morris Parloff, in Abzug, *Vicious Heart*, p. 42.
20. Abzug, *Vicious Heart*, p. 58.
21. Paul Kemp, 'The Liberation of Bergen-Belsen Concentration Camp in April 1945: The Testimony of Those Involved', *Imperial War Museum Review* 5 (1990), pp. 28–41.
22. Film Reel and Dope Sheet A 700/335/4: Belsen Concentration Camp. 'Harrods', 15–16 May 1945, Photographer: Sgt Hewitt. Film & Video Archive (FVA), Imperial War Museum, London (IWM).
23. Dope Sheet A 700/335/4. See also similar captions to cameraman Hewitt's photographs from the same occasion. BU 6365, Photograph Archive (PA), IWM.
24. Joanne Reilly, *Belsen: The Liberation of the Concentration Camp* (London: Routledge, 1998), pp. 39–40.
25. Hagit Lavsky seems to be not principally opposed to ascribing a concern about clothes and outer appearance to female survivors. Without reference to the Harrods episode, her argument gives the stereotype another turn, however: 'Their sense of shame and modesty returned, and the women started paying attention to how they looked'. Hagit Lavsky, *New Beginnings: Holocaust Survivors in Bergen-Belsen and in the British Zone in Germany, 1945–1950* (Detroit: Wayne State University Press, 2002), p. 48.
26. Sgt. Hewitt, BU 6369–71, 16–17 May 1945, Belsen Concentration Camp, PA, IWM, reprinted in Hôtel de Sully, *Mémoire des Camps: Photographies des camps de concentration et d'extermination nazis, 1933–1999* (Paris: Marval, 2001), pp. 164–5.
27. See Jean Mohr's vivid examples of ambiguity and John Berger's theorisation of the phenomenon in their book, *Another Way of Telling* (London: Writers and Readers Publishing Cooperative Society, 1982).
28. 'Material Needed for Proposed Picture on German Atrocities', NARA.
29. Legend to Sgt Hewitt, B U 6369–6371, 16–17 May 1945, Belsen Concentration Camp, PA, IWM.
30. Barbie Zelizer is mistaken when she describes Margit Schwartz in the third photograph as 'looking alluringly at the camera, as she has been photographed before the war'. Not even in the old photograph did 'sex appeal' seem to have been an issue. It is out of the question for the later one. Barbie Zelizer, 'Gender and Atrocity: Women in Holocaust Photographs', in Barbie Zelizer (ed.), *Visual Culture and the Holocaust* (New Brunswick: Rutgers University Press, 2001), pp. 247–71, here p. 264.

31. Annette Kuhn, *Family Secrets: Acts of Memory and Imagination* (London: Verso, 1995), pp. 12, 15. See also Berger and Mohr, *Another Way of Telling*, esp. pp. 86–9, 108, 280.
32. The third photograph appeared with the caption 'A very old woman of 31 years, driven mad by hunger and maltreatment' in the US Military Government's photo brochure *KZ*, distributed in autumn 1945 in Germany's American zone of occupation for re-education purposes. Cornelia Brink, *Ikonen der Vernichtung: Öffentlicher Gebrauch von Fotografien aus nationalsozialistischen Konzentrationslagern nach 1945* (Berlin: Akademie Verlag, 1998), p. 69. The first and third photographs with the insert 'C'est la même personne' were printed in Eugène Aroneanu, *Konzentrationslager. Tatsachenbericht über die an der Menschheit begangenen Verbrechen* (Baden-Baden: Arbeitsgemeinschaft 'Das Licht', 1947).
33. Kemp, 'The Liberation of Bergen-Belsen Concentration Camp', pp. 32, 33.
34. The *List of Names* at the Memorial Bergen-Belsen does not record whether Margit Schwartz died in the hospital or could be discharged.
35. Parts of the 'Harrods' material do appear in the not-screened hour-long British compilation later entitled *Memory of the Camps* (see below). The commentary claims that the inmates gossiped about clothes 'as women love to do' but then went on, 'There was something symbolic about new clothes. New clothes meant renewed hope. They donned them with pride'. All quotations from the commentaries are my own transcriptions from the films.
36. For information on the various films, including hints on where to find copies today, see the database 'Cinematographie des Holocaust' of the Fritz Bauer Institut, Frankfurt: <http://www.cine-holocaust.de/>.
37. See the seminal work in sensualistic film theory: Siegfried Kracauer, *Theory of Film: The Redemption of Physical Reality* (New York: Oxford University Press, 1960), esp. pp. 157–9 and its insightful interpretation by Miriam Hansen, '"With Skin and Hair": Kracauer's Theory of Film, Marseille 1940', *Critical Inquiry* 19 (1993), pp. 437–69.
38. These are the following: *Atrocities–The Evidence* in *Movietone News*, GB, 24 April 1945; *Welt im Film*, No. 5: *KZ*, US/GB, 15 June 1945; *Les Camps de la Mort*, F, 1945; *Nazi Concentration Camps*, US (Counsel for Prosecution of Axis Criminality), 1945, dir. George Stevens; *Your Job in Germany*, US (War Department), 1945, supervised by Frank Capra; *Deutschland Erwache (Germany Awake)*, US (War Department), 1945; *Die Todesmühlen*, US (Information Control Division), 1945, dir. Hanus Burger, supervised by Billy Wilder; *Death Mills*, US (War Department), 1946; *Memory of the Camps*, GB (Ministry of Information), 1946, dir. Stewart McAllister, supervised by Alfred Hitchcock, preview (of fragment), 1983.
39. Abzug, *Vicious Heart*, p. 138.
40. Sven Kramer calls the gaze of the photographers shameless and accuses them of repeating Nazi dehumanisation through their pictorial strategy of shock. Sven Kramer, 'Nacktheit in Holocaust-Fotos und -Filmen', in Sven Kramer (ed.), *Die Shoah im Bild* (Munich: edition text + kritik, 2003), pp. 225–48, here p. 235.
41. See the request to delete shots of exposed genital organs quoted by David Culbert, 'American Film Policy in the Re-education of Germany after 1945', in Nicholas Pronay and Keith Wilson (eds), *The Political Re-education of Germany and her Allies after World War II* (London: Croom Helm, 1985), pp. 173–202, here p. 176, n. 9.
42. All films and commentary versions except one have a male voice-over. The exception is *Di Toit Milen*, a Yiddish-language version of the American film *Die Todesmühlen*, produced for German viewers (see below). It is strange enough that such a version for survivors was produced at all; even more strangely, the Yiddish commentary is a literal translation of the original German one that clearly addressed *Mitläufer* (bystanders).
43. All reopened movie theatres of a region had to show this twenty-minute film for an entire week and not in conjunction with any feature film. On the history of the film's production see Brewster S. Chamberlin, '*Todesmühlen*: Ein früher Versuch zur Massen-"Umerziehung" im besetzten Deutschland', *Vierteljahrshefte für Zeitgeschichte* 29 (1981), pp. 420–36.

44. Quotations from German-language commentaries are my own translations. In English-language versions of the same films the commentary may be different.
45. The children in a famous film sequence from Auschwitz, who all roll up their sleeves in order to show to the camera the numbers tattooed onto their arms, are atypical as well. They only survived because as twins they were used for 'medical' experiments.
46. *Welt im Film*, No 5: *KZ*.
47. Bourke-White, '*Dear Fatherland, Rest Quietly*', pp. 76–80.
48. *Die Todesmühlen*.
49. The estimated 100,000 Jewish survivors of the mass killings made up no more than 20 per cent of the entire concentration camp population at the end of the war. Nevertheless, it is striking that without exception, in these early films Jews are not yet referred to as those whom the Nazis persecuted and murdered most systematically and in the largest number. Most films classified the victims predominantly by nationality. The Allies argued that they meant to avoid perpetuating Nazi classifications. Foregrounding nationality and not ethnicity undoubtedly also helped the Allies in regard to repatriation issues to limit Jewish survivors' emigration to Palestine, which was the concern of the British. Anti-Semitic resentment at governmental level also cannot be ruled out. See Henry Friedlander, 'Darkness and Dawn in 1945: The Nazis, the Allies and the Survivors', in *1945: The Year of Liberation* (Washington, DC: US Holocaust Memorial Museum, 1995), pp. 11–35, esp. pp. 24–7.
50. My assessment of the significance of gender in the films differs from Barbie Zelizer's theses about strategic presentations of photographs in the contemporary British and American press. In her view, pictures of female victims were hardly ever used for accurate documentation but 'as markers of a larger story', that is to say in a symbolic and metaphorical way. Zelizer criticises this larger atrocity story as a master-narrative that failed to reflect the full range of female experiences in the camps. Zelizer, 'Gender and Atrocity'.
51. In a letter, one of the liberators of Bergen-Belsen noted his consternation when women, peeling potatoes among hundreds of corpses, smiled when he lifted his camera. See Caiger-Smith (ed.), *The Face of the Enemy*, p. 14.
52. Sussex, 'The Fate of F3080'.
53. Jeffrey Shandler, *While America Watches: Televising the Holocaust* (New York: Oxford University Press, 1999), pp. 16–18, makes a similar observation with regard to various American newsreels.
54. See the known cases of reconstruction and their discussion in, Clémont Chéroux, '"L'Epiphanie négative": Production, diffusion et réception des photographies de la libération des camps', in Hôtel de Sully, *Mémoire des Camps*, pp. 103–27, here pp. 115–17.
55. Appearances clearly still male also mark those Buchenwald survivors whom Margaret Bourke-White staged behind barbed wire in her famous shot. Though it is interesting that a female photographer took this picture of intact masculinity, the fact should not be over-interpreted in terms of a 'female gaze'. Like Lee Miller, Bourke-White visited only places where men had been imprisoned. What distinguishes their photographs from the pictures of army cameramen is their professionalism and personal style. On the reprocessing of this and other images in other genres see Marianne Hirsch, 'Surviving Images: Holocaust Photographs and the Work of Postmemory', *Yale Journal of Criticism* 14 (2001), pp. 5–37.
56. The idea that sexual significance had been erased from many bodies is briefly raised in Zelizer's analysis of the photographs. But she focuses more on what can be seen in the pictures than on what might have happened to these people in reality. Zelizer, 'Gender and Atrocity', pp. 263–4.
57. Susan Sontag, *Regarding the Pain of Others* (New York: Farrar, Straus & Giroux, 2003), p. 42.

58. Produced to give evidence to the tribunal, *Nazi Concentration Camps* was the documentary that displayed the most efforts to include the survivors' perspective, presenting them as witnesses.
59. 'Material Needed for Proposed Picture on German Atrocities', NARA.
60. Peter Tanner quoted in Elizabeth Sussex, 'The Fate of F3080', p. 96. Photographs of lynched SS men do exist though.
61. The German-language original does without irony, presumably because one did not expect the German audience to catch it. Instead the commentary on the perpetrators is harsh but factually oriented.
62. Silke Wenk, 'Rhetoriken der Pornografisierung. Rahmungen des Blicks auf die NS-Verbrechen', in Insa Eschebach, Sigrid Jacobeit and Silke Wenk (eds), *Gedächtnis und Geschlecht: Deutungsmuster in Darstellungen des nationalsozialistischen Genozids* (Frankfurt and New York: Campus, 2002), pp. 269–94.
63. I do not agree with Barbie Zelizer's characterisation of the SS women as 'genderless' who had 'pushed the boundaries of female gendered behaviour beyond the category itself'. Since Zelizer designates 'over-gendered' and 'genderless' representations of women according to their correspondence with stereotypes of femininity, she can only conclude that stereotypes dominated in the photographs' presentations of women. Zelizer, 'Gender and Atrocity', p. 264.
64. Zelizer, 'Gender and Atrocity', p. 251.
65. 'The Showing of the Atrocity Film to Ps/W', 1 August 1945, The National Archives, Kew (TNA), FO 939/352.
66. On the reception of Ilse Koch see Alexandra Przyrembel, 'Transfixed by an Image: Ilse Koch, the "Kommandeuse of Buchenwald"', *German History* 19 (2001), pp. 369–99.
67. For an interesting, though debatable, interpretation of these artefacts and their function in the courtroom see Lawrence Douglas, 'The Shrunken Head of Buchenwald: Icons of Atrocity at Nuremberg', in Barbie Zelizer (ed.), *Visual Culture*, pp. 275–99.
68. See the following titles: Browning, *Ordinary Men*; Gisela Bock, 'Ordinary Women in Nazi Germany: Perpetrators, Victims, Followers and Bystanders', in Dalia Ofer and Lenore J. Weitzman (eds), *Women in the Holocaust* (New Haven: Yale University Press, 1998), pp. 85–100; Daniel J. Goldhagen, *Hitler's Willing Executioners: Ordinary Germans and the Holocaust* (New York: Alfred A. Knopf, 1996).
69. I found this expression in Marianne Hirsch and Leo Spitzer, 'Gendered Translations: Claude Lanzmann's *Shoah*', in Miriam Cooke and Angela Woollacott (eds), *Gendering War Talk* (Princeton: Princeton University Press, 1993), pp. 3–19, here p. 3.

3 Images of Virtuous Women: Morality, Gender and Power in Argentina between the World Wars

María Fernanda Lorenzo, Ana Lía Rey and Cecilia Tossounian

Early in 1823 the Minister for Home Affairs and president-to-be of Argentina, Bernardino Rivadavia, created the Beneficent Society and established the Awards for Virtue (*Premios a la Virtud*). In his speech at the opening ceremony of the Beneficent Society, Rivadavia claimed that the new institution should pursue 'moral perfection and spiritual work in the fair sex, dedication to industrious activities, which results from the combination of these attributes'.[1] This philanthropic institution, made up of women belonging to the Porteño (Buenos Aires) elite, took up the beneficent side of the state. As a true representative of the Argentine liberal tradition, Rivadavia intended to deprive the Church of its central role in charitable activities and to give a new role to *damas laicas* (lay ladies)[2] in taking care of other women and improving them both intellectually and morally.

This early and strong alliance between public power and the most renowned elite women had the main goal of developing civic virtues in future citizens by raising and educating them within the scope of the moral qualities these women embodied. The rules of the Awards for Virtue read,

> Every prize awarded for real merits is, apart from a rigorously fair tribute, a trigger promoting social perfection. Honour, dear to public awards, generally represents much more than its intrinsic value and it is a permanent way to encourage a practical life of virtue and attempts to acquire the qualities leading to such a reward.[3]

The idea of social perfection had its material realisation in four different prizes: one each for moral virtue and for industry in the case of adult women and two awards for dedication in the case of orphan girls, all of them to be financed by the national state. Eventually, the scope of these awards came to be widened, thanks to the private financial support to the institution, legacies in memory of relatives and donations meant to ratify the 'respectable name and honour' of donors. As a result, other categories of virtue and virtuous women were added to the list, such as filial and fraternal love, humility, unselfishness, marital love, outstanding tidiness and organisation in the home, poor widow shamed by her reduced social status and poorest and most long-suffering woman, among others.[4] All the awards reinforced what the Society saw as the intrinsic values of feminised poverty.

One of the most striking characteristics of the prizes is how regularly they were awarded. Every 26 May, in an unequivocal homage to the emancipating campaign that had culminated in the May 1810 Revolution, the Beneficent Society held its most important ceremony, the Virtue Ceremony (*Fiesta de la Virtud*); different dignitaries were invited every year. The ceremony came to a halt only during the Juan Manuel de Rosas administration (1835–52); then it continued without interruption until the Society had to accept greater governmental intervention during the administration of General Juan Domingo Perón (1946–55) in 1947. For more than 120 years, the 'ladies' in the Beneficent Society and the government formed a powerful alliance: the government acknowledged the Society's role as the moral guide of the nation and put the Society in charge of many health and welfare institutions.

However, the swift changes that took place between the late nineteenth and early twentieth centuries transformed the foundations and meaning of the alliance. Immigration, industrialisation and urbanisation led to the emergence of new patterns of social behaviour. This can clearly be seen in the increasing number of working women and in feminists' 'emancipation' from traditional female roles, which was reflected in tango lyrics and the language of the press. By the 1930s, many had come to the conclusion that these new identities dangerously threatened traditional morals. In this context, the moral role of elite women became the most secure guarantee supporting 'decent customs'.

On the other hand, during the 1920s and more clearly during the 1930s, there were changes in state policies of social intervention due to the emergence of the social issue in public discussion and the spread of a more scientific concept of social assistance. Gradually, the state took over popular social assistance, undermining the role that the ladies had played for a century.

This gradual process reached its peak in the period between the wars. While the Beneficent Society found that its charitable activities were being severely questioned, the moralising endeavour of rewarding virtue continued undiminished in visibility and public support. Analysing the contradiction between these two dimensions can help explain both the changes in female identities and the new views on social assistance emerging in this period. Based on the visibility of the award ceremony in the period between the wars, this essay investigates the role of the Society in those years. In addition it interrogates how the women belonging to the Beneficent Society constructed a representation of themselves which became the hegemonic model for Argentine women. Lastly, it discusses the ways in which women from popular sectors burst into this space of bourgeois representation.

The discussion and analysis included in this article are based mainly on the photographs taken at the Virtue Ceremony at the Colón Theatre. The corpus analysed is a continuum of institutional images picturing the prize-giving ceremony – images which were published on the front page of the most important media in those years.[5]

The *Fiesta de la Virtud*

European and American historiography has extensively studied the agency of women's associations in the formation of early social policies and in the development of welfare states. The women's social movements that arose in the late nineteenth and the early twentieth centuries throughout Europe and the United States[6] were mainly concerned with the needs of mothers and children, for whom they set up institutions and devised programmes. Between 1880 and 1920, states relied on the initiatives of these organisations to provide poor women and children with assistance and relief. The organisations also exerted their influence on the design and operation of welfare programmes.[7] From this historical perspective, what is peculiar about the Beneficent Society is that it is neither a completely private nor a totally public institution. From 1880, when state institutions in Buenos Aires acquired jurisdiction over the whole national territory, onwards, it was under the jurisdiction of the national Ministry of Internal Affairs, but it was funded by both the national government and private donations and it had no formal links with the Catholic Church.[8] In this sense, Argentina was one of the few countries where a voluntary association of politically active, elite women became an administrative agency of the Republican government without losing its full autonomy.

The activities of the Beneficent Society had two main channels. On the one hand, it tackled poverty and health issues among women and children from the popular sectors. It was in charge of managing the *Hospital Nacional de Alienadas* (Asylum for Insane Women), the *Hospital de Niños* (Children's Hospital), the *Colegio de Huérfanas de la Merced* (Mercy School for Orphan Girls), the *Casa de Expósitos* (Foundling Home) and the Hospital Rivadavia, among other institutions. On the other hand, it managed two financial aid programmes for poor families. The ladies distributed aid from this 'Poor Fund' (*Fondo de Pobres*) on a monthly basis, as well as giving out the Awards for Virtue, money rewards handed over in the sophisticated annual ceremony to women who were their household's chief income earners.[9]

From its inception, the Virtue Ceremony was an important occasion for the Beneficent Society for several reasons. For one thing, it was the only opportunity the Society had to publicise the daily activities of the institutions it managed. Apart from the celebration, it was only possible for the Society to make statements that were published in newspapers every now and then. Besides, the ritual represented by the ceremony was the only moment when the ladies' values and beliefs shone in the public light. The catalogue of virtues that the ladies embodied, which were considered specific to their class and gender, propelled them to seek those very virtues in the lower-class women who received the awards. The ladies wanted to see those women's personal qualities reflected in the popular classes as a whole. The criterion for choosing virtuous women, established in 1823, was based on the idea that 'virtue is more meritorious and praiseworthy in women of the middle classes than in distinguished ladies, since the former lack the education and aspirations, which lead the latter to comply with the principles imparted to them'.[10] These virtues were embedded in maternalist discourse as an ideology highlighting women's capacity for motherhood and extending the values of care and morality to society as a whole. Several social actors have resorted to maternalist discourse, among them women's movements in the late nineteenth and mid-twentieth centuries. By extolling the private virtues of the domestic sphere, maternalist discourses legitimised the intervention of women in the public domain.[11] Thus, the ladies used the prize-giving ceremony as a visual display of their social role, namely, being the moral guide of the nation. Never was this role so evident, nor was its application so perfectly achieved as with the girls from the Beneficent Society's orphanages. In the 1937 Virtue Ceremony, President Carmen María del Pilar de Rodríguez Larreta pointed out,

> as for the girls, I believe we should improve their education and link them to new labour patterns. Our orphanages for girls produce outstanding nurses, baby-sitters, seamstresses, hygiene workers. It is our goal to educate women who are ready to perform various tasks and support their future husbands ... In this way, we are forming the core of families built upon the communion of feelings as well as on the collaborative attitude necessary to have thriving homes. We need to turn them into useful women, for we know they will make wonderful mothers and set a good example of Christian virtues for their offspring to follow.[12]

In this way, each 26 May, elite ladies hosted a variety of prestigious public figures and women from popular sectors attending the ceremony to receive their prizes. Both the protagonists and the audience took part in this celebration 'uniting the rich and the poor', as defined by Inés Dorrego de Unzué in 1921:

> I know that the distinguished audience listening to my words has not attended this celebration with the indifference of the public at a banal show ... Most of our guests come here every year as if they were attracted to the virtue of humble people, feeling close to our work because they share our ideals and keep careful track of our activities, almost in the need to assess them because they are considered to be part of the works of the nation.[13]

The press gave ample coverage to the ceremony: photographs of it appeared on the front page of the newspapers with the highest circulation in the country, such as *La Nación*, *El Mundo* and *La Prensa*, as well as in the magazine most widely consumed in the popular sector, *Caras y Caretas*. Even though their targets were different sectors of the population, these media taken together can be said to appeal to a wide urban public, increasingly eager to read and be well informed.[14] By the early 1930s, the print press had become modernised and in the new reading contract between readers and publishers, newspapers began to include photographs to illustrate news and to make informative texts more compact. In this context, by the end of the decade, the ladies had already appeared on the front pages. Later, in the late 1930s, the recognition of virtue was given only minor space in the overall organisation of newspapers, with a small, non-illustrated column referring to the ceremony in the society section.

Information about the photographers who took the pictures is altogether omitted in the newspapers. Besides, the captions below the photographs are highly repetitive throughout the whole decade and across newspapers, typically including the same adjectives: 'The "Awards for Virtue" ceremony was magnificent' or 'One aspect of the magnificent ceremony' and so on, followed by a list of the figures in the photograph. Articles, on the other hand, provide general descriptions of the ceremony and sometimes include snippets of the speech delivered by the Society's president or by a representative of the government, in addition to the ever-present list of prize-winners and the name of each prize.

Given their symbolic significance, public authorities who were present tended to be mentioned in newspaper chronicles,[15] but presidents did not appear in the photographs, thus highlighting the ladies' central position. They attended the ceremony and watched it from the 'avant scene' box assigned to the government at the Colon Theatre, the most important theatre in Argentina, devoted to satisfying the elite's taste for opera. Earlier ceremonies had been held at less socially significant places, such as the Templo San Ignacio (Saint Ignacio Church) first or the Colegio de Huérfanas de la Merced (Mercy School for Orphan Girls) or the Politeama Theatre later (Figure 1).

Attenders also changed over time. Until 1880, they were mainly women belonging to other charitable institutions and prominent churchmen. By the 1900s, the ceremony had become more opulent. Several government officials tended to be present, beginning with members of

Figure 1: Politeama Theatre. Awards for Virtue Ceremony.
Source: *Caras y Caretas*, year II, N°35, 3 June 1899, p. 12.

parliament. Gradually officials higher up the political ladder began attending, until the late 1920s when the Head of State also began to attend regularly. The ascending level of official attendance is a measure of the increasing importance of the ceremony. As the Awards for Virtue ceremony gained in importance, other charitable institutions such as the Damas de la Caridad (Charitable Ladies) decided to have their own ceremony and awards. Even one of the most popular social clubs, the Club Atlético Boca Juniors (Boca Juniors Athletic Club) began to award prizes to meritorious and selfless men in the neighbourhood on 25 May.[16] By 1913, these institutions held ceremonies very similar to the ones organised by the Beneficent Society at the end of the nineteenth century.

Another important guest at the ceremony, placed in the centre of the stage, was the Minister of Foreign Affairs and Religion, present because the Society had been under the jurisdiction of this Ministry since 1908. The presence of Minister Carlos Saavedra Lamas in the photographs should also be mentioned, because his wife had a prominent role in the Beneficent Society of the city of Buenos Aires (Figure 2). Other important visitors that can be seen in the pictures are Monsignor Santiago Luis Copello, Monsignor José Frietta and Catholic Nuncio Felipe Cortesi, all of them joining in the ladies' work (Figure 3).[17] Further in the background of both photographs, a group of women can be seen, all dressed in indistinguishable white: they are the orphan girls and the nurses looking at the centre of the stage.

In this elitist frieze where politics and religion appear intertwined, the outstanding central figures are the Society's officers. Following the yearly customary practice, the Society's president read out a detailed account of the activities carried out in each institution managed by the Society and presented the tasks ahead. Ever-present were also the usual tribute to Rivadavia and the secretaries' reading of the proceedings describing the work of the 'ladies who visited the poor' (*visitadoras de pobres*) and the list of prize-winners.[18]

The choice of lower-class women for the prizes depended solely on the annual selection made by the *Comisión de visitadoras de pobres*. These ladies were minor society members who visited the homes of the candidates for the awards and checked the truthfulness of their stories, as well as inspecting how they lived. Family sacrifice, love of work and acceptance of one's own social condition were highly valued. According to the criteria established in 1823:

> The real target of the awards should be virtue in poverty, focused on personal work without resources or relationships with pious people. Anyone who finds herself in extreme poverty, so as not to be a social burden, should rely upon her

Figure 2: Distribution of the Awards for Virtue in the Teatro Colón. Mrs Adelia Harilaos de Olmos pronouncing her speech in front of the first lady of the Republic, and the Minister of Foreign Affairs and Religion of External Relationships, 1932. Source: AGN. Inventory 82500.

Figure 3: Awards for Virtue Ceremony, 1938. Source: AGN. Inventory 157943.

own labour only and, when earnings are not enough, dispose of her belongings and accept with resignation what Providence holds: this is undoubtedly what informs the spirit of the law and it is our duty to find sublimity in moral behaviour.[19]

One of the poor visitors explained that she had found 'many good examples of altruism, faithfulness, modesty and self-denial, embarrassing but noble poverty, resigned misfortune and we have tried to comfort them, helping those in need and rewarding the virtuous ones'.[20]

In 1930, the committee reported that they had visited 553 homes and given seventy-eight Awards for Virtue.[21] The increasing number of prizes was a result of the ever-growing number of donations to the Beneficent Society from prominent families, which allows for an interesting reading of the elite's attitude towards 'poor women with dignity'. Most of the rich who gave away money did not do so anonymously but with the aim that some of the prizes be named after them or their relatives.[22]

Nevertheless, apart from these very general references at the ceremony, in both newspaper articles and the Society's proceedings there appeared only the names of the women honoured and their corresponding prizes. This can be contrasted with prize-giving ceremonies before the Great War, when a detailed account of the women's way of living was the central part of the celebration and was later included in news articles,[23] usually accompanied by the relevant pictures (Figures 1 and 4).

The Virtue Ceremony: the old Republican ritual revisited

For more than 120 years, the Virtue Ceremony was held in accordance with, as one of the Society's ladies put it, 'the tendencies and demands of the social environment in each age, without changing the assumptions its purpose is based on'.[24] In this view, what could have led to the ceremony gaining in public pre-eminence as it did in this period? In order to answer this question, it is necessary to enquire into the new role the ceremony played in the 1930s.

The years between the wars have a number of characteristics that can be applied to an analysis of the ceremony. The economic crisis and the growing conservative opposition in politics brought the era of Radical rule – which had begun in 1916 in the aftermath of the first election with compulsory secret ballot for men only, because of the 1912 Sáenz Peña Law – to an end. In September 1930, a civil-cum-military *coup d'état* brought General José F. Uriburu to power. Uriburu's rule ended in

Figure 4: Josefina Brisalda, Eduarda Bernal and María Bajarano. Beneficent Society of Buenos Aires. Balcarce Award for filial love, 1908. *Source:* Archivo *Caras y Caretas*, AGN. Inventory 263441.

February 1932. He was followed by General Agustín P. Justo, who governed from 1932 to 1938 as a result of the electoral fraud that gripped the country for more than a decade. Besides these political changes, from the late nineteenth century onwards, Argentina's social structure became increasing complex, concomitant with the growth and diversification of the country's production structure.[25] In the first decades of the twentieth century, this industrialisation and urbanisation process brought about new social issues related to the population's standards of living and sanitation, the emergence of workers' unions and strikes.

More to the point, in the 1920s, this social modernisation process resulted in conflicts stemming from gender differences, the new role of women and the emergence of a new female figure: the so-called 'modern woman', nourished by the visible, active presence of working women, feminists and female intellectuals in the public sphere. Simultaneously, in Argentina, as in other societies, women walking along the streets on their own, smoking and going out to dances appeared in urban spaces. They came to be associated with consumption in advertisements for household appliances and beauty and cleaning products.[26] The gender system was therefore reformulated to accommodate these changes, at least to some extent. This process slowed down at the end of the 1920s and came to a halt in the 1930s.[27]

This new feminine figure represented a moral threat to some social sectors. Many times it was associated with excesses: this woman's body oozed sexual evils and social aberration. Moral and sexual themes turned into public issues thanks to the circulation of serial romance novels, plays and women's magazine articles. Tango and *milonga* lyrics also reflected the association of female attributes with urban disorder and, many times, efforts to correct this deviant behaviour. These tango lyrics by Homero Manzi are a good depiction of moral changes:

> Moralists grumble – but they're not right–/that the world is turned upside down in moral matters/that women in the past, as compared to modern ones/used to be modest and all that./So, at a glance, we can accept that/ but on a closer look what we see is different/ ... What is difficult is to be *virtuous* in today's clothing.[28]

Both popular and scientific discourses emerged at the time to control women and their bodies – an increasing number of representations warning women in particular and society in general against the dangers of sexual excesses and recommending the virtues of economy, work and providence.[29] An era of progressive conservatism began as regards the social roles of women an example of which can be seen in the Justo administration's attempt to reform the 1924 Law on Women's Civil Rights. The proposed reform would have taken the country back to the moment when married women were legally considered minors, with no right to work outside their homes unless their husbands granted a permit and no right to own real estate or be members of commercial partnerships or civil associations.

As Kathleen Newman suggests, a considerable sector of Argentinean society did not accept the representations of femininity that had emerged in the previous decades. They substituted the image of a woman who kept up with the times and yet preserved an eternal, i.e. nineteenth-century, femininity. Porteño aristocratic women were the perfect example of those values and so their pictures started to appear in general interest magazines.[30]

In this way, moral values were safely preserved by showing what was considered lost, exposing the female virtues of poor women and especially of not-so-poor women, to public opinion. Elite women found an empty space, a slot to be filled by this functional representation of femininity, which appeared in the public sphere through their portraits and in the photographs taken at the ceremony, both published in the media.

At the same time as Porteño aristocratic women gained pre-eminence as the best representatives of Argentinean femininity, conflicting views on how to design and manage social policies emerged. In the 1930s, the good relationship that had existed until then between the government and the Beneficent Society started to crack. Through the national Secretary of Hygiene (Departamento Nacional de Higiene, established in 1880) the state had initially tackled mainly urban sanitation problems; assistance programmes had originally been delegated to the Beneficent Society. From the late nineteenth century until the 1920s, the state and the ladies performed complementary tasks.[31] The new era, however, brought about a change in the state's pattern of social intervention.

The relationship with the Beneficent Society started to turn from complementarity to rivalry. The incipient clash in domains can be seen in the government's criticism of the lack of organisation in the Society's assistance system and in attempts to control the association. The debate between the advocates of public social assistance and the supporters of private charity had a long tradition, but it gained momentum in those years. The staunchest critics of private charity were a group of physicians working in the public sphere known as the 'hygienists', whose opinions were based on a scientific view of social issues. Their perspective led them to criticise beneficent actions, for they considered it to be associated with Christian charity, with trying to alleviate social evils without seeking to eradicate their causes. According to the hygienists, social assistance, on the contrary, should be based on prevention and this was the role of the state. As both groups were positioned in the same sphere, the ladies and the advocates of public social assistance fought for the funds provided by the state, generally allotted to the Beneficent

Society. The first steps in the creation of a centralised social assistance system were three converging factors set into motion in the late 1920s and early 1930s: a set of laws rationalising state subsidies,[32] the growing number of social services provided by the doctors and nurses in public hospitals, who replaced private charity in its old responsibilities[33] and a series of social laws intended to meet the needs of working women.[34]

But even though emerging social policies included efforts to control and replace the ladies in the work they had traditionally done, this tendency did not have enough strength or consensus yet to become established.[35] So, the 1930s were marked by a permanent struggle for power, and it was only in the following period of the Perón administration that the welfare state came into full force. The fact that elite women managed to keep some of their old power can explain why public social assistance was a latecomer in Argentina when compared to other South American countries.[36]

Oddly enough, when the alliance between the state and the Beneficent Society began to crack, as the criticisms of the former about the latter's work and institutions intensified, the Virtue Ceremony reached its peak in visibility and public support. These were the years when photographs of the ceremony appeared on newspaper and magazine front pages and the attendance of the president and other high-ranking officials was mentioned in the articles.

The emphasis on the ladies' moralising role led to some degree of understanding between the Beneficent Society and the state, turning the relation into a complex combination of conflict and complementarity, only resolved with the increased intervention in the Society's affairs and its subsequent dissolution during the Peronist administration.

The construction of virtuous bodies

The prize-giving ceremony can also be analysed as a fixed, performative ritual, since year in, year out, the same event was performed as a series of activities reinforced in each repetition of the ceremony. For each act, the Society ladies chose a political figure to deliver the main speech on behalf of the national authorities; every year, the Society's president reviewed the activities carried out. As the photographs show, year in, year out, the protagonists and the general public were located in a similar fashion, the four prizes provided by the government were awarded and the effort implied in the private prizes was praised.

Paul Connerton defines this kind of repetitive ritual as a 'liturgical language'. Rituals are performative – they crystallise meaning in words, gestures and postures repeated as a sequence of stereotypes.[37] Following this type of analysis, photographs are an apt artefact for reading the ceremony. Since rituals are cultural forms where performance has a central role, it is in the bodily substratum that some meanings can be found.

On the other hand, as Gillian Rose writes, the concept of a photograph's *representational space* 'connects the fictive spaces of the image with the spaces of its interpretation by considering the relations between image and audience implicit in particular spatial configuration'.[38] The pictures analysed show the work of the Society's ladies in Buenos Aires. Apart from creating a specific image of the ladies, the photographs give information about how the popular sectors were captured by the anonymous photographer. As noted by Luis Príamo in his study of the relation between photography and private life, when photographed, individuals from popular sectors 'hand over their intimacy', willingly or unwillingly, without having much control over the forms into which their images have been captured.[39]

The pictures, then, are a suitable means to reconstruct the ritual and performative aspects condensed in the ceremony and to enquire into the way in which bourgeois and popular sectors are represented in them.

The ladies as mothers of the nation

The prize-giving ceremony was a space where the ladies' values were enacted. The photographs show a ceremony that followed a script in which bodies were organised in a hierarchical order. All cultures express the choreography of authority in the body: power and rank can be seen in postures that reveal aspects of the relationship to others. The hierarchical organisation can also be seen in the position of all the social actors participating in the ceremony, as if they were a polyphonic choir.

In the photographs, the Beneficent Society's representatives are in the centre of the stage, their president flanked by male figures from the Church and the government. Before them lies the desk with the certificates to be awarded. These characters appear fore-grounded and considerably higher than the general public, who are excluded from the pictures' frame. In the background, there are minor social characters and low-level government officials. Behind those characters is a crowd of women: the orphan girls and the nurses. The choir-like display has a special effect. The central position is occupied by the nurses, who surround Bernardino Rivadavia's bust, with the orphans standing at both sides, as if they were a kind of internal audience on the stage, watching the parade of prize winners and authorities and, at the same time, being observed as the culminating product of the ladies' efforts as if in a game of symmetrical observation.

On the whole, the photographs reveal a role game in terms of gender. The ladies are the only female authorities at the ceremony and as such, they have a prominent place, together with the government authorities, all of them men, emphasising a clear role division. The state, then, is represented with two faces: a male one, that of the government's representatives and a female one, the ladies. By staging values such as altruism, effort and sacrifice – the values the ladies embody, which are considered inherently female – the ceremony highlights the motherly dimension of their activities. At the same time, it personifies the state in its roles of both the mother and the father of the prize winners (Figure 5).

From this perspective, the different places assigned to the characters can be seen to be arranged in a kind of female family tree constructed by the ladies in relation to those surrounding them. The lineage begins with the orphans, who will some day take part in the numerous philanthropic activities with their work and spiritual self-denial. Maybe some day they will also be rewarded for their virtues, but at the moment when the picture was taken, they symbolically represents the role of promise, the safeguard of the beneficent institution's greatness in the future. The nurses are the virtuous women of the present *par excellence*, spending their time in taking care of others. Last but not least, there are the poor, prize-winning women, the guests of honour in the ceremony, who are the symbolic embodiment of all the values distributed among the rest of the women in the event. In this sense, the ladies can be seen as the roots of this tree, transmitting the traditional values of the past to the professional women, the orphans and the prize-winning women. Taken together, these groups of women represents the past, present and future of the Beneficent Society. At the ritual's pinnacle, the Society's ladies bless the recreation of the lineage. Thus, they take on the role of moralising mothers of the nation.

Popular-sector women as virtuous women

The photographs showing the awarding of prizes reveal the marginality of the prize winners. While there are hundreds of pictures featuring the award certificates on the authorities' desk, only three portray the women who received them. In the corpus of photographs analysed, no caption saves those women from their anonymous status. Their individual virtues are unknown. When they were called to receive their award, some of the ladies belonging to the Society's board escorted them to the place where they would get the certificate proving their virtue. Even when they were being given the award, they did not get a close-up but a long shot or profile picture (Figure 6). However, this subordinate place within the photographs,

Figure 5: The stage of the Teatro Colón during distribution of the Awards for Virtue, 1939. Source: AGN. Inventory 162368.

Figure 6: Minister of External Relationships, Carlos Saavedra Lamas giving the Awards for Virtue to two ladies in the Teatro Colón, 1933. Source: AGN. Inventory 52514.

corresponding to the ladies' prominence in the ceremony, is not a hurdle to analysing how women from popular sectors are represented. This analysis begins from the observation that the images of virtuous women play a role that is in marked contrast to other representations of working women in those years, such as the image of the heroic and long-suffering labourer and, from a different perspective, the prostitute.[40]

The images of working women posed a challenge, since work, the paradigmatic realm of men, was considered a threat to femininity. One of the strategies employed to offset this perception was the maternalisation of feminine working-class figures. The threat posed by a woman associated with the sphere of work was thus toned down by linking her to the maternal condition.[41]

It is surprising that, in contrast, the photographs of virtuous women do not include indications of their condition as actual or potential mothers. The award-holders are never accompanied by their children when they come on stage. In fact, the only children present at the ceremony are those 'saved from being an orphan' by the ladies. This is perfectly consistent with the purpose of the ceremony, for the awards are given not for motherhood or for the values associated with it, but for having overcome life's hurdles with dignity and virtue.[42]

While in this period, the modern woman became a disturbing figure as regards moral customs and, therefore, for the nation's future, the ceremony represented prize winners as women who could not threaten the gender and social order, which was then reproduced successfully. How is this identity of poor but respectable women constructed in the photographs? First of all, these women can be recognised in the pictures through bodily differences denoting social differentiation. Besides, since the photographs have been taken in a de-contextualised setting, without reference to these women's daily lives, or to the tenements (*conventillos*) or districts from which they come, their otherness cannot be recognised in their spatial or social localisation. What differentiates them is rather shown in a distinct appearance as compared to the elite ladies. Prize winners are wearing simple clothes that emphasise their humble origins and their willingness to get past them, clothes that intentionally suggest sobriety and simplicity. The long shot captures the idea that their way of dressing shows some toned-down poverty rather than pauperism. Their simplicity is not expected to be diminished or transformed in order to be more in accordance with the opulence of the aristocratic space of the Colón Theatre. Thus, prize winners are represented as outside the event's magnificence. Their clothing is in sharp contrast to the elegant fur stoles, the opulent jewellery and the big hats that are part of the ladies' attire.

However, even though prize winners are clearly distinguished by the absence of overt symbols denoting their social status – an absence that consequently marks social class differences – they are trying to imitate the tastes and clothes of the matriarchs in their sobriety, identifying themselves with the ladies' values. Both groups are attired in long, dark coats covering their whole bodies and they are both wearing hats, which in those years signalled social cachet. These signs are part of representation codes of a type of femininity which confirm that these women are respectable as a group. Their bodies adhere to a rigid codification of what a virtuous woman should look like.

Some symbols, however, emphasise the differences, even when they are shared by both groups: the ladies' hats are bigger and in a highly ornate style and their coats are accompanied by furs and jewellery, elements worn moderately, if at all, by the virtuous women (see Figures 2 and 3). In this sense, Nancy Armstrong points out that 'image by image, popular photography produced a stereotypical body image that came to represent the female. Against this standard, any variation could be measured: promiscuous women, working class women'.[43]

The lack of information on the selection of prize winners, their living conditions and the reasons why they were chosen can be understood when their photographed bodies are analysed in the framework of the ceremony. The values rewarded emanated from the virtuous bodies, as they were constructed in these photographs, without the need to justify the selection explicitly.[44] The press of the period displayed the ceremony's photographs as evidence of model bodies, which did not need to be changed because they were naturally praiseworthy. It is precisely the fact that the prizes were awarded to these women for what they were and not for what they had been in the past or could be in the future that rendered them an apt representation to project virtues (Figure 5).

In this sense, the virtuous woman can be understood as the counterpart of the representation of the prostitute. Both were public women, but the former is constructed as the epitome of the woman who, by way of persistence and effort, has managed to overcome the trials of her social background and forge a decent future for herself. The latter, on the other hand, represents the woman who has fallen prey to social pressure, lacking the necessary willpower to get out of indecency. Thus, the poor but virtuous woman emerges as one of several identities – certainly the most reassuring one – that the representation of working women can take.

The ceremony's ritual was designed to favour the prize winners' identification with the canonical virtue proposed by the ladies. This was achieved through an appropriate mixture of emotional appeal and reaffirmation of codified social norms. One of the goals of a ritual is to get some rules to be naturally accepted, making them universal and desirable. As Victor Turner suggests, in a ritual, norms and values are loaded with emotion and emotions, in turn, become nobler through the contact with social values.[45]

In this respect, the fact that the ceremony was held at the Colón Theatre in Buenos Aires allowed prize-winning women to enter a harmonious space, isolated from other contexts marked by the pollution of social conflict and mixture. The ladies escorted the winners to get their certificates and bowed to them, making the contrast between their magnificence and the simplicity of the virtuous women's attire emerge. The 'enacted' distance makes the theatrical nature of the event evident. The fact that the ceremony took place in a deliberately unreal scenario, within the context of conflict-free coexistence, was a means to promote the ladies' social norms and to intensify the emotional appeal to the public. The temporal reiteration of these values produced a naturalisation of those virtuous bodies, with the result that 'annoyance of moral repression turns into love of virtue'.[46]

New readings: virtue and parody

A look at the photographs that can only recognise disciplinary discourses runs the risk of placing the representation exclusively on the side of authority. Nevertheless, this tendency can be reversed if discourses are deliberately allowed to proliferate and the meaning of the pictures is reconstructed accordingly.[47] This observation raises the question of how women from popular sectors might have reacted to the prizes and the photographs of the ceremony published in the newspapers and magazines of the period. Probing into subordinate classes' representations is fraught with difficulties and it is even more so in the case of women, given the invisibility that has characterised their history. The scarcity of direct sources and testimonies makes an indirect approach and a counter-reading necessary and especially valuable. Together with photographs, other non-traditional sources can be a suitable means to accomplish this goal.

In this vein, a play published by *La Escena* magazine, entitled *Premios a la Virtud*, can be analysed.[48] Drama, especially the so-called *sainete* (satirical farce), was one of the genres in which popular traditions found expression. As opposed to highbrow drama and together with bullfighting, cockfighting and *pato* (a sport played on horseback), the *sainete* was part of popular entertainment in those years. One of its main characteristics was a generally sardonic and stereotypical presentation of characters.[49]

The plot of this play develops out of the vicissitudes of a family made up of a mother, two daughters and a son, after their economic collapse. The backbone of the play is the contrast between the sisters: one of them has been selected to be awarded the prize for her virtue, whereas the other has fallen into the disgrace of prostitution. The play is useful as a source to analyse how the Virtue Ceremony was conceived of among the popular classes. In a satirical tone, the play offers an inversion of the traditional values represented by the characters. Rosa Blanca, the older sister, the one in the 'disgraceful' trade, is in fact virtuous, for her 'sacrifice' provides for the whole family. They live on her earnings, but she is looked down upon and marginalised because she has an immoral job. The son, who is expected to take on the social responsibility of maintaining his mother and sisters after the death of the *pater familias*, is depicted as a lazy man who lives off his sister. All the characters are revealed in their true nature and their fake morals are criticised in the play.

The play's climax comes when the Society's ladies arrive at the house to meet the sister chosen for the prize. In a scene appealing to the spectator/reader's complicity, one of the ladies complains at the arrival of a photographer from *Caras y Caretas*, even though later it is found out that the ladies were the ones who called him. The ladies, who do not know about Rosa Blanca's trade and are led to believe that she is also involved in charity, insist that she appear in the group photograph, 'so that people can see how good deeds are rewarded'. Rosa Blanca agrees, reluctant at first, but later pleased with the ironic situation. In the end, the photograph captures the ladies and the two poor but 'virtuous' sisters. Knowing that there is one daughter who 'chose a mistaken path' yet not realising that that daughter is Rosa Blanca herself, the ladies criticise her severely and praise the other daughter's virtue. After listening to the ladies' criticism for some time, Rosa Blanca cries, 'And don't you think it must be really hard for a woman born with a good nature to become bad? ... As far as I know, that daughter became a sinner to prevent her family from falling into poverty; they were hungry and hunger knows nothing about virtue'. The play ends with Rosa Blanca's rebellion against her family's disdain and her running away with Federico, her fiancé, who is an anarchist and does not care about her allegedly immoral past. As he puts it, 'it is unfair not to reward so much self-denial'.

As a parody of the norms in force, the *sainete* manages to debunk them. By mocking what virtue and the ladies' work mean, the play shows how unnatural this type of gender behaviour is. The parodic staging of what are natural norms for the ladies is used precisely to reveal their performative nature. Rosa Blanca embodies all the moral values despised by the ladies and by society in general. She symbolises the prostitute that has been labelled in other spaces as the origin of all the nation's social evils. In this play, however, prostitution is rather the painful trade of a virtuous woman. This re-signifying practice whereby the prostitute gets rid of the condemnation associated with the word and becomes the 'true' virtuous woman reveals the subversive potential of the parodic appropriation of discourse. In the process, the virtuous identity so laboriously constructed by the ladies is also dismantled. In an ironic play of symmetries, the disciplined bodies of the women portrayed by the *Caras y Caretas*'s photographer, analysed in the previous section, acquire a different meaning here. The *representational space* of this photograph has changed, since a different public now reads the same picture with new and critical eyes.

Before disappearing, every star has its zenith and the Awards for Virtue, the most important public ceremony of Porteño elite women in the years between the wars, were no exception. A few years after the period analysed in this paper, the Beneficent Society's ladies lost the position they had held secure for more than 120 years.

This article has provided an analysis of the prize-giving ceremony of the Awards for Virtue and the representation of femininity constructed by Porteño elite ladies through those prizes in the years between the wars. The photographs of the ceremony published in newspapers proved to be one of the most significant sources for the analysis.

For more than a century, the structure of the ceremony changed little. The same virtues that Rivadavia had identified in 1823 were rewarded, the same well-known homage to the Beneficent Society's founder was paid and the same staging of the ladies' efforts was performed, with the hope that the institution had a promising future and with the emphasis on the importance of its activities for the nation's moral perfection. Throughout the nineteenth century, the state left important social assistance programmes in the hands of the Society's ladies, a process which started to be reversed in the first decades of the twentieth century. Even as the state questioned their charitable activities, the ceremony gained in renown, as testified to by the use of increasingly magnificent spaces and the presence of Heads of State. Prizes also grew in number, as a result of the increase in private donations made to the institution.

The ceremony's public visibility reached its peak in the 1930s, especially as a result of the photographs published in the media. The ladies' visual prominence in the pictures was so great that prize winners, allegedly the protagonists of the event, could barely be seen, let alone recognised. Thus, the analysis of the pictures allows for the reconstruction of the representations of femininity displayed at the ceremony.

In their role as mothers of the nation, the ladies personified a type of femininity that guaranteed the permanence of traditional moral standards just when changes in customs seemed to be threatening them. Altruism, effort and sacrifice were the values they embodied and projected onto prize winners. The Awards for Virtue were the tool to construct the representation of women from popular sectors as poor but virtuous. Such a representation, enacted in the artificial harmony of the Colón Theatre, yielded a reassuring image for the traditional gender and social order, in contrast to the disturbing representations of women that arose from the profound and conflicting social changes that characterised Argentina's social modernisation.

These other possible representations contain a potential for criticism of the female identity defined by bourgeois femininity. The image of Rosa Blanca, the virtuous prostitute, appearing in a photograph for *Caras y Caretas* with the 'beneficent ladies', is emblematic of the multiplicity of discourses that can be read from the same photograph.

Notes

We wish to thank Patricia Hayes, who organised the International Workshop on Gender & Visuality, University of the Western Cape, 26–29 August 2004, where this paper was originally presented; SEPHIS (The South-South Exchange Programme for Research on the History of Development), which made our trip to South Africa possible; and our colleagues from the Archivo Palabras e Imágenes de Mujeres (APIM) for their insightful comments.

1. In María Inés Passanante, *Pobreza y Acción Social en la Historia Argentina: de la Beneficencia a la Seguridad Social* (Buenos Aires: Humanitas, 1987), p. 11.

2. The members of the Beneficent Society, representing the elite classes, were referred to and referred to themselves as *damas*, translated as 'ladies' in this essay.
3. Government decree to implement the Awards for Virtue, Buenos Aires, 1 March 1823. In Karen Mead, 'Oligarchs, Doctors and Nuns: Public Health and Beneficence in Buenos Aires, 1880–1914' (unpublished doctoral thesis, University of California, Santa Barbara, 1994), p. 152.
4. 'Premios a la Virtud', *Sociedad de Beneficencia, Memorias* (Buenos Aires: Imprenta de la Escuela de Artes y Oficios del Asilo de Huérfanos, 1911–43).
5. All the photographs analysed in this paper are kept at the Departamento de Documentos Fotográficos in the Archivo General de la Nación, Buenos Aires.
6. For the European case, see Seth Koven and Sonya Michel (eds), *Mothers of a New World: Maternalist Politics and the Origins of Welfare States* (London: Routledge, 1993); Gisela Bock and Pat Thane (eds), *Maternity and Gender Policies: Women and the Rise of European Welfare States 1880s–1950s* (London: Routledge, 1991). For the American case, see Theda Skocpol, *Protecting Soldiers and Mothers: The Political Origins of Social Policy in the United States* (Cambridge: Harvard University Press, 1992); Linda Gordon (ed.), *Women, the State and Welfare* (Madison: University of Wisconsin Press, 1990); Linda Gordon, 'Social Insurance and Public Assistance: the Influence of Gender in Welfare Thought in the United States, 1890–1935', *American Historical Review* 97 (1992), pp. 19–54.
7. Seth Koven and Sonya Michel, 'Womanly Duties: Maternalist Politics and the Origins of Welfare States in France, Germany, Great Britain and the United States, 1880–1920', *American Historical Review* 95 (1990), pp. 1076–1108.
8. Religion was an important factor motivating the ladies' charitable activities, in spite of the liberal secularism that the Beneficent Society represented as an institution. For associations of Catholic women, see Karen Mead, 'Gender, Welfare and the Catholic Church in Argentina: Conferencias de Señoras de San Vicente de Paul, 1890–1916', *The Americas* 58 (2001), pp. 91–119; Omar Acha, 'Catolicismo Social y Feminidad en la Década del 30', in Paula Halperin and Omar Acha (eds), *Cuerpos, Géneros e Identidades: Estudios de Historia de Género en Argentina* (Buenos Aires: Del Signo, 2000), pp. 197–227; Sandra McGee Deutsch, 'The Catholic Church, Work and Womanhood in Argentina, 1890–1930', in Gertrude Yeager (ed.), *Confronting Change, Challenging Tradition: Women in Latin American History* (Washington: Scholarly Resources, 1994), pp. 127–51.
9. Mead, 'Oligarchs, Doctors and Nuns', pp. 151–3.
10. 'Premios a la Virtud', *Sociedad de Beneficencia, Memorias, del año 1923* (Buenos Aires: Escuela de Artes y Oficios del Asilo de Huérfanos, 1923), pp. 43–4.
11. Koven and Michel, 'Womanly Duties', p. 1079.
12. 'Discurso de la Presidenta de la Sociedad de Beneficencia', *Sociedad de Beneficencia, Memorias del año 1937* (Buenos Aires: Escuela de Artes y Oficios del Asilo de Huérfanos, 1938), pp. 52–3.
13. 'Discurso de la Presidenta Inés Dorrego de Unzué', *Sociedad de Beneficencia, Memorias del año 1921* (Buenos Aires: Escuela de Artes y Oficios del Asilo de Huérfanos, 1921), pp. 43–4.
14. *La Nación, La Prensa, El Mundo* and *Caras y Caretas* make up a media corpus with different audiences and, therefore, with different ways of handling information. However, in the late 1920s and the 1930s, they significantly shared the use of images to convey news *La Nación*, a 'periodical of ideas' founded by Bartolomé Mitre in 1870, addressed itself in the 1930s as before to the country's intellectual and economic elites. *La Prensa*, founded by José C. Paz in 1869, a pioneer in introducing printing techniques, was the most widely read newspaper in Argentina at the beginning of the twentieth century, since its readership was a mixture of different social classes. At the end of the 1920s, *El Mundo* had become one of the most important Argentinean morning newspapers. Characterised by widespread use of photographs in its daily edition, it belonged to the Heynes publishing house, which owned other large-circulation newspapers and magazines. *Caras y Caretas* (1898–1939), the first magazine to use photographs and to become a modern publication,

was directed to a popular audience and especially to women, who were seen as potential consumers both of the products advertised on its pages and of the subjects of the articles. See Jorge B. Rivera, *El Escritor y la Industria Cultural* (Buenos Aires: Atuel, 1998); Sylvia Saítta, *Regueros de Tinta: El Diario Crítica en la Década de 1920* (Buenos Aires: Sudamericana, 1998); Sylvia Saítta, *El Escritor en el Bosque de Ladrillos* (Buenos Aires, Sudamericana, 2000); Beatriz Sarlo, *El Imperio de los Sentimientos* (Buenos Aires: Catálogos, 1985).

15. The first President to attend the ceremony was Figueroa Alcorta in 1910 as part of the centennial of the May Revolution, accompanied by Infanta Doña Isabel de Borbón from Spain and the Chilean President, Dr Montt. During the 1910s and part of the 1920s, the presidents did not tend to attend the ceremony. They began to attend again in the late 1920s. 'Premios a la Virtud' in *Sociedad de Beneficencia, Memorias* (Buenos Aires: Escuela de Artes y Oficios del Asilo de Huérfanos, 1920–39).

16. *El Diario*, 21 May 1933. Mead points out that in the 1910s, the ceremony organised by the Charitable Ladies was simpler and less ostentatious than that of the Beneficent Society. Mead, 'Oligarchs, Doctors and Nuns', p. 290.

17. The presence of ecclesiastical authorities at the prize-giving ceremony is closely related to the internal changes affecting the Catholic Church in the 1920s, especially to Social Catholicism. Among other consequences, this resulted in the Church becoming more acquainted with the charitable activities of several associations of Catholic women. The Church's attempt at re-organisation included the creation of Catholic culture courses in 1922, the appearance of *Criterio*, a Catholic magazine, in 1928, the foundation of the Acción Católica in 1931 and, in particular, the creation of its Socio-Economic Secretary, conceived of as a means to meet social needs. See Loris Zanatta, *Del Estado Liberal a la Nación Católica: Iglesia y Ejército en los Orígenes del Peronismo, 1930–1943* (Buenos Aires: Universidad Nacional de Quilmes, 1996).

18. 'Acta de Sociedad' and 'Informe de la Comision Visitadora', *Sociedad de Beneficencia, Memorias* (Buenos Aires: Escuela de Artes y Oficios del Asilo de Huérfanos, 1911–43).

19. Speech delivered by President Sofía Arning de Bengolea when the institution celebrated its centennial anniversary. 'Premios a la Virtud', *Sociedad de Beneficencia, Memorias 1923* (Buenos Aires: Escuela de Artes y Oficios del Asilo de Huérfanos, 1923), pp. 43–9.

20. 'Informe de la Comisión Visitadora', *Sociedad de Beneficencia, Memorias del año 1928*, (Buenos Aires: Escuela de Artes y Oficios del Asilo de Huérfanos, 1928), p. 63.

21. *Sociedad de Beneficencia, Memorias del año 1930*, Archivo General de la Nación, file 9883/2. By way of comparison, in 1910, forty-four prizes were awarded and 800 homes were visited.

22. In 1931, an annual $1,000 prize donated by María del Carmen Sala de Demona in memory of her mother, a former Society president, Etelvina Costa de Sala, was to be awarded to two orphan girls from the Beneficent Society who were worthy of such a reward. See *El Diario*, 27 May 1931.

23. Mead, 'Oligarchs, Doctors and Nuns', pp. 292–4.

24. Speech delivered by President Sofía Arning de Bengolea when the institution celebrated its centennial anniversary. 'Premios a la Virtud', *Sociedad de Beneficencia, Memorias 1923* (Buenos Aires: Escuela de Artes y Oficios del Asilo de Huérfanos, 1923), pp. 43–9.

25. Although population numbers had increased dramatically because of immigration – Argentina had 1.8 million inhabitants in 1869 and 7.9 million in 1914 – this growth rate came to a halt as a result of international crises. During the 1930s, the net migration balance was the lowest in the country's history since the beginning of modernisation. Economic growth, based mainly on the exports of primary goods, was also spectacular: between the late nineteenth and early twentieth centuries, GDP increased by a 5 per cent mean annual rate. Even though the economy remained dynamic, the growth rate decreased in the years 1914–30. A new cycle began in the 1930s, when the relation

between the rural sector and industry shifted after the 1929 crash and the Second World War. Such an economic boom, however, was never reached again.
26. There is consensus among historians as regards the progressive insertion of women into the so-called light industries (food and clothing) and into the service-producing sector in the 1920s. This decade is also marked by the height of feminist organisations, especially those devoted to the demand for women's suffrage. See Marcela Nari, 'El Feminismo frente a la Cuestión de la Mujer en las Primeras Décadas del Siglo XX', in Juan Suriano (ed.), *La Cuestión Social en la Argentina 1870–1943* (Buenos Aires: La Colmena, 2000), pp. 277–99.
27. Kathleen Newman, 'Modernization of Femininity: Argentina 1916–1926', in UC-Stanford Seminar on Feminism and Culture in Latin America, *Women, Culture and Politics in Latin America* (Los Angeles: University of California Press, 1990), pp. 74–89.
28. Lyrics of the tango song 'De Ayer a Hoy' by Homero Manzi (1907–51). In *Homero Manzi: Cancionero* (Buenos Aires: Torres Aguero Editor, 1979), pp. 24–5, emphasis added.
29. See Francine Masiello, *Between Civilization and Barbarism: Women, Nation and Literary Culture in Modern Argentina* (Lincoln and London: University of Nebraska Press, 1992), pp. 167–71; Dora Barrancos, 'Moral Sexual, Sexualidad y Mujeres Trabajadoras en el Período de Entreguerras', in Fernando Devoto and Marta Madero (eds), *Historia de la Vida Privada en Argentina*, vol. 3: *La Argentina entre Multitudes y Soledades: De los Años Treinta a la Actualidad* (Buenos Aires: Taurus, 1999), pp. 198–225.
30. Newman, 'Modernization of Femininity', p. 87. The author points out that in 1926, the magazines *Plus Ultra* and *Caras y Caretas* published a special supplement on Argentinean women, where the photographs of feminists, intellectuals and actresses were replaced with rather anachronistic and static pictures featuring some of the representatives of the Porteño aristocracy in delicate poses and brandishing Argentinean traditional values.
31. For authors who emphasise complementarity and overlook conflict, see Ricardo González, 'Caridad y Filantropía en la Ciudad de Buenos Aires durante la Segunda Mitad del Siglo XIX', in *Sectores Populares y Vida Urbana* (Buenos Aires: CLACSO [Consejo Latinoamericano de Ciencias Sociales], 1984), pp. 251–9, esp. pp. 256–7; Eduardo Ciafardo, *Caridad y Control Social: las Sociedades de Beneficencia en la Ciudad de Buenos Aires, 1880–1930* (unpublished MA dissertation, Facultad Latinoamericana de Ciencias Sociales, Buenos Aires, 1990), pp. 16–18.
32. In 1932, the Social Assistance Fund (Fondo de Asistencia Social) was created to regulate the granting of subsidies; in 1933, the Government organised the First National Convention on Social Assistance; in 1940, the National Assistance Roll (Registro Nacional de Asistencia) was created; and in 1944, the Social Assistance Direction (Dirección de Asistencia Social) was instituted under the jurisdiction of the Labour and Welfare Secretary (Secretaría de Trabajo y Previsión Social). See Emilio Tenti Fanfani, *Estado y Pobreza: Estrategias Típicas de Intervención*, vol. 1 (Buenos Aires: Centro Editor de America Latina, 1989), pp. 72–4.
33. The first social assistance programmes including maternal services were provided by the Maternity Institute of the Rivadavia Hospital, under the jurisdiction of the Beneficent Society, in 1928. See Ciafardo, *Caridad y Control Social*, pp. 167–211.
34. Maternity benefits, which were first regulated in 1934, were a $200 subsidy for working women payable only to mothers themselves. Women were also entitled to free medical assistance during delivery. The money came from the compulsory quarterly contributions of both working women and their employers. In 1937, the National Direction of Maternity and Infancy was established, with the aims of creating shelters for single mothers, health-care centres and kindergartens and supervising all the institutions devoted to the protection of mothers and children, except for those under the jurisdiction of the Beneficent Society.
35. This can be seen in the National Direction of Maternity and Infancy's failure to control the institutions under the jurisdiction of the Beneficent Society, a victory the ladies won

after pressing the government hard. See Donna Guy, 'La Verdadera Historia de la Sociedad de Beneficencia', in Barbara Potthast and Eugenia Scarzanella (eds), *Mujeres y Naciones en América Latina: Problemas de Inclusión y Exclusión* (Madrid: Iberoamericana, 2001), pp. 249–69, esp. p. 261.

36. Christine Ehrick, 'Affectionate Mothers and the Colossal Machine: Feminism, Social Assistance and the State in Uruguay 1910–1932', *The Americas* 58 (2001), pp. 121–39, argues that Argentina's Beneficent Society's power was stronger and longer-lived than that of its Uruguayan counterpart, which favoured the growth of the Battlist state and the emergence of an early welfare assistance system.
37. Paul Connerton, *How Societies Remember* (Cambridge: Cambridge University Press, 1989), p. 43.
38. Gillian Rose, 'Engendering the Slum: Photography in East London in the 1930s', *Gender, Place and Culture* 4 (1997), pp. 277–300, esp. pp. 277–8.
39. Luis Príamo, 'Fotografía y Vida Privada 1870–1930', in Fernando Devoto and Marta Madero (eds), *Historia de la Vida Privada en la Argentina*, vol. 2: *La Argentina Plural 1870–1930* (Buenos Aires: Taurus, 1999), here p. 276.
40. Omar Acha, 'Catolicismo Social y Feminidad en la Década del 30', p. 200.
41. Gillian Rose analyses photographs of slums which depict women doing the household chores or posing for the camera, surrounded by their children and relatives. This can be read as a form of domestication and feminisation of the sphere of daily life. See Rose, 'Engendering the Slum', pp. 277–300.
42. According to Karen Mead, prizes did not appeal specifically to mothers for they could also be awarded to daughters and sisters, a striking selection pattern if considered in the wider context of maternalist discourse in the 1930s, which emphasised the importance of the mother–child dyad as the foundation for the nation's future. See Karen Mead, 'La Mujer Argentina y la Política de Ricos y Pobres al Fin del Siglo XIX', in Omar Acha and Paula Halperin (eds), *Cuerpos, Géneros e Identidades* (Buenos Aires: Editorial del Signo, 2000), pp. 31–59, esp. p. 50; Mead, 'Oligarchs, Doctors and Nuns', pp. 158–9; Marcela Nari, *Las Políticas de la Maternidad y el Maternalismo Político: Buenos Aires 1890–1940*, (unpublished PhD thesis, Universidad de Buenos Aires, 2000), pp. 181–3, 201.
43. Nancy Armstrong, 'Modernism's Iconophobia and What it did to Gender', *Modernism/Modernity* 5 (1998), pp. 47–75, here p. 51.
44. Griselda Pollock analyses several representations of working women and points out that, as a new type of disciplinary technology, photography led to the development of a discourse linking truth to vision. Thus, degradation and immorality became visible in the physical bodily appearance. Griselda Pollock, 'With My Own Eyes: Fetishism, the Labouring Body and the Colour of its Sex', *Art History* 17 (1994), pp. 342–82, here p. 362. Opposing values, such as morality, can also be seen in the body.
45. Victor Turner, *La Selva de los Símbolos: Aspectos del Ritual Ndembu*, tr. Ramón Valdés del Toro and Alberto Cardín Garay (Mexico City: Siglo XXI, 1999).
46. Victor Turner, *La Selva de los Símbolos*, p. 33.
47. Pollock, 'With My Own Eyes', p. 15; Rose, 'Engendering the Slum', p. 2.
48. Ulises Favaro, 'Premios a la Virtud (Awards to Virtue)', *La Escena* (Buenos Aires) 3 (1920), n.p. The play was first put on by the Muiño-Alippi Theatre Company at the Buenos Aires Theatre on 30 July 1920, n.p.
49. Jorge Lafforgue, *El Teatro Argentino* (Buenos Aires: Centro Editor de América Latina, 1979), pp. 83, 87.

4 The General View and Beyond: From Slum-yard to Township in Ellen Hellmann's Photographs of Women and the African Familial in the 1930s

Marijke du Toit

Illustrations to South African social anthropologist Ellen Hellmann's monograph *Rooiyard: A Sociological Study of an Urban Native Slum Yard* include a page showing readers a 'General view' and 'The yard surface after rain'. The snapshot quality of the first photograph is accentuated by the slight angle at which the picture was taken, also adding to its strong sense of movement (Figure 1). A man looms past the frame, a woman bends over her washing. An original print, carefully preserved in Hellmann's manuscript copy, has an arresting profusion of detail. In the narrowing gap between two rows of buildings, men and women are visible as small figures receding or advancing in the distance. A young girl stands just off the centre of this activity in a posture of apparent thought or contemplation, perhaps of the pile of branches in front of her. In the second picture, two women pause for the camera in front of washing draped from lines, while another stands, perhaps watching them, at the left edge of the frame. One woman, holding a pole in one hand, also points her finger at the photographer. Half the pictorial surface is taken up by the trampled expanse of furrowed, water-filled mud. More careful examination of the print reveals small figures in the distance and – in still separation from the trajectories of looking in which photographer and some of those photographed are engaged – another woman who sits almost hidden from view by pale garments and a weathered tin drum.[1]

This article investigates the use of photographs for Hellmann's research and her representation of African women within the context

Figure 1: Page from *Rooiyard* manuscript. Photos by Ellen Hellmann. Ellen Hellmann Papers, William Cullen Library, University of the Witwatersrand, South Africa (EHP).

of the South African visual economy of the 1930s. *Rooiyard* is well known in southern African studies. An early appraisal of research on 'Women in Southern Africa' by historian Deborah Gaitskell included Hellmann in her discussion of 'the contribution of pioneering female academics' – sociologists and anthropologists – long before historians paid attention to female experience.[2] Hellmann's work has also been regarded as ground-breaking for its focus on African families struggling to subsist in an urban environment, particularly by social and cultural historians who, from the 1980s, sought to recover the politics of an early twentieth-century black proletariat. Hellmann's writing was mined for research on 'oppositional' working-class cultures forged in Johannesburg slums.[3] Efforts by academics to popularise research on the making of an African working class also included pictures from *Rooiyard*. But while these richly illustrated books comprised a strong re-imaging of South African history, scholars involved in this project were not concerned with exploration of how photographs may be said to document the past – with 'their particular roles ... in inscribing, constituting and suggesting pasts'.[4]

The 'pictorial turn' in southern African historical studies[5] is relatively recent and the regional visual economy remains under-researched, especially as regards twentieth-century South Africa. This article begins to map out the local photographic context for Hellmann's picture-taking, also attempting a conscious exploration of the possibilities for reading Hellmann's photographs as historical documents. One strategy for doing so is to consider these pictures against a range of contemporary images that circulated at the time, across ostensibly separate genres of photography. My focus is on photographic practices incorporated into publications aimed primarily at white-imagined South African publics. I discuss Hellmann's photography in relation to pictures that circulated in popular and academic books, magazines and newspapers – publications that included official and amateur commemorative and touristic photography, ethnographic and anthropological picture-taking as well as early forms of social documentary photography and photo-journalism. I do so with specific attention to questions of gender discourse as articulated through photographs and image-text.[6] How did taking photographs involve presenting and how does looking at Hellmann's photographs involve seeing raced and gendered bodies and spaces in particular ways? Did her photographic framing and textual positioning of photographs produce meanings that cohere with, or may be read as, stepping 'beyond' the 'general view' of her time?

A number of historians have asked questions about gendered subjectivities while analysing images produced by cameras harnessed as part of colonial administration and the popular cultures of settler societies and empire.[7] Hellmann took her photographs in a period of rapid and accelerating urbanisation. Increasing numbers of African women moved to South African towns with the intent to settle, frustrating urban local authorities that wanted African labour but could only envisage tolerating a small and well-controlled black familial presence.

This was also a time when images of African men and women circulating in the regional visual economy framed a narrow range of stereotypes that were seldom destabilised. I argue that, considered from the perspective of the present, a number of Hellmann's pictures do not conform to the 'general view' of black and particularly African, female subjectivity current in South Africa of the 1930s. I suggest that this departure was closely linked to her documentary intent – to how she, as a social anthropologist, mobilised the photograph's indexicality – that is, the idea of the photograph as chemical trace, 'a physical, material emanation of a past reality'.[8] Hellmann never discussed her use of a camera as a tool for her research. Even so, my strategy for reading photographs as historical documents includes a detailed exploration of authorial intent, through a reading of how she built her argument via an inter-relationship of words and images. Textual analysis, however, only gathers historical depth through close attention to political and social context, for example, to Hellmann's increasing immersion in local networks of research and interaction with government structures. Moreover and crucially for a paper concerned with gender and visuality, analysis of the photographs as historical documents must also involve considering Hellmann as woman photographer – looking at how this researcher's raced and gendered subjectivity shaped her work. A careful reading of the pictures – again together with Hellmann's own comments – suggests how Hellmann's social identity and position helped shape the photographic encounter, not least as a 'European' woman who chose to research and photograph 'Native' men and women.

Besides these historically specific questions of how one woman used visual technology for her purposes and in what relationship with South African inter-war policies of racial segregation, questions about the particularity and difference of photographic texts as documents of 'pastness' remain important. How can, how do we write photographs into feminist history? What exactly happens when the historian scrutinises, describes and combines with words certain photographs – two-dimensional tracings with powerful, deeply rooted, widely shared cultural associations as imprints of reality – as spaces for memory-making and imaginings of identity, placing them into her own arrangement of image-text?

Hellmann's urban social anthropology and the visual celebration of white South African modernity

The Golden City, a commemorative volume about Johannesburg published c. 1933, includes a picture taken by editor Allister MacMillan in a neighbourhood long singled out as a notorious slum and targeted by a municipality intent on using slum-clearance legislation for purposes of racial segregation.[9] It shows an anonymous black family attentive to the camera as they might have been for a studio photographer (Figure 2). The seated couple with their baby are centred in a triangulated space formed by lines of washing on a makeshift pole and smoke drifting from two of several buckets and tin drums. The melancholy atmosphere of the picture is accentuated by the separate figure of a young girl. Apparently unaware that she is included in the camera's field of vision, or assuming that she is excluded from attention, she leans against some object so that her posture contrasts to the upright self-awareness of the parents.[10]

It was in late 1933 that Ellen Hellmann, sometimes supplementing her notebook with a camera, spent her mornings visiting homes in nearby Doornfontein, where landlords rented rooms to black families in need of living space near central Johannesburg. Considered as photographic framings of African subjects and urban space, MacMillan's picture and several of Hellmann's have much in common. All show inner city enclaves of African-occupied living spaces. All show the presence of African women in the city. The assembly of man, woman and child in MacMillan's Ferreirastown photograph clearly signified familial relationship and included evidence of domestic endeavour; Hellmann's pictures (Figure 1) also show a girl child, possibly engaged in domestic chores and a woman with a toddler on her hip next to lines of washing. However, when these pictures are considered as components incorporated into two books comprising words and images, participant in wider image-worlds, important differences of intent and emphasis become apparent.[11]

What is most striking about Hellmann's photographs is their consistent pictorial focus on black women, men and children engaged in the everyday tasks of living in a South African city, embedded in text discussing the facts of urban African family life. When she began her research, commercial prints of colonised African subjects had circulated in southern Africa for some seventy years, pasted into settler albums and printed as postcards. More than half a century before she launched her project, racial anthropologists had begun to systematise their use of photography. Popular ethnographic picture-taking was well established by the 1930s, as was official touristic photography with strong compulsions to present 'native life' to local and foreign audiences.[12] *The Golden City* fitted neatly into the mainstream of white, English South African

Keeping the Home Fires burning in Ferreirastown.

[Photo: Allister Macmillan.

The Editor had the pleasure of accompanying Miss Spurr on a tour of exploration of Ferrierastown for the purpose of her article in this volume. The photograph reproduced above illustrates admirably her reference to the life of that district. The couple with their baby kindly posed for the picture; and behind the camera was a crowd of the residents of the court, who evinced great interest in the proceedings from their position of assurance. The black object suspended on a wire on the left of the illustration is a piece of dried meat.

Figure 2: Allister Macmillan, *Golden City* (London: W. H. & L. Collingridge, 1933), p. 204.

visual culture. As such, MacMillan's view of a black working-class couple of little means in a poor part of town was exceptional. The description of Ferreirastown (which included several additional pictures of its poor, white inhabitants) represented a rare instance when MacMillan's 'tour' (as he described it) included a slum neighbourhood. This was a publication intended to instruct and entertain while celebrating the white, modern city of Johannesburg as a place where civilisation met and moulded the tribal picturesque. The book also presented Johannesburg in ways that cohered with dominant race and gender discourse. The only other picture that showed an African woman in city space was a tiny uncaptioned picture in which Africans boarded a train, presumably for their home. If MacMillan's caption to the Ferreirastown picture made ironic or jocular reference to familial struggle to survive ('Keeping the home fires burning in Ferreirastown'), this publication scarcely presented any pictures of African wives with husbands, relentlessly presenting African men as migrant, properly disciplined and half-civilised warrior-workers living in single-sex compounds on the Rand's gold mines. African women featured as rural maidens clad in 'tribal' dress, posing as if engaged in 'traditional' women's work, half-nude in the well-established trope of the colonised, traditionally decorous and available black female body.

As regards officially produced photography, representations of the black female subject largely remained the purview of touristic imaginings, produced by the South African Railways and Harbours. These included a core group of favoured images that were printed and re-printed in books and magazines of the 1920s and 1930s and that continued to present African women almost exclusively as exemplifying tribal tradition and culture and often engaged in 'traditional' domestic tasks in the Union's rural reserves, sometimes also as workers on white-owned farms (Figure 3).[13]

Hellmann's photographs were exceptional for recording the presence of African women, men and children in the less-easily regulated spaces of Johannesburg. Of course, it was precisely because she was not participating in projects that invited armchair touring of imagined colonial reaches or that celebrated civilisation as exemplified by white South Africa that Hellmann's pictures did not cohere with these visions of tribal subjectivity. It is therefore instructive specifically to consider Hellmann's visual records of Doornfontein against those taken by other scholars of the 1930s also engaged in her chosen documentary enterprise, that of anthropology. In fact, Hellmann's 'General view' and 'The yard surface after rain' differed significantly from most photographs taken by scholars intent on studying African cultures, even though her pictures were also recognisably shaped by the young

A Native Rebecca.

Figure 3: South African Railway and Harbours photo reproduced in Allister Macmillan, *Golden City*, p. 189.

researcher's induction into a recently established school of *social* or *cultural* anthropology. Comparison with photographs from a contemporary volume of anthropology and ethnography, *The Bantu-speaking Tribes of South Africa* (1937), in which some of her *Rooiyard* pictures were first published, reveals that Hellmann's picture-taking coincided with a larger shift in the documentary use of cameras by South African social anthropologists who engaged in new forms of observation and recordkeeping.[14]

The book confirms that ethnographers working in South Africa who were intent upon using the camera in order to create records of bodily adornment maintained a serious interest in photography well into the twentieth century. Their photographs often involved de-contextualising and positioning bodies in a manner very similar to that of racial anthropology. Thus, for example, van Warmelo's full frontal and profile head and shoulder photographs, classified into a typology of tribes, have a shallow depth of field so that his subjects are presented against blurred or uniformly patterned backgrounds. Where this ethnographer for South Africa's Native Affairs Department presented men and women performing an aspect of their culture within a physical environment, the frame tended to exclude signs of modernity that could place his subjects in historical time. Bodies were often placed in balanced relationship to each other or in the regulated patterning of ritual movement, emphasising a sense of order and stasis.[15]

Hellmann's *Rooiyard* pictures show a lack of interest in recording human physical features; her almost arbitrary framing of street scenes does not focus attention on signs of cultural specificity. As such, they are identifiable as belonging to a strand of social anthropological photography in which the camera was used neither to establish or confirm a racial or ethnic typology nor to isolate cultural performance. Isaac Schapera's edited volumes on African culture included carefully staged pictures produced by the publicity department of the South African Railways and Harbours, presented as evidence of cultural practice. However, a different form of visual documentary was also emerging – one in which it was important to present human subjects in a physical environment descriptive of both cultural and socio-economic practice. Schapera's own photographs in *Bantu-speaking Tribes* and in *Western Civilization and the Natives of South Africa* exemplify this approach.[16] In contrast to the more carefully orchestrated photographs taken by ethnologists associated with colonial administrative structures, the camera recorded the presence of material objects, whatever their supposed cultural origin.[17] Indeed, the study of 'culture contact' and of how 'western' commodities were absorbed into indigenous cultures was now a central preoccupation. If cultural anthropologists still sought to describe cultures of 'origin', their photographs often incorporated signs of change and hybridity.

Hellmann was among the first of the new generation of anthropologists – and unusual within the broad spectrum of South African social science – to study and also to photograph black persons in the immediate vicinity of their homes in the city. Indeed, the newly established discipline of social anthropology was yielding its first examples of photographs intended to document socio-economic circumstances. Hellmann set out to explore not only to what extent 'the Native in the towns' was adopting 'European material culture', but also to document the conditions in which Africans living in the city struggled to subsist. As she explained, 'the desire of the urban Native to acquire European goods is limited only by his poverty. And poverty is one of the most outstanding characteristics of those Natives whose families have taken up residence in an urban area'.[18] How and why the majority of Rooiyard residents were desperately poor was an important aspect of an investigation that included camera-work.

Hellmann's own intention with her photographs was to create illustrations for her written text. Photographs are referred to briefly in her monograph, for example as illustrations to the layout of the yard or in her discussion of economic activities such as beer brewing – belying a more complex relationship between image and word. For Hellmann, the camera enabled a form of visual note-taking in the field, subordinated to pen and paper. Verbal explanation based on fieldwork provided a necessary interpretation of the visual, while photographs helped illustrate her argument.[19] By reading them as components of visual-verbal description and discussion, the pictures acquire new layers of meaning, as part of an argument about urban African cultural practice and economic survival.

Perusal of the pictures in her book show several that provide views of people walking, standing and working in the spaces between buildings, similar to the pictures in Figure 1, and several more that show the spaces without apparent focus on persons at all. In fact, it seems as if Hellmann took a number of pictures while not specifically intent on showing people in her photographs. She wanted to record living spaces visually; people often appear as if almost incidentally present in these pictures. The partial presence of a man who had walked into the frame of 'Rooiyard alleyway' seems accidental, arbitrary (Figure 4). The eye has to search for other distant or shadowy figures among objects that seem to litter the space between the corrugated iron structures and the brick building at the back – wooden poles, bags, basins, sheets of tin, drums and a bicycle. But to eyes tutored by Hellmann's textual discussion, certain objects that may first appear as incidental clutter become visible as receptacles essential for women's role in economic survival and for their domestic tasks. Hellmann's caption for this photograph indicated 'the assortment of tins used for beer-brewing, soap-making, washing, etc.', thus illustrating the detailed discussion of women's work elsewhere in her book.[20] The surface of communal yards and alleyways prominent in a number of Hellmann's photographs also hid subterranean cellars crucial (so she explained) to women's livelihood and at the centre of struggles with police.

This visual-textual representation becomes all the more interesting when considered against early twentieth-century strands of discourse concerning slums and 'native' women in South Africa. From early in the century and particularly from the 1920s, official reports and correspondence articulated strong stereotypes of 'native' women as prostitutes and brewers of illicit liquor. African women (beer brewing was traditionally women's work) could not legally brew any alcoholic beverage within the jurisdiction of South African municipalities and raids to prevent this were a regular feature of attempts at urban social control. *The Golden City* described 'Skokiaan Queens' (named after a potent alcoholic home brew) as significant figures in the city's underworld, echoing a more widespread condemnation by middle-class whites

Figure 4: Photo by Ellen Hellmann from *Rooiyard* manuscript, EHP.

(and, for that matter, missionary-educated blacks) of immoral African city women.[21] Particularly from the mid-1920s – when Johannesburg city officials declared the city 'European' according to the Native Urban Areas Act of 1923 and attempted to remove black slum-dwellers – African women were identified as 'disproportionately responsible for the ills of slums'. As the chairman of the Johannesburg Native Affairs Committee explained in 1929, 'the large influx of women' was 'a danger and a menace to society and the fair name of Johannesburg. They are either liquor sellers or prostitutes, or they are living an illegal life with a man'.[22]

However, it seems that such notions had little impact on visual representations of African women in South African magazines and newspapers, publications that reflected back to their readers the orderliness and decorous sociability of a safely white world. Occasional pictures taken in slum areas in Johannesburg had been featured in South African illustrated magazines of the 1920s, specifically showing the results of raids against illicit alcohol manufacture. At least one of these showed an unidentified black woman watching as policemen destroyed their find. More often the pictures showed deserted expanses of churned-up earth next to which officers of the law displayed trophies – the caches of illicit alcohol that they had found hidden underground.[23] Although these pictures showed no actual culprits, middle-class white readers may have associated such scenes of lawful destruction with the shadowy figures of *skokiaan* queens. One picture essay from 1920 ('Police dig up over 8 000 Gallons at Prospect Township ... the liquor is a highly intoxicating concoction prepared from Kaffir corn, by native women') also included a drawing showing a woman with subterranean receptacles for brewing.[24]

As one Rooiyard woman explained to the researcher, 'we eat from beer'.[25] This, as Hellmann explained, was a marginal but crucial economic activity that relied on the patronage of domestic servants (men and women) from nearby white homes, workers whose meagre wages made them 'the prosperous section of the native populace'.[26] Hellmann's study focused on households comprising a man living with a woman, usually with children. While the official stereotype of African city women presented them outside of the realm of the respectably familial, Hellmann therefore firmly inscribed women into familial contexts, although her research on beer-brewing emphasised that widows and single women also made their living in this way.[27]

In this respect, the gender dimension of Hellmann's photographs bears an interesting resemblance to another social documentary photographic project focusing on urban slums. In an analysis of how women were pictured as 'figured bodies in fictive spaces' in photographs depicting London's East End of the 1930s, Gillian Rose discusses how some photographers refigured female inhabitants of the slum as 'bringing order, cleanliness and sociability to the poor'.[28] Hellmann discussed what she saw as the destructive repercussions to family life of an alcohol-based economy of survival. Even so, she emphasised that women were perforce 'breadwinners' together with husbands who were paid below subsistence wages. What legitimate work was available to them was usually incompatible with caring for their children.[29] Hellmann refigured Rooiyard as a domesticated space of arduous female labour for survival, through words and images that also presented women neither as idealised carriers of tribal identity nor as prostitutes and beer brewers at the immoral centre of slum living.[30]

In fact, it is also important to compare Hellmann's pictures – taken to illustrate a 'sociological study' – to contemporary South African pictures of spaces identified as slums, taken for the purposes of social reform. Such initiatives were part of the beginnings of a new documentary approach to photographing poor people that demonstrated the need for rescue and state social welfare support.

In South Africa before the 1930s, photography had been used by charities and (from the mid-1920s) state-driven projects in order to present rehabilitated poor whites as their beneficiaries. If the camera was conventionally understood as an instrument of uncomplicated truthfulness, it was also seldom that photographers set out to contextualise people as *being* poor. It was only in the late 1920s that a coherent, photographic project of documenting poverty emerged, as part of racialised research, peripheral to published, written texts.[31] Moreover, black persons were only accidentally included within these framings of the problematically poor. By the early 1930s, in the context of economic depression and intense politicisation of the 'poor white problem', some campaigners for the establishment of subsidised housing projects for working-class whites were beginning to incorporate photographs into their efforts to expose 'the evil of the slums', 'the dark places of our city'.[32] This was, of course, before the launch in 1935 of the US Farm Security Administration's photography project – the initiative most famously associated with a widely disseminated genre of photography called 'social documentary'. Most likely, South African social reformers' first efforts to use photography to expose slum conditions were influenced by British literature and projects incorporating photography.[33]

It is possible that Hellmann saw pictures such as those reprinted from the *Rand Daily Mail*, a Johannesburg newspaper, in 'To Hell with Slums', a pamphlet that also referred the reader to a range of mostly British publications on this topic. The photographs showed narrow alleyways and closed, bleak, dilapidated surfaces as part of arguments as to how (quoting Ruskin) 'the soul of the nation is expressed by its architecture' and how 'improved conditions and surroundings' would create better citizens.[34] Pictures and text attempted to project the poignancy of abandonment ('Half the world knows not how the other half lives') through their intense focus on young children in otherwise empty courtyards. One photograph, placed next to a picture of small children in a neglected backyard, framed several figures in the narrow space between the corrugated iron wall and the discoloured plaster of two buildings. A woman in a threadbare dress faces the photographer, one hand holding a cloth against the rim of a tin wash basin, the other resting on her hip. Above her hangs some washing, behind is a young girl and a toddler. In the distance, also looking towards her and the camera, is the figure of a black man. Text accompanying the photograph discussed the plight of white families – mothers forced to work for a pittance, fathers unemployed, children sent begging. If these were 'European Slum Conditions', they involved whites living in problematic juxtaposition 'to coloured persons, Asiatics and a certain number of natives not as yet removed as a result of the Proclamation of the whole of Johannesburg [as European]' (Figure 5).[35]

Figure 5: Photo from the pamphlet 'To Hell with Slums' (1933) published by the Johannesburg Housing Utility Company.

None of the pictures in 'To Hell with Slums' conveys the striking sense of movement and activity that characterises such photographs of Hellmann's as 'The General View'. Instead, the photographs seem intentionally framed and captioned so as to convey a sense of hopelessness, of still bodies in bleak space. As a social anthropologist, Hellmann was intent on a more complex investigation of everyday living than were these campaigners for racialised social reform. A comparison between her project and those used in segregationist campaigning against slums underscores that for Hellmann, documenting poverty and inadequate living conditions was one, albeit crucial, aspect of her study. In fact, it would be Hellmann's detailed attempt to describe not only how women tried to balance their budgets but also the cultural beliefs and practices of urbanising Africans that attracted late twentieth-century social historians to her work.

Most people in Hellmann's study remained anonymous, much like the people in the photography of supposedly 'European' slums. But while the woman in the pamphlet photo (Figure 5) remains an anonymous symbol of helpless motherhood in need of rescue, Hellmann's book – which mostly features women standing at some distance or framed more closely but looking down at one or another task – also included one closer portrait of a woman whose personal history is used to present a narrative of resilience and determination (Figure 6). In 'Angela with her daughter' the woman stands holding her baby, surrounded by the cheap metal surfaces and cloth of urban living: corrugated iron rooms, tin drums, a tin basin, a woven sack (on which happens to be printed, enigmatically, the word 'land'). Hellmann's 'case history' relates a story of tenacious motherhood. 'Angela' lost two babies while living with her in-laws in the countryside before choosing to remain in the city for her third pregnancy. Through strenuous effort and by making use of all resources available to

Figure 6: Photo by Ellen Hellmann from *Rooiyard* manuscript, EHP.

her in the city – traditional remedies and beliefs as well as Western primary health care – she kept her third, pictured, child alive and strong.

What was the interaction between researcher and researched, as 'Angela' told her story and posed for a photograph? In fact, how much of this can these photographs tell? Analysing photographs of poor neighbourhoods in London, Rose draws on Victor Burgin in order to emphasise that photographs are cultural texts, 'structured and structuring spaces', 'places of work' for the viewer. Photographs are 'fictive spaces', which (following Griselda Pollock) are also 'spaces of representation'. As Rose explains, 'the fictive space of the image and its relation to particular audiences is what Pollock has called the space of representation of an image'. A photograph 'organises a view of a specific body and of the space of and around that body; but that fictive space also invites a certain reading of the image in the way that it structures a relation between the fictive spaces of the photograph and the audiences of the photograph'.[36] Hellmann's photographs were intended for a white, academic audience and as additional evidence of slum yard conditions, perhaps also for officials of the city's native affairs department. But how can a twenty-first century historian read the photographs as 'places of work', while asking questions regarding (gendered, raced, class-inflected) interaction and the dynamics of power?

More comparison between Hellmann's photographs and those published in 'To Hell with Slums' begins to clarify some general questions as to how the photographers positioned themselves in relation to their subjects. Pictures from the pamphlet placed human subjects well within the frame, at a clear distance from the photographer. Hellmann's camera also often placed figures at considerable distance – possibly when she was mapping out architectural space. Hellmann was certainly capable of careful framing, as the photograph of 'Angela' testifies. The energy of some of her pictures, however, is created by seemingly arbitrary framing that show some objects and bodies only partly within the frame (Figures 1 and 4). In fact, this was because Hellmann, holding her box camera, had moved into the space of the slum yard's lived parameters – she was in the midst of people going about their business, so that some literally brushed past her as she took her pictures. And precisely because people walk 'into' the resulting frame, these snapshots also reduce the distance between viewer and viewed. Whether intentionally or not, the photographs indicate the continuum of activity and people 'beyond' Hellmann's general view.

Writers on photography have emphasised how the spatial organisation of bodies and objects in photographs shapes the way the viewer may understand them. Some have also, however, emphasised that how the subject looks at, beyond or away from the photographer is an important pictorial component from which the viewer makes meaning. Here (Figures 1 and 4), the lack of interaction between photographer and subject means that no meeting of eyes between photographer and subject can be imagined as taking place between viewer and viewed, across time and space. Sometimes, when subjects seem to look towards the camera, as does the woman pictured in the pamphlet (Figure 5) or when their gazes seem to reach beyond the photographer, as does that of 'Angela' (Figure 6), the direction of the eyes almost compels attention to the consciousness or perception of an indeterminate other, beyond the border of the photograph, involved in that process of looking.

In a few of Hellmann's pictures, however, she recorded women specifically looking at and clearly, judging by their facial expressions, paying attention to her. One such example is 'Yard Surface after Rain' (Figure 1), with the woman smilingly pointing her finger. Hellmann's verbal description matches the direction of her camera, focused low on muddy dirt. This, then, is a picture that is meant to illustrate the yard's unsanitary conditions, amply discussed in Hellmann's book. Graham Clarke, discussing Roland Barthes's idea of the *punctum*, suggests that a disconcerting detail may disturb 'the surface unity and stability' of an image and 'like a cut, begin the process of opening up that space to critical analysis. Once we have discovered our *punctum* we become, irredeemably, active readers of the scene'. As Barthes would have it, the reader *animates* and is *animated* by the photograph.[37] Here, for this reader, the *punctum* is a moment of heightened contact of eye and gesture between photographer and photographed. The object of research – even as she is pointed out by the camera – draws attention to Hellmann herself.

However, when considered not only in conjunction with the caption but also in the larger context of the book, this detail in the photograph coheres with Hellmann's own reflections on her dealings with Rooiyard residents. Discussing the high level of suspicion with which she was regarded by local women when doing her research, Hellmann explained that she was eventually judged a friend by some, but that 'the general attitude was one of amused indifference, every now and then changing into resentment and antagonism'. It was the 'continuous conflict with the authorities' about illegal beer brewing that had made 'especially the women ... very suspicious of all Europeans', who were all regarded as police agents unless proven otherwise.[38] Hellmann also commented that she perforce dealt more with women than with men because she visited the yard during the morning. She mentioned that she had decided to avoid the more volatile evenings: 'at night, especially, in the gloomy alleyways in which the swaying and stumbling forms of drunken Natives were dimly discernible, I felt compelled to agree that Rooiyard is a difficult place for a woman fieldworker'.[39]

Hellmann did not comment on this dynamic of distrust related to her social status and identity, other than commenting on perceptions of 'Europeans'. Married and twenty-six years old at the time, she was from a socially prominent and well-to-do Jewish family that had probably settled on the Rand at the turn of the twentieth century. She conversed in English and Afrikaans – languages of communication between mistress and servant – with her research subjects and used an interpreter when necessary.[40] There were huge gaps of socio-economic status, political power and culture between herself – a white, middle-class, recently enfranchised woman on her way to acquiring a post-graduate qualification – and her black, disenfranchised, economically marginal subjects. Moreover, upon her preliminary visit to Doornfontein, she was accompanied not only by a church social worker but also by the district health inspector, an official who would often have been involved in liquor raids.

If Rooiyard's inhabitants were suspicious of her note-taking, Hellmann's intention as a researcher of the yard is in fact difficult to determine. Perhaps she hoped to support liberal efforts to shape 'native' policy by emphasising the fact of black urban poverty.[41] She had been a founding member of the South African Institute for Race Relations (SAIRR) in 1929, the body formed in order to coordinate collection of evidence on Africans' socio-economic position for the Native Economic Commission of 1932. But what was her political response to the City of Johannesburg's efforts in favour of racial segregation, vehemently resented by slum-yard residents who did not want to live in an officially designated township for Africans, as she herself documented? Hers was a record, in word and image, of a place in the city that, within the year, ceased to exist as a *native* slum. The last picture in Hellmann's book was of 'Departure from Rooiyard: A woman's personal possessions outside her room'. When her monograph on Rooiyard was published in 1948, Hellmann, now president of the South African Institute for Race Relations, referred elliptically to the study as 'revealing a naivety of outlook particularly in regards to its political immaturity and unawareness of the implications of national policy in this country'. Writing this introduction at the end of a decade when World War Two had precipitated dramatic urbanisation, at a time of great tension around the provision of living space for Africans in Johannesburg and in the year of the Nationalist Party victory on a platform of apartheid, Hellmann may have had in mind official reluctance to substantially accommodate urban Africans in the early 1930s. Then, as in 1948, most officials had insisted that all except a closely policed minority would only be accepted as temporary urban sojourners. Her Rooiyard research asserted the growth of African urban culture and indicated the relationship between slum clearance and segregation, but Hellmann never discussed the policy itself.

By 1935, the year after she completed her work on Rooiyard and in an article on fieldwork methodology for urban-based anthropological research, Hellmann was already emphasising the importance of grasping the political and economic context in which one conducted fieldwork. Researchers had to understand 'the Native policy of the municipal authorities' and the impact of the 'economic structure of Western civilisation' on African lives. 'I do not hereby maintain that it is the duty of the field-worker actively to plunge into the field of politics nor that it is his duty to become a political advocate in the cause of justice. I merely submit that he must take cognizance of practical politics in so far as they affect the group with which he is concerned'.[42]

In fact, Hellmann was herself at the beginning of a long career as a researcher and liberal activist, in the course of which she rejected key aspects of segregationist policy and publicly worked for reform towards a just political dispensation. She was establishing herself as part of a small liberal network of researchers intent on shaping aspects of state policy. While her next research project was commissioned by the SAIRR, it was also financed by the National Bureau of Educational and Social Research, a governmental institution headed by educationist E. G. Malherbe, recent co-author of the report of the Carnegie Commission of Investigation into the Poor White Problem (1932).[43] Once again, Hellmann's method of research included camera work.

Social anthropology in public and private: Hellmann's photography of the late 1930s

Perusing Hellmann's published book of 1940, *Problems of Urban Bantu Youth*, the researcher could well conclude that Hellmann had become less interested in photography by the late 1930s.[44] Only seven photographs, captioned but otherwise never referred to in the text, are interleaved with her discussion. The first, taken in Johannesburg's oldest official African township, is 'Pimville Play'. Two young boys of perhaps five or six years, clad in worn shirts, sit on bare, littered earth next to corrugated iron structures, using their hands to dig furrows in the dirt. Overleaf and juxtaposed to her introduction to 'The Causes of Early School Leaving' are two pictures captioned 'Childhood Environment, Sophiatown' showing children and women in unkempt streets and yards or on the verandas of dilapidated houses. This first chapter has four more pictures, all of boys and young men on township streets or of children attending primary school.

Problems of Urban Bantu Youth, however, was based on Hellmann's doctoral research (also presented as a report to Malherbe's bureau), which has some twenty-eight original photographic prints included as an appendix. The pictures from the book version are all present, as are several more pictures of boys enjoying 'location leisure', 'gambling' and 'playing truant'. A group of 'non school-goers' are shown cradling toddlers on their laps, a girl 'nurse' stands with a baby on her back. A picture of two small girls and a woman bent over her work in front of a brick house is explained as 'Helping to settle in at Orlando'; three pictures show 'The Creche, Orlando' and several more show teenage boys and young men waiting to enter and exercising at 'The day club. Orlando'.

Besides these two public presentations of research, Hellmann included an album containing over 150 photographs in the documents that she donated to the University of the Witwatersrand's collection of historical papers in 1981 (she died a year later). Details of ink and handwriting suggest that she compiled the album at or shortly after the time of her research. The album includes almost all of the pictures used for her thesis and research report. Photographs, arranged chronologically, were taken from 1937 to 1938, the period of fieldwork for her doctoral study. In addition to the themes already mentioned, several other sequences of photographs are clearly discernable in the album. While it opens with several pictures of impoverished Sophiatown streets (the freehold urban area where Africans could still own land) showing women and children, the album moves on to several more views of homes, streets and children at play in Prospect, a slum finally scheduled for destruction. These are followed by pictures variously captioned 'Moving Prospect' and 'Shifting Prospect', complemented by the sequence 'Settling in – Orlando'. Hellmann then re-focused on the specifics of her research topic with pictures of Township street views and more youths at play in Orlando and the older Pimville. The rest of the album contains several other sequences interspersed with more views of official and freehold township streets and houses. These comprise an outdoors 'Sunday Grievances meeting' in Orlando, 'Pimville election scenes', a long sequence detailing a wedding ceremony, portraits of her research assistant C. Setlogelo and a number of variously named and unidentified individuals.

Hellmann included no photographs from *Rooiyard* in her gift of documents to the archive other than those pasted into the manuscript for her book – these also correspond exactly to the published version. The survival of distinct texts – album, PhD thesis and published book – from different stages of research and writing for her next project allow for questions about Hellmann's choice of certain photographs for inclusion in the public versions. As a component of now publicly available historical papers at a university library, the once privately kept album comprises the layer of image-text privileging the visual most strongly, least directly juxtaposed to textual discussion. It poses particular challenges for historical interpretation.

Hellmann once wrote that the clear terms of reference of her doctoral study, limiting her to 'dealing with only one aspect of the urban Native problem, brought home to me more clearly than work on a more comprehensive problem could have done the disruption in Native family life'.[45] By the late 1930s, Hellmann's research was centrally informed by preoccupations more specifically shared by South African liberal politicians and researchers – what Deborah Posel has termed 'the politics of the urban African family'. Enormous poverty amongst Africans and 'the debilitating pressures on family life in the urban African townships' were the defining and interlinked features of the 'urban native question' as it was articulated at this time. Several years before, Carnegie Commissioner E. G. Malherbe's pictures of poor whites were informed by a politics of social welfare that 'insisted and believed in the power of state-driven initiatives to intervene positively in economic and social life'. Similar beliefs informed 'a different set of initiatives to manage the dual problems of poverty and family instability in urban African communities, spearheaded by various groupings of liberals, missionaries, academics, urban African leaders and urban administrators'. What was imagined was 'a racialised welfare state, with racially differential – if improved – investment on the part of the state in the "upliftment" of all the country's racial groups'.[46]

The two sets of published photographs are clear illustrations of the fact of black children and youth playing and socialising on township streets, of the lack of parental supervision of city-living black children. In Hellmann's book and thesis, general views of township spaces communicate the high levels of poverty and social neglect. Specific framings of youths function to convey the inadequacy of township amenities and familial socialisation.

The album interweaves additional, albeit overlapping, interests and concerns, for example the narrative sequence of pictures about 'moving' and 'shifting' (as Hellmann put it) Prospect and the pictures of families 'settling' at Orlando. The relationship between these pictures and a particular understanding of the crisis of the 'native' familial is, perhaps, not discernable from the pictures themselves. At first glance, her juxtaposition of images seems to reproduce a recognisable visual format that celebrated the triumph of orderly town planning, contrasting the slum with the regulated spaces of the township, familiar from a sprinkling of newspaper reports and pamphlets on slum clearance in order to build white housing projects.[47] 'Shifting Prospect' also has a deliberately low focus that foregrounds churned-up mud, an open drain, a scrounging dog, rusted metal and other discards, with brick houses and people appearing in the background (Figure 7). Here, Hellmann returned to her concern with insanitary slum conditions, one that she shared with city health officials. The first of the two pictures of Orlando show the

Figure 7: Page from Ellen Hellmann's personal photo album, EHP.

Figure 8: Page from Ellen Hellmann's personal photo album, EHP.

expanse of dry, empty ground that fronts neat freestanding brick houses of the new township. In the second (selected for her book) a house appears within a tighter frame, so that the woman and children labouring at moving into their new home are more clearly visible (Figure 8). While the photographs are unusual for their time as documents of removals from black 'slum' to 'township', considered by themselves they do not seem to question official policy and popular white support for the need to keep African families out of towns, except for, at best, a well-segregated minority.

A different reading of the photographs becomes possible, however, when they are brought into relationship with Hellmann's public, civic activities. She took a keen interest in the affairs of Orlando, the older Pimville (subject of frequent discussions about inadequate sewage provisions and its proximity to a sewage plant) and the freehold areas of Sophiatown and Alexandra. She did so not only from within the SAIRR but also as member of the (Johannesburg) Joint Council of Europeans and Natives, an organisation founded several years before to combat poverty amongst Africans and improve 'race relations'. Hellmann may have commented that researchers need not work for justice, but by 1937 she did not conform to this idea. Even as Hellmann wielded her camera in Pimville, Prospect and Orlando, photographing, inter alia, the unexplained 'grievance meeting' (dated September 1937 on the photograph), she was attempting to publicise her views on the inadequate provision of 'native' housing in the local press: 'E. Hellmann. We have made careful inquiries into the "six points" on which your letter is based and are satisfied your information is not correct', noted Johannesburg's *Star*, also in September 1937.[48] In this letter (never published by the newspaper), Hellmann agreed that 'native slums' had to be removed since they were 'veritable plague spots ... a source of danger to the white populace of Johannesburg'. Orlando's municipal houses also improved upon the 'miserable slum rooms' from which people were being moved. But Hellmann insisted that 'real facts' must not be 'completely distorted by illusion'. Her six points concerned defects in the houses that had been overlooked by newspaper reports in which Orlando had been described as a model township. Her list mentioned such defects as the lack of ceilings, floors, insulation and adequate cement binding for bricks.

> I watched Prospect Township Natives arriving and being deposited with their belongings in the dreary desolation of Orlando. The first matter which of necessity claimed their attention was the floors, bare veld. The heaped up sand swirled with every movement in the room. To make the place at all tolerable they had first to drench their floors with water and thereafter commenced the arduous job of stamping and hardening them. And in these damp and draughty rooms they had to sleep ...[49]

Hellmann explained that the provision of 'houses, the poorest and cheapest of their kind ... to accommodate people whose former habitations were a menace to the health of the city', together with inadequate transport facilities, corresponded to the administrative agreement 'to treat our urban natives as temporary labourers from the rural districts and not as part and parcel of our population'. It was the 'smug and complacent' acceptance of this status quo that had to be challenged.[50]

This, then, was the context for Hellmann's photograph of a woman and children 'settling in', probably at work on the inadequate flooring of their new house (Figure 8). While the book and the thesis both include this picture (and neither raises the issues discussed in Hellmann's letter), they scarcely divert the reader's attention from the strong focus on youth, particularly on boys and young men. Neither book nor thesis pictures women, except as small figures in the few street scenes included. By contrast, the album has a number of pictures specifically featuring women in township settings. If Hellmann had focused strongly, in text and pictures, on women's work in a Johannesburg slum yard, her album proceeded to a visual note-taking of women's lives in the city's official townships.

Some of these pictures suggest that Hellmann's vision was shaped by the discourses of contemporary social science as well as by other, familial modes of amateur photography, perhaps because this was also a personal record of relationships with people whom she met through her research. At least one of Hellmann's contemporaries associated with the Department of Bantu Studies compiled an album and most (possibly all) took photographs. If Max Gluckmann used a similar, basic camera for the pictures that he took from 1936 to 1937 in Northern Zululand, his was a systematic visual record of cultural practices and economic activity, described in detailed captions.[51] Hellmann pursued her own interests in the adaptation of African custom by picturing a 'Makoti wearing a Hlonipha shawl. Oct. 37'. However, while Gluckmann never names his subjects, the appropriately dressed daughter-in-law is also named as 'Lena Mapumula. Pimville'. Hellmann's photograph closely frames the crisply dressed young woman, patterned shoes matching her dress, leaning slightly against the door frame of a wood-and-iron home. Possibly simply by virtue of the chronological placement of the photographs, perhaps through more deliberate selection and placement, Hellmann also created an unusual juxtaposition of woman and bare township landscape by pasting Mapumula's picture next to one of women visible in the distance, hurrying across an open expanse with loads balanced on their heads (captioned 'Women returning from station. Orlando Oct '37') (Figure 9).

What could these photographs be said to 'mean', how could they be read as 'history'? Certainly, the context of field-work and civic involvement suggest possible interpretations, for example that Hellmann explored, pictorially, women's lives in the segregated spaces of Johannesburg, including long hours spent on public transport and the almost impossible obstacles this placed in the way of women's earning a

Figure 9: Page from Ellen Hellmann's personal photo album, EHP.

Figure 10: Page from Ellen Hellmann's personal photo album, EHP.

living. But the album, more obviously than photographs chosen to illustrate extensive textual discussion, confronts the historian with the excess and opacity of photographs as objects from the past.

Perhaps the relative lack of words functioning as anchors also allows more space for the imagination, for the photographs themselves to assume power as 'revenants', as visual memory that recalls and associates images from different times and places. One striking page is unusual for its juxtaposition of township vista and the portrayal of an individual. Far-off small houses form straight lines in the veld, under a large sky bleached of its blueness in the photograph. A woman watches mildly as she sits in her chair, dressed in black, her face and the hands in her lap lined with age. Hellmann captioned the first picture 'Orlando', the second with the words 'Mourning' and 'Ester Dineko's mother' (Figure 10).

Understanding how these photographs are animated as image-texts conveying information about the past to one twenty-first century reader requires careful disaggregation of how meaning is made in the process of looking. With a longer sweep of South African history in mind, my own eyes note the resemblance between Hellmann's picture and conventional, official photographic representations of townships as spaces for the proper control of Africans in South African cities, sometimes also printed in postcard form or published in illustrated magazines.[52] Knowledge of Hellmann's scholarly interest brings awareness that she probably took the second picture while seeing through the eyes of a social anthropologist fascinated with questions of 'Westernised' African customs associated with a death in the family. But if I note this as, possibly, a photographic study of 'native' ritual within the context of family, the photograph also recalls contemporary conventions of familial portraiture. As a closely framed portrait of an elderly black woman, perhaps a widow, respectfully named according to her maternal status, sitting comfortably, looking directly at the camera, this is an unusual picture for South Africa at this time. The inscription 'Mourning', read within the longer history of the cultural uses of visual technology, also invokes photography's long association with loss, with death and with (often familial) remembrance of loved ones.[53] Perhaps the poignancy of these images results from the visual contrast of the regulated sameness of isolated township homes placed next to the closely framed individuality of portraiture. More likely, this is a personal reading of two photographs into a history of spatial segregation. Written into this past, the photographs recall the struggles of black families to survive in the face of racist policies. More specifically, they evoke the difficulties forced upon women by policies of urban segregation, which denied African women (including widows) any access to homes in the city other than through a man.

Figure 11: Page from Ellen Hellmann's personal photo album, EHP.

It is the presence of sharply focused pictures, so reminiscent of numerous early twentieth-century amateur family snapshots pasted onto the black pages of other Kodak-type albums that is most startling when you first turn these pages, not least because very few personal portraits of African families from the early twentieth century have survived.[54] Among a number of pictures taken on her wedding day is one of an uncomfortable looking 'Lena Mapumula in bridal attire'. Formal group photographs of family celebrating the event also appear in tiny prints. A Pimville picture of an unidentified mother and sons shows more relaxed participation from Hellmann's subjects, certainly from the two boys, who obviously enjoy the symmetry of their stance. The final pages of the album combine photographs of homes in Orlando with separate portraits of several women in the neat living rooms of small township homes. Lena Mapumula is shown seated with trunks and packing cases arranged along the walls; in another tiny picture sits 'Winnie Nolefi' of Pimville together with her child, a book and sewing machine on the table, a dressing table with plates carefully arranged against the wooden walls of her home (Figure 11). Apparently, Hellmann never used these outside the pages of her album, that conventional space for private contemplation, personal remembrance, the collection of the colonial picturesque and the systematic arrangement of visual evidence relating to social scientific research. Perhaps Hellmann was drawn to take pictures of women seated within their neat small houses, because she was a proponent of reforms that would provide adequate housing for Africans in the city and that rewarded perceived efforts of familial self-discipline. The homes she photographed in Pimville were likely self-built, as Africans living in this small township had been allowed to build their own houses on plots provided on a ninety-nine year lease.[55] Perhaps Hellmann took some pictures for the pleasure of her interviewees and made them copies. Whatever the political intent, research-related motivation and personal dynamics of her picture-taking, these slivers of time and space are possibly the most unusual of Hellmann's photographs, not least as portraits of black women and their children in a racially segregated South Africa.

Conclusion

Hellmann's pictures are variously found in her published work, appended to her manuscripts and pasted into an album. As such, they had limited circulation in the visual economy of the 1930s, an economy in which pictures by ethnologists, as well as similarly structured photographs produced by the prolific publicity division of the state-owned railway system South African Railways and Harbours, were not only printed in books intended for a scholarly audience but were also circulated much more widely.

For all their limited contemporary impact, Hellmann's pictures are historically significant as imaginings of 'native' space and particularly of African women. Hellmann's photographs refocused attention away from women's decorated bodies as evidence of ethnic specificity onto the living spaces that constituted Johannesburg's slum-yards. As image-text, *Rooiyard* presented evidence of African women's efforts to survive in the city, refusing to reproduce the dominant official discourse of slum-yards as breeding ground for criminals with *skokiaan* queens at the corrupt centre. Through words and images, Hellmann refigured a 'native urban slum-yard' into a domesticated space of arduous women's work for the survival of their families.

As pictures of poverty, Hellmann's photographs added to a more complex investigation of everyday living than did those published as part of campaigns for racialised social reform. Her intention to use the camera for visual note-taking – her effort to mobilise the camera's capacity to record – sometimes prompted her to move in amongst the people whom she photographed. But if the images that resulted were unusual for the way in which they conveyed the energy and activity of city life in slum conditions, Hellmann also often placed her white-imagined, academic audience at a distancing perspective from African subjects. When reading these photographs in order to investigate them as gendered and historical texts, it is important to ask how Hellmann's social identity as a woman living and working in South Africa of the 1930s could have shaped her photography. It is by following trajectories of looking within her photographs that one may investigate how class and racial privilege and hierarchies of power enabled the points of view from which Hellmann framed her African subjects, even as she pursued reformist political aims.

Compiled as a form of record-keeping, perhaps also for remembrance, Hellmann's album contains images of African women that are unusual for their focus on urban-based domesticity and on life in newly established, segregated township spaces. Photographic albums compiled by social scientific researchers, particularly by those sociologists and social anthropologists of the early twentieth century who themselves privileged words above pictures, remain unexplored in South African historical studies and indeed neglected within the broader history of photography. This initial reading of photographs from Hellmann's unpublished album in the context of her archived papers and publications suggest possibilities and difficulties for historical interpretation of text that privileges images above words.

The historian who attempts to place photography at the centre of her research and analytical endeavour is time and again confronted with questions about how photographs are (and are not) different from written text – as mute documents that seem to summon an exact, severed sliver of time and space into the present for our contemplation. For all their insistent immediacy of presence, the 'ambiguity' of visual language and the inherent slipperiness of visual signifiers have often been noted in discussions of photography and history. I have only begun to explore the questions raised by Elizabeth Edwards about the 'kind of past inscribed in photographs' and how photographs' 'apparently trivial incidental appearance of surface [can] be meaningful in historical terms'. Edwards (curator of the Pitt Rivers museum and its collection of colonial ethnographic photographs) suggests that photographs are 'very literally raw histories in both senses of the word – unprocessed and painful. Their unprocessed quality, their randomness, their minute indexicality, are inherent to the medium itself'. As documents that present 'a levelling of equivalence of information, with the trivial and the significant intertwined and shifting places', they present particular difficulties for historical interpretation and opportunities for the articulation of alternative histories.[56] Gillian Rose reminds us that numerous writers on photography – Barthes, John Berger, Jean Mohr and others – have argued that 'photographies, perhaps more than any other visual text, do persistently exceed the discursive'.[57] We follow Hellmann's line of sight as we look into the flat surface of an old photograph, trying to imagine what she saw, animated by details that she perhaps never noticed; we try to visualise the world beyond this frame, the before and after of a woman sitting behind the washing line.

Notes

1. Ellen Hellmann, *Rooiyard: A Sociological Study of an Urban Native Slum Yard* (Oxford: Oxford University Press, 1948). Ellen Hellmann Collection (EHC), A1419, 3.5, 9–10. Historical Papers, University of the Witwatersrand Library (UWL).
2. Deborah Gaitskell, 'Introduction', *Journal of Southern African Studies* 10 (1983), pp. 1–16, esp. pp. 2–3.
3. Eddie Koch, '"Without Visible Means of Subsistence": Slumyard Culture in Johannesburg 1918–1940', in Belinda Bozzoli (ed.), *Town and Countryside in the Transvaal* (Johannesburg: Ravan Press, 1983), pp. 152–75.
4. Elizabeth Edwards, *Raw Histories: Photographs, Anthropology and Museums* (Oxford: Berg, 2001), p. 5. Luli Callinicos, *A People's History of South Africa* vol. 2: *Working Life, 1886–1940: Factories, Townships and Popular Culture on the Rand* (Johannesburg: Ravan Press, 1987).
5. Patricia Hayes, Jeremy Silvester and Wolfram Hartmann, 'Photography, Memory and History' in Wolfram Hartmann, Jeremy Silvester and Patricia Hayes (eds), *The Colonising Camera: Photographs in the Making of Namibian History* (Cape Town: University of Cape Town Press, 1998), pp. 2–9, esp. pp. 2–3.

6. My use of the term 'image-text' is influenced by Marianne Hirsch, *Family Frames: Photography, Narrative, and Postmemory* (Cambridge: Harvard University Press, 1997), pp. 3–8.
7. For example, Malek Alloula, *The Colonial Harem* (Minneapolis: University of Minnesota Press, 1986); Suren Lalvani, *Photography, Vision, and the Production of Modern Bodies* (Albany: State University of New York Press, 1996); Deborah Poole, *Vision, Race, and Modernity: A Visual Economy of the Andean Image World* (Princeton: Princeton University Press, 1997); Hartmann, Silvester and Hayes (eds), *The Colonising Camera*; Elizabeth Edwards, *Photography and Anthropology* 1860–1920 (New Haven: Yale University Press, 1992); Christraud Geary, 'Different Visions? Postcards from Africa by European and African Photographers and Sponsors', in Christraud Geary and Virginia Webb (eds), *Delivering Views: Distant Cultures in Early Postcards* (Washington DC: Smithsonian Books, 1998), pp. 147–77; Ciraj Rassool and Patricia Hayes, 'Science and Spectacle: Khanako's South Africa, 1936–1937', in Wendy Woodward, Patricia Hayes and Gary Minkley (eds), *Deep hiStories: Gender and Colonialism in South Africa* (Amsterdam: Rodopi, 2002), pp. 117–61.
8. Hirsch, *Family Frames*, p. 6.
9. Susan Parnell, 'Race, Power and Urban Control: Johannesburg's Inner City Slum-yards, 1910–1923', *Journal of Southern African Studies* 9 (2003), pp. 615–37.
10. Allister MacMillan, *The Golden City* (London: W. H. & L. Collingridge, 1933), p. 204.
11. Here I draw on Deborah Poole's use of the term 'image world' in Poole, *Vision, Race, and Modernity*, esp. p. 7.
12. Geary, 'Different Views?'; Andrew Bank, 'Anthropology and Portrait Photography: Gustav Fritsch's "Natives of South Africa", 1863–1872', *Kronos* 27 (2001) pp. 43–76.
13. *Die Huisgenoot*, 28 December 1923; 7 December 1923; 28 March 1924. Examples of state tourist bureau publications that re-circulated images, including Figure 3, are 'Native Life in South Africa' (1936), 'South Africa' (*c*. 1934) and 'South African Native Studies' (1934), George G. Gubbins Africana Library (GAL), UWL.
14. Isaac Schapera (ed.), *The Bantu-speaking Tribes of South Africa: An Ethnographical Survey* (London: G. Routledge, 1937).
15. Schapera (ed.), *The Bantu-speaking Tribes*, Plates VIII and XXI.
16. Isaac Schapera (ed.), *Western Civilization and the Natives of South Africa: Studies in Culture Contact* (London: G. Routledge, 1934).
17. See also Patricia Hayes, 'Northern Exposures: the photography of C. H. L. Hahn, Native Commissioner of Ovamboland 1915–1946', in Hartmann, Silvester and Hayes (eds), *The Colonising Camera*, pp. 171–87, here pp. 177–8.
18. Ellen Hellmann, 'The Native in the Towns', in Schapera (ed.), *The Bantu-speaking Tribes*, pp. 405–34, here p. 407.
19. South African anthropology of this period was strongly influenced by British trends. Edwards discusses a similar shift in British social anthropology towards a perception of photography as 'a less satisfactory mode of recording and expression', Edwards, *Raw Histories*, pp. 38, 47.
20. Hellmann, *Rooiyard*, illustration no. 3, n.p.
21. MacMillan, *The Golden City*, p. 158.
22. Katherine Eales, 'Gender Politics and the Administration of African Women in Johannesburg 1903–1939', unpublished MA dissertation (University of the Witwatersrand, 1991), pp. 6, 19.
23. *S. A. Pictorial*, 24 January 1920, p. 7; *Die Huisgenoot*, 6 March 1925.
24. *S. A. Pictorial*, 24 January 1920.
25. Hellmann, *Rooiyard*, p. 39.
26. Hellmann, *Rooiyard*, p. 17.
27. Hellmann, *Rooiyard*, pp. 51–3.
28. Gillian Rose, 'Engendering the Slum: Photography in East London in the 1930s', *Gender, Place and Culture* 4 (1997), pp. 277–300, here p. 287.

29. Hellmann, *Rooiyard*, pp. 47–8.
30. Hellmann, *Rooiyard*, p. 40.
31. Marijke du Toit, 'Interior Journeys: Photographs from the Carnegie Commission of Investigation into the Poor White Problem (1929/32)'. Available at <http://www.history.ukzn.ac.za/Sempapers/DuToit2002.pdf>.
32. Johannesburg Housing Utility Company, 'To Hell with Slums', 1933, GAL, quotes from p. 1.
33. Johannesburg Housing Utility Company, 'To Hell with Slums'.
34. Johannesburg Housing Utility Company, 'To Hell with Slums', pp. 24, 32.
35. Johannesburg Housing Utility Company, 'To Hell with Slums', pp. 10, 42.
36. Gillian Rose, 'Engendering the Slum', pp. 277–8.
37. GrahamClarke, *The Photograph* (Oxford: OxfordUniversity Press, 1997), p. 32; RolandBarthes, *Camera Lucida: Reflections on Photography*, tr. Richard Howard (London: Fontana 1984), p. 9.
38. Hellmann, *Rooiyard*, p. 1.
39. Manuscript copy of 'Rooiyard', p. 1. The printed copy omitted the word 'woman'. EHC, A1419/34.
40. Manuscript copy of 'Rooiyard', p. 1. EHC, A1419/34.
41. Hellmann published several articles based on her research in specialist academic journals (*Africa, Bantu Studies*) in the 1930s.
42. Hellmann, 'Methods of Urban Fieldwork', *Bantu Studies* 9 (1935), pp. 185–202, here p. 199.
43. E. G. Malherbe, *The Poor White Problem in South Africa: Report of the Carnegie Commission* (Stellenbosch: Pro Ecclesia, 1932).
44. Ellen Hellmann, *Problems of Urban Bantu Youth: Report of an Enquiry into the Causes of Early School-leaving and Occupational Opportunities amongst Bantu Youth in Johannesburg* (Johannesburg: South African Institute of Race Relations, 1940).
45. Ellen Hellmann, 'Early School-Leaving and African Juvenile Occupational Opportunities', undated ms., EHC, A1419/51.
46. Deborah Posel, 'The Case for a Welfare State: Poverty and the Politics of the Urban African Family in the 1930s and 1940s', in Saul Dubow and Alan Jeeves (eds), *South Africa's 1940s: Worlds of Possibilities* (Cape Town: Double Storey, 2005), pp. 64–86, here pp. 66, 68.
47. Gary Minkley, '"Corpses behind Screens": Native Space in the City', in Hilton Judin and Ivan Vladislavic (eds), *Blank: Architecture, Apartheid and After* (Cape Town: Philip, 1998), section D11, n.p.
48. *Star* (Johannesburg), 1 September 1937, p. 21.
49. Hellmann, letter to the editor, the *Star*, 17 August 1937. Institute of Race Relations Collection, AD1433, Cj2.1.17 (file 2) JBG Joint Council correspondence. Historical Papers, UWL.
50. All quotes from Hellmann's letter to the editor, *Star*, 17 August 1937.
51. Max Gluckmann, 'Photographs taken in Nongoma and Hlabisa districts of Northern Zululand, September 1936–April 1937 by M. Gluckmann'. Art Galleries Collection, University of the Witwatersrand. The unnumbered collection has been absorbed into the University of Witwatersrand Art Galleries and includes a large number of index cards with photographs apparently mounted in the 1930s, comprising work by anthropologists Monica Hunter, Eileen Krige, Audrey Richards and others.
52. Minkley, 'Corpses behind screens'.
53. Hirsch, *Family Frames*, pp. 5, 19–20; Marijke du Toit, 'Blank Verbeeld, or the Incredible Whiteness of Being: Amateur Photography and Afrikaner Nationalist Historical Narrative', *Kronos* 27 (2001), pp. 77–113, here p. 87.
54. Santo Mofokeng, 'The Black Family Album', in *Anthology of African and Indian Ocean Photography* (Paris: Revue Noire, 1999), pp. 68–75.
55. I am grateful to Phil Bonner for pointing this out to me.
56. Edwards, *Raw Histories*, p. 5.
57. Rose, 'Engendering the Slum', p. 13.

5 Racialising the Virile Body: Eadweard Muybridge's Locomotion Studies 1883–1887

Elspeth H. Brown

In 1883, the photographer Eadweard Muybridge was invited to the University of Pennsylvania to conduct one of the first sponsored research projects of the modern American university. The investigations concerned the sequential photography of human and animal movement, resulting in over 100,000 images and 781 published collotype plates containing more than 20,000 figures of moving men, women, children, animals and birds.[1] Dr William Pepper, the University's provost, and others, including the American realist painter Thomas Eakins, were instrumental in bringing Muybridge to the university, a move that allowed Muybridge to continue the motion studies that he had completed with Leland Stanford in 1879. The university provided Muybridge with space, extensive equipment and assistants in order to undertake the project, which he conducted between 1884 and 1887.[2] Dr Pepper also created a commission to oversee Muybridge's research, consisting of nine professionals, seven of whom were doctors or engineers employed by the University of Pennsylvania (the other two were Thomas Eakins and Edward Coates, both of the Pennsylvania Academy of Fine Arts). As film historian Tom Gunning has recently remarked, Muybridge was a bit of a 'crazy uncle' whose project straddled 'intersections between photography, science, art and new forms of mass entertainment'.[3]

The Muybridge project's immense scope and complexity has been further documented in archival material concerning Muybridge's University of Pennsylvania work recently made available to scholars at the Smithsonian's National Museum of American History (NMAH). NMAH Photographic Specialist Michelle Delaney has helped to build scholarship on a group of 850 cyanotype, or 'blueprint', contact proof sets that Muybridge made from his Animal Locomotion negatives.[4] The original glass-plate negatives for these images have never been found.[5] Most of the NMAH cyanotypes are sheets of blue, non-enlarged photographs, printed directly from the lost glass-plate negatives onto thin, off-white paper and cut to size. This process replicates the long, thin strips of glass-plate negatives, which are usually about 30 cm long and 1.2 cm wide. These blue-tinted contact prints are mounted on 850 separate thin sheets of cardboard and labelled using pre-printed sheets with blanks for the Animal Locomotion plate number, title, classification, as well as the negative series number and the number of views taken (Figure 1).

In Figure 1, we see a young woman, artist model Blanche Epler – paid for four hours of work on this autumn day of 25 September 1885 – walking up and down a short flight of stairs with a water vessel.[6] The sequence of images here, which most Westerners would read from left to right, suggests a filmic narrative of small, incremental changes in time, captured through the instantaneous photography of Muybridge's multi-camera apparatus. But as Marta Braun has so brilliantly demonstrated, a close analysis of the printed plates reveals curious temporal gaps, usually ignored in the viewer's effort to render the series a narrative of discrete and temporally contained, motions.[7] Here, for example, Miss Epler apparently turns about face in the third image; whereas the first two images show her moving up the stairs, in the third image she is darting down to the final step. Further viewing time reveals that perhaps these images are not a connected sequence after all; in the fourth image, an earthenware vessel, which had been on the ground in the first three images, has replaced the dish of water that Miss Epler obligingly carries before the camera. Below the top row of images, other contact prints show the results of rear and frontal views; Muybridge usually photographed each subject simultaneously from three different positions, using a battery of twelve cameras for the lateral view and another two cameras with twelve lenses for the front and rear views. The label on the top of the image shows additional information not available in the printed collotype plates. Most importantly, the inclusion of the series negative number (here, number 1419) allows the researcher to match the images to the remaining extant Muybridge workbooks, now located in the International Museum of Photography, George Eastman House in Rochester, New York. In this case, for example, we learn that immediately after this series of images Miss Epler disrobed, performing a related series in the nude. Although the printed plates reflect the cyanotype proofs in every detail, revealing that the negatives that made the cyanotypes were used for the final printed version, the inclusion of additional information in the cyanotypes allows for further research into the Muybridge project. The discovery of these

Racialising the Virile Body   111

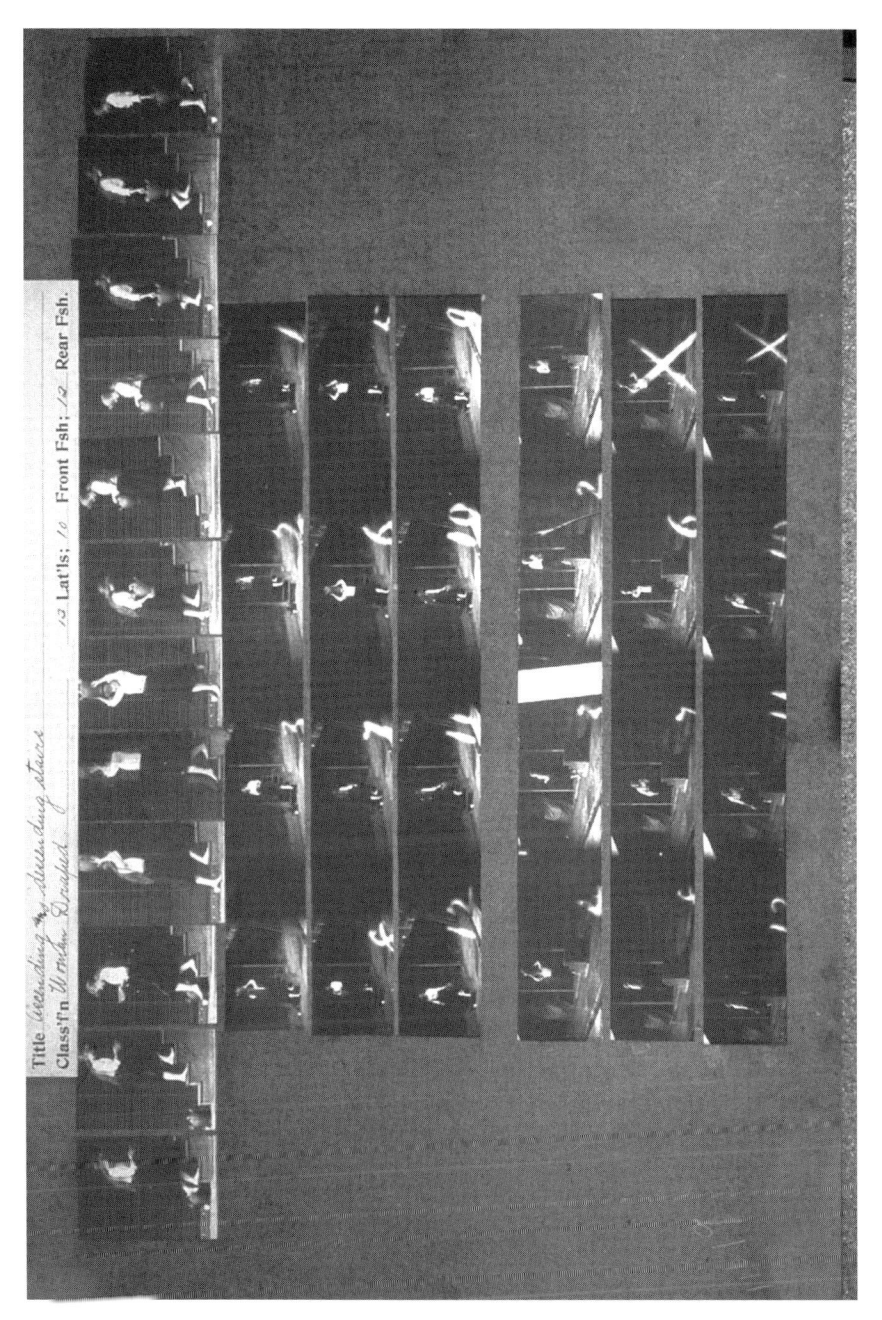

Figure 1: Eadweard Muybridge cyanotypes (Ascending and Descending Stairs; proof print for what became PL 504); (1885). Photographic History Collection, National Museum of American History, Smithsonian Institution, Washington D.C. (NMAH).

proofs has sparked a renewed interest in Muybridge's University of Pennsylvania work, for now scholars have new visual evidence for his working methods.[8]

Despite the complexity of this project as a site for competing discourses concerning science, art and mass culture, Muybridge straightforwardly declared his own interests in the University of Pennsylvania project. His studies of both human and animal movement would be of value, he claimed, to both 'the Scientist and the Artist'. Muybridge seemed especially interested in effectively bringing science and art into close dialogue with each other. In his press scrapbook from the project, the one theme that is consistently underlined, by what looks like Muybridge's hand, is the necessary interrelationship between science and art. A typical underlined sentence: 'Science can never furnish a substitute for the artistic sense. But there is no reason why the artist should not avail himself of all that science can teach him'.[9]

Some readers may be familiar with at least some of the historiography concerning this famous project, which has included arguments over the origins of cinema, the discourse of science and art, Muybridge's relationship to Eakins and nineteenth-century realism, feminist critiques of pornographic visuality and, more recently, pathological locomotion.[10] The cacophony of scholarly voices here can be partly attributed to the complexities of the text. Despite Muybridge's central role in the project, others were also involved in the work; he cannot properly be understood as the project's sole 'author'.[11] The polysemic nature of the photographic text also opens the project to a number of readings, both historical and theoretical; these readings are informed, in part, by the tumultuous history of late nineteenth-century race and gender politics.

As a generation of photographic critics has argued, the history of photographic meaning is necessarily a history of institutions and of structures of power relations of dominance and subordination that have specific histories that shape the ways in which photographic meaning is produced. John Tagg, working within an Althusserian and Foucauldian framework, has argued that photography has no intrinsic identity, that what is real is not just the material item but more importantly 'the discursive system of which the image it bears is part'.[12] Allan Sekula, working with the assertion that 'photographic meaning depends largely on context', has sought to understand how photography 'serves to legitimate and normalise existing power relationships'.[13] Tagg and Sekula, in particular, have shown how 'instrumental' photographic images, such as mug shots, anthropological records, medical images and even documentary photographs were central to managing the new forms of governance intrinsic to colonial expansion, the second industrial revolution and state formation in the late nineteenth century.[14] Their efforts have been joined by a generation of cultural and photographic historians who have become suspicious of modernism's allegiance to 'the thing itself' (the term is John Szarkowski's, former curator of photography at the Museum of Modern Art), instead focusing on how the photograph, in Abigail Solomon-Godeau's formulation, has been made subject to the 'grids of meaning imposed upon it by culture, history, language'.[15]

In this article I wish to attend, literally, to the photographic 'grid' by resituating Muybridge's University of Pennsylvania work in relationship to ideas concerning the gendered nature of racial progress in the late nineteenth century. Borrowing from Michael Omi and Howard Winant's work on racial formation, I want to think through the University of Pennsylvania work as a historically situated racial project in which 'human bodies and social structures are represented and organized' in order to create, inhabit, transform or destroy racial categories.[16] Race and gender are not ontologically given; they are categories that signify and symbolise relations of power, categories that are articulated and contested in the realm of culture, in relationship to human bodies whose racial and gender specificity becomes knowable, in part, through visual representation. In this essay, I argue that the University of Pennsylvania Muybridge project reveals an investment in gendered evolutionary race science, an investment that we can retrieve through an investigation into three related sites, all connected to anthropometry. The first site concerns the anthropometric grid; the second site concerns scientists' investment in this research; and the third concerns the racialising and gendering of some of the male models engaged for this project.

The first site: anthropometry and the grid

A key aspect of an alternative reading of this project as inflected by nineteenth-century race science concerns the role of anthropometry in the University of Pennsylvania project. By the second half of the nineteenth century, measurement technologies of the body's external features had become increasingly standardised in an anthropological sub-discipline known as anthropometry, 'the technique of expressing quantitatively the form of the human body'.[17] In the United States, the Civil War marked what one historian has called a 'watershed' in anthropometric developments, not only because of the widespread anthropometric examination of Union soldiers, but also because nearly all post-bellum theories of racial inferiority focused upon war anthropometry for scientific validity.[18] While Samuel Morton's work in this field, which had been used as a justification for slavery, lost its influence in the United States in the wake of the Civil War, his work took root and flourished in Europe, especially in the work of polygenesist Paul Broca. As C. Loring Brace has argued, 'The techniques that Broca elaborated from Morton's beginnings were adopted in England ... and later, Hrdlička and Hooton [founders of American physical anthropology] saw to it that these returned to American anthropology as it grew in the twentieth century'.[19] Anthropologists continued to pursue anthropometric methodologies throughout the nineteenth and into the twentieth centuries, avidly measuring bodily and facial characteristics, such as stature, arm length, head length and width and nose length.[20] Anthropologists were most likely to study either institutionalised or non-white populations, such as the 'feeble-minded', school children, Native Americans, blacks or colonised subjects. The idea was that the measurement of anatomical differences could help define racial types and that the isolation of these racial types could help (for some investigators) illuminate not only physical differences, but cultural, mental and moral differences as well. Through measurement, racial typologies and hierarchies – of both body and mind – were constructed and naturalised. This work continued through the 1920s among eugenicist scientists. As one concluded in 1928, 'the reason for using the stature-capacity index is fairly clear. The brain very evidently has something to do with intelligence and it would seem only reasonable to suppose the larger the brain relative to the size of the individual, the greater would be his or her intelligence'.[21]

Photography became central to this enterprise of constructing and mapping somatic difference.[22] In physical anthropology, photography's principal contribution through at least the 1920s was the documentation of distinct racial types. Historians of physical anthropology, photography and empire have noted several of the major efforts to use photography as a means of taxonomising racial types. In 1850, the prominent American natural scientist Louis Agassiz arranged for Joseph T. Zealy to daguerreotype five South Carolina slaves in order to document somatic evidence of tribal difference.[23] In 1873, the year after Muybridge began his work with Leland Stanford in California, two photographic projects designed to chart racial difference got underway in Europe: the Hamburg photographer Carl Dammann's *Ethnological Gallery of the Races of Men* (published in English in 1875); and the British Lieutenant Colonel William Marshall's study of South Indians, entitled *A Phrenologist among the Todas*, which was illustrated by photographs of residents of Madras and Simla.[24] Whereas some of this work represented more fluid approaches that were dictated as much by moments of encounter as by systematic mapping, other efforts were underway to standardise photographic methodologies across subjects. In 1869, J. H. Lamprey proposed the photographic incorporation of the metrological grid system, long used by artists seeking to accurately portray bodily proportions (Figure 2). Although some French systems predate Lamprey's approach, his grid system was published in the London-based *Journal of the Ethnological Society* and was thus made available to English-speaking professional

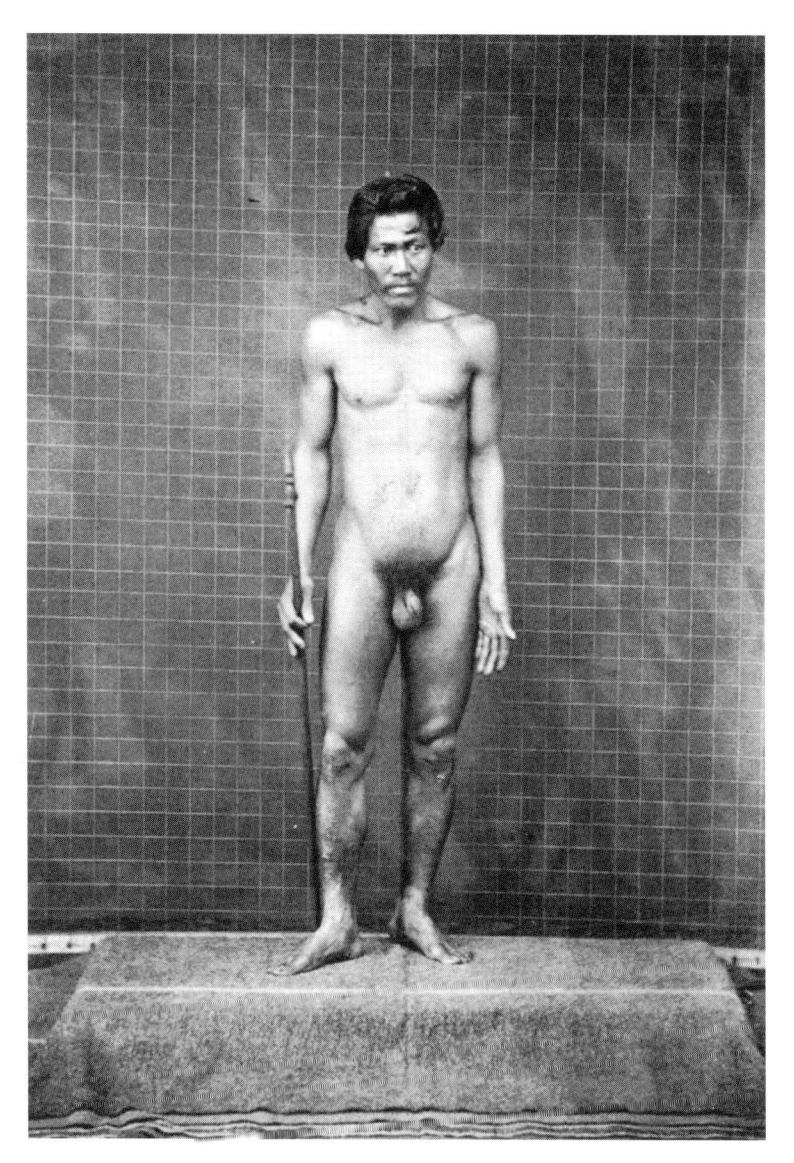

Figure 2: Front view of a Malayan male, photographed by J. Lamprey, *c.* 1868–9. Royal Anthropological Institute of Great Britain and Ireland (no. 2116).

audiences.[25] The system allowed some generalised comparisons across subjects and was widely followed.[26]

The introduction of photography to the emerging discipline of physical anthropology helped define a new genre in visual culture, the anthropological photograph. Despite the variations in approach that continued to frustrate those scientists who sought a standardised methodology, the anthropological photograph emerged during the late nineteenth century with a recognisable set of visual signs. For example, the American polygenesis advocates J. C. Nott and George R. Gliddon urged those interested in 'ethnic iconography' that 'the same portrait should be photographed both in *front view* and in *profile* [emphasis in original]'. M. V. Portman, a colonial officer in the Andaman Islands, wrote that when photographing 'savages', the subjects should be 'stark naked, a full face and a profile view should be taken of each and the subject should touch a background painted in black and white chequers, each exactly 2 inches square'.[27] In Figure 2, for example, a Malayan male stands before the camera, his right hand holding a staff while his left palm opens towards the camera in a gesture of cautious vulnerability. As in many of these photographs of racial 'types', the subject avoids returning the camera's gaze. The power relations of looking that structure such photographs imply a nineteenth-century white viewer allowed to enact the colonising gaze without risking the confrontational gesture of the colonial subject's 'looking back'.[28] The subject's powerful legs are slightly parted away from the centre of his body, while his arms and hands are held away from the torso; the overall attitude of the model, slightly elevated on a fabric-covered platform, suggests a puzzled, though not necessarily hostile, reluctance. Behind him, the grid of silk threads at two-inch intervals helps construct an emerging iconography of visual empiricism, where signs of measurement signal the rhetoric of a disinterested scientific endeavour. Lamprey argued that the vertical silk lines would allow the comparison of height between, for example, a 'good academy figure or model of six feet' with 'a Malay of four feet eight in height' (the image of Lamprey's model in Figure 2, however, suggests a height of five feet, three inches). The horizontal lines would allow the comparative study of anatomical structure and contour.[29] As critics of photography, the state and empire have argued, however, the joining of photography and science, especially in this period, was central to the creation of instrumental images where state power was masked by the discourse of photographic objectivity.[30]

That Lamprey's anthropometric grid shows up for the first time in American photography in Muybridge's University of Pennsylvania project suggests that a racialised narrative informed the project. Lamprey's system posed the body against a gridded backdrop divided into two-inch squares by means of silk threads; Muybridge's grid was composed of threads dividing the field into five-centimetre squares (Figure 3).[31] Even

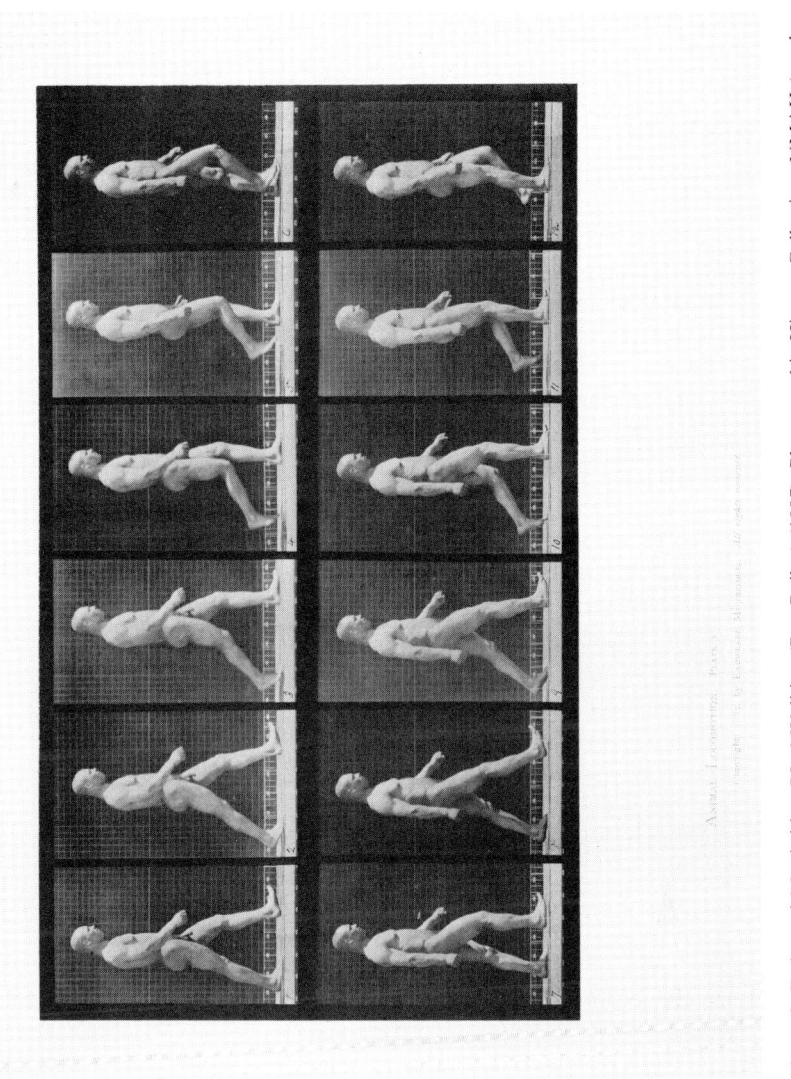

Figure 3: Eadweard Muybridge, Pl. 6 Walking (Ben Bailey) (1887). Photographic History Collection, NMAH (catalog no. 2430).

more relevant, Muybridge did not begin his work at the University of Pennsylvania using the metrological grid. As Marta Braun shows, his earliest images, taken in the spring and summer of 1884, were made on the University Veterinary Hospital grounds against a solid background, the same as he had used in California for his earlier motion studies (Figure 4).[32] In Figure 4, we see a sequence of images of a woman spanking a child; unlike the later sequences, where human and animal models move in a direct course past a bank of cameras, in this case the models remain stationary while six cameras arrayed in an arc covering 180 degrees describe the models from six different points. This method of working was abandoned by the early summer of 1885, when Muybridge was finally able to perfect the system for which the series is best known, batteries of twelve cameras placed at three different angles to the model.[33] The unlined backdrop suggests that the implicit goal was the visual description of the models and their activity, rather than their measurement.

As Braun shows, the metrological grid appears for the first time in Muybridge's work on 2 June 1885 when, while working in the 524–31

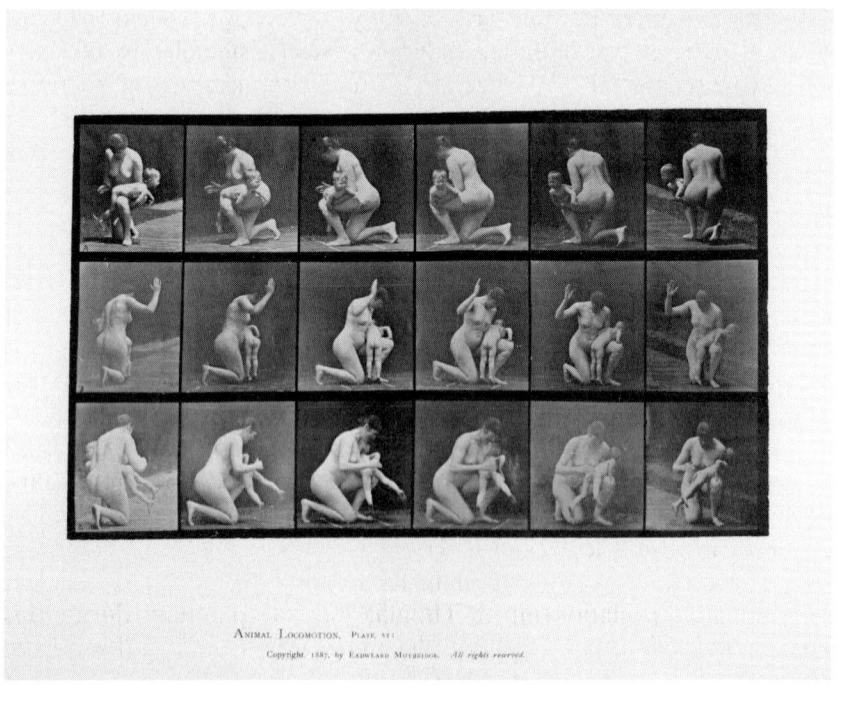

Figure 4: Eadweard Muybridge, PL 527 Spanking a Baby (1887). Photographic History Collection, NMAH (catalog no. 2896).

negative series, Muybridge photographed Ben Bailey.[34] Ben Bailey, a 'mulatto' pugilist, was the only model of African descent among the ninety-five models photographed for Muybridge's work at the University of Pennsylvania; Bailey walked, ascended and descended stairs, struck a blow and threw a rock for Muybridge's cameras.[35] Bailey appears to have been one of the numerous black and mixed-race boxers in the Philadelphia area who made the city a centre for boxing during the period, fighting in athletic clubs and bars for whatever the spectators would donate (professional boxing was highly lucrative at the top, though still illegal).[36] With Ben Bailey, we have the introduction of the anthropometric grid into American photography; although the other ninety-four models were white, the anthropometric grid first appears behind the only model who was African American. It is as if the non-white 'other' cannot be understood, scientifically, without the anthropometric grid, a technology for mapping racial difference. The fact that Bailey was mixed-race raises the question of what role he may have played in addressing late nineteenth-century anthropological inquiries into racial hybridity and evolution.[37] Once introduced, Muybridge retained the grid for all of the series after negative number 524, where Bailey was first introduced.

Figure 3 represents the first activity that Bailey performed for Muybridge's cameras: walking. Maleness is clearly signalled by the genitalia, while masculinity is articulated through the absence of narrative that defines many of the female series. For example Miss Epler's task for 15 September 1885 was crossing a brook on stepping-stones. From the perspective of the 1880s implied white, male, middle-class viewer, Bailey's musculature would have seemed unusually developed. His powerful upper arms cast small shadows in the full sunlight, while his quadriceps muscles suggest a coiled power. The decision to include this plate early in the published series, as number six, suggests that Muybridge, or others, considered it to be exemplary – but of what, is unclear. Bailey's physique stands in marked contrast to that of the comparatively slight bodies of the male students, whose athletic accomplishments were also photographed as model movements (discussed below). Bailey's articulation of a muscled, racialised body represents, perhaps, an emerging model for a new embodied masculinity, marked by a cross-racial investment in musculature as a visible marker of masculine gender identity. As Gail Bederman has argued and as Martin Berger has discussed in relationship to Thomas Eakins's paintings during this same period, Victorian ideals of the male gender were shifting from older notions of 'manhood', characterised by inner virtues and adult responsibilities to emerging ideas of modern 'masculinity', where self-control became legible through the muscled body.[38] Bailey's powerful physique signals an emerging masculine ideal that was, at the time, identified with both working class and African American male body types, but which would soon emerge as a white, middle-class ideal as well.

The hegemony of white cultural identity, as numerous historians and critics have argued, is grounded in its invisibility as a racial category, but, like all forms of difference, the consolidation of one aspect of the binary (for example, whiteness) is predicated on the identification of the other (for example, blackness). Ben Bailey's impressive display of physical prowess as – significantly – a boxer situates him as the object of desire and of admiration for the implied nineteenth-century white viewer. At the same time, the history of violence against American blacks in late nineteenth-century America, when an average of 188 lynchings occurred per year during the 1890s, suggests a violent affirmation of racial difference, reinforced by the official inequality of law and social practice, which these images quietly ignore. In the context of nineteenth-century race politics, the admiration of a physical embodiment of whites' corporeal ideal suggested by the photographs was strenuously contradicted by the racial hierarchies promulgated by the same emerging disciplines, further described below, that supported the Muybridge project. This is the 'dialectic of love and theft' detailed, for example, by Eric Lott in his work on nineteenth-century blackface minstrelsy: whites' fascination with an invented black vitality, always shadowed by a panicked, envy-laced disgust.[39] This splitting is constitutive of white racial identity in nineteenth-century American history. In a period of complex racial formation, where white racial identity was being redefined as 'Caucasian' to include the provisional whites of nineteenth-century immigration, while being consolidated against definitions of blackness integral to Jim Crow segregation, the anthropometric grid discursively situates Bailey as a racialised object of anthropological inquiry, against which narratives of racial progress can be mapped and measured.[40]

The second site: anthropometry and the scientists

One could argue that the grid emerged at this point because of the project's link to realism in the visual arts, for example through Thomas Eakins. Eakins is unlikely to have been much concerned with the grid, however, because he appears to have ended his association with the Muybridge work well before June 1885, when the grid appeared. Another alternative might be seen in the involvement of Francis Xavier Dercum, who was interested in the documentation of pathological locomotion. However, the project's second linkage to anthropometry, through the research interests of many of the scientists on the Muybridge advisory commission and their associates, suggests an alternative interpretation.[41] These influential professors may have seen Muybridge's work as an evidentiary source for their own scholarly claims in the fields of comparative anatomy and physical anthropology.

A first clue concerning the relationship between the Muybridge project scientists and the study of comparative racial anatomy is the discovery that some of them were also founders of the American Anthropometric Society. The American Anthropometric Society was founded in 1889 – three years after the completion of Muybridge's project – by Harrison Allen, Francis X. Dercum, Joseph Leidy, William Pepper and Edward Charles Spitzka.[42] Allen, Leidy and Pepper were all members of the Muybridge advisory commission. Francis X. Dercum, head of the neurological clinic at the university, was Muybridge's collaborator in photographing pathological locomotion as part of the Pennsylvania project; he also reviewed 20,000 of Muybridge's photographs in the fall of 1885 as part of the university's supervision arrangement.[43] These scientists all had various linkages to shifting ideas of race science in the nineteenth century.[44]

Pepper, an important figure in the history of medical education in America in addition to his roles at Penn, was extraordinarily ambitious for the university. He asserted that he 'undertook the patronage of Muybridge, believing that it could promote the general recognition of the university' as well as produce 'an important piece of useful work being done under scientific control'. Both of these goals were realised in his estimation.[45] Pepper founded the first university teaching hospital in the United States in 1874 at Penn. As provost of the University of Pennsylvania from 1881–1894, Pepper was instrumental in shifting Penn towards the European model of a research university. During his tenure as provost, the university grew from a site of fifteen acres to fifty-two, while the number of students more than doubled from 981 to 2,180.[46] The development of a system of physical education and hygiene was one of Pepper's key goals; for him, the development of the white, male student body was directly linked to white racial progress, as manifested in the Anglo-Saxon and in what Pepper labelled a new American race. On the occasion of a University of Pennsylvania student winning the world record for the high jump in 1887, Pepper pronounced that physical education was nothing less than central to the 'cultivation of manly and courageous qualities ... among those two great branches of the English speaking races [Britain and America] that the world has most to hope for in the maintenance of peace and in the ultimate triumph of liberty'.[47] Such rhetoric was not necessarily unusual at a time when 'race' was also used to refer to what would now be understood as cultural or social qualities of a nation or people.

Joseph Leidy was one of the more senior members of the scientific commission. Professor of anatomy for thirty-eight years at the university, he was a key founder of American vertebrate palaeontology, as well as the foremost anatomist of his time. Although some aspects of vertebrate palaeontology concerned the collection and classification of human fossils, including skulls, in an effort to map racial difference, Leidy's work focused for the most part on extinct vertebrate forms, including the ox, horse, and – most famously – the dinosaurs. Unlike his close colleague at the American Philosophical Society, Samuel Morton, Leidy generally avoided the mid-nineteenth-century investment in human skull collection and measurement as a scientific basis for racial hierarchies and for slavery. When given an opportunity to take over Morton's work after Morton's death in 1851, Leidy declined; as he later wrote, 'after the death of Dr Morton, it was proposed to me to take up the investigation of the cranial characteristics of the human races, where he had left it, which I omitted, not from a want of interest in ethnographic science, but because other studies occupied my time'.[48] Instead, Leidy was one of the earliest American supporters of Darwin's controversial ideas concerning evolution. As a result of Leidy's advocacy, the Academy of Natural Sciences in Philadelphia became the first American scientific society to recognise Darwin's work through admitting Darwin to membership in 1860.[49] In his role as anatomist Leidy became the director of the university's first Department of Biology in 1884, where his title changed to Professor of Comparative Anatomy and Zoology. His research in comparative anatomy rendered Leidy an ideal member of the Muybridge commission, even though he apparently did not a take a direct role in the photographic work.

Harrison Allen, a member of the Muybridge commission and president of the American Anthropometric Society after his teacher and colleague Joseph Leidy's term, was Professor of Comparative Anatomy and Zoology, as well as (at various points) Physiology, at the University of Pennsylvania from 1865–96. Allen was more involved in the project than Leidy and contributed an essay entitled 'Materials for a Memoir on Animal Locomotion' to the volume on the project published in 1888.[50] Allen's own research concerned comparative racial and vertebrate anatomy and physical anthropology. He produced a number of scientific papers on bats as well as on human anatomy and, especially in his later years, crania and the classification of skulls.[51] According to his contemporary, anthropologist and University of Pennsylvania professor

Daniel Brinton, Allen was especially interested in the anatomical differences 'between races or varieties of the human species' and sought to understand these differences, in part, through an investigation of animated structures – through movement. His investigations into the lower jaw, as a 'test character of race', Brinton argued, 'should be committed to memory by every student of racial anatomy'.[52] For Allen, anatomical characteristics could be traced to evolutionary development of racial types, the study of which was known as comparative racial morphology. In the assessment of physical anthropologist Aleš Hrdlička, Allen stood, after Samuel Morton and another nineteenth-century colleague, as 'the foremost American representative of our branch of science before the end of the nineteenth century'. Allen's interest in cranial measurements and comparative racial anatomy, Hrdlička reported in this laudatory assessment of 1919, stemmed primarily from 'the works of [Samuel] Morton and J. Aitken Meigs, the latter of whom he knew personally'.[53] Allen attributed distinctions in anatomy to diversity in nutrition and other environmental conditions and, like other contemporary anthropologists, his work represented the post-bellum rapprochement between Neo-Lamarckian ideas of the inheritability of acquired characteristics and an environmental determinism that provided morphological evidence for Spencerian notions of racial hierarchy.

As Lee Baker has argued, Philadelphia, and the University of Pennsylvania in particular, played an important role in the 'Faustian bargain' made between anthropology and race in the late nineteenth century. In 1886, a few years after he had invited Muybridge to the university, Provost William Pepper hired Daniel G. Brinton as the first professor of anthropology at a US university. The hiring of Brinton was designed to support Pepper's interest in creating a museum of ethnology on the campus and Brinton was appointed Professor of American Archaeology and Linguistics; once at Penn, he quickly became the head of the emerging field of anthropology in the Philadelphia area.[54] Brinton, like other neo-Lamarckian anthropologists, argued that all human beings had a common psychic heritage, but that differences in environment produced, over time, different races, which could be clearly charted in a hierarchy from savage at the foot to civilised at the head. In 1884, Brinton became Professor of Ethnology and Archaeology at the Academy of Natural Sciences of Philadelphia (ANSP). In his popular, fee-based lectures to Main Line (elite) Philadelphians, most of whom were women, Brinton contrasted the perfect development of the 'Aryan American woman' to her over sexed 'savage' sisters. His influential books *Races and Peoples* (1890) and *The American Race* (1891) grew out of the ANSP lectures.[55] For Brinton, ethnography was the science of mapping and classifying races and peoples; the physical differences measured by comparative anatomists such as Harrison Allen were the means through which these racial taxonomies could be constructed. According to Aleš Hrdlička, although Brinton's personality was 'widely different' from Harrison Allen's, the two associated 'as friends and each doubtless exercised an influence on the other's thought and scientific production'.[56] He popularised the scientific investigation of comparative racial anatomy using an explicit discourse of racial hierarchy that placed the European or white race at the top and Africans and American Negroes at the bottom. Brinton's arguments did not prevent *Races and Peoples* (1890) from being positively reviewed on both sides of the Atlantic, including by the young Franz Boas, who reviewed the work for *Science* in 1890.[57]

The racial assumptions of the emerging field of physical anthropology, known during the period as 'somatology' or 'comparative racial anatomy' were legitimised through technologies of measurement and visualisation. By 1883, the year that University of Pennsylvania scientists extended the invitation to Muybridge, still photography was widely accepted as a key technology in mapping somatic difference and classifying the static body on scales of racial hierarchies. Muybridge's work in documenting motion, however, corresponds with a new direction in physical anthropology where movement emerged as a key indicator of racial evolution. Late nineteenth-century French anthropology became especially interested in mapping movement, particularly human locomotion, as an index of racial types. Felix-Louis Regnault, the French anthropologist who pioneered ethnographic film in the 1895, turned to film as a means of recording racial difference; for Regnault, the still camera could not capture the body in motion, which he believed provided essential clues concerning racial typologies. As Fatimah Tobing Rony persuasively argues, '[i]n searching for an index of race – the unfashioned clue – Regnault chose to explore *movement*, that which is "in between" culture and nature, acting and being'.[58] Each race, Regnault argued, had a particular posture while in motion and only studies of sequential movement could capture what the eye failed to detect unaided. Might Muybridge, long disputed 'father' of the motion picture, be an influence in ethnographic film, where kinesiology, as well as physiology, was seen to index racial difference?

The third site: anthropometry and Penn athletics

The third appearance of anthropometry in the project concerns the fourteen male university student models who performed many of the athletic feats for the University of Pennsylvania work. The students were part of a broader category that included Penn student record-holding athletes, professional athletes, mechanics who were 'experts in their particular trades' and labourers; the female models, Muybridge claimed, 'were chosen from all classes of society'.[59] In general terms, Muybridge wanted the female models to demonstrate what he considered to be everyday activities accomplished with grace and poise, whereas the male models were intended to represent the perfect, or champion, motions of a given athletic or work-related activity.[60] The gendered representation of some of these quotidian tasks trafficked in the visual discourse of the erotic.[61] Just one of numerous examples was Catherine Aimer, an artist's model whom Muybridge paid for five hours on 18 July 1885 to bathe and pour water over her head, dry herself, step out of the bath and put on stockings. These performed activities could be read simultaneously as mundane and pornographic, depending upon the reading practices of the viewer.[62] Although Muybridge paid the artist models to disrobe, he was frustrated that their working-class origins prevented them from producing the class-inflected poise that he sought from his female locomotion studies. 'I have experienced a great deal of difficulty in securing proper models. In the first place, artists' models, as a rule, are ignorant and not well-bred', he complained to a reporter in the summer of 1885. 'As a consequence, their movements are not graceful and it is essential for the thorough execution of my work to have my [female] models of a graceful bearing'. The working-class male models, however, could not be induced to remove their clothing at any price, according to Muybridge.[63]

Muybridge was more successful at getting the male student models to disrobe. Most of the male Penn models were students in the mechanical engineering programme or in the medical school; outside class, they were often team mates on a variety of amateur athletic teams at Penn, including baseball, cricket, track, football, rowing and cycling. For example, the Penn athletic model and student Randolph Faries graduated with a BA in 1885 and received an MD in 1888. During these years, he became prominent in athletics and held the championship for the mile run in 1884, 1885 and 1886; he was also on the baseball team for four years. In 1890, he was made Director of Physical Education at Penn, a post he kept until 1897.[64] Percy C. Madeira, the model for Plate 59, 'Starting for a Run' and Plate 60, 'Running at a Half-mile Gait', among other plates, was the 1884 amateur one-mile champion of America for 1884. In addition to modelling running for Muybridge, Madeira also high-jumped, long-jumped, ran hurdles and participated in other physical activities.[65] Many of the other athletic models were also champions or record holders of their various sports: for example, Albert Cline, who received his BS in 1887 and ME (post-graduate engineering degree) in 1888, set a college record for the pole vault in 1886. During the same meeting, classmate and fellow Muybridge model Randolph Faries won

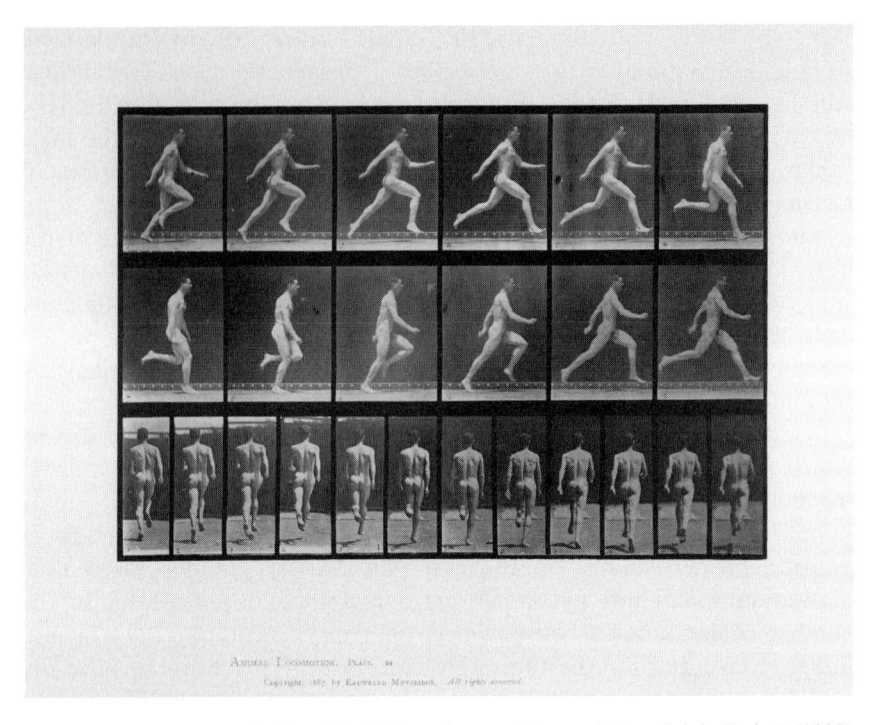

Figure 5: Eadweard Muybridge, PL 64 Running at full speed (Randolph Faries) (1887). Photographic History Collection, NMAH, (catalog no. 2480).

the mile (Figure 5), while Thomas Grier, another Muybridge model and a project assistant, won the mile walk.[66]

When Muybridge arrived at the university in 1883, the university was at the start of a rapid process of modernising its athletic programme. Led primarily by Penn alumni, the Athletic Association ran Penn's teams; because these alumni no longer had a formal relationship to the school, sports became a way to maintain loyalty. They recruited players from local athletic clubs and other colleges and then enrolled the athletes in a Penn course in order to make them eligible to play football, for example.[67] In 1884, this long-standing practice was curtailed by the passage of new regulations from the Intercollegiate Athletic Sports association, to which Penn belonged. In the 1880s, the university, led by Provost Pepper, modernised its athletic facilities, which were seriously underdeveloped in comparison to those of Penn's athletic rivals, especially Harvard, and established a new department of physical education.[68]

In December of 1885, just after Muybridge had completed the bulk of his photos, the new gymnasium was formally opened.[69] The facilities and programmes were directed by White, with Robert Pennell, a well-known trainer from the New York Athletic Club, in charge of the gymnasium. Founded in 1866, the New York Athletic Club established the standard rules for amateur athletics, including the American innovation of barring paid athletes from membership, thereby preventing competition from working-class athletes, who might pursue athletics as a form of paid labour.[70] The goal of the new University of Pennsylvania gymnasium was not principally to build strength, a concern of later athletic programmes, but to build physical health and vigour. As the *Regulations for Intercollegiate Athletic Sports* argued in 1884, 'the object of physical training is to confirm health, correct morbid tendencies, strengthen weak parts, give a symmetrical physical development and secure as far as possible a condition of perfect physical vigor'.[71] D. Hayes Agnew, a professor at the university and the subject of Thomas Eakins's well-known painting of his surgical theatre, argued before a university meeting that the intellectual capacities of many students were limited by their feeble bodies, a problem that the proposed Department of Physical Culture would address.[72]

The university's new department was inspired by the developments at Harvard, where Dudley Allen Sargent had been hired in 1879. Sargent designed and built, with Harvard's support, advanced versions of the mechanical fitness machines he had pioneered in his previous position at Bowdoin College. Sargent designed his fifty-six exercise machines to mimic movements from everyday life, especially those concerning manual labour. Thus, a student could 'chop wood' with a pulley exercise, or saw wood by moving the weights from front to back.[73] These exercises were designed to give an even overall muscular development, rather than the overdeveloped muscles of a worker engaged in regular manual labour, such as a blacksmith or lumberjack. Although motions of these workers could provide useful models for exercise form, their muscular development was not to be emulated. The advent of exercise machines in college athletics introduced a new trained body, a body whose *even* development signalled the class status of someone with the time to devote to building muscles effectively removed from productive labour.

This evenly developed, trained white male body emerged as an ideal type for enervated middle-class professional men during the 1880s. As the Committee formed to raise the funds to create Penn's athletic programme in 1883 argued concerning the merits of the Harvard approach, through Dudley's system 'the ideal student has been transformed from a stooping, weak and sickly youth into one well-formed, robust and healthy'.[74] The medical professors who were behind the move to physical culture in the Ivy League schools had long noticed that the most accomplished academic students were often the most physically underdeveloped. At Yale, for example, anthropometric measurements had revealed that the highest-ranking students had more than their fair share of spinal curvature. The medical directors of the athletic facility there responded by requiring that all scholarship students submit to physical examinations and they acquired a set of Muybridge photographs of University of Pennsylvania athletes for comparison study. Eventually, the directors began making their own photographs of physical deformities, which they exhibited at the International Hygiene Exhibition at Dresden in 1911.[75] Using the Muybridge photographs as guides, Yale advocates of physical culture sought to blend the over-developed musculature of the manual labourer with the mental acuity of the sunken-chested scholar to create a new, vigorous upper-class body, immune from neurasthenia and over-civilisation.

At the University of Pennsylvania, the new department and facilities were directly modelled on the anthropometric systems in place at Harvard, Amherst and other elite colleges. As at Penn, these modern athletic departments were directed by medical doctors, who sought to introduce new scholarship in physiology and the physical sciences into college athletics. Edward Hitchcock of Amherst College, the founder of the first college department of physical education, advocated new corporeal standards; he researched Francis Galton's anthropometric work in England and published in 1888 the widely used *Anthropometric Manual*.[76] As the first president of the Association for the Advancement of Physical Education in 1885, Hitchcock helped to make anthropometric measurement a major methodology of the new profession.

At Penn, White introduced required anthropometrical measurements as a key element of his athletic system. As he described in his remarks at the opening of the gymnasium in 1885, 'each student is stripped and carefully examined as to his weight, height, the circumference of his chest, the size and condition of his legs, thighs, arms and forearms'.[77] The student engaged in a series of tests: a dynometer, for example, measured back and loin strength, while a spirometer tested lung capacity. While the doctor was making the measurements, 'the physical peculiarities are observed and the special weaknesses, if any exist, are noted'.[78] The sum of these measurements was the quantified index of a student's 'development', which White used, along with the student's detailed personal and family medical history, to diagnose weaknesses that an athletic programme could address. Students were then directed to the 'chest weights, chest expanders, high and low pulleys' and other exercise machines that Harvard's Dr Sargent had personally arranged for the new facilities.[79]

The athletic models' participation in the University of Pennsylvania Muybridge project was part of a larger nineteenth-century endeavour to engender manliness in upper-class white men. Social commentators as well as young men themselves felt that their generation had become excessively refined; they longed for the manly challenges that their fathers had faced during the Civil War. Indeed, as sport historian Steven A. Reiss has observed, 'upper-class young men looked to sport as a means to prove their manliness'.[80] The 1880s interest in athletics and the training of the upper-class male body also stemmed from the American adaptation of British ideals of 'muscular Christianity', elaborated in 1850s Britain as part of the rise of empire and popularised in the United States by Protestant ministers such as Thomas Wentworth Higginson and Henry Ward Beecher.[81] In the United States, the 'strenuous life' advocated by Teddy Roosevelt became part of prep school and college athletics as a prophylactic against the gender and sexual degeneracy of an excessive intellectualism, a decline that within the period's discourse of civilisation and progress meant a racial regression as well.[82]

American advocates for physical education in American colleges and universities drew on European biometrics, including Galton's anthropometric work, to argue for the importance of sport in battling male neurasthenia, the 'American nervousness' that Charles Beard, S. Weir Mitchell and other prominent physicians argued was threatening to overwhelm America's 'brain workers' – the college educated, professional managerial class.[83] Although hysteria is often associated with women, as the Greek etymology of the word would suggest, in the last quarter of the nineteenth-century American nervous disease doctors diagnosed neurasthenia as being on the increase among 'the business and professional men who were most committed to the competitive ethic'.[84] The illness was a difficult one to diagnose, because it lacked a definitive pathology in an era when doctors required predictable, physical aetiologies in order to prescribe treatment. But most specialists, including the well-known Philadelphia physician S. Weir Mitchell, followed George Beard's analysis that the disease was caused by the shock of modernity: the advent of new technologies, such as steampower and electricity; the frenzied increase in the pace of life; and the overwork of an accelerating market economy. Neurasthenia, in this analysis, was a badge of civilisation, a sign of racial progress. According to Beard, the prevalence of neurasthenia among America's brainworkers was an indication that American civilisation was the most advanced in the world.[85]

Neurasthenia was also a difficult malady to cure and many doctors, including Francis Dercum, followed the Weir Mitchell rest cure, developed during the Civil War for soldiers suffering from battle fatigue. The rest cure consisted of complete, isolated bed rest for six to eight weeks, passive exercise in the form of massage or electrotherapy and a strict diet that emphasised protein and dairy.[86] Male neurasthenics were rarely prescribed the full rest cure; the doctors' assumptions about class and gender privilege prevented them from prescribing treatment that would fully cut off their male patients from their work. Instead, male neurasthenics were often prescribed healthful forms of exercise, along with a reduced work schedule. Mitchell, whose 'rest cure' prompted Charlotte Perkins Gilman to write the short story 'The Yellow Wallpaper', was sufficiently involved in the Muybridge project at the University of Pennsylvania to be thanked by Muybridge in the preface to his 1899 book on animal locomotion.[87] As Rachelle A. Dermer has shown, Plates 556 and 557 document the case of Robert Connelly, a male patient of Dr Mitchell's who suffered from the 'functional spasms' that Mitchell understood to be a 'typical example of hysteria in the male'.[88]

Anthropometry, like photography itself, was an instrumental technology marshalled to legitimise a variety of truth claims over the course of the late nineteenth century. Its appearance in three sites central to the Muybridge work at the University of Pennsylvania suggests its centrality in efforts to enact and stabilise late nineteenth-century racial and gender hierarchies in the age of colonial expansion, Jim Crow segregation and white middle-class women's increasing engagement with the public sphere. The Muybridge project's complexity, with its 100,000 images, ninety-five models and numerous personnel, eludes – once again – any one scholar's claim to a definitive reading. The period's racialised discourse of anthropometry, joined with Gilded Age redefinitions of white, middle-class masculinity, overdetermines the Muybridge University of Pennsylvania work, yielding a new reading of the research as an imperfect racial project in which human bodies are represented and organised in order to consolidate historically situated racial formations specific to the late nineteenth-century discourses of manliness and civilisation.

Notes

I would like to express my thanks for the important contributions of Marta Braun to my thinking in this work; we have engaged in countless discussions as this project takes shape as part of each of our research. I owe an enormous debt to her fine scholarship, visual acuity and intellectual companionship. Many thanks to Michelle Delaney of the National Museum of Photographic History; the American Philosophical Society, which funded my stay in Philadelphia as a Fellow at APS; and audiences at the Muybridge symposium at Stanford University in May 2003, the Institute for Historical Studies at the University of Maryland (College Park), as well as the University of Manitoba conference on 'The Photograph' in March 2004, for their comments. Lastly, I would like to express my appreciation for the anonymous readers for *Gender & History*, who have helped to make this a stronger article.

1. In 1887 Muybridge offered Eadweard Muybridge, *Animal Locomotion: an Electrographic Investigation of Consecutive Phases of Animal Movements, 1872–1885* (Philadelphia:

University of Pennsylvania, 1887) as a selection of 100 plates, held in a leather portfolio, or as individual prints. The full series of images is reprinted in Eadweard Muybridge, *Muybridge's Complete Human and Animal Locomotion* (New York: Dover, 1979). The collotype was a preferred method for high-quality mechanical printing of photographic images in the 1880s. The resulting commercially printed images were lush, with great tonal gradations. Collotypes were expensive and were associated with luxury publications such as *Animal Locomotion*. Visually, the published collotype plate was difficult to distinguish (for most observers) from the original photograph.

2. Eadweard Muybridge, 'Original Prospectus and Catalogue of Plates' (1887), reprinted in Muybridge, *Muybridge's Complete Human and Animal Locomotion*, vol. 3 (New York: Dover, 1979), pp. 1585–97, here p. 1585. Muybridge's assistants, paid by the university, were students, all but one of whom were also models for the project. For further details on the assistants and their work, see Thomas G. Grier to G. E. Nitzsche, 4 March 1929 and H. L. Bell to G. E. Nitzsche, 7 December 1923, UPA 9 Box 2, FF26, University of Pennsylvania Archives, (UPA).

3. Tom Gunning, 'Never Seen this Picture Before: Muybridge in Multiplicity', manuscript in author's possession, p. 3. Muybridge's zeal in documenting motion has led another researcher, a psychologist by training, to suggest that the project provides evidence for an obsessive-compulsive disorder. See Arthur P. Shimamura, 'Muybridge in Motion: Travels in Art, Psychology and Neurology', *History of Photography* 26 (2002), pp. 341–50, here p. 349.

4. Michelle Delaney, with Marta Braun and myself as guest co-curators, also curated an exhibition focused on this collection: 'Freeze Frame: Eadweard Muybridge's Photography of Motion', Smithsonian's National Museum of American History (NMAH), 7 October 2000 – 15 March 2001: <http://www.americanhistory.si.edu/muybridge/index.htm>.

5. Thus, the cyanotypes at NMAH represent the closest thing we have to the original negatives for the project. Muybridge's correspondence with Erwin F. Faber, the Philadelphia artist who drew the elongated animals for Muybridge's zoopraxiscope plates, describes the shipment of the negatives to Glasgow for the purpose of making lantern slides. This late correspondence (March 1901) suggests that further detective work might be in order. See Eadweard Muybridge to Erwin L. Faber, 16 June 1899 and 11 March 1901, Eadweard Muybridge Papers, UPT 50, M993, Box 1 Folder 37, UPA.

6. Muybridge Notebooks, Notebook 3, negs. 1322–1540, 15 September–28 October 1885, International Museum of Photography, George Eastman House, Rochester, New York (IMP).

7. Marta Braun's 1984 article on the Pennsylvania work redefined Muybridge scholarship. Working with the published plates alone, she convincingly argued that despite 100 years of arguments to the contrary, Muybridge's Pennsylvania work, as compared to that of Marey, was more concerned with narrative than it was with scientific accuracy. See Marta Braun, 'Muybridge's Scientific Fictions', *Studies in Visual Communication* 10 (1984), pp. 2–21; Marta Braun, *Picturing Time: The Work of Etienne-Jules Marey (1830–1904)* (Chicago: University of Chicago Press, 1992).

8. The newly discovered archive is especially important to historians. In 1896, Muybridge made an agreement with William Pepper of the University of Pennsylvania to transfer the remaining 33,000 collotype plates and negatives to the University. For discussion of the transfer of material concerning the project from New York to the University of Pennsylvania in 1896, see H. G. Ward to William Pepper, 25 June 1896 and Eadweard Muybridge to William Pepper, 24 June 1896, in William Pepper Papers, Annenberg Rare Book and Manuscript Library, University of Pennsylvania, (Annenberg). For a description of the NMAH collection (Acc. No. 98743), see Marta Braun, 'Muybridge's Animal Locomotion: The Director's Cut', *History of Photography* 24 (2000), pp. 52–4; as well as an undated, untitled document in the Muybridge 'Outline of Collection' vertical files, Division of Photographic History, National Museum of American History, Smithsonian Institution, Washington, DC.

9. L. F. Rondinella, 'More About Muybridge's Work' (July 1929), quoting Muybridge's 'Descriptive Zoopraxography' (1893), in Eadweard Muybridge Papers, UPT 50 M993, Box 2 Folder 6, UPA. Muybridge scrapbook, p. 139/157, Kingston Museum, Kingston-upon-Thames, Britain (KM).

10. For the arguments concerning Muybridge and the origins of cinema, see Kevin MacDonnell, *Eadweard Muybridge: The Man Who Invented the Moving Picture* (Boston: Little Brown, 1972); Gordon Hendricks, *Eadweard Muybridge: The Father of the Motion Picture* (New York: Grossman Publishers, 1975); Anita Ventura Mozley, 'Introduction to the Dover Edition', *Muybridge's Complete Human and Animal Locomotion*, pp. vii–xxxviii; for the competing discourses of science, narrative and academic art, see Braun, 'Muybridge's Scientific Fictions'; Braun, *Picturing Time*; and Janine A. Mileaf, 'Poses for the Camera: Eadweard Muybridge's Studies of the Human Figure', *American Art* 16 (2002), pp. 30–53; for the relationship between Thomas Eakins, Muybridge and nineteenth-century realism, see Elizabeth Johns, *Thomas Eakins, The Heroism of Modern Life* (Princeton: Princeton University Press, 1983); Susan Danly and Cheryl Leibold (eds), *Eakins and the Photograph: Works by Thomas Eakins and his Circle in the Collection of the Pennsylvania Academy of the Fine Arts*, (Washington, DC: Academy by the Smithsonian Institution Press, 1994); for a reading of the female nude as pornographic visuality, see Linda Williams, *Hard Core: Power, Pleasure and the 'Frenzy of the Visible'* (Berkeley: University of California Press, 1999); for pathological locomotion, see H. L. Gibson, 'The Muybridge Pictures of Motion', *Medical Radiography and Photography* 26 (1950), pp. 18–24; Michael Rogers McVaugh, 'Francis X. Dercum and Animal Locomotion', *Caduceus: A Museum Quarterly* 3 (1987), pp. 1–35; Marta Braun and Elizabeth Whitcombe, 'Marey, Muybridge and Londe: The Photography of Pathological Locomotion', *History of Photography* 23 (1999), pp. 218–24; Rachelle A. Dermer, 'Photographic Objectivity and the Construction of the Medical Subject in the United States', PhD dissertation (Boston University, 2002).

11. For more on the others involved in the project, see Rondinella, 'More About Muybridge's Work'.

12. John Tagg, *The Burden of Representation: Essays on Photographies and Histories* (Amherst: University of Massachusetts Press, 1988), p. 4; John Tagg, 'Power and Photography: Part One, A Means of Surveillance: The Photograph as Evidence in Law', *Screen Education* 36 (1980), pp. 17–27. See also Elspeth H. Brown, *The Corporate Eye: Photography and the Rationalization of American Commercial Culture, 1874–1929* (Baltimore: Johns Hopkins University Press, 2005), p. 15.

13. Allan Sekula, 'Photography between Labour and Capital', in Leslie Shedden, *Mining Photographs and Other Pictures, 1948–1968: A Selection from the Negative Archives of Shedden Studio, Glace Bay, Cape Breton*, ed. Benjamin H. D. Buchloch and Robert Wilkie (Halifax: Press of the Nova Scotia College of Art and Design, 1983), pp. 193–268, here pp. 193–4; Allan Sekula, 'The Body and the Archive', *October* 39 (1986), pp. 3–65; Allan Sekula, *Photography against the Grain: Essays and Photo Works, 1973–1983* (Halifax: Press of the Nova Scotia College of Art and Design, 1984).

14. This work has sparked a number of compelling projects including Sandra S. Phillips, Mark Haworth-Booth and Carol Squiers, *Police Pictures: The Photograph as Evidence* (San Francisco: Chronicle Books, 1997); Shawn Michelle Smith, *American Archives: Gender, Race and Class in Visual Culture* (Princeton: Princeton University Press, 1999); Laura Wexler, *Tender Violence: Domestic Visions in an Age of U.S. Imperialism* (Chapel Hill: University of North Carolina Press, 2000).

15. Abigail Solomon-Godeau, *Photography at the Dock: Essays on Photographic History, Institutions and Practices* (Minneapolis: University of Minnesota Press, 1991), p. xxviii. Solomon-Godeau, in the same passage, is also the source for the attribution of the phrase to Szarkowski. For a classic collection of essays in postmodern photographic criticism, see Victor Burgin, *Thinking Photography* (London: Macmillan, 1982). For a recent

rapprochement between postmodern photographic criticism and modernism's allegiance to the object, see Geoffrey Batchen, *Burning with Desire: The Conception of Photography* (Cambridge: MIT Press, 1997), pp. 4–21. See also Sarah Bassnett, 'Photography, Instrumental Discourse and City Planning in Early Twentieth Century Toronto and Montreal', PhD dissertation (Binghamton University, 2003).

16. Michael Omi and Howard Winant, *Racial Formation in the United States: From the 1960s to the 1990s* (London: Routledge, 1994), pp. 55–6.
17. Charles Davenport, *A Guide to Physical Anthropometry and Androscopy* (New York: Cold Spring Harbor, 1927), p. 7. Anthropological measurement practices began their route to international standards in 1874 with the publication of *Notes and Queries on Anthropology*, a traveller's guide designed to promote standardised measurements of the human form. British Association for the Advancement of Science, *Notes and Queries on Anthropology, for the Use of Travellers and Residents in Uncivilized Lands* (London: E. Stanford, 1874). The more generalised study of body proportions, especially for the purposes of art, has a much older history; see, for example, Albrecht Dürer's works on human proportion in Albrecht Dürer, *Von menschlicher Proportion* (1528; repr. Nördlingen: A. Uhl, 1980).
18. John S. Haller, Jr, *Outcasts from Evolution: Scientific Attitudes of Racial Inferiority, 1859–1900* (Urbana: University of Illinois Press, 1971), especially pp. 3–40.
19. C. Loring Brace, 'The Roots of the Race Concept in American Physical Anthropology', in Frank Spencer (ed.), *A History of American Physical Anthropology* (New York: Academic Press, 1962), pp. 11–30, here p. 19.
20. This (partial) list of measurements is drawn from Louis Sullivan, 'Anthropometry of the Siouan Tribes', *Anthropological Papers of the American Museum of Natural History*, 23 (New York: American Museum of Natural History, 1920), p. 89. Sullivan conducted measurements of 1,431 individuals from various Sioux tribes at the World's Columbian Exposition in Chicago, 1893. See Louis Sullivan, *Essentials of Anthropology: A Handbook for Explorers and Museum Collectors* (New York: American Museum of Natural History, 1923).
21. G. H. Estabrooks, 'The Relation between Cranial Capacity, Relative Cranial Capacity and Intelligence in School Children', *Journal of Applied Psychology* 12 (1928), pp. 524–9, here p. 529. For the relationship between eugenics, racism and the 1924 Immigration Act, see Daniel Kevles, *In the Name of Eugenics: Genetics and the Uses of Human Heredity* (New York: Knopf, 1985), pp. 96–112.
22. Sekula, 'The Body and the Archive'; Smith, *American Archives*.
23. On the 'Zealy daguerreotypes', see Elinor Reichlin, 'Faces of Slavery', *American Heritage* 28 (June 1977), pp. 4–12; Melissa Banta and Curtis M. Hinsley, *From Site to Sight: Anthropology, Photography and the Power of Imagery* (Cambridge, MA: Peabody Museum Press, 1986), pp. 57–8; Alan Trachtenberg, *Reading American Photographs: Images as History, Mathew Brady to Walker Evans* (New York: Hill and Wang, 1989), pp. 54–6; Brian Wallis, 'Black Bodies, White Science: Louis Agassiz's Slave Daguerreotypes', *American Art* 9 (1995), pp. 39–62.
24. Carl Dammann and F. W. Dammann, *An Ethnological Photographic Gallery of the Various Races of Men* (London: Trübner, n.d.); William E. Marshall and George U. Pope, *A Phrenologist among the Todas or, The Study of a Primitive Tribe in South India: History, Character, Customs, Religion, Infanticide, Polyandry, Language* (London: Longmans Green, 1873) Martin Kemp, '"A Perfect and Faithful Record": Mind and Body in Medical Photography before 1900', in Ann Thomas (ed.), *Beauty of Another Order: Photography and Science* (New Haven: Yale University Press, 1997), pp. 120–49, here p. 129. See Paul S. Landau, 'Empires of the Visual: Photography and Colonial Administration in Africa', in Paul S. Landau and Deborah D. Kaspin (eds), *Images and Empires: Visuality in Colonial and Postcolonial Africa* (Berkeley: University of California Press, 2002), pp. 141–71.
25. J. Lamprey, 'On a Method of Measuring Human Form for Students of Ethnology', *Journal of the Ethnological Society* new series 1 (1869), pp. 84–5.

26. See Frank Spencer, 'Some Notes on the Attempt to Apply Photography to Anthropometry during the Second Half of the Nineteenth Century', in Elizabeth Edwards (ed.), *Anthropology and Photography, 1860–1920* (New Haven: Yale University Press, 1992), pp. 99–107; David Green, 'Classified Subjects', *Ten/8 Photographic Journal* 14 (1984), pp. 30–37; Elizabeth Edwards, 'Photographic Types: The Pursuit of Visual Method', *Visual Anthropology* 3 (1990), pp. 235–58; Russell Roberts, 'Taxonomy: Some Notes Towards the Histories of Photography and Classification', in Chrissie Iles and Russell Roberts (eds), *Invisible Light: Photography and Classification in Art, Science and the Everyday* (Oxford: Museum of Modern Art, 1998), pp. 9–52; Elizabeth Edwards, *Raw Histories: Photographs, Anthropology and Museums* (London: Berg, 2001); Shawn Michelle Smith, *Photography on the Color Line: W. E. B. Du Bois, Race, and Visual Culture* (Durham: Duke University Press, 2004), pp. 49–50.
27. Josiah C. Nott and George R. Gliddon, *Indigenous Races of the Earth* (Philadelphia: J. B. Lippincott, 1857), p. 612; M. V. Portman, 'Photography for Anthropologists', *Journal of the Anthropological Institute of Great Britain and Ireland* 25 (1896), pp. 75–87, quote on p. 76.
28. For a discussion of the politics of 'looking back' at the camera, see bell hooks, 'The Oppositional Gaze: Black Female Spectators', in *Black Looks: Race and Representation*, pp. 115–31 (Boston: South End Press, 1992); Coco Fusco and Brian Wallis (eds), *Only Skin Deep: Changing Visions of the American Self* (New York: International Center of Photography Harry N. Abrams, 2003); see also Alan Trachtenberg's reading of the Zealy daguerreotypes in Trachtenberg, *Reading American Photographs*, pp. 52–6.
29. J. Lamprey, 'On a Method of Measuring Human Form for Students of Ethnology', pp. 84–5; see also Elizabeth Edwards, 'Ordering Others: Photography, Anthropologies and Taxonomies', in Iles and Roberts (eds), *Invisible Light*, pp. 54–68, here p. 56.
30. See for example, Tagg, *The Burden of Representation*; David Green, 'Veins of Resemblance: Photography and Eugenics', *Oxford Art Journal* 7 (1985), pp. 3–16; Sekula, 'The Body and the Archive'.
31. Edwards, 'Ordering Others', p. 55; Robert Taft, 'An Introduction to Eadweard Muybridge and his Work', in Muybridge, *The Human Figure in Motion*, pp. vii–xiv, here p. x.
32. The original arrangements stipulated that the work would take place in the enclosure of the Veterinary Department of the University of Pennsylvania during the spring and summer of 1884. Eadweard Muybridge to William Pepper, 3 September 1883. William Pepper Papers, Annenberg; Marta Braun, 'Leaving Traces', in Nancy Mowll Mathews (ed.), *Moving Pictures: The Un-Easy Relationship between American Art and Early Film* (New York: Hudson Hills Press, 2005).
33. Although there are some inaccuracies in Gordon Hendrick's chronology (for example, he incorrectly argues that the published plates contained up to twenty-four, rather than thirty-six photographs), his discussion remains an important grounding for a close analysis of the period when Muybridge was working at the University of Pennsylvania. He reconstructs in detail the technical changes made during the summer of 1884 and the university's frustration with the resulting slow progress. Muybridge finished most of the photography by 15 December 1885, though he did continue to re-shoot motion studies until May 1886. Gordon Hendricks, *Eadweard Muybridge*, pp. 167–72.
34. Muybridge Notebooks, Notebook 2 Negs. 524–1084, 2 May–4 August 1885, IMP. The notebook covering the negative series 1–523 is missing, but Marta Braun 'Leaving Traces', has shown that as late as series negative number 520, which was of pathological locomotion, there was no grid. We have not been able to match/find nos. 521–3, which are detailed in the missing notebook.
35. The category of 'mulatto' was dropped from the census in 1920 as the 'one drop' rule of the Jim Crow era eradicated mixed-race legal identities. On mulattoes during this period, see Joel Williamson, *New People: Miscegenation and Mulattoes in the United States* (New York: Free Press, 1984); for the antebellum era see Howard Bodenhorn, 'The Mulatto Advantage: The

Biological Consequences of Complexion in Rural Antebellum Virginia', *Journal of Interdisciplinary History* 33 (2002), pp. 21–46. For a listing of Bailey's activities, see 2 June 1885 entries for negative series numbers 524–31 in Eadweard Muybridge, Lab Notebook Number 2, 2 May–4 August 1885, IMP. It does not appear that Bailey was photographed after this date. Muybridge referred to Bailey (model 22) as 'a mulatto and professional pugilist'; he does not note the racial status of any other model. See Eadweard Muybridge, *Animal Locomotion Prospectus and Catalogue of Plates* (Philadelphia: J. B. Lippincott, 1887), p. 12.

36. For black boxing in late nineteenth-century Philadelphia, see Roger Lane, *The Roots of Violence in Black Philadelphia, 1860–1900* (Cambridge: Harvard University Press, 1986), pp. 118–19. Philadelphia city directories and census for 1880–5 reveal a large number of men named Ben Bailey, some listed as mulatto, in occupations such as waiter, plasterer, brick-maker; it is impossible to tell which might have been the Muybridge model. Bailey was apparently not a particularly well-known boxer, historically; he is not mentioned in Nat Fleischer, *Black Dynamite: The Story of the Negro in the Prize Ring from 1782 to 1938* (New York: C. J. O'Brien, 1938).

37. The question of racial 'hybridity' was central to the formation of physical anthropology as a discipline in both the United States and Europe, as scientists debated the relative fecundity of mixed-race offspring as a measure of civilisation or degeneration. For example, Nott and Gliddon credited Philadelphia's Samuel Morton for showing that 'the mulatto would seem to fall into that condition of hybrids, where they continue to be more or less prolific for a few generations, but with a constant tendency to run out … mulattos are less prolific than either pure race; suffer much from tubercular affections; their children die young; and … their average duration of life is very low'. Nott and Gliddon, *Indigenous Races of the Earth*, p. 367; see also Brace, 'The Roots of the Race Concept in American Physical Anthropology'.

38. Gail Bederman, *Manliness and Civilization: A Cultural History of Gender and Race in the United States, 1880–1917* (Chicago: University of Chicago Press, 1995); Martin A. Berger, *Man Made: Thomas Eakins and the Construction of Gilded Age Manhood* (Berkeley: University of California Press, 2000).

39. Eric Lott, *Love and Theft: Blackface Minstrelsy and the American Working Class* (New York: Oxford University Press, 1993).

40. Matthew Frye Jacobson, *Whiteness of a Different Color: European Immigrants and the Alchemy of Race* (Cambridge: Harvard University Press, 1998); Grace Elizabeth Hale, *Making Whiteness: The Culture of Segregation in the South, 1890–1940* (New York: Pantheon Books, 1998).

41. It is worth stressing that there can be more than one reason for the introduction of the grid in the summer of 1885. While this essay stresses its racial meanings, the grid may have other instrumental purposes. For further discussion of Eakins, Muybridge, Marey and the development of photographic apparatuses at the University of Pennsylvania, see William Dennis Marks, 'The Mechanism of Instantaneous Photography', in University of Pennsylvania, *Animal Locomotion: The Muybridge Work at the University of Pennsylvania* (Philadelphia, J. B. Lippincott company, 1888), pp. 9–33; William I. Homer, 'Eakins, Muybridge and the Motion Picture Process', *Art Quarterly* 26 (1963), pp. 194–216. Dercum helped Muybridge in two successive summers, probably 1885 and 1886. The Dercum letter is cited in Hendricks, *Eadweard Muybridge*, pp. 162–3.

42. Edward Anthony Spitzka, 'A Study of the Brains of Six Eminent Scientists and Scholars Belonging to the American Anthropometric Society …', *Transactions of the American Philosophical Society* new series 21 (1908), pp. 175–308, here, p. 176.

43. Mozley, 'Introduction to the Dover Edition', p. xxvi, see also Rogers McVaugh, 'Francis X. Dercum and Animal Locomotion'; Braun and Whitcombe, 'Marey, Muybridge and Londe'.

44. Haller reports that the American Anthropometry Society was organised for the preservation of the brains of its members. Haller, *Outcasts from Evolution*, p. 37.

45. William Pepper to H. Galbraith Ward, 15 June 1896, William Pepper Papers, Annenberg.
46. Joshua Lawrence Chamberlain, William Torrey Harris, Edward Potts Cheyney and Ellis Paxson Oberholtzer, *Universities and their Sons: University of Pennsylvania, its History, Influence and Characteristics* (Boston: R. Herndon Company, 1901), pp. 135–72.
47. Newspaper clipping of remarks that Pepper made on the occasion of student Page setting the world record for the high jump (dated 17 October 1887), vol. 3, p. 466. William Pepper, MD Collection, Van Pelt Library Special Collections, University of Pennsylvania.
48. As quoted in Aleš Hrdlička, 'Physical Anthropology in America, an Historical Sketch', *American Anthropologist* 16 (1914), pp. 508–54, here p. 516.
49. Leonard Warren, *Joseph Leidy, The Man who Knew Everything* (New Haven: Yale University Press, 1998); Martin Meyerson and Dilys Pegler Winegrad, *Gladly Learn and Gladly Teach: Franklin and his Heirs at the University of Pennsylvania, 1740–1976* (Philadelphia: University of Pennsylvania Press, 1978), pp. 89–97.
50. Harrison Allen, 'Materials for a Memoir on Animal Locomotion', in University of Pennsylvania, *Animal Locomotion*, pp. 35–102.
51. 'Harrison Allen', in American Association of Anatomists, *Proceedings of the Tenth Annual Session, Ithaca, N.Y., December 28–30, 1897* (Washington, DC: Beresford, 1898) pp. 12–26. See also Harrison Allen, 'Crania from the Mounds of the St. John's River, Fla. A Study Made in Connection with Crania from Other Parts of North America', read 12 June 1894, *Journal of the Academy of Natural Sciences of Philadelphia* new series 10 (1896), pp. 367–448; Harrison Allen, 'A Study in Hawaiian Skulls', *Proceedings of the Wagner Free Press Institute of Science* (1898), p. 55.
52. Daniel G. Brinton, 'Dr. Allen's Contributions to Anthropology', American Association for the Advancement of Science, Springfield meeting, August 1895, *Proceedings of the American Association for the Advancement of Science* 44 (1897), pp. 522–9, quote from pp. 523–4. For further information about Daniel G. Brinton, a key figure in the history of American anthropology, see Lee D. Baker, 'Daniel G. Brinton's Success on the Road to Obscurity, 1890–99', *Cultural Anthropology* 15 (2000), pp. 394–423. Baker argues that Brinton's work provided a modern foundation for the reciprocal relationship between race and anthropology in the period after the flourishing of the 'American School' of anthropology, whose central figure was Samuel Morton, in the mid-nineteenth century.
53. Aleš Hrdlička, *A History of American Physical Anthropology* (Philadelphia: Wistar Institute, 1919), pp. 59–60; see also Aleš Hrdlička, 'Physical Anthropology in America, an Historical Sketch'. J. Aitken Meigs, also associated with Philadelphia-area scientific establishments, wrote a number of works in early American physical anthropology, including an essay in a racist anthology by Nott and Gliddon. J. Aitken Meigs, 'The Cranial Characteristics of the Races of Men', in Josiah C. Nott and George F. Gliddon (eds), *Types of Mankind: or, Ethnological Researches, Based upon the Ancient Monuments, Paintings, Sculptures and Crania of Races and upon their Natural Geographical, Philological and Biblical History* (Philadelphia: Lippincott, 1854). Meigs took over Morton's skull collection when Joseph Leidy demurred.
54. Lee D. Baker, 'Daniel G. Brinton's Success on the Road to Obscurity', pp. 395, 399. Pepper succeeded in establishing the Department of Archaeology and Palaeontology and its museum in 1891; the museum is now the University of Pennsylvania Museum of Archaeology and Anthropology. Edward P. Cheyney, *History of the University of Pennsylvania* (Philadelphia: University of Pennsylvania Press, 1940), p. 351; Steven Conn, *Museums and American Intellectual Life, 1876–1926* (Chicago: University of Chicago Press, 1998), pp. 75–114.
55. Daniel G. Brinton, *Races and Peoples: Lectures on the Science of Ethnography* (New York: N. D. C. Hodges, 1890); Daniel G. Brinton, *The American Race: A Linguistic Classification and Ethnographic Description of the Native Tribes of North and South America* (New York: N. D. C. Hodges, 1891).
56. Hrdlička, 'Physical Anthropology in America', p. 539.

57. My discussion of Brinton is indebted to Lee D. Baker, 'Daniel G. Brinton's Success on the Road to Obscurity'. For the Boas review, see [Franz Boas], 'Review of *Races and Peoples*', *Science* 16 (1890), pp. 276–7.
58. Fatimah Tobing Rony, 'Those Who Squat and Those Who Sit: The Iconography of Race in the 1895 Films of Felix-Louis Regnault', *Camera Obscura* 28 (1992), pp. 262–89, here p. 267.
59. Muybridge, *Animal Locomotion Prospectus*, p. 12.
60. Muybridge, *Animal Locomotion Prospectus*, p. 13.
61. Williams, *Hard Core*.
62. See the 18 July 1885 entries for negative series numbers 937–42, as Muybridge described them in his workbooks. Eadweard Muybridge, Lab Notebook Number 2, 2 May–4 August 1885, IMP. For a further reconstruction of what the models were doing when, see Marta Braun, 'Muybridge le Magnifique', *Études Photographiques* 10 (November 2002), pp. 34–50.
63. 'Animal Motion', *The Times*, Philadelphia, 2 August 1885.
64. See vertical file on Randolph Faries at the UPA, including clippings from *Philadelphia Inquirer, Philadelphia Evening Bulletin* and other sources.
65. Percy C. Madeira, 'Not So Fast', *Saturday Evening Post*, 11 July 1936, pp. 16–17, 77–78, 80. Madeira seems not to have been a Penn student.
66. George W. Orton, *A History of Athletics at Pennsylvania, 1873–1886* (Athletic Association of the University of Pennsylvania, n.d.), pp. 25–7. For the list of models, see Eadweard Muybridge, Lab Notebooks, IMP; for information about the students, see the UPenn Master Alumni List and vertical files, UPA.
67. Dan Rottenberg, *Fight on Pennsylvania: A Century of Red and Blue Football* (Philadelphia: University of Pennsylvania, 1985), p. 27; Athletic Association of the University of Pennsylvania, *Fortieth Anniversary, 1873–1913 (Franklin Field May 17, 1913); An Illustrated Account of what the University of Pennsylvania Achieved in all Branches of Sport* (Athletic Association of the University of Pennsylvania, 1913).
68. For Pepper's key role in Penn's athletics, see note from Pepper, 4 April 1882, seeking to help organise University athletics; letter from Pepper to John C. Sims, 12 April 1882; letter from Pepper to John C. Sims, 25 April 1882; John C. Sims clippings books, vol. 1 (1 January 1883–31 December 1886); General Administration Records, 1749–1930, Box 19, 1883 'Physical Culture', UPA. 'Physical Education: The New Department at the University of Pennsylvania', 1885 clipping, in John C. Sims Clipping Books, vol. 1; William M. Stewart to Samuel Dickson, Esq., 1 December 1884, General Administration Records, 1749–1930, Box 19, 1884 'Athletic Department', UPA. 'A University Gymnasium', *Inquirer*, 23 November 1883; *Telegraph*, 23 November 1883. According to Mr Pennell, the person in charge of the athletic grounds, Harvard's Dr Sargent oversaw the arrangements concerning the gymnasium's equipment. 'Athletics at the University', 27 August 1885 clipping, John C. Sims clipping books, vol. 1, UPA; see also 'Athletic Development', *Evening Telegraph*, 23 April 1885.
69. 'A University Gymnasium', *Inquirer*, 23 November 1883; *Telegraph*, 23 November 1883.
70. Steven A. Reiss, *Sport in Industrial America, 1850–1920* (Wheeling, IL: Harlan Davidson, 1995), p. 51; see also Benjamin Rader, *American Sports: From the Age of Folk Games to the Age of Televised Sports* (Upper Saddle River NJ. Prentice Hall, 2004).
71. 'Regulations for Intercollegiate Athletic Sports', 7 February 1884; see also printed circular beginning 'Dear Sir', dated March 1884, John C. Sims clipping books, vol. 1, UPA.
72. 'Important Project', newspaper clipping, 22 March 1884 and 'Local Affairs', newspaper clipping, 22 March 1884, John C. Sims clipping books, vol. 1, UPA.
73. Carolyn Thomas de la Peña, *The Body Electric: How Strange Machines Built the Modern American* (New York: New York University Press, 2003), p. 57; see also Donald J. Mrozek, *Sport and American Mentality, 1890–1910* (Knoxville: University of Tennessee Press, 1983), pp. 36–7, 69–71.

74. Circular of the building committee of the Athletic Association of the University of Pennsylvania, 20 November 1883, John C. Sims clipping books, vol. 1, UPA.
75. For more information about Sargent's career, as well as his role in bringing his system to Yale, see George W. Pierson, 'Apostles of Physical Culture', *Yale Alumni Magazine* (1973), pp. 11–17.
76. Edward Hitchcock and H. H. Seelye, *An Anthropometric Manual, Giving the Average and Mean Physical Measurements and Tests of Male College Students and the Method of Securing Them* (Amherst, MA: Williams, 1887); Roberta J. Park, 'Healthy, Moral and Strong: Educational Views of Exercise and Athletics in Nineteenth-Century America', in Kathryn Grover (ed.), *Fitness in America: Images of Health, Sport and the Body, 1830–1940* (Rochester: Woodbury Strong Museum, 1989), p. 142. For a report on Galton's Anthropometric Laboratory's measurement of 9,337 visitors in seventeen different ways, see Francis Galton, 'On the Anthropometric Laboratory at the Late International Health Exhibition', *Journal of the Anthropological Institute of Great Britain and Ireland* 14 (1885), pp. 205–21.
77. 'The University Gymnasium: Prof. White on College Athletics', *Evening Telegraph*, 3 December 1885.
78. 'The University Gymnasium', *Evening Telegraph*, 3 December 1885.
79. 'The New Gymnasium', *Inquirer* clipping, 4 December 1885; see also 'The University Gymnasium', *Press*, 3 December 1885, John C. Sims clipping books, vol. 1, UPA; see also 'Athletic Development', *The Evening Telegraph*, 23 April 1885, J. William White scrapbooks, 5 April 1883–2 August 1884, UPA.
80. Reiss, *Sport in Industrial America*, p. 47.
81. Clifford Putney, *Muscular Christianity: Manhood and Sports in Protestant America, 1880–1920* (Cambridge: Harvard University Press, 2001), pp. 23–4; Harvey Green, *Fit for America: Fitness, Sport and American Society* (New York: Pantheon Books, 1986), pp. 181–216.
82. Theodore Roosevelt, *The Strenuous Life: Essays and Addresses* (New York: Century Company, 1901); see also Bederman, *Manliness and Civilization*; E. Anthony Rotundo, *American Manhood: Transformations in Masculinity from the Revolution to the Modern Era* (New York: Basic Books, 1993); Green, *Fit for America*, pp. 219–58.
83. Green, *Fit for America*, p. 138; T. J. Jackson Lears, *No Place of Grace: Antimodernism and the Transformation of American Culture, 1880–1920* (Chicago: University of Chicago Press, 1994).
84. Francis G. Gosling, *Before Freud: Neurasthenia and the American Medical Community, 1870–1910* (Urbana: University of Illinois Press, 1987), p. 10.
85. George M. Beard, *American Nervousness, Its Causes and Consequences* (New York: G. P. Putnam's sons, 1881), p. 176; see also Tom Lutz, *American Nervousness, 1903: An Anecdotal History* (Ithaca: Cornell University Press, 1991), p. 7.
86. Gosling, *Before Freud*, p. 110.
87. Jayne Morgan, 'Eadweard Muybridge and W. S. Playfair: An Aesthetics of Neurasthenia', *History of Photography* 23 (1999), pp. 225–31. According to Dermer, 'Photographic Objectivity', p. 43, Mitchell was one of the attending physicians for the work on abnormal movement, concerned primarily with the physical manifestations of hysteria.
88. S. Weir Mitchell and William G. Spiller, 'A Case of Uncomplicated Hysteria in the Male Lasting Thirty Years, with Post-Mortem Examination', *Transactions of the Association of American Physicians* 19 (1904), pp. 433–45, here p. 433, as cited in Dermer, 'Photographic Objectivity', p. 57.

6 History, Memory and Trauma in Photography of the *Tondues*: Visuality of the Vichy Past through the Silent Image of Women

Alison M. Moore

In numerous surveys of modern European history one can find examples of iconic visual representations of the '*tondues*': French women targeted as collaborators and whose heads were shaven in rituals of public disgrace during and after the defeat of German forces at the end of World War II.[1] As images of humiliation, popular retribution, implicitly sexualised but muted corporeal violence, the *tondue* photos are striking, arresting and confounding to scholars and non-academic viewers alike. Frequently in these images the shaven-headed women appear to stare blankly, faces silent with shock or with sadness or with a refusal to perform the shame the crowd demands. But while thousands of such photographs exist in archives, only a small number are repeatedly disseminated to a broad academic and general public, predominantly through their reproduction in modern Europe survey books, popular historiography of the French Occupation and Liberation, in historical exposés in French news magazines and textbooks, and in recent academic critiques of the politics of retribution in post-war Europe.[2] While a substantial body of scholarship has remarked upon the striking nature of *tondue* visual representation, the status of the *tondue* photographs as texts within the politics of historical memory remains under theorised.[3] This article is not based on a study of the process by which such photographs were taken and first circulated, but rather on their post-war, especially recent, usage in works of both scholarly and popular representation of the past. The reproduction, contextualisation and captioning of *tondue* photographs in such texts has frequently been complicit in a reductive mythology of collaboration as feminine sexual betrayal. There is thus an unacknowledged dimension of visuality in the politics of memory about the Vichy past in which gender features voicelessly and implicitly. Barbie Zelizer has shown that the high level of selection and repetition in Holocaust photographic representation has had profound implications for historical remembering of the Shoah by assisting in a reduction of genocidal practices to an aestheticised 'Auschwitz experience'.[4] Likewise the selective and repetitious use of *tondue* photographs in representing French collaboration has supported a reductive mythologisation of the Nazi Occupation of France – in this instance, the implication that collaboration was a question of a passive and feminised compromise to the Nazi occupiers rather than a product of the self-defined, anti-Semitic and right-wing regime that was Vichy France. To unravel this silent manipulation, the *tondue* photos need to be specifically examined as texts in their own right, texts in which something fundamental is revealed about the relationship between gender, visuality and historical memory. Photography of the *tondues*, or rather the selection and repetition of particular images, has been complicit in a post-war mythologisation of collaboration as specifically feminine and as uniquely sexual. The *tondue* photographs have seen much broader dissemination in the wave of French historiographic confrontation with the Vichy past that has occurred since the late 1980s, in particular since the birth of specialised historical scholarship about the practice of the *tonte*.[5] However the 1990s and turn of the twenty-first century have also seen the revival of highly contested public debates in France about the meaning of the World War II past through war crimes trials of Vichy officials such as Paul Touvier and Maurice Papon. Evocations of the tragedy of the *tondues* have at times formed part of right-wing attempts to anathematise the Resistance and the Liberation as an indirect means of reviving the status of Vichy in historical memory.[6] But in reproducing the *tondue* photographs, the danger is less that the Vichy state will be relativised by a delegitimisation of the Liberation that followed it, but rather that the self-defined complicity of Vichy in the Nazi anti-Semitic programme will be mediated by a perpetuated discourse that constructs the Vichy era as an aberration in French history, as a feminised moment of weakness in which the French nation 'got into bed with the Germans'.[7]

Critical analysis of the political agendas implied in contemporary visions of the European past generally rely heavily upon the verbal articulations of these agendas in historiographic writing, in fiction, film, monuments and in various forms of official state memorialisation. Photographs present a unique challenge in relation to critical analysis of the politics of 'memory' because the sense in which they 'speak' to us is via a visual encoding that is decipherable only through broader consideration of how the motifs captured in the photo relate to pre-existing cultural understandings. Implicitly sexual images of women are an especially fertile ground for embedding non-verbal narratives of the past because the generalised post-war fetishisation of female bodies (promoted through advertising, women's magazines, popular film, etc.) means that such images have an automatic voyeuristic currency that allows for their ubiquitous reproduction, without visual theorists noticing anything unusual about this. The *tondue* images are texts particularly open to this variety of manipulation in the ongoing contestation of the Vichy past precisely because of the nature of the victims they depict – unlike Holocaust victims, there are no testimonials of the *tondues'* experience to counterbalance the overwhelming photographic colonisation of their image. As mute objects, moreover surrounded by the moral ambiguity of their position as collaborators, the women in these photos can be made to stand for a non-explicit, non-verbal assertion about the character of the Vichy regime in a way that is difficult to deconstruct because it is never clearly articulated in the first place. As such the *tondue* photos have fed into prevailing discourses of memory without any sustained critical examination by historians or gender scholars. And while Holocaust photographs and other images of atrocity form the basis of contemporary (often psychoanalytically informed) theorisation of the role of photography in historical memory,[8] consideration of the *tondue* photographs has remained absent from this field of discussion. This is surprising because although the *tondue* images depict something clearly not of the order of an 'atrocity', they are nonetheless archetypal representations of trauma at the heart of contested historical memories of World War II. The image of the *tondue* woman is both a reminder of reactionary excesses that muddy the glory of the Liberation in collective memorialisation, and a symbol of the sexualised humiliation imputed to the trauma of Occupation. Yet both of these meanings are an expropriation of the individual trauma experienced by the women who were victims of the *tonte* and who are the passive objects of the photographic gaze. Is it then possible, as theorist Ulrich Baer (following Fatimah Rony) asks, to 're-see' the victims photographed in images of trauma, unencumbered by the agendas to which they are subject?[9]

The sexualised nature of the *tondue* photographs begs analysis precisely because sexualised and gendered motifs have been central to visual representation of the French nation since the time of the French Revolution. The French nation is perhaps more than any other European nationality constructed as a feminine body. Although one speaks of *la Patrie* (or fatherland), *la République* was popularly configured as Marianne throughout the nineteenth century: a semi-bare-breasted virgin, draped in white cloth as depicted in the 1830 painting by Eugène Delacroix, *Liberty Leading the People*.[10] As Leah Hewitt notes, the image of the French nation as a woman saved from the Germans by Charles de Gaulle remained a staple image during the Fifth Republic.[11] But the notion of female collaboration as inherently sexual is particularly important to consider in relation to post-war constructions of the Vichy state because the Vichy regime itself used gender to legitimise its authority by invoking images of Joan of Arc, and by emphasising pro-natalism and conservative family roles.[12] Visual media featured heavily in Vichy pro-natalist campaigns, as attested to by the large number of posters to celebrate Mother's Day and encourage French women to bear children in the service of the nation by representing happy glowing mothers, and healthy babies juxtaposed with valiant soldier-males. Visions of France as a woman were invoked with posters depicting the war in terms of French women threatened sexually by leering, dirty British and Soviet soldiers, and rescued by benevolent clean-cut Germans.[13] Moreover, as Jean-Paul Sartre remarked as early as 1947, fascist writers under the Vichy regime had consistently deployed a sexualised metaphor to describe the collaborationist arrangement with Nazi Germany, speaking of the 'union' of France with Germany, and of France as symbolised by the notion of the 'eternal feminine'.[14] Indeed anti-republicans reportedly referred to the destruction of the republic under German occupation as 'the death of the whore' (*la gueuse*).[15]

But sexual metaphor too was instrumentalised during the Liberation precisely to de-legitimise the Vichy regime. In the trial of collaborationist writer Robert Brasillach in 1947, imputations of Brasillach's homosexuality were suggested by the prosecution by way of explanation for, indeed proof of, his treacherous stance.[16] On the whole though, explicit accusations of sexual collaboration with the Nazis were reserved for women – homosexuality does not appear among the official charges levelled against male collaborators.[17] As François Rouquet has remarked, the notion of '*collaboration horizontale*' is a construction of national betrayal through the metaphor of (hetero)sexual interaction with German soldiers – the crime of having represented the military penetration of the French nation by Germany, via the passive reception of the German phallus into the French female body.[18] But the term also suggests that the crime of sexual 'collaboration' resided specifically in the presumed passive sexuality of women: their act of treason is that they lay on their backs and let themselves '*se faire faire chez les boches*'.[19] Little wonder then that the details of how the *tondue* is supposed to have collaborated have often been assumed, her passive body acting as the metaphoric site upon which the contamination of the Occupation is exorcised, in a way that is both obvious and taboo in French collective understanding.[20] Therefore in helping to sustain the myth of the *tondues* as sexual traitors, and of the Vichy past as a passive sexualised treason, photographic representation holds profound implications for the place of feminine sexuality in historical memory of the Vichy legacy. But clearly also there is a continuity across French representations of the nation as a feminine body that complicate aligning either the *tondue* phenomenon itself or its photographic representation with any one stance in relation to republicanism, Vichy, the Resistance, Gaullisme, or any other political tendency. While photographs of the *tontes* must be appreciated in this broader historical context, as texts in themselves they do not properly belong to any one version of the past any more than does the motif of the French nation as a feminine body. Where the *tondue* photos do begin to support a politicised narrative about Vichy is in their repetitive reproduction as generic images of the Occupation and Liberation. As the primary form of visual image reproduced to represent the absolute divisions within French society that the Occupation embodied, the *tondue* photo becomes the arbiter of a continued alignment of female sexuality with national betrayal, and of passive femininity as an explanation for the weakness of the French nation state during World War II. This both supports a denigration of women and of feminine desire in post-war French culture, and suggests an excuse for why Vichy cooperated with the Nazis in a way that expiates the shame of this legacy in collective memorialisation.

Trauma visualised as a silent woman

The *tondue* photographs assist in the traumatic fixing of the humiliation of the Occupation by sustaining mythologies of female collaboration as inherently sexual, and in so doing sustaining the gendered discourse about Vichy as a feminine compromise to the penetration of Nazi masculinity. The image of the *tondue* acts as the vessel through which this particular trauma of the past (that of defeat, emasculation and the failure of national consensus) is kept an open wound, a past that cannot pass precisely because the mythologies of its own historical moment are reiterated continually through a visual representation which repeats the metaphor of sex as national betrayal that operated both during and at the end of the war. But the *tondue* image also holds a fetishised status in cultural visions of the Occupation as a psychoanalytic trauma because the photographic text itself acts as a metaphor for the frozen moment that stops the flow of memory. Thus the *tondue* photographs show us that there is an implicitly gendered dimension to visuality in historical memory of Vichy France. These iconic images of shaven-headed women have served a unique function in representing as 'trauma' the issues embedded in French denial about the Vichy past, something that has eluded scholarly analysis both because the agent is a voiceless image, and because it is not necessarily the photographs themselves, nor even the photographers who took them, that are the agents behind the message they emit. Rather the power of these photos to echo the older discourses of women's sexuality as the vehicle for national danger suggests that memory and memorialisation are governed by a politics not only of what is said and argued, or what is not said or denied, but indeed also by what is shown and seen, and specifically by what is seen and not heard. Images of women who are silent in history are an especially pliable medium for this particularly slippery form of representation both because of the fetishistic cultural currency that allows for their repetition, and because their subjects can be relied upon to stay silent and let the photographs 'speak for themselves' – in other words, speak for whatever agenda mysteriously results from their unexplained reproduction.

The *tondue* images are an ideal source through which to interrogate psychoanalytically framed theories of visuality. They allow us to reinsert gender into theoretical considerations of photography and memory (as these have been articulated by Roland Barthes, Susan Sontag and Ulrich Baer), by examining the concrete way in which gendered visual imagery aids in the historical remembering of trauma in a society where these concerns have been explicitly constructed through a psychoanalytic metaphor: memory as a flow and trauma as a fixing of this flow, something symbolically similar to what occurs in the mechanism of photography itself. In *Spectral Evidence: The Photography of Trauma*, Ulrich Baer interrogates the nature of Holocaust visuality by recalling the psychoanalytic imagination of photography as a metaphor through which to construct the concept of 'trauma'. As Baer notes, psychoanalytic trauma was first theorised in relation to a body of gender-specific imagery – the photographs of 'hysterical' women patients documented by Jean-Martin Charcot in the Salpêtrière hospital in the 1890s and reflected upon in Sigmund Freud's early writings.[21] Memory and trauma as terms in psychoanalysis and psychiatry are thus inherently bound up with the photographic representation of women who were silenced by the visual expropriation of their experience in the context of a pathologising construction of feminine hysteria at the end of the nineteenth century. But if, as for Baer, this observation is a useful platform from which to interrogate the relationship between collective historical memory and photography of victimisation in the Holocaust, clearly it is doubly relevant to a study of the *tondue* photographs. Invoking psychoanalytic terms like 'memory' and 'trauma', that were designed to explain individual psychic function, and proposing them as terms that apply to collective historical memorialisation has the danger of obscuring understanding of how versions of the past are propagated by conscious political agents.[22] However, here indeed is an important observation that a study of the *tondue* photos may help to suggest, since they point to the way in which discourses about the past are reiterated via both conscious and unconscious processes, in particular in relation to visuality. Images can be reproduced without any clear awareness or intent on the part of the author in whose work they are situated, or even on the part of the publisher, whose interests often reflect a concern for marketability above other considerations. But acknowledging these unconscious processes need not dilute critique of the politicised consequences of such reproduction.

Discussion of collective 'trauma' and 'memory' are also appropriate to an analysis of the French Vichy legacy because psychoanalytic ideas have been reflected in French filmic, literary and scholarly explorations of the Occupation since the early post-war era, in particular those relating to gender and sexual issues. Nowhere is the sense of memory, trauma and sexual collaboration more linked than in *Hiroshima mon amour*, a film of minimal narrative in which the focus is a poetic script, and a highly visual cinematography centred on the inter-cultural lovers' bodies, faces and re-enacted memories, in which sexual intimacy functions to unravel the traumatic freezing of the French woman's trauma of being a victim of the *tonte*.[23] In his seminal 1987 work *Le syndrôme de Vichy*, Henry Rousso similarly framed the denial of French complicity in Nazi agendas in terms of a blocked, frozen memory. Positioning himself as both historian and psychotherapist of the living corpse that is the Vichy past, Rousso suggested that the Occupation and Liberation have remained moments that defy the flow of time and function as a kind of screen upon which the realities of subsequent generations are projected like a photographic image.[24] In Rousso's metaphor, the Vichy past thus lives on as a traumatic blockage in the flow of French collective memory.[25] But though Rousso's use of psychoanalytic terminology functions more within his writing as a linguistic device than as a methodological framing, the problem of the *tondue* photos suggests that a more complex relationship may exist between visions of the Vichy past as 'trauma' and visual depictions of women collaborators. Like the hysterical women in Charcot's Salpêtrière photographs, the *tondues* do not speak for themselves. Indeed the metaphoric language of psychoanalytic trauma and feminine silence is widely observable across post-war French reflections of the Vichy past, in particular in *mode rétro* literature that indirectly critiques post-war denial about the Vichy past such as novels by Evelyne Le Garrec and Marie Chaix.[26] And of course in the work of Rousso, denial about French complicity in the Holocaust is framed as a 'syndrome', as frozen memory or trauma.[27] But as in Rousso's writing, the concept of trauma presented here is one defined less as an emotive incapacity to confront the past than by a network of politicised narratives designed to expiate the messier problematics posed by national legacies such as that of Vichy. In attempting to fix some sort of finality in the flow of time, the traumatic response freezes its moment and in so doing condemns that moment to endure and repeat, reproducing itself in new forms. Considering then the way in which notions of 'trauma' and memory were constructed by Charcot and Freud through the metaphor of photography, and considering also the way that psychoanalytic metaphors of memory as flow and trauma as a frozen moment have entered French reconstructions of the Vichy past, the status of the *tondue* images as photographs begs discursive analysis.

In her highly influential study, *On Photography*, Susan Sontag suggested that photographs of victims repeat the violation of their subject through the aggressive possession implied in the capturing of a photographic image.[28] In her recent reconfiguration of the problem of photography and victimhood, *Regarding the Pain of Others*, Sontag again speculated on the inherent character of photojournalistic complicity in war and violence by virtue of the voyeuristic pleasure such photographs inevitably invite.[29] During the Liberation *tondue* photographs were made into postcards and sold as souvenirs, as surviving examples attest.[30] They were ubiquitously plastered across newspaper headlines throughout France during the summer of 1944, and indeed this visual representation participated in the violation of women through ongoing *tonte* rituals over the following year. In attempting to explain how the idea of the *tonte* spread to all regions of France in the aftermath of the German defeat, an examination of the photographs in the Liberation press is an obvious possibility to consider. As numerous historians muse, there was no official directive to shave the heads of women collaborators. While Fabrice Virgili has argued that rumour networks established under the Occupation conveyed the idea of the *tonte* across France,[31] only further research will allow us to determine whether press photography of the *tontes* was not in fact also instrumental to their spread in the later stages of the Liberation.[32] As Virgili notes, photographers themselves played a dubious role in relation to the scenes they documented: the *tonte* rituals were above all enacted specifically for the eye of the camera and thus the photographs form as much part of their theatre as they are record of the *tontes*.[33] Indeed even during the early years of the Occupation, long prior to the existence of photography of any *tonte* action, visual representation in the form of drawings appeared in clandestine propaganda that indicated to the reader how disgraced Frenchwomen should be humiliated with swastikas painted on their foreheads at the moment of the German defeat.[34] For these reasons the *tondue* photographs hold a unique status as 'documents' of post-war retribution. Unlike most other photographic record of World War II, the *tondue* images are not merely documentary but were themselves complicit in encouraging further repetitions of the acts depicted. During the Liberation era they acted simultaneously as historical record, journalistic report and an infectious call to action by virtue of the fetishistic appeal of the humiliation they depicted. This then makes the *tondue* photographs problematic texts in the politics of historical memory since in our gaze upon them we are potentially complicit in an ongoing symbolic violence against the visually captured *tondues*. If, as Susan Sontag claims, the voyeuristic appeal of photographs of violent suffering makes the viewer of them inherently partisan to that violence, then the *tondue* images offer a particularly concrete example of this complicity.

But missing from Sontag's work (and from the work of others who theorise a relationship between photography and the memory of World War II) is any consideration of the interplay of gender and the photographic gaze, something the *tondue* images also offer us an opportunity to consider. Between photographer and subject in relation to the *tondues* there was often a gendered dimension. With the notable exception of the female American photographer Lee Miller, men constituted the overwhelming majority of those who 'captured' images of the *tontes*. But the violence within the *tondue* image lies less in the gendered demarcation of the role of subject and object and more precisely in the motifs of the silence of the women depicted and of the traumatic interruption of the flow of time and memory that the photograph itself symbolises. As images of the specifically gendered trauma of Occupation and collaboration, the *tondue* photos form an apex that links the voiceless feminine subject to the wound that is the Vichy past. Alain Brossat has remarked on the irony that in attempting to recover the truth of the *tonte* phenomenon, it would be a shame if all viewpoints were presented except that of the victim.[35] Yet both Brossat and Virgili explicitly rejected the possibility of interviewing any surviving victims of the *tonte* – Brossat on the advice of acquaintances of the women who felt it would be unkind to ask a *tonte* victim to relive this often secret and buried trauma, as well as difficult to encourage anyone to come forward,[36] Virgili because the object of his analysis was the head-shaving practice, a re-situating of the historical object that he shows has been over-personified through the stereotype of the *tondue* as a sexual collaborator.[37] In the face of the silence and absent subjectivity of the *tondues* women, a comparison of their image with visuality in historical memory of the Holocaust can only be taken so far: while Holocaust photography since the 1970s must compete with the vastly more influential 'vector of memory' generated by first-person autobiographical accounts of survivors,[38] the visual image of the *tondue* stands virtually alone as a representation of the experience of the victim. Moreover, while Holocaust victimisation is a universally vindicated suffering, the trauma of the *tondues* is an altogether murkier form in the moral stakes of World War II complicity. Indeed, since the high-profile trials of ex-Vichy officials for crimes against humanity in relation to anti-Semitic persecution, the stigma surrounding the (assumed) horizontal collaborator has become something much more internationalised in its moral implications than the original charge of national betrayal.[39]

The year 2004 saw the reappearance of *tondue* photographs in the international press because of the deaths of Henri Cartier-Bresson and Carl Mydans, both members of the self-administered cooperative Magnum agency most often associated with professional photography of the *tontes*, and founded by Cartier-Bresson and Robert Capa in France during 1947. In revealing language one press obituary of Cartier-Bresson described him as a 'Master of the Moment', invoking the image of the photographer as a masculine proprietor of the passive visual object.[40] In fact both Bresson and Mydans were renowned for acknowledging their own potential complicity in the events they captured by virtue of the voyeuristic appeal of images of war and violence.[41] But if the Magnum photographers are the masters, then who are the slaves in the moment that was the Liberation of France, in the moment frozen by the image of the *tondue*? While it would be problematic to assume that there is anything inherently disruptive to historical remembering about a voyeuristic gaze, the *tondue* photographs pose a unique set of problems in that the subjectivity of the women depicted appears now more than ever condemned to an infinite silence. If photographic images of shaven-headed women are to be shown as frequently as they were between the 1970s and the 1990s without there being any sense in which a voice was matched to that visualisation, what are the implications for the way in which we look at the women in these photographs, and correspondingly, for the way in which women are, or more specifically feminine sexual desire is, situated within historical memory of collaboration?

Photography and the myth of sexualised collaboration

Scholarly study of the punishment of women in the Liberation period was virtually non-existent prior to the end of the 1980s, and indeed the most detailed and substantial contributions have occurred only since then.[42] Throughout the entire period from the end of the war until this recent blossoming of interest, the *tondues* remained largely a void within historical understanding of the Occupation and Liberation. In the face of this analytic lacuna, *tondue* imagery nonetheless held a constant place in non-academic 'vectors of memory', in literature, music but most saliently in the visual domains of photography, documentary and cinema. In other words, for nearly fifty years the image of the *tondue* was visually memorialised, and implicitly mythologised via this visual archive, without any counterbalancing verbal analysis.

Throughout this period of visual representation, the *tondues* were entirely collapsed with the notion of sexual collaboration – what Virgili calls the stereotype of '*young-girl-whose-head-was-shaved-by-the-crowd-because-she-slept-with-a-German*'.[43] But as numerous historians have revealed, the head-shaving was inflicted upon women as a punishment for all varieties of collaboration, on women who had served German soldiers as shopkeepers, domestic servants or acted as informants, or even women who simply had the misfortune to belong to an ethnic minority associated with the Axis powers, or of being the wife of a collaborator.[44] By Virgili's estimate, only 42 per cent of *tontes* inflicted on women nationally were punishment for sexual, as opposed to other types of collaboration,[45] and while in French Forces of the Interior (Forces Françaises de l'Intérieur, FFI) and civic courts the charge of 'intimate relations with the enemy' was indeed often accompanied by the order to undergo the *tonte*, there were also clearly known sexual *collaboratrices* who were not subjected to the same punishment, as we can gather from the autobiography of the high-profile, high-society sexual collaborator Corinne Luchaire.[46] Professional prostitutes themselves were not, in contrast to the World War I Belgian experience, the primary targets of the *tonte*.[47] And yet both at the time of the Liberation and subsequently the *tondues* have been characterised as sexual traitors. In contrast, Virgili rejected the emphasis on the woman shorn as opposed to the act of shearing since the object of specialist inquiry is precisely the action inflicted upon the women in question, an intellectual project that specifically attempts to deconstruct existing stereotypes about the *tondues* as sexual collaborators and to contextualise historically the events surrounding them.[48] The stereotype of the *tondues* as sexual collaborators is at best a half truth; the shearings represented not a punishment for sexual collaboration, but rather a sexualisation of female collaboration during the Liberation and in post-war memory.[49] Thus Virgili's own image selection in *La France 'virile'* reflects this emphasis with the use of photos that resituate viewer attention on the perpetrators and reveal something of the mechanics of the ritual, bypassing the more common and over-represented images in which the shaven-headed women are the central and fetishised objects of the photograph.

If the myth of the *tondue* as a sexual collaborator was frequently assumed throughout the post-war era, it was specifically asserted through another form of visual representation, namely cinema. The central character in *Hiroshima, mon amour* is a woman whose relived trauma is both to have suffered the shaming of the *tonte* and to have seen her German lover killed during the Liberation. In the 1966 Claude Berri film *Le Vieil homme et l'enfant*, the moment of Liberation is represented as the scene of a *tonte* in which we are led to understand the sexual nature of the woman's crime by the presence of the 'suspect' baby in her arms.[50] The treatment by Marcel Ophuls in the influential documentary *Le Chagrin et la pitié* equally links the *tondues* to sexual collaboration by situating documentary footage of a *tonte* ritual in Paris alongside interviews with inhabitants of Clermont-Ferrand in which he asks them how they felt seeing French girls on the arms of German soldiers in the street.[51] This is in spite of the fact that Madame Solange, the one woman he interviews as an ex-collaborator, was accused not of any kind of sexual collaboration but of denunciation. But the replay of footage of Paris prostitutes being shamed in 1944, accompanied by the 1964 Georges Brassens satirical song '*La Tondue*' ties the patently sexless charges levelled against Mme Solange with the sexual collaboration imputed to the *tondues*. The masculine words by Brassens are offset by feminine images, while the words of Mme Solange are made to sound dismissive.[52] In other words, while the evidence before Ophuls suggests a breakdown in the relationship between female collaboration, sexual collaboration and the *tontes*, he maintains the slippage through editing and the selection of visual archive. Moreover, the documentary footage reinforces the myth of the *tondue* as a sexual collaborator, since in the instance depicted in the footage (not at all representative of the majority of *tontes*) clearly the women in question were having sexual relations with German soldiers because this was their job.[53] As Miranda Pollard notes, in generally privileging masculine recollections of the Occupation, *Le Chagrin et la pitié* feeds into the discourse of women as 'victims, dupes or opportunists' in relation to the Nazi Occupation, and of collaboration as a feminised act of submission.[54] But if Ophuls was reflecting the prevailing assumptions of the time, he reiterated them specifically, perhaps albeit unconsciously, through visual assertion.[55]

The *tondue* photographs in particular can be made to coalesce with the slippage between collaboration and feminine sexuality because in depicting the women naked, in their underwear or other various states of partial undress in a public space they renew the spectacle of sexual humiliation that was itself exorcised through the *tonte* – in reminding the viewer of the women as sexual beings, we are seduced into an all-too-easy imagination of their supposed sexual collaboration. In popular histories the captions that accompany such photographs sometimes explicitly describe the women as sexual collaborators: a photograph of a lone *tondue* in Ian Ousby's book on Occupation is captioned, 'A *collabo horizontale* after ritual punishment in Gisors'.[56] (How does Ousby know this was her crime? Or does he simply assume it?) In his epic *Grande histoire des Français sous l'Occupation*, journalist Henri Amouroux reproduced an example of the more graphic type of depiction of the sexualised humiliation of *tondues* – a photograph in which six women stand naked, heads shaven, mud smeared on their breasts and genitals, forced to imitate the Nazi salute. Below this is another (smaller) photograph of a single male collaborator, clothed and blindfolded unspectacularly being prepared for execution. Amouroux's captioning of the two photographs is revealing: '*Les nues et les morts*' – naked women and dead people (though the gender-neutral *morts* in this context clearly refers to the man about to be executed) – a dichotomy in which women's collaboration and punishment are distinguished as questions of sexuality and nudity, while that of men is tied to death.[57] The sizing and positioning of the photographs reinforces the symbolic order in which the more visually lurid and striking punishment of women is given primary place next to the rather drab, visually discountable ritual of the punishment of men. But the 'nues' versus 'morts' dichotomy of Amouroux's photo selection is intriguing in its construction of the finality and completeness of retribution against male collaborators, in opposition to the sexualised, generative punishment of women. The mud on the women's bodies in this image defiles but also accentuates the sexual zones of their bodies. Amouroux's selection of these especially contrasting photographs captioned in such a way shows how visual images can assist in a memorialisation of post-war retribution in which the sexualised projection on women collaborators is perpetuated and reinforced, and in which a fetishisation of their humiliation is sustained in historiographic accounts, particularly those of the less scholarly (and therefore also probably more widely distributed) variety like Amouroux's.

Gender-differentiated photographs reproduced in this fashion 'speak' to a discourse in which retribution against men is constructed as a brutal but final, fatal but unequivocal settling of accounts, while that against women is constructed as a gratuitous spectacle of ongoing repetition. As Virgili remarks, while state officials after 1946 took pains to record the number of collaborators killed during official retribution (predominantly men), no one bothered to ask how many had been 'shaven' (predominantly women).[58] But if shaven-headed women were privileged as fetishised visual objects in the Liberation press, they have been doubly so in post-war reproductions of retribution photography. While head-shaving formed only one of the punishments enacted against female collaborators, and while it was not uniquely reserved for women, the image of the shaven-headed woman is nonetheless the singular representation of female collaboration throughout post-war representation, and indeed has become the most iconic visual image of collaboration generally. Two questions then must be asked about this. First, what is it about these photographs that gives them such an ongoing appeal for a generation that can no longer be said to remember the war through direct experience? Second, what are the implications of this singular (and gendered) visuality of collaboration for historical 'memory' of the Vichy and Liberation periods?

As Virgili notes, head-shaving was not infrequently part of rituals of defilement to punish male collaborators, though never on accusation of sexual collaboration, nor ever discursively interpreted as a form of sexual humiliation either within the press and resistance propaganda of the time, nor at any stage in post-war memory.[59] Although photographs of shaven-headed men do exist,[60] it appears to have been above all the photographs of shaved women that dominated press coverage during the Liberation period itself. This may reflect the discrepancy in the quantity of photographs taken of men compared to women (and indeed the quantity of *tontes* directed at men compared to women), but it was also perhaps because of the perception by photographers and by press editors at the time that the shaven-headed woman represented a more 'striking' photographic spectacle.[61] This is a logical supposition in light of the way women's hair was contested in France during the interwar period. As cultural historians such as Mary Louise Roberts and Carolyn Dean have discussed, Victor Margueritte's 1922 novel *La Garçonne* initiated a discourse within the French press and in social hygienist writing in the 1920s and 1930s about the danger to the health of the French nation posed by the new boyish career girl. 'La Garçonne', or 'New Woman' (as the British equivalent was called), was seen as neglecting her national duty of bearing children in favour of sexual indulgence and selfish ambition.[62] Not only was the androgyny of the *garçonne* frequently cited as one of the prime explanations for the alarming decline in birth-rates in France during the interwar period (a revival of older Third Republic anxieties about sexual morality and the health of the nation), but was also decried as a sign of a degenerate collapsing of gender differentiation. Pro-natalist writers and fashion commentators discussed women's short haircuts alongside the new more revealing fashions of short skirts (i.e. above the ankle) and slinky figure-hugging dresses. Both were read as signs of a new lascivious female sexuality, dangerous because virile, excessive because androgynous, encouraging a

Les nues et les morts

Cette photo n'est pas belle, mais il s'agit d'un document qui rappelle quel spectacle fut offert dans trop de villes françaises à des foules sadiques. Quels que soient les griefs que l'on pouvait avoir contre certaines femmes, la volonté de les dégrader, de les souiller, jusqu'à les obliger à un dérisoire salut nazi, condamne ceux qui s'étaient, sans mandat, érigés en justiciers. Plusieurs mois s'écouleront avant le retour à une justice « normale », celle qui condamne et fait exécuter l'accusé « dans les règles »
(Coll. Diret Angel et B,N. Paris, Arch. E.R.L.)

Figure 1: Page from Henri Amouroux, *La grand histoire des Français sous l'occupation*, vol. 8 *Joies et douleurs du peuple libéré, 6 juin-1er septembre 1944* (Paris: Editions Robert Laffont, 1988). Used with the permission of Editions Robert Laffont.

vision of woman not as child-bearer and wife, but as disruptively both aroused and arousing.[63] Curiously, as Jean-Yves le Naour has noted, one interwar journalist's objection to *garçonne*-type women cutting their hair short was precisely on the grounds that it evoked the treachery of prostitutes whose heads were shaved as punishment for sleeping with German soldiers along the Belgian border in 1918.[64] The shaving of women's heads then would have been clearly understood by the French wartime generation as an act of violence that specifically sexualised female collaborators in a manner linking them to perversion and to a form of sexuality and femininity deemed outside the nation.[65]

Voyeurism and memory

Alain Brossat has speculated that historiographic reluctance to write about the *tondues* until very recently was a product of aversion to the voyeuristic appeal of the subject – voyeurism understood as visual pleasure but also understood metaphorically as pleasure in all forms of perception. It may be the fear of engaging in a voyeuristic indulgence that has resulted in the selection and repetition of a single *tondue* image by Robert Capa. In other words, to be seen digging up either histories or (rather particularly) visual images of the *tontes* has often been perceived as participating in 'a sort of pornography'.[66] It is perhaps for these reasons that specialised scholars of *tonte* history have displayed little inclination to reproduce images in the manner of Amouroux and Ousby, and yet in more popular representation the *tondue* photographs abound. What then is so voyeuristically appealing about the visual image of the *tonte*? Roland Barthes, in his landmark 1980 study of photographic representation, *Chambre claire* (*Camera Lucida*), noted that all photographs have the quality of perpetuating infinitely and mechanically a moment in time that cannot itself ever be repeated.[67] As such they give rise to a 'fetishised' gaze, a sense of oneself as a spectator taking pleasure in the photograph as an object.[68] Barthes identified within this gaze two themes that bear upon a photograph; the 'studium' and the 'punctum'. The *studium* aspect of photographic gaze is that which allows the viewer to state whether they like the photo or not; it is a calculated aspect of the gaze and invites the gazer to consider the content of the photo and study the nature of the event that it records.[69] As such the *studium* aspect is that which dominates in photographic analysis. The *punctum* is that aspect that 'strikes' ('pierces') the gazer, the aspect that evokes something inexplicable in the viewer, an instantaneous impression that coexists alongside the *studium*. It may often be a tiny detail within the photo that repeatedly

Photography of the Tondues

Figure 2: Photograph by Robert Capa, 1944. Used with the permission of Magnum Photos, Inc.

draws the eye back to it, and without which the photograph would have an altogether different impact upon the viewer.[70] This detail may reside within the content of the photograph, or in what the viewer knows about the photographed subject, in the narratives that either explicitly or unconsciously accompany the viewing of the photograph, and which are often alluded to in their captions. The *punctum* of the *tondue* photographs lies in the false narrative of 'she slept with a German'. The *tondue* photo's principal voyeuristic appeal lies precisely in its status as a living part of the violence it depicts because in so far as photography helps to sustain the myth of collaboration as a feminine sexual compromise, the injustice of the *tonte* is perpetuated in the present.

It would be false to assume though that the unspoken narratives implied by reproductions of *tondue* images are singular or consistent. As Bernard Fride remarks, Amouroux's pseudo-scholarly history frequently presents a relativised image of the Vichy era in which ideological divisions, and the sticky issue of responsibility for French complicity in the Holocaust, are subsumed under a collective memorialisation of the suffering of 'the French people'.[71] Here the *tondue* stands as a tragic figure, a sign that a whole range of truly terrible things happened of an order of complexity too great to disentangle, a dismissing stance that clearly cushions those, like Amouroux, whose own complicity during the Vichy period may not stand up to closer scrutiny. But while in such accounts the *tondue* appears as a tragic figure of national non-consensus for which gender acts as an unspoken alibi, in other texts the *tondue* photograph's greatest appeal lies specifically in the false narratives of national consensus and redemption that its visual language suggests. While specialists emphasise the role of the *tonte* rituals in affirming the authority of the Resistance in the aftermath of the Liberation,[72] more generic scholarship has assumed local populations to have been instrumental in if not entirely responsible for the shearings.[73] Indeed the image of the *tontes* as a form of spontaneous and therapeutic collective celebration of Liberation is one of the stereotypes that specialised scholarship has attempted to debunk.[74] Virgili notes the dynamic relationship between gendarmes, FFI men and local populations in the targeting of women collaborators, an interpretation borne out in many *tondue* photographs that document multiple variations of actors and perpetrators.[75] In numerous photographs the perpetrators are identifiable through signifiers such as uniforms, patches and hats, while in others the men who lead their victims are ambiguous; in many cases crowds of onlookers appear actively engaged in the ritual: chasing, following, shouting and cheering as the *tonte* activity unravels.[76]

But while the mass of photography indicates a wide variation in the character of *tonte* rituals, in who led and supported them, the repeated reproduction of one image in generic histories of the period suggests that one version of the *tondue* story has dominated the post-war era both within France and beyond. Rare indeed is the historian (either professional or amateur, either French or other) who when asked about the *tondues* does not recall Robert Capa's August 1944 photograph of the anonymous French woman with child in arms, her head shaved, pursued by a jeering mob of all genders and ages through the streets of Chartres.[77] The *punctum* of this photograph (and probably the reason for its reproduction) relates to the look of selfless concern that the victim displays towards the child in her arms. Though never stated in any captions to this photo, the *punctum* phrase is universally understood: this child is the progeny of the *tondue*'s sexual collaboration with a German. The presence of the baby promotes conflicting and ambiguous narratives that both problematise and feed into the discourse that produced the *tonte*. The baby is the absolute proof of the *tondue*'s betrayal, the product of the penetration of German blood into the French nation symbolised by the penetration of the German phallus into the French woman's body, of German semen into French blood.[78] And yet the Capa photograph also disrupts these narratives of misogyny. Reproduced throughout the post-war era it suggests the sad injustice of the retribution against the victim who may simply have been a woman in love, like the *tondue* of *Hiroshima, mon amour*, or like that of Régine Desforges's *La Bicyclette bleue*.[79] The Capa photo has also clearly been a common choice because of the 'tasteful' nature of a *tonte* ritual it captures in which, unlike many, there appears no nudity, no apparent sexual violation, no physical damage or forceful coercion.[80] It privileges the role of other women in encouraging the *tonte* since the victim, though led by a uniformed FFI man, is surrounded by civilian women and children. In this way the photograph supports a vision of the *tonte* not as a simple question of violence against women committed by men but rather of a generalised social consensus to punish a particular group of women deemed outside the nation.[81] As such the viewer is reassured that if a brutal justice was inflicted on the woman in the photograph, it was inflicted by all, man, woman and child,[82] that it was done in a spirit of nationalism (the tricolour flag features in the background of the photograph), and was done in an orderly and civilised manner. As numerous other *tondue* photographs attest, this was clearly not always the case.[83] Indeed the real *punctum* of this photo is not the image of the woman's relationship to her child (that occupies the centre of the photograph), but rather the faces of the women in the foreground – the woman closest has her head turned completely towards the *tondue*, the others are partially visible enough to discern an intent regard that might suggest both a support for the action, and a concern for the wellbeing of mother and child. In invoking a gender-equity of perpetrators of the *tonte* and an ambiguity surrounding the attitude of the participants, the photograph silences questions about the Liberation, about who was punished and why and by whom. It invokes a sense of post-war retribution as a moment in which all participated willingly and played out their respective roles for the benefit of a collective catharsis. The repetition of this photograph then acts as a tool for regrouping national collectivity in the post-war era, reflecting the unstated dismissal of the *tontes* as violence against women within the larger interest of post-war national cohesion.

Conclusion

The *tondue* photographs began reappearing in historical picture books and glossy news magazine articles during the explosion of discussion in the 1990s surrounding new claims of the extent of collaboration, and about French complicity in the Nazi programme of Jewish genocide. As the work of historians such as Henry Rousso and H. R. Kedward has revealed, whereas the justice of the people's tribunals and military and Resistance courts may have been imprecise, brutal and swift, the justice of the Supreme court in prosecuting known French war criminals over the past sixty years has been highly selective, delicate and slow. Even the otherwise very unforgiving ex-resistance fighter and historian Célia Bertin remarked that in spite of her disgust for female collaborators, she couldn't help feeling that it was nonetheless somewhat unjust that all those women had been so brutally traumatised, while men such as Maurice Papon were able to walk away from the Vichy era not only free but reintegrated into French state power structures and privilege.[84] The *tondue* images then, reappearing as they did during the 1990s, may be read a nagging reminder that until the controversial trials of high-profile collaborators, those who had received the fiercest justice were not in fact those most accountable for the worst that Vichy had to offer. There is no doubt that the use of the *tondue* photos by professional historians commonly forms part of an agenda designed to show the injustice of settlements driven by Cold War political imperatives and in which it was often the most vulnerable not the most responsible who were punished.[85]

But while *tondue* photographs may often be reproduced in historical books in order to problematise mythologies of the Liberation as a joyous moment, such depictions actually assist in the construction of the World War II past as precisely too different and too distant to be contemporarily relevant. The most common form of captioning of the *tondue* images in books by non-specialist historians frames them in terms of barbarism and the unleashing of darker passions, and in this way too the *tondue* photos are made complicit in an othering of the past, a construction of France of the Liberation moment as 'another country'.[86] This function is suggested too by photographic theories of viewer distance which argue that photographs fracture reality by freezing one moment that was part of a flow of time, and are thus a mechanism for constructing difference in historical memory, making the present safe from the horrors of the past.[87] But in fact there is something incredibly present about what the *tondue* images depict, about women's heads as the locus of contested nationhood, as the recent furore over the Islamic headscarf in French public education indicates. As Neil MacMaster and Toni Lewis have shown, photographs of veiled Islamic women were contextually misused in the French press throughout the 1990s to promote associations of the veil with the threat of violence imputed to Islamic fundamentalism. Images of women wearing the more extreme head-to-foot covering of the Iranian *chador* have often appeared alongside news exposés about the headscarf debate, in spite of the fact that most Muslim women in France are of North African origin and are hence more likely – if they wear anything at all – to wear a scarf that covers merely their hair.[88] Here again women are suggested as an alibi for a form of national non-consensus this time presented by fears of Islamic influence on French culture. Here again gender acts as a vehicle for a politics that is invoked not (or not only) by verbal assertion but by visual repetition. The *tondue* photographs are striking because of the silent myth that the women as objects within them are made to embody: the myth that says that Vichy 'got into bed with' the Germans because the French nation state is a woman and was penetrated by the masculine Nazi war-machine, something no one needs to 'say' anymore, both because it is understood through the legacy of past nationalist imagery, and because the visual message of the photographs sustains the myth and communicates it non-verbally to subsequent generations. Representation of the headscarves debate shows that women's bodies remain a question of national self-definition in France, and that gendered visuality is a persistent medium through which to assert a politics that might hold less power if forced to articulate itself only verbally. No clearer proof exists to show that the *tondue* memory is part of 'a past that will not pass',[89] a memory relived and recreated in the present, than the fact that its pattern is reinvented through a resonant politics of the present.

Notes

1. *Tondue* = shorn/shorn one (feminised). As Fabrice Virgili notes, the use of the noun *la tonte* is quite particular in this instance, suggestive of dehumanisation. Fabrice Virgili, *La France 'virile': des femmes tondues à la Libération* (Paris: Payot, 2002, p. 12. Readers

interested in the English translation can consult Fabrice Virgili, *Shorn Women: Gender and Punishment in Liberation France*, trans. John Flower (Oxford: Berg, 2002), p. 12.
2. On the 'staggering' gap between the quantity of photographs taken and the small number commonly reproduced see Michael Griffin, 'The Great War Photographs: Constructing Myths of History and Photojournalism', in Bonnie Brennen and Hanno Hardt (eds), *Picturing the Past: Media, History, and Photography* (Urbana & Chicago: University of Illinois Press, 1999), pp. 122–57, here p. 125.
3. Corran Laurens, '"La femme au turban": les femmes tondues', in H. R. Kedward and Nancy Wood (eds), *The Liberation of France, Image and Event* (Oxford & Washington DC: Berg Publishers, 1995), pp. 155–79, here p. 174; Virgili, *La France 'virile'*, pp. 116–19; Alain Brossat, *Les Tondues, un carnaval moche* (Paris: Manya, 1992), pp. 25–30.
4. Barbie Zelizer, *Remembering to Forget: Holocaust Memory Through the Camera's Eye* (Chicago: University of Chicago Press, 1998).
5. *Tondue* photos appear in Henri Amouroux, *Joies et douleurs du peuple libéré, 6 juin-1er septembre 1944* (Paris: Editions Robert Laffont, 1988); John Ardagh and Colin Jones, *Atlas de la France: histoire, culture, société* (Paris: Nathan, 1991), p. 93; Colin Jones, *The Cambridge Illustrated History of France* (Cambridge & New York: Cambridge University Press, 1994), p. 278; Ian Ousby, *Occupation: The Ordeal of France 1940–1944* (New York: St Martin's' Press, 1998), images between pp. 174–5; Nick Yapp, *Nineteen-Forties: The Hulton Getty Picture Collection, Decades of the Twentieth Century* (Cologne: Könemann, 1998), p. 165; Nancy Wood, *Vectors of Memory: Legacies of Trauma in Postwar Europe* (Oxford & New York: Berg, 1999), p. 188; Jacques Marseille and Carl Aderhold *et al.* (eds), *Journal de la France du vingtième siècle* (Paris: Larousse, 1999), p. 285; István Deák, Jan T. Gross and Tony Judt (eds), *The Politics of Retribution in Europe: World War II and Its Aftermath* (Princeton NJ: Princeton, University Press, 2000) – cover image on the paperback edition. Pascal Garnier's novel *Parenthèse* (Paris: Plon, 2004) also has a well-know *tondue* image on the front cover.
6. Brossat, *Les Tondues*, pp. 90–91, 233.
7. Clearly this is a larger cultural phenomenon of the sexual slippage in this French expression and the corresponding English expression 'to get into bed with' as a term for describing some form of corrupt cooperation with an enemy, though it is beyond the scope of this paper to consider the origins of such terms. Such expressions have often been used in invectives against collaborators, for instance in the trial of Robert Brasillach. See Alice Kaplan, *The Collaborator: The Trial and Execution of Robert Brasillach* (Chicago: University of Chicago Press, 2000), pp. 162–4.
8. Zelizer, *Remembering to Forget*; Ulrich Baer, *Spectral Evidence: The Photography of Trauma* (Cambridge, MA: MIT Press, 2002); Andrea Liss, *Trespassing Through Shadows: Memory, Photography, and the Holocaust* (Minneapolis & London: University of Minnesota Press, 1998), Janina Struk, *Photographing the Holocaust: Interpretations of the Evidence* (London & New York: I.B. Tauris, 2004); Susan Sontag, *On Photography* (London: Allen Lane, 1973); Susan Sontag, *Regarding the Pain of Others* (London: Penguin, 2003).
9. Baer, *Spectral Evidence*, p. 22.
10. Indeed visual representation of the French nation and republic as a feminine body is as old as the nation/republic itself. See Barbara Caine and Glenda Sluga, *Gendering European History* (London & New York: Leicester University Press, 2000), pp. 55–65; Maurice Agulhon, *Marianne au combat: L'Imagerie et la symbolique républicaines de 1789 à 1880* (Paris: Flammarion, 1979); also Joan Landes, *Visualizing the Nation: Gender, Representation, and Revolution in Eighteenth-Century France* (Ithaca & London: Cornell University Press, 2001).
11. Leah D. Hewitt, 'Vichy's Female Icons: Chabrol's *Story of Women*', in Melanie Hawthorne and Richard J. Golsan (eds), *Gender and Fascism in Modern France* (Hanover, NH: University of New England Press, 1997), pp. 156–74, here p. 161.

12. Francine Muel-Dreyfus, *Vichy et l'éternel féminin* (Paris: Seuil, 1996), Miranda Pollard, *Reign of Virtue: Mobilizing Gender in Vichy France* (Chicago: University of Chicago Press, 1998).
13. See Pollard, *Reign of Virtue*, p. 198.
14. François Rouquet, 'L'épuration, Résistance et représentations: quelques éléments pour une analyse sexuée', in Jacqueline Sainclivier and Christian Bougeard (eds), *La Résistance et les Français: enjeux stratégiques et environment social* (Rennes: Presses Universitaires des Rennes, 1995), pp. 285–94, here p. 287. Also Andrew Hewitt, 'Sleeping with the Enemy: Genet and the Fantasy of Homo-Fascism', in Hawthorne and Golsan, *Gender and Fascism in Modern France*, pp. 119–40.
15. In Robert Gildea, *Marianne in Chains: Daily Life in the Heart of France During the German Occupation* (New York: Picador, 2002), p. 3.
16. Kaplan, *The Collaborator*, pp. 162–64.
17. Virgili, *La France 'virile'*, p. 29.
18. Rouquet, 'L'épuration, Résistance et représentations', p. 294.
19. As depicted in one example of wartime graffiti painted on the outside of a *tondue's* house: '*Va te faire faire chez les boches!*' (Go get done in the German style), a play on the traditional slang expression which uses '*chez les grecs*' (in the Greek style) and approximates the English language expression 'Bugger off'. See Brossat, *Les Tondues*.
20. Virgili, *La France 'virile'*, p. 57.
21. Baer, *Spectral Evidence*, p. 9.
22. See Jay Winter, 'The Memory Boom in Contemporary Historical Studies', *Raritan* 21:1 (Summer 2001), pp. 52–67.
23. Alain Resnais and Marguerite Duras, *Hiroshima, mon amour* (France/Japan, 1959). See Nancy Wood, 'Memory by Analogy: Hiroshima mon amour', in Kedward and Wood (eds), *The Liberation of France*, pp. 309–21.
24. Henry Rousso, *Le syndrome de Vichy: 1944–198* … (Paris: Editions du Seuil, 1987), pp. 11–15.
25. Rousso, *Le syndrome de Vichy*, p. 20.
26. See Claire Gorrara, 'Une prise de conscience féministe? L'Occupation vue par les femmes écrivains en France après 1968', *Clio: Histoire, Femmes et Sociétés* 1 (1995), pp. 200–204. Evelyne Le Garrec, *La Rive allemande de ma mémoire* (Paris: Editions du Seuil, 1980). Marie Chaix, *Les Silences, ou la vie d'une femme* (Paris: Editions du Seuil, 1976).
27. Rousso, *Le syndrome de Vichy*, pp. 11–12.
28. Sontag, *On Photography*, p. 14.
29. Sontag, *Regarding the Pain of Others*, pp. 60, 100.
30. Virgili, *La France 'virile'*, p. 117, footnote 16.
31. Virgili, *La France 'virile'*, pp. 195–200.
32. Further archival research is necessary to substantiate this claim.
33. '*Ces photographies s'insèrent totalement dans le déroulement de la tonte, constituent l'événement autant que son témoignage*'. Virgili, *La France 'virile'*, p. 117.
34. Virgili, *La France 'virile'*, p. 96.
35. Brossat, *Les Tondues*, p. 14.
36. Brossat, *Les Tondues*, pp. 13–14.
37. Virgili, *La France 'virile'*, pp. 11, 12; Also: 'Rencontre avec Fabrice Virgili', Manuscrit.com, October 2001: <http://www.manuscrit.com/Edito/invites/Pages/OctHisto_Vigili.asp> (sic), accessed 28 September 2004.
38. See Rousso, *Le syndrome de Vichy*, pp. 233–86.
39. See Claire Gorrara, *Women's Representation of the Occupation in Post-'68 France* (London: Macmillan, 1998), pp. 12–15.
40. Adam Bernstein, 'The Acknowledged Master of the Moment', *Washington Post*, 5 August 2004, p. A01.
41. 'Carl Mydans, pioneer of the photo essay, dead at 97', *Sydney Morning Herald*, 19 August 2004; this question divided Cartier-Bresson from Moholy-Nagy, who claimed the impersonal stance of documentarian. Sontag, *On Photography*, p. 123.

42. In addition to works cited above, see Luc Capdevila, 'La "Collaboration sentimentale": antipatriotisme ou sexualité hors-normes? (Lorient mai 1945)', *Cahiers de l'institut du temps contemporain* 31 (2002). pp. 1–22; Luc Capdevila at Fabrice Virgili, 'Tontes et repression de la collaboration: un antiféminisme?' in Christine Bard (ed), *Un siècle de antiféminism* (Paris: Fayard, 1999), pp. 243–55; Fabrice Virgili, 'Les "tondues" à la Libération: le corps des femmes, enjeu d'une réappropriation', *Clio: Histoire, Femmes et Sociétés* 1 (1995), pp. 1–11; Françoise Leclerc et Michèle Weindling, 'La repression des femmes coupables d'avoir collaboré pendant l'Occupation', *Clio: Histoire, Femmes et Sociétés* 1 (1995), pp. 129–50; Karen Adler, 'Reading National Identity: Gender and "Prostitution" during the Occupation', in *Modern and Contemporary France* 7, 1999, pp. 47–57.
43. Virgili, *La France 'virile'*, p. 11.
44. Adler, 'Reading National Identity', p. 47; Virgili, *La France 'virile'*, p. 29; Leclerc and Weindling, 'La répression des femmes …', p. 132.
45. Virgili, *La France 'virile'*, p. 23.
46. Célia Bertin, *Femmes sous l'Occupation* (Paris: Stock, 1993), pp. 104–12.
47. Virgili, *La France 'virile'*, p. 42.
48. Virgili, *La France 'virile'*, pp. 10–15.
49. Virgili, *La France 'virile'*, p. 58.
50. See Brossat, *Les Tondues*, p. 29.
51. Marcel Ophuls, *Le Chagrin et la pitié: chronique d'une ville française sous l'Occupation*, part 2 (France, 1969–71).
52. Compare Gildea, *Marianne in Chains*, p. 5.
53. See Virgili, *La France 'virile'*, pp. 42, 50–52; Alison Moore, 'Female Flesh and Boundaries of the French Nation: A Theoretical Intervention into Recent Historiography of the "tondues"', in Stephan Atzert and Andrew Bonnell (eds), *Europe's Pasts and Presents* (Unley, SA: Australian Humanities Press, 2004), pp. 361–2.
54. Miranda Pollard, 'Whose Sorrow? Whose Pity? Whose Pleasure? Framing Women in Occupied France', in Hawthorne and Golsan (eds), *Gender and Fascism in Modern France*, pp. 145–8. See also Sian Reynolds, 'The Sorrow and the Pity, or Be Careful, One Train Can Hide Another', *French Cultural Studies* 1 (1990), pp. 149–59.
55. Ophuls did make another film in 1988, *Hôtel terminus*, which includes an interview with a woman who did undergo the *tonte*.
56. Ousby, *Occupation*, Illustration 14.
57. In some regions almost as many women were executed for collaboration as men, and the percentage of female collaborators executed increased significantly after January 1946. Leclerc and Weindling, 'La répression des femmes …', pp. 132–47.
58. Virgili, *La France 'virile'*, p. 74.
59. Virgili, *La France 'virile'*, p. 83.
60. Male *tondus* do appear in a rare number of photographs. See Brossat, *Les Tondues*, images between pp. 192–3.
61. A suggestion that requires further research to substantiate.
62. Carolyn J. Dean, *The Self and Its Pleasures: Bataille, Lacan, and the History of the Decentered Subject* (Ithaca & London: Cornell University Press, 1992), pp. 70–73. Victor Margueritte, *La Garçonne* (Paris: Flammarion, 1922).
63. Mary Louise Roberts, *Civilization without Sexes: Reconstructing Gender in Postwar France, 1917–1927* (Chicago & London: University of Chicago Press, 1994), pp. 69–72.
64. Jean-Yves Le Naour, 'Femmes tondues et répression des "femmes à boches" en 1918', *Revue d'Histoire Moderne et Contemporaine* 41 (2000), pp. 149–50.
65. See Adler, 'Reading National Identity', pp. 50–1. This dichotomy is clearly reflected in the writing of Bertin, *Femmes sous l'Occupation*, p. 112.
66. Brossat, *Les Tondues*, p. 19. For an insightful discussion of claims about images of suffering as 'pornographic', see Carolyn J. Dean, *The Fragility of Empathy after the Holocaust* (Ithaca & London: Cornell University Press, 2004), pp. 16–42.

67. Roland Barthes, *La Chambre claire: note sur la photographie* (Paris: Editions de l'Etoile, 1980), p. 15.
68. Barthes, *Chambre claire*, p. 54.
69. Barthes, *Chambre claire*, pp. 50–51.
70. Barthes, *Chambre claire*, pp. 73–8.
71. Bernard Fride, 'Henri Amouroux et l'histoire', *Le Monde Juif* 163 (1998), pp. 243–51.
72. Capdevila, 'La "Collaboration sentimentale"', pp. 7–8.
73. See Amouroux, *Joies et douleurs du peuple libéré*, photo caption between pp. 394–5. For critique, see Laurens, '"La femme au turban" …', p. 176. Herbert Lottman, *The People's Anger: Justice and Revenge in Post-Liberation France* (London: Hutchinson, 1986), p. 17.
74. See Brossat, *Les Tondues*, pp. 187–90, Virgili, *La France 'virile'*, pp. 195–200.
75. Virgili, *La France 'virile'*, pp. 123–8.
76. Virgili, *La France 'virile'*, p. 128.
77. This photograph appears in Jones, *The Cambridge Illustrated History of France*, p. 278; John Merriman, *A History of Modern Europe*, vol. 2: *From the French Revolution to the Present* (New York & London: W.W. Norton & Co., 1996), p. 1300. It is also commonly reproduced in the press. See Véronique Chauvin, 'Pourquoi les femmes tondues? Le châtiment des "collaboratrices horizontals"', *Evénement du jeudi*, 19–25 August 1993, pp. 80–82.
78. See Brossat, *Les Tondues*, pp. 85–6; Virgili, *La France 'virile'*, p. 56.
79. Régine Desforges, *La Bicyclette bleue* (Paris: Livre de poches, 1987). Bertin, *Femmes sous l'Occupation*, p. 100, states that the image of the genuine young woman who had the misfortune to fall in love with an enemy soldier was hardly true to reality.
80. Brossat, *Les Tondues*, p. 26.
81. On the complicity of the Capa photo in supporting a denial of the *tonte* as specifically gendered violence see Laurens, '"La femme au turban" …', p. 174.
82. Noted also by Brossat, *Les Tondues*; p. 26.
83. Much more violent and violating images can be found in Brossat, *Les Tondues*; Amouroux, *Joies et douleurs du people libéré* and Laurens, '"La femme au turban" …'.
84. Bertin, *Les femmes sous l'Occupation*, pp. 103–4.
85. István Deák, 'Introduction', in Deak, Gross and Judt (eds), *The Politics of Retribution in Europe*, pp. 1–13.
86. Tony Judt, 'The Past is Another Country: Myth and Memory in Postwar Europe', in Deak, Gross and Judt (eds), *The Politics of Retribution in Europe*, pp. 293–323.
87. See Baer, *Spectral Evidence*, p. 2.
88. Neil MacMaster and Toni Lewis, 'Orientalism: From Unveiling to Hyperveiling', *Journal of European Studies* 28 (1998), pp. 121–36.
89. Term borrowed from the title of: Eric Conan and Henry Rousso, *Vichy, un passé qui ne passe pas* (Paris: Gallimard, 1996).

7 A Glance into the Camera: Gendered Visions of Historical Photographs in Kaoko (North-Western Namibia)

Lorena Rizzo

On an early morning in June 1951 a group of fifteen men in a convoy of jeeps, trucks and vans left Windhoek heading for Kaokoveld reserve situated in the north-western part of what was then South West Africa. Among the group was Heinz Roth, a businessman and amateur photo-grapher. Roth had been charged to take photographs by the expedition's head, the Cape Town-based Bernard Carp, an adventurer, hunter and collector of Dutch origin.[1] Commissioned and financed by the Transvaal Museum, the King Williamstown Museum and National Museum of Southern Rhodesia, the expedition's purpose was the collection of flora and fauna.[2] In the course of the journey, Heinz Roth took more than 170 black and white photographs and produced a 16 mm film. Collecting left only a marginal imprint on Roth's visual production; photographs of animal and vegetal species would eventually make up a minimal proportion of the images. The camera was directed mainly towards Kaoko's landscape and people and towards the expedition as a social event in itself.[3] After several days' drive past the white farming area and a few scattered towns, the men would cross into the 'native reserve' and explore a territory beyond the so-called Police Zone or Red Line, beyond the margins of the white settler area. They would have the privilege of entering a region they perceived as inaccessible and unknown to all but a very few Europeans, where Africans lived according to their own 'customs'.[4] Indeed, their hopes and expectations were based on a vision of Kaoko rooted in a repertoire of colonial mythologies rather than in knowledge of the region, its inhabitants and their past.[5]

Mythology, more than history, shaped the vision of Kaoko far beyond the 1950s. It was only after Namibia's independence in 1990 that a post-Apartheid historiography began to emerge in the country. Even within this rapidly growing literature, Kaoko has remained on the margin. Far into the 1990s a South African Government publication, N. J. van Warmelo's *Notes on the Kaokoveld (South West Africa) and its People*, published in 1951, circulated as the main reference work on the region's history.[6] Kaoko continued to occupy, now within scholarship, a peculiar place associated with the persistence of African tradition rather than with the dynamics of historical change. Hence, it was anthropology (and the natural sciences) that determined the scholarly approach to Kaoko and its inhabitants, the Ovahimba. This anthropological approach went hand in hand with a continuously growing photographic coverage of Ovahimba people and a popularisation of Ovahimba culture beyond academic domains. In contemporary Namibia, images of Ovahimba and particularly of Ovahimba women, circulate both in commercial advertising and tourism and represent the country's cultural heritage to an outside audience.[7] The more a static vision of Kaoko and its inhabitants spreads, the less need there seems to be to explore the region's past.

To date, the historiography on Kaoko consists of scattered work by a small number of scholars and is far from being the subject of multi-vocal debate.[8] The focus of this essay is not to 'fill in the gap' in this historiography, but rather to explore a particular event through a very specific medium – historical photography. The shape of the narrative, emphasising some issues and neglecting others, is determined by the selection of photographs discussed. Background information is supplied correspondingly, depending on the historical contexts of the images.

The photographs taken by Heinz Roth in Kaoko in 1951 are kept in the National Archives of Namibia, as part of its photographic archive. Compared to the huge and well-known collection of photographs taken by C. H. L. Hahn in northern Namibia over three decades in the first half of the twentieth century, the Roth photographs seem at first sight of limited interest, if not ephemeral: they form a loose and relatively small corpus, neither systematised nor catalogued by the photographer, and accompanied by limited written documentation.[9] Roth spent a very short period in the region and was not known as a photographer or scientist, nor was he important within the colonial administration. Although the Carp expedition in general did gain some publicity, Roth's images were not included or recognised in it.

In the context of Namibian historiography and visual history in particular, it is precisely the de-contextualised, unsystematic and ephemeral state of the Roth collection that is more typical of archival resources than the exceptional ones, such as the Hahn collection. This is particularly true when it comes to the history of photography in Kaoko in the first half of the twentieth century, both in the period of German colonial rule (1884–1915) and under South African administration (1915–90). The photographs produced in the region were usually by-products of activities with a variety of other purposes, such as military control and policing (e.g. by Colonel Victor Franke in the early twentieth century), commercial exploration (by Julius Kuntz and Georg Hartmann in the 1910s), missionary work (Bernard Trey and Heinrich Vedder in 1914) or (pseudo)scientific documentation (the Denver Africa expedition in 1925 or N. J. van Warmelo in 1948), all of which involved non-professional photographers. Consequently, the question of whether and where these photographs were published and in what contexts they circulated remains.

The analysis consists of roughly two parts. First I sketch out some theoretical and methodological concerns within colonial visual history. The discussion tries to illustrate the kinds of problems we face when using colonial photographs in Namibian history in general and in an historical inquiry on Kaoko in particular. I contextualise Roth as a photographer within photographic activities in Kaoko in the first half of the twentieth century and specify some of the consumption spaces where the photographs were used. The second, larger part of the paper is concerned with an analysis of the photographs themselves. I explore the various genres and themes relevant to a visual narrative on Kaoko in that period. Beyond this thematic structure, the analysis of the photographs moves from an interpretation based mainly on archival material and historiography towards one that is predominantly informed by oral information on some of the photographs.

The way the photographs were framed by the photographer strongly suggests a specific interpretation of the images, as does the story of their circulation and eventual cataloguing within the archive. Yet visuals have a peculiar potential to draw attention to inconsistencies and fractures that blur these interpretative paradigms. The article explores these 'intermediate tones', although it necessarily follows the logics of Roth's gaze to an extent. While the written sources on Kaoko reinforce colonial historical narratives, contemporary Kaoko residents' engagement with the photographs allows alternative perspectives on people and places in the images to emerge.

Colonial photography in Kaoko[10]

The photographs of Heinz Roth discussed in this paper are 'colonial' – in the sense that they were taken by a member of the Namibian settler society in a reserve under colonial rule. This situation created observers and observed, subjects and objects. In a very material sense, it determined author – and ownership – and it structured the ways in which the images circulated and how they have been used, consumed and archived. A very fragmentary kind of information results from the trajectories of colonial photographs.[11] We may find out who the photographer was, when the images were taken and sometimes in what area, but there is often limited information on people in the images, let alone on the photographic situation, which might help to contextualise them. The analytical theme 'colonial photographs' does not suggest that these photographs were 'signature images' of a colonial practice or vision.[12] Visual representations from a colonial context – photographs or others – do emerge from and relate to particular truth regimes. They are shaped by uneven power relations and compulsory forms of knowledge production. But there is no predictability or inevitability in the dynamics of the relationship between photography and colonialism.[13] The potential meanings generated through these visual representations remain part of the story to be told.

Kaoko first experienced South African military intervention with Major Charles Manning's expeditions to the region in 1917 and 1919.[14] These expeditions were meant to disarm the local population, collect information about the region and its inhabitants and identify and involve local leaders in future administration. Manning's Kaoko tours resulted in voluminous reports on and photographs of Kaoko's natural features, strategic places and routes, local resources such as game, water and minerals, European presence and illegal hunting,[15] arms and potential political resistance and not least on the history and social organisation of the various 'tribes'.[16]

In 1923 northern Kaoko was divided into three reserves, meant to associate the population with three designated headmen. The identification of these three leaders, their claim to the control of people and land and their involvement in the colonial administration patterned the visual narrative of Kaoko.[17] One of them, Vita Tom, occupied the visual field most successfully, featuring prominently as a strong man with access to the main insignia of political and social status: numerous followers, arms, horses, cattle and women. From the beginning of South African rule he had managed to establish himself as the main political figure in the region. By attaining a privileged status vis-à-vis his immediate rivals, he won recognition by the administration as the only chief in the area.[18]

Throughout the 1920s, the administration gradually began to delineate the borders of the north-western reserve, yet colonial presence and rule in the region remained rather limited. The weakness of the colonial state corresponds to the few written sources and exceptionally scarce visual information from this period, consisting of scattered references in the governmental reports to the League of Nations.[19] A tiny but continuous photographic production, which may be labelled as the visual representation of Indirect Rule – based on two gendered narrative pillars, nature and natives – began to represent Kaoko in the 1930s.[20]

Individual men, represented as 'traditional' leaders and political authorities the administration relied on, were visually juxtaposed with groups of anonymous women, who signified the pre-modern cultural life in the northern areas.[21] Landscape photography naturalised the spatial structure of the territory and visually inscribed the reserve as an absent presence, enabling colonial rule without undermining African 'virgin' nature and culture. Paralleling this administrative narrative in the 1930s a further genre gradually emerged within the visual appropriation of Kaoko: the photo-safari.[22] In Kaoko it was mainly made up of privileged members of the southern African settler societies, usually men and seldom women, adventuring on hunting and leisure tours to the area.[23] The parallel itinerary of guns and cameras came into play here,[24] and both wildlife and hunting trophies prominently entered the visual field, evoking visions of colonial and settler masculinities.[25]

The photographer

Heinz Roth belonged to a German-speaking settler society tradition of amateur photographers who professionalised their photography in the context of scientific journeys and safari trips throughout colonial Namibia from the mid-1930s onwards. The importance of Kaoko as a destination for such travelling gradually increased in the decades following World War II. In contrast to neighbouring Owambo, where most Africans lived, the north-western part of Namibia, with a much smaller population, had not been a serious target of neither labour recruitment nor missionary expansion. Migrations from and to Kaoko, as well as trade with neighbours, had been increasingly difficult. Control was reinforced in 1946 when foot-and-mouth disease broke out in the region. Economic activities beyond ensuring subsistence were limited in the reserve, except for small-scale trade to southern Angola and eastern Owambo.[26]

The expedition led by Bernard Carp entered a frontier zone, which by the late 1940s was increasingly conceived of as 'Africa untamed'; as a place where African life allegedly developed untouched by modernisation and colonial economics. This perception of Kaoko resulted in a popularisation of the region as a consumption asset of the settler elite. The difficulties of overcoming administrative restrictions on 'white' access to the area only added to its appeal. Carp himself was denied permission to enter Kaoko on several occasions,[27] and it was only owing to the intervention of members of the settler community in Namibia that his project was recognised.[28] The administration's reluctance to open the way was rooted in distrust of the motivations and aims of groups of 'white' urban-based civilians wanting to venture on such tours. That the expedition, as planned by Bernard Carp, was at the same time a scientific, commercial and leisure enterprise only increased official suspicion.[29] Indeed, by the 1920s, this 'jumelage' of hunting, commerce and science had spread significantly in southern Africa.[30] Its photographic documentation acquired economic viability in a time of expanding institutionalised visual consumption. Carp's desire to have a proper and extended visual record of the expedition and to entrust Roth as photographer and filmmaker was linked not least to the museums' sponsorship of the expedition. The museums, as we shall see, provided a future market for the visuals – of people and of wildlife.

Social biographies of the Roth photographs

The involvement of South African museums as the funders of Carp's expedition to Kaoko is of particular relevance for what Elizabeth Edwards has called the social biographies of photographs; the term is intended to stress the use, circulation and archiving of images for the ways they become meaningful.[31] In the planning phase of the Kaoko tour, conflicts regarding the disposition of the expedition's material output emerged, as Roth and other Namibian-based participants stressed the need to prevent an exclusive South African profit. Yet, in the long run, uneven patterns of use emerged, at least with regard to the photographs. While Roth spread his images within the rather narrow space of his private networks and his expedition fellows, it was the South Africans and Europeans who successfully used the photographs in publications and in museums as arenas of public and popular expertise. Dennis Woods displayed the Roth photographs for talks at the Wildlife Protection Association; Bernard Carp did so during a number of lectures he gave in the Transvaal Museum, the Mountain Club in Cape Town and similar public and semi-public institutions, establishing himself as an expert with entrepreneurial flair.[32] Lawrence Green most prominently used the photographs in his widely read book *Lords of the Last Frontier*, published shortly after the tour in 1952.

Roth tried to commercialise his photographic activity and to establish himself as a professional photographer, yet his hopes of continuing his collaboration with Carp did not materialise.[33] This may have been one reason why he decided, by the late 1950s, to offer his photographic skills to the Southwest-African administration and ended up taking aerial photographs of the northern border rivers. Much later, in the 1970s, he deposited his photographic collection in various Namibian and European archival institutions, such as the Windhoek Scientific Society and the National Archives of Namibia.[34] As the photographs entered these institutions, processes of de-contextualisation and re-contextualisation commenced. In the National Archives the photographs were arranged in a cataloguing system in which photographs in general are made accessible in a uniform format, material appearance – as black and white positive prints – and numerical order. Heinz Roth's photographs have been furnished with captions, which synthesise information and knowledge available within the archives and are limited to the identification of the 'white' male members of the Carp expedition, often along with a general attribution of the images to the Kaoko reserve. As in the case of most visuals, the photographs have been separated completely from the written sources. These archiving procedures have further obliterated the inter-relatedness of the various documents and their historical conditions due to the specific representational strategies of the colonial state and selected members of the colonial society. As will be shown, discussions of the Roth photographs with residents of Kaoko blurred some of these archival constraints. The identification and naming of individuals, places and sites in the images interrupted their confinement to ethnographic and segregation narratives. On the other hand the photographs were re-contextualised and given new meanings, now within local memory and local historical narratives.

The photographs: nature and natives

As I mentioned above, both thematic foci and methodological concerns shape my selection and analysis of the nine photographs, eight of them from the Roth collection. While some photographs are related to written sources, others will be related to oral information. All the photographs discussed were shown to residents in Kaoko in 2001 and 2002, yet their reactions to the images varied significantly. While the photographs showing people, i.e. 1951 residents of Kaoko, sparked strong interest and animated debates, landscape photographs and those showing members of the Carp expedition were of less interest. My own concern with the social history of the region, rather than with issues of landscape or 'interracial' perception, enforced this selective approach to the images.

The Roth expedition photographs roughly followed two patterns of representation, an outward gaze, towards nature and Kaoko's 'native' population and an inward gaze, focused on the everyday nature of the expedition, that is, the male participants and their cars and trucks. Within these two strands, various genres are evident, suggested not least by the accompanying captions. 'Nature' includes panoramic views of open landscapes as well as focused framings of waterholes, single trees and sections of riverbanks, while 'natives' labels all photographs of local people, as individuals or groups. On the other hand, the expedition's journey itself is captured: images of single members of the expedition group, vestiges of earlier white presence such as ruins of colonial buildings or monuments, cars, lorries and roads reflecting the men's trajectories; hunting photographs are abundant. As will be shown, both visions were deeply interconnected, referring to each other implicitly and explicitly.

The main genre for representing nature visually is landscape. Landscape photographs are images of physical nature or space; they mediate specific visions of the natural world and express value and meaning.[35] Heinz Roth's photographs of natural spaces in Kaoko emerged in a post-war colonial context in which Kaoko's association with particular visions of landscape and its significance as a frontier zone strongly occupied the visual field. In fact, as a colonial periphery, the territory remained disputed and was claimed by various agents. Roth's landscape photographs responded to these local contests over the power to occupy and appropriate space and land – both physically and symbolically.[36] As we shall see, in the way they codify nature and space, these photographs can be interpreted as emblems of the social and particularly the gender relations concealed within them.[37]

Heinz Roth took a number of panoramic views of open landscapes (Figure 1). This photograph shows a vast grass plain lying in front of a

Figure 1: 'Mountain range at Sesfontein', Heinz Roth, 1951 (National Archives of Namibia) (NAN 2902).

massive mountain range forming the horizon; in between a subtle line of trees indicates a river. The grass, the structure of the mountain, the river and parts of a tree on the upper right-hand corner lead our eye in an ecliptic movement towards the right-hand frame of the image. There are no people, no animals – neither game nor stock, no visible signs of any economic or social activity. It is an empty land, natural scenery, lying calmly, passively, but wild and untamed before the viewer's eyes. Such a vision of a place makes viewers forget the presence of the camera, naturalising the image's frame by suggesting infinity of openness.[38] Vacant land is a well-known *topos* in imperial and colonial imagery, suggesting the absence of indigenous people and visualising territorial claims by the colonisers. Colonial spaces appear as if willing to be appropriated and occupied by particular groups – in southern Africa, ideally male settlers.[39] Correspondingly, these images are inflected with gendered discourses – written and visual – based on analogies between lands and women as objects of appropriation and control.[40] But this photograph by Roth allows further readings beyond the vision of an idealised disposable, conquerable female landscape. The photograph was taken at Sesfontein, on the southern margins of Kaoko and the river flowing through the plains is the Hoanib. Although the riverbed is dry most of the year, it is a site of permanent underground water flows and surface waterholes. The Hoanib traverses a huge mountain gorge before reaching the plains of Sesfontein and continuing westward down to the Atlantic coast. It roughly delineates the southern border of what was then considered to be Kaokoveld reserve[41] yet it also represents the trajectory of north–south migrations. In the early 1950s it was the most common way to reach Kaoko from the south or to leave the reserve going south. So the photograph is about borders and confinement and about movement and migration, its axes sketching out the frame for the emergence of colonial societies in the northern areas. It is the expression of a colonial discourse that was predominantly conceived of as male, affecting white and African men in particular. As a representative of settler society, Roth could claim the privilege of moving beyond the northern margins of the white settler area into what he may have considered a 'virgin African space', juxtaposing his mobility with that of African men, who were theoretically and ideologically confined to labour migration. River photographs have yet a further meaning, related to Kaoko's natural resources, namely water.

'Scenery near Onganga' is one of these images (Figure 2). A variety of vegetation, grasses and trees, mostly the palm trees, sketch the course of the river bed and its peculiar vegetation through stony, rocky lands. The photograph was taken at Onganga, a waterhole on the Hoarusib (Owaruthe) river in central Kaoko. Again, there are no people or

Figure 2: 'Scenery near Onganga', Heinz Roth, 1951 (NAN 2973).

animals in the image; it is at first view an image of a natural landscape with palm trees. We may – and should – argue for a romanticised vision of natural beauty, of fragile and peculiar vegetation in a semi-arid surrounding, devoid of any signs of disruption or civilisation – an idealised vision that eradicates the conflicts and contradictions of colonialism.[42] Besides being an image of a waterhole, it evokes the significance of the appropriation of water resources by southern African settler societies throughout the nineteenth and twentieth centuries.[43] Waterholes and water resources in general were knots of social and economic life and had a strong symbolic meaning, for both Africans and settlers.[44] The series of images by Heinz Roth sketches a topography of water sites that constitutes one matrix of symbolic appropriation of Kaoko as a space. The discursiveness of these photographs emerges from inter-visuality, from their cross-reference to other images, earlier photographs and paintings and, more importantly, maps and cartographic sketches. On one of the oldest South African maps of Kaoko, Major Manning's map, based on his tours through the region in 1917 and 1919, Onganga is indeed marked as the place of the palm trees on the Hoarusib River. Seen from this angle, Roth's landscape photographs anchor him in a genealogical line of male colonials appropriating Kaoko not only by military penetration, as in Manning's case, but increasingly through knowledge,[45] codified in the visual symbolism of a genealogy of interdependent images.

Roth's photographs of nature and space are characterised by the absence of Africans. They enabled Roth as a photographer to reassert himself as a settler and traveller in contrast to African men and women in the reserves. It is indeed in the way he represented women in Kaoko where these references become most striking, since it was women and particularly female bodies that mediated nature and stood at the centre of the settlers' visions of Kaoko as a contained landscape materialising in the post-war period. Roth's expedition photographs were taken during a period of transition. Kaoko was still considered to be a 'nature reserve' in contrast to neighbouring Owambo.[46] The shift towards a perception of the region as a 'native reserve' was made only gradually.[47] These parallel ideas influenced Roth's selection and visual documentation of themes.

The photographs of Kaoko residents in the collection fit only partially into contemporary visual discourses on African men and women in the colony. This is a result not least of the fact that the involvement of these men and women in the 'photographic occasions' (the interaction between photographer and photographed in a particular spatial and temporal setting) helped shape the visual output. At the centre of a photograph taken in Sesfontein in southern Kaoko, a group of women and children gathered close to a hut (Figure 3). In the background there are trees, a few scattered huts and a fence enclosing gardens or stock. On the far right, shadowy hills or mountain ranges mark the horizon. On the lower frame of the image a tiny shadow suggests the presence of a further person, probably the photographer. Neither the women nor the children seem to have been involved in any activity. This 'lack of action'

Figure 3: 'Owahimba women & children, Sesfontein', Heinz Roth, 1951 (NAN 2891).

was characteristic for ethnographic photography of women in Kaoko in the 1930s and 1940s. Roth took a whole series of such images, feeding into a repetitive genre and underlining the increasing exposure of women and their bodies to visual intrusion and observation.[48] There is a double repetition in this photograph. First, it relates to the aforementioned ethnographic narrative, in which women represent idealised signs of cultural continuity, of naturalised corporeality and inscriptions of a historical past. As such, culturalised women would guard and mediate the northern frontier.[49] This narrative guaranteed the images' value in colonial and international spaces of consumption.[50] Second, the image depicts a group instead of a single person. Picturing a group stresses the de-individualisation of these nameless women, who represent tribal or ethnographic types (see caption 'Owahimba women').[51] The staging of this tribal scene is further sustained by its domestic anchoring among children and huts. The social identity of the women inscribed through this photograph was a reproductive and objectified one. It defined them in relation to African men via the children and the domestic, andmale settlers, as potential objects of sexual fascination and of scrutinised observation.[52]

The intrusiveness of the camera becomes even more evident in the close-ups of some of the women in the group (Figure 4). Here Roth celebrated the visual mapping of the female bodies and enforced the scrutiny of his observing eye.[53] It is this blunt exposure of the power

Figure 4: 'Owahimba women', Heinz Roth, 1951 (NAN 2897).

relations that positioned the women as passive objects offering themselves to the camera and Roth as the observer with privileged control of the colonised body that makes these images crude. The slight and thievish presence of the photographer on the lower frame of the group image was indeed intended as a signature of his intrusive privilege. But what is somehow provocative about these photographs is that both the group and the single women did not return the gaze. Most of the women and children directed their view towards something or someone beyond the frame of the image. Heinz Roth confirmed that he was not supposed to take these photographs and that he hid his camera while he photographed the women.[54] This prohibition probably emerged from the general restriction placed on the Carp expedition, which limited them to interaction within a male sphere; contacts between expedition members and local women were to be supervised and controlled by local intermediaries.[55] The question of whether Roth considered the negotiation of a photographic encounter inappropriate or disturbing remains open to speculation. Whatever his attitude, there was no photographic occasion for this image in the sense of a negotiation between the photographer and the photographed. The women themselves were observing from a distance and probably directed their view towards Carp and his fellows. In such a situation, their gathering in front of the hut could be interpreted as a performance of collective strength and as a refusal to enter the visual field. The series of photographs taken by Roth in fact suggests that the overt photographic occasion, involving photographing the men, took place close to the women, beyond the frame of this photograph.

'Headmen of Kaoko Otavi' was taken in one of the main residential centres in central Kaoko (Figure 5). It shows a group of people gathered close to one of the many scattered trees structuring the open spaces of the stony grounds. The frame of this image is open, referring on both

Figure 5: 'Headmen of Kaoko Otavi', Heinz Roth, 1951 (NAN 2968).

sides to what lies beyond. The group included men and women of different ages, all dressed in 'European style' clothes. Their engagement with the camera varied; some of them returned the gaze directly, others seemingly ignored the photographer, others again directed their glances beyond the frame. This variety provides the image with a slight informality or non-staged atmosphere, a snapshot character. The photograph is part of a series Roth took in Kaoko Otavi consisting of portraits of single persons and groups in various constellations. In a few images, local people were joined by Bernard Carp and other members of the expedition. Photographs of groups of headmen in the reserves were widespread in the post-war era.[56] They contrast with earlier images of individual men, such as Vita Tom, who had occupied the visual field as cosmopolitan, powerful individuals owing their strength and influence to their control of various pre-colonial and early colonial resources. The headmen councils, however, very often consisted of men with differing bases of legitimisation; yet in the 1940s and 1950s most of them drew their authority from the colonial administration. In this context, Roth's photograph visualised the workings and functioning of an administrative system that guaranteed the diversification of power structures in the reserves and the emergence of a socially well-off political elite with access to Western commodities. In relation to the visual representation of women, such images made up the opposite pole in a narrative that pretended to modernise African societies without undermining traditional social structures. This change-in-continuity-discourse addressed both the growing international attention to South Africa's operations in its Namibian colony[57] and intra-Namibian control of remote African frontier spaces.[58] In this visual codification, the headmen, as the African counterparts to the colonial administration, mediate both African society[59] and the reserve as socially constructed space. These men provided Bernard Carp and his companions with information, with access to particular places and people and with the knowledge required to move through the area safely.[60]

Yet, the photograph somehow averts the evidential force of such an interpretation through its strong reference to what lies beyond its frame and especially through the presence of the two women on the right-hand margin of the image. The caption is misleading, since only some of the men in the photograph were in fact members of the headmen council in 1951. The council system in Kaoko had been introduced in the late 1930s and had been part of an effort to assimilate the system of indirect rule in this region to the one in neighbouring Owambo.[61] Yet this body, which through the 1940s included a growing number of men from the demarcated tribal areas within Kaoko, i.e., Herero, Himba and Tjimba, turned out to be unsuitable for administrative purposes.[62] In Kaoko Otavi local power plays and conflicts over access to natural and social resources became particularly virulent in the late 1940s, not least because of the deteriorating economic and ecological conditions.[63] Two main parties opposed each other. According to the administration's logic, the conflict was conceived in tribal terms, as one between Herero and Tjimba. What was at stake locally were questions of political and residential legitimacy going back to migrations into Kaoko in the early twentieth century as well as increased pressure on settlement options in the reserve due to colonial intervention in the late 1920s and 1930s.[64] From this perspective, the photograph becomes an expression of tribal politics, of Herero claims to authority and power. Correspondingly, a view beyond the frame of the image would refer to Tjimba residents of Kaoko Otavi – to that part of the population which in 1951 remained economically and socially disadvantaged because of its lack of access to Western commodities such as cloth, and which had no political representation on the headmen council.[65]

Yet, the presence of the women in the image raises questions. Their repeated appearance in several photographs from the Kaoko Otavi series suggests a social definition of the group rather than a political–administrative one. This line of argument is supported by oral information and the following identification of individuals in the images. Indeed, the group pictured was one of the families in Kaoko Otavi that were deeply involved in competition over local economic and political control in the late 1940s and early 1950s. The most prominent man in the photograph is second from the left, Katjitoha Thomas Mutate, who in 1951 had lost the colonial administration's recognition as headman, but who remained one of the leading economic and political figures in Kaoko Otavi.[66] The woman on the right is his wife Jogbeth Inazongara Unomuingo.[67] Viewed from this perspective, the photograph could be interpreted as a local performance of a socially, not tribally, based interest group, which included women and used the presence of the camera to visualise their political and residential claims.

The photographic occasions for the production of the images discussed above were determined by both colonial power relations,[68] and pre-existing visual narratives. Roth's photographs encode these discourses of power and rule, of observation and classification. They mirror the photographer's vision of African life in an African space, as well as his awareness of privileged access to the means of appropriating land and people both physically and discursively. As such these photographs contributed to elite visions of apartheid, providing the settler society with its geographical and symbolic frontiers.

Yet there was a further ingredient in the visual representation of Kaoko and its African population, namely images showing the expedition members, their cars and the symbols of white presence in the region. These images may have served to construct biographical or personal records in contrast to the ethnographic and landscape photographs. It will be shown that they were part of one and the same project of visual appropriation and representation, that the photographs reflected the internal gaze *and* constantly referred to the reserve and its people. They also visually inscribed, reproduced and enforced gender identities. Nevertheless, some of the photographs open up a space for alternative interpretations, as they allow fractured and contested visions of gender to unfold.

The internal gaze: photographs of the expedition

Roth's images of the expedition visually inscribed a whole range of settler society claims to Kaoko. First, they are about the physical and symbolic appropriation of land and natural resources. Kaoko had been the target of settler ambitions since the beginnings of colonial rule. Economic activities such as mining, agriculture, hunting and commercial trading, as well as white settlement, remained an issue up to the 1930s when an independent Kaoko native reserve was established.[69] Photographs of ruined abandoned farmhouses, of former military and police posts, of vestiges of explorers and adventurers figured prominently in Roth's series, as they did repeatedly in most photographic work on Kaoko from the 1930s onwards.[70] They sketched the settlers' visual literacy of the landscape and mapped a spatial structure of the region, identifying the nodes and coordinates of 'white' trajectories through the reserve.

There were other forms of penetrating and appropriating African spaces and resources too. 'White' mobility in the colony in the mid-twentieth century was ideally and symbolically connected to motorcars. In one image, Eberhard von Koenen, one of the expedition members, was sitting in a Jeep, dressed in leisure clothing, a briefcase on his left, holding up a rifle (Figure 6). The back of the car was loaded with boxes, probably containing expedition equipment or von Koenen's personal belongings. On the front of the car, we see a dead antelope skilfully fixed to the radiator. Cars were symbols and assets of male status and expressions of ruling-class identity in Namibia. In the 1950s they were the *sine qua non* of any tour to the northern areas, whether private or official. Indeed, providing the Jeep had been one of the material conditions of von Koenen's participation in the expedition.[71] It was cars and lorries that empowered Carp and his fellows symbolically to conquer and subdue the wilderness of Kaoko.[72] This photograph celebrates male

Figure 6: 'E. von Koenen with shot springbok', Heinz Roth, 1951 (NAN 2901).

physical force and male control of nature. Cars were part of the ritual of conquest, as much as arms and cameras were, especially when these technologies were put together in the field of hunting. Photographs of hunting trophies, such as the one here, were a popular genre of colonial rule and self-representation.[73] They symbolised the 'white' male elite's claim to a privileged ability to conquer space and exploit the land. The most significant rivals to this elite masculinity were Africans and particularly African men. Their absence from the photograph hides their likely involvement in the hunt and the arrangement of the trophy on the car. Furthermore, it is an absence negating Africans' involvement in game management and hunting[74] in the region, their access to arms and trading networks and their knowledge of game stocks.[75]

Some images produced by Roth show expedition members involved in leisure and pleasure activities (Figure 7). In this photograph Bernard Carp, Lawrence Green, Dennis Woods and Harry Hall were having a bath in a waterhole in central Kaoko. All appear to be more or less naked. The men's reaction to the camera varied; while Carp remained standing uncomfortably in the middle of the pool, Green and Hall protected themselves against the camera's intrusion into their intimacy by glancing towards each other. Woods immersed his body in the water. The image gave the waterhole an alternative significance – no more a site of social and political contest, but rather a locus of ease, pleasure and intimacy, a place where specific forms of male solidarity and

Figure 7: 'Water hole, Onganga, L. Green, B. Carp, H. Hall, D. Woods', Heinz Roth 1951 (NAN 2975).

familiarity could be played out, an environment of homosocial enjoyment.[76] We may argue that such tours to the northern areas enabled men to participate in a different set of gendered social relations: homo-eroticism, corporeal intimacy and an exposed vulnerability that might be coded feminine. Captured in their nakedness, the men appeared as fellows, regardless of any differences in their social and individual identity, willing to merge into an intimate collective ritual. Furthermore, their 'nakedness'[77] resonates with Roth's representations of naked bodies in Kaoko – those of Africans, particularly women. The authority of this image lies precisely in the presence of the 'white' men. Its visual statement about bodies and race operates through cross-reference to particular discursive contexts in which African nakedness functioned as a sign of primitivism and wilderness, while 'white' nakedness signified socially controlled body performance within modern society. On the other hand, by placing a harmonious leisure activity in an area determined by the daily political, social and economic struggles of its inhabitants, the image gains significance as a representation of elite exclusiveness and arrogance of power. This line of argument is reinforced if we compare the photograph with other images in which Roth placed the men in harmony with a peaceful environment, in a condition of complete bourgeois satisfaction with themselves and their world. Therein, Roth masterfully relied on repertoires such as reading, writing, painting and 'proper' clothing, which were of particular interest to the urban-based, cosmopolitan settler elite, distinguishing them from uncivilised wild Africans (and Boers) from the bush. Eventually, we see images of Eberhard von Koenen painting, of Lawrence Green meditating, or of the group, dressed for dinner, enjoying their meal near a nightly fire.

Gendered visions: discussing the Roth photographs in 2002[78]

Heinz Roth's photographs, like most colonial photography produced in Kaoko, were not intended for consumption in the region, but for private and public audiences within the Namibian and southern African settler societies. Although the Roth photographs were used by various members of the Carp expedition and in various institutions, ending up in a number of Namibian archives, they did not circulate within the region.[79] In 2002 we showed the Roth photographs in a small exhibition in Sesfontein[80] and discussed them with interviewees in Sesfontein and Kaoko Otavi. The aim was to identify people and places in the photographs and to find out more about the photographic occasions from which these images resulted. Furthermore, questions of circulation and accessibility of images in the region and the role of photographs in local personal archives were taken up. Central to discussions was that interviewees used the photographs as points of departure to comment and reflect on normative narratives and on the role of visuals in recording and representing the past and to place themselves in particular contexts. Two points are of importance here. First, showing the Roth photographs to Kaoko residents, who would have had personal relationships to the people in the images,[81] or would know places and sites Roth had captured with his camera, does not mean that the images were returned to an 'original' context. It was rather a re-contextualisation, a reframing of the visuals in new and alternative interpretations, a further chapter in the social lives of these photographs.[82] It was not a point of closure, but one of opening. Second, the aim is not to juxtapose a visual narrative on the past with an oral one.[83] Roth's photographs did not simply deliver historical evidence, nor did the information given during the interviews necessarily correspond with knowledge of the past.[84] Using the photographs in interviews was about exploring the potentials of images to take on various meanings. An exposure of the Roth images to debates within the region, even though rather limited by the interview situation, opened up ways to alternative, not authentic, 'readings' and to reflections on both the contingencies and the hierarchies of different forms of representing the past.

Missionary Heinrich Vedder took a number of photographs in Kaoko Otavi during his stay in 1914 and published them in 1928 in *The Native Tribes of South West Africa*.[85] This book is an example of how images used in interviews become representational resources in a context of conflicting visions of the past and in attempts to have male individuals especially recognised in historical accounts.

The caption to one photograph in particular identifies a figure in a trio of men as 'Tjimba headman'. This photograph was not part of the collection we showed during the interviews, but emerged as a photocopy in the course of our discussions with some of the local men.[86] One of the main issues in these interviews had been conflicts in Kaoko Otavi emerging in the aftermath of immigration to the region from southern Angola in the late 1910s and 1920s. In Kaoko Otavi the immigrants met an impoverished population that had just begun to recover from decades of extended raids in the region and which was slowly building up herds again.[87] Yet this process of re-pastoralisation was interrupted by the arrival of well-armed immigrants with comparatively large herds of animals. It eventually led to the expulsion of the old political elite by invading young men who,[88] taking advantage of Portuguese colonialism in southern Angola, had built up political, social and economic capital and managed to take control over their new place of residence.[89] In the consolidation of their claim to local power, they skilfully used options resulting from the gradual establishment of a colonial administration in the region. During South African colonialism these conflicts over diverging historical experiences, economic inequalities and local political control were transformed into inter-ethnic rivalries, resulting in an antagonistic discourse of 'Tjimba' subordination and 'Herero' overrule. In contemporary debates over the past and in post-independence power struggles within Kaoko, these issues continue to play an important role.

The Roth photographs picture members of the so-called Herero elite, including the above-mentioned Katjitoha Thomas Mutate, exclusively. The images reflect uneven access to the colonial state, to settler society and to forms of representation within colonial Kaoko.[90] By introducing the photocopied Vedder photograph, the local people could make statements challenging the dichotomies and hierarchies structuring local politics, identity and ethnicity. In contrast to perceptions and representations of so-called Tjimba as that group in Kaoko Otavi without access to European commodities or to economic wealth, education and political power,[91] male interviewees used the photograph of 1914/1928 as a visual reinforcement of their own oral representation of the past. It became an image blurring the dominant narratives that conceptualise the history of Kaoko Otavi in ethnic terms and along the axis of rulers and ruled. Starting from the photograph, the men unfolded male genealogies explaining the immigration as a result of their rivals' family networks. They attributed the political power plays to generational rather than ethnic conflict.[92] The existence of a photograph of Tjongoha (also known as Hinunu), taken by one of the most prominent missionaries in South West Africa and published in various books,[93] and his identification as 'Tjimba headman' made him a relevant historical agent, who, among other things, stood for an early engagement with forms of visual self-representation. A comment by one of the local residents of Kaoko Otavi in 2002 underlined this concern: 'When the missionary came he made Tjongoha chief by taking a photograph of him'.[94]

Beyond the narratives of big men's political careers, the photographs could also suggest other ambiguous perceptions of these prominent male figures. The women particularly used alternative readings of the photographs to question the status and popularity of headmen and chiefs, both in the past and in current historical debates. Indeed, they remembered the shifts in the social organisation of gender relations that had resulted from the increasing formalisation of power and the involvement of male members of the community in colonial policies.[95] The women interviewed stressed increasing control over their mobility, their labour and their reproductive functions.[96] The re-intensification of raids in Kaoko caused by immigration from southern Angola put young women at particular risk since they were one of the targets of these assaults.[97] The photographs of prominent men became emblems of early colonial male rule and the privileging of men within colonial society. On the other hand, the fact that women in the visual field were not identified as individuals – as in most colonial representations of Kaoko[98] – mirrors the ideological programme that gradually assigned women to the domestic and reproductive sphere, to the role of collective representatives of 'tribal' life bound to the reserve.[99] Nevertheless, the analogy between political and economic status, performed visually by men such as Vita Tom, was questioned and challenged by reconstructing the strategies of women in the 1920s and 1930s to acquire wealth and social status in sites other than colonial structures such as the administration, the military or the mission.[100]

Discursive ambiguities concerning the role of women and their historical experiences in colonial Kaoko developed around various photographs, such as the portrait of a woman near Kaoko Otavi (Figure 8).[101] She was riding a donkey and was part of a group including a man and another woman, with the second woman on foot. In the interviews this image was used to take up issues of gender and mobility, ownership of horses and donkeys and reasons for travelling within and beyond Kaoko. The construction, by both men and women, of riding and

Figure 8: 'Woman with child (Herero), on donkey', Heinz Roth, 1951 (NAN 2984).

long-distance mobility as a male activity or as one confined to groups living in other areas was reflected in one interviewee's comment on the image: 'The woman is not from our place. Women did not ride on horses in those days'.[102] Indeed, throughout the colonial period, mobility had been gradually restricted. Colonial policy tried to limit men's mobility to labour migration and to prevent the migration of women altogether. Travel permits and passes issued to women in the 1930s and 1940s usually named private reasons for travelling, such as medical examinations or funerals,[103] and only a few men left the region to look for work.[104] Furthermore, discourses constructing African societies in the reserves as static and the inhabitants of Kaoko as particularly reluctant to engage with 'modern life' – i.e. with labour migration[105] – increasingly fed into the implementation of laws restricting migration. Uneven options and varied forms of moving and travelling in the region were the result; gender was one factor determining them, place of residence another. The reference to women from other areas in the interviews may be interpreted as the local reproduction of a normative discourse on women. In addition, the association of the woman in the photograph with southern Kaoko and particularly Sesfontein, neighbouring the settler area, reflected that locality's closer access to employment, trading partners, commercial commodities and to donkeys, the most widespread means of transport in the 1950s.[106] In a local context, Roth's photograph unintentionally opened up counter-narratives to exclusive 'white' mobility in the region and enabled interviewees to engage with a social history of African mobility.

At the same time, gendered narratives about female mobility emerged. The women we interviewed in fact concentrated less on the donkey than on the woman's appearance and the caption, labelling her as a 'Herero' woman. Repeatedly stating that Herero dress was far from 'traditional' in 1951, they questioned the ethnic classification model, which would make daily dress into a cultural marker.[107] In contrast, the women stressed the socio-economic significance of European-style dress in Kaoko in the 1950s. Access to cloth and similar commodities had become increasingly difficult and not least a question of availability of cash. In this view, Heinz Roth's photograph referred to a particular form of mobility, namely a social one: the woman in the photograph was first of all someone considered to be wealthy.[108] The clothing style of the woman induced the interviewees to place the image in the contexts of education and Christianisation, of independent local churches and the resulting social options for women. European-style clothes would then suggest an association with Christians. In the early 1950s, Christianity was less bound to missions than to a social network of independent evangelists and teachers who supplied the congregations in the region with religious services, but also with products and goods not available locally.[109]

Using photographs in Namibian history

Historical photographs are visual enunciations about the past. They can be interpreted as documents, as material products resulting from a social interaction, or as an encounter between photographer and photographed at a particular moment in time. Yet, it is an asymmetrical relationship, dictating the terms under which subjects get access to the means and mode of production and objects are constituted within particular knowledge regimes. Heinz Roth used his privileged status as a member of Namibian settler society to enter a northern 'native' reserve and the technology of the camera to unfold his vision of Kaoko and its African population. At the same time, Roth positioned himself as a 'white' man in relation to African men and women, reproducing and reinforcing the political and social organisation of colonial Namibia, increasingly coming under pressure in the post-World War II period.

I have examined Heinz Roth's production of photographs in order to analyse their historical relevance and the ways his camera sketched the field of documentation and representation. I have argued that colonial photography in Kaoko, as it developed during the first half of the twentieth century, was bound to the dynamics of colonial appropriation and control of a region and a society, both of which were gradually being transformed by the needs of an emerging colonial state. This context of production gave the images a pattern that made them meaningful and 'readable' to their intended local and international audiences. Photographs functioned as ever-realistic, authentic and immediate signs of a genuine African space, which increasingly threatened to disappear behind the veils of modernity and African emancipation. Nevertheless, the Roth photographs do not merge into a coherent narrative of colonialism and the coming of apartheid. Their potential meanings are multiple and open, historically suggestive but not clear. It is this ambiguity and openness of the images that conceals the agency of the photographed, the men and women returning the gaze of Roth and his camera. Indeed, historical photographs, both as material objects and as forms of representation, can be understood as contested grounds of social interaction, raising questions about the accessibility and use of the medium by various agents involved. The photographic occasions from which the photographs of Heinz Roth emerged depended on the social relations that framed the moment of production. Therein lay the vulnerability of women in front of the camera, their exposure to visual scrutiny and objectification mirrored their increased marginalisation in colonial Kaoko by the mid-twentieth century. Although Roth's hidden camera expresses the limitations and constraints limiting Africans' – women's – ability to determine the terms of the visual encounter, there were moments of refusal, of active resistance to the camera and the colonial gaze. The hierarchies underlying the production of the photographs continued to affect their circulation and consumption. The photographs of Heinz Roth travelled through time and space, moving between private and public spaces of consumption, but always remaining beyond the borders of Kaoko. It is this history of colonial decontextualisation and dominance of the images and their interpretation, their closure within the archive, which creates the need to recontextualise historical photographs in local, oral narratives about the past.

Notes

My thanks for support of research done in Namibia in 2001–2 go to the Schweizerische Nationalfonds; Jeremy Silvester, University of Namibia; Patricia Hayes, University of the Western Cape; and the National Archives of Namibia. Giorgio Miescher and Dag Henrichsen of the Basler Afrika Bibliographien have critically contributed to discussions on this article from the beginning.

1. Roth was a soil inspector for the South African administration. Interview with Heinz Roth, Windhoek, 18 March 2002. The fifteen members include only the 'white' men. Several 'coloured and native' skinners and 'camp servers' took part in the expedition. Lawrence Green, *Lords of the Last Frontier* (Cape Town: Howard Timmins, 1952), pp. 12, 27. With one exception, Green, also an expedition participant, does not mention the guides and translators Carp and his fellows relied on at all.
2. B. Carp to Dr Martin, Windhoek Museum, 10 November 1949; B. Carp to the secretary of SWA, 21 February 1951. National Archives of Namibia (NAN), Windhoek, Accession 340.
3. There are 172 photographs on Kaoko in the NAN Roth collection. Roth gave some of his photographs to the Scientific Society in Windhoek and to the Wolfskehlen/Rietstadt, Hessen library in Germany where his ex-wife lived. Interview with Heinz Roth, Windhoek, 18 March 2002. Most of the photographs are images of local people (43) and their houses (8), or of the natural environment (53). Only three are of animal species and plants. Thirty-eight depict the members of the Carp expedition and their cars. The rest (28) are images of colonial monuments, of game and of colonial personnel. It has not been possible to trace a copy of the film in NAN, the South African Film Archives, or the Transvaal Museum.
4. The rarity of 'whites' entering Kaoko in 1951 is confirmed by von Koenen, one of the expedition members. See Heidi and Eberhard von Koenen, *Das alte Kaokoland* (Göttingen, Windhoek: Klaus Hess Publishers, 2004), p. 13.
5. For a detailed discussion of the Kaoko myth, see the editors' 'Epilogue', in Giorgio Miescher and Dag Henrichsen (eds), *New Notes on Kaoko: The Northern Kunene Region (Namibia) in Texts and Photographs* (Basel: Basler Afrika Bibliographien, 2000), pp. 237–45.
6. N. J. Van Warmelo, *Notes on the Kakaoveld (South West Africa) and its People* (Pretoria: Government Printer, 1951).
7. Giorgio Miescher and Dag Henrichsen, 'Foreword', in *New Notes on Kaoko*, pp. vii–xi, here p. vii.
8. See Michael Bollig, 'The Colonial Encapsulation of the North-Western Namibian Pastoral Economy', *Africa* 68 (1998), pp. 506–36; Michael Bollig, 'Zur Konstruktion ethnischer Grenzen im Nordwesten Namibias: Ethnohistorische Dekonstruktion im Spannungsfeld zwischen indigenen Ethnographien und kolonialen Texten', in Heike Behrend and Thomas Geider (eds), *Afrikaner schreiben zurück: Texte und Bilder afrikanischer Ethnographen* (Cologne: Rüdiger Köppe, 1998), pp. 245–74; Michael Bollig and Tjakazapi Janson Mbunguha, *'When War Came the Cattle Slept–': Himba Oral Traditions* (Cologne: Rüdiger Köppe, 1997). Steven van Wolputte, 'Subject Disobedience: The Colonial Narrative and Native Counterworks in North-western Namibia, ca. 1920–75', *History & Anthropology* 15 (2004), pp. 151–73, generally follows Bollig's argument.
9. Interview with Heinz Roth, Windhoek, 18 March 2002.

10. On the history of photography in Kaoko see Michael Bollig and Heike Heinemann, 'Nomadic Savages, Ochre People and Heroic Herders: Visual Presentations of the Himba of Namibia's Kaokoland', *Visual Anthropology* 15 (2002), pp. 267–312; Michael Bollig and Heike Heinemann, 'Visual Presentations of the People and Land of North-western Namibia in German Colonial Times', in Wolfram Hartmann (ed.), *Hues between Black and White: Historical Photography from Colonial Namibia 1860s to 1915* (Windhoek: Out of Africa, 2004), pp. 259–78, dealing mainly with cartography; Patricia Hayes, 'Camera Africa: Indirect Rule and Landscape Photographs of Kaoko, 1943', in Miescher and Henrichsen, *New Notes on Kaoko*, pp. 48–73, on the photographs of C. H. L. Hahn.
11. See Patricia Hayes and Andrew Bank, 'Introduction', *Kronos*, Special Issue: Visual History 27 (2002), pp. 1–14.
12. Elizabeth Edwards, *Raw Histories: Photographs, Anthropology and Museums* (Oxford: Berg, 2001), p. 12.
13. Patricia Hayes, Jeremy Silvester and Wolfram Hartmann, 'Photography, History and Memory', in Wolfram Hartmann, Jeremy Silvester and Patricia Hayes (eds), *The Colonising Camera: Photographs in the Making of Namibian History* (Cape Town and Athens, OH: University of Cape Town Press and Ohio University Press, 1999), pp. 2–9, here pp. 4–6.
14. NAN ADM 156 W32, 'Report on Kaokoveld by Major C. Manning (Resident Commissioner Ovamboland)', 15 November 1917; NAN SWAA 2516, 'Report by Major C. N. Manning re. Second Tour Kaokoveld; Disarmament; General', 25 August 1919.
15. See NAN ADM 139 C74, 'Illicit trading of Portuguese subjects'; NAN A 450, Manning to secretary of South West Africa, 4 October 1921.
16. The main issue preoccupying the South African military administration and the few settlers in the early years were rumours of armed conflicts in Kaoko – a potential threat to colonial rule. NAN OCT 17 ZI, 'Native unrest Zessfontein'. Although immigration into the region from Angola in the 1910s did cause political friction, fears of armed resistance in the north were limited to Kaoko and reflected the unsteadiness of colonial rule and control in this period.
17. In 1925 the Denver African expedition made a short trip to Kaoko, which resulted in images taken in Kaoko Otavi, some of which have been published in Robert J. Gordon, *Picturing Bushmen: The Denver African Expedition of 1925* (Athens, OH: Ohio University Press, 1997).
18. NAN SWAA 2516, Major Eadie to the secretary of the protectorate, 20 March 1919; NAN NAO 28, NC Ovamboland to NC Windhoek, 3 May 1928.
19. Union of South Africa, *Reports Presented by the Government of the Union of South Africa to the League of Nations Concerning the Administration of South West Africa* (Pretoria: Government Printer, 1921–39). The publication of photographs in these reports started in 1926.
20. On the homology of nature and natives for the photography of C. H. L. Hahn, see Patricia Hayes, 'Northern Exposures: The photography of C. H. L. Hahn, Native Commissioner of Ovamboland 1915–1946', in Hartmann, Silvester and Hayes (eds), *The Colonising Camera*, pp. 171–87. For a history of the *topos* of nature and natives in European thinking about overseas societies and regions from the sixteenth century onwards, see Wolfgang Marschall, *Klassiker der Kulturanthropologie: Von Montaigne bis Margaret Mead* (Munich: Beck, 1990).
21. Hayes, 'Northern Exposures', p. 178.
22. See e.g. F. Nink, 'Auf Wildfährten im Kaokoveld', *Meinerts Monatsmagazin* 6 (1930), pp. 259–74.
23. On adventure travel by German-speaking settlers to north-western Namibia see Dag Henrichsen, 'Pilgrimages into Kaoko: Herrensafaris, 4x4s and Settler Illusions', in Miescher and Henrichsen (eds), *New Notes on Kaoko*, pp. 159–85.
24. Motorised hunting and photographic trips or safaris emerged as a settler activity in East Africa during the 1930s and became popular in Namibia during the 1950s. See Henrichsen, 'Pilgrimages into Kaoko', p. 164.
25. See Hayes, 'Northern Exposures', pp. 173–4; Wolfram Hartmann, 'Performing Gender, Staging Colonialism: Camping it up/Acting it out in Ovamboland', in Hartmann, Silvester and Hayes (eds), *The Colonising Camera*, pp. 156–63. Hartmann does not unfold the

entanglement of colonial masculinity – and homoeroticism – with big game hunting, even though the photographs he discusses would be very suggestive in this context.
26. NAN SWAA 1168, Vol. 3; NAN NAO 61 12/3.
27. NAN A 340, Bernard Carp to Heinz Roth, 30 January 1950 and 14 March 1950.
28. Mainly Heinz Roth, Eberhard von Koenen and a representative of the Windhoek Museum, Dr Martin. NAN A 340, B. Carp to Dr Martin, 3 March 1950 and Carp to the secretary of SWA, 26 April 1951.
29. NAN A 340, Bernard Carp to Heinz Roth, 9 May 1951. Roth confirmed that they shot at least one animal per day. Interview with Heinz Roth, Windhoek, 18 March 2002. The multiple interests and agendas of the Carp expedition are reinforced by von Koenen. Heidi and Eberhard von Koenen, *Das alte Kaokoland*, pp. 14–16.
30. Paul Landau, 'Empires of the Visual: Photography and Colonial Administration in Africa', in Paul Landau and Deborah Kaspin (eds), *Images and Empires: Visuality in Colonial and Postcolonial Africa* (Berkeley: University of California Press, 2002), pp. 147–71.
31. Edwards, *Raw Histories*, p. 12.
32. NAN A 340, Bernard Carp to Heinz Roth, 13 November 1951.
33. NAN A 340, Bernard Carp to Heinz Roth, 14 May 1950.
34. Interview with Heinz Roth, Windhoek, 18 March 2002. It has not been possible up to now to reconstruct archiving strategies in the Namibian institutions mentioned. It seems to have been common for settlers to deposit collections in various institutions. Information given by Werner Hillebrecht, NAN archivist, March 2003.
35. Peter Burke, *Augenzeugenschaft: Bilder als historische Quellen*, tr. Matthias Wolf (Berlin: Wagenbach, 2003), p. 49 English language original, Peter Burke, *Eyewitnessing: The Uses of Images as Historical Evidence* (Ithaca: Cornell University Press, 2001); W. J. Thomas Mitchell, 'Imperial Landscape', in W. J. Thomas Mitchell (ed.), *Landscape and Power* (Chicago: University of Chicago Press, 1994), pp. 5–34, here p. 17.
36. For a similar point for landscape images in the Cape Colony in the 1820s, see David Bunn, '"Our Wattled Cot": Mercantile and Domestic Space in Thomas Pringle's African Landscapes', in Mitchell (ed.), *Landscape and Power*, pp. 127–74.
37. Mitchell, 'Imperial Landscape', p. 17.
38. Edwards, *Raw Histories*, p. 120.
39. See Bunn, 'Our Wattled Cot', even though the author does not elaborate on gender.
40. See Nink, 'Auf Wildfährten'; Green, *Lords of the Last Frontier*, pp. 37–9; H. W. Stengel, 'Eine kleine Landeskunde des Kaokoveldes', *Die Muschel: Ein Almanach für das Jahr 1966* 1 (1966), pp. 29–9. Most authors compare Kaoko to female protagonists from fairytales, such as Sleeping Beauty. For a detailed analysis of written discourses on Kaoko, see Giorgio Miescher, 'Epupa, Kaoko, Namibia: Analyse einer öffentlichen Debatte im postkolonialen Namibia – Kontinuitäten und Diskontinuitäten kolonialer Konzepte', unpublished master's thesis, Basel University, 1997.
41. NAN SWAA 1168 Vol. 2, Gov. Notice No. 374 of 1947, in the official Gazette No. 1331, 4 November 1947.
42. For a broader discussion see Mitchell, 'Imperial Landscape', p. 21.
43. See William Beinart, 'African History and Environmental History', *African Affairs* 99 (2000), pp. 269–302, here p. 272.
44. Dag Henrichsen, 'Herrschaft und Identifikation im vorkolonialen Zentralnamibia: Das Herero- und Damaraland im 19. Jahrhundert', unpublished doctoral thesis (University of Hamburg, 1997) pp. 54–8.
45. A similar point regarding America in the 1860s and 1870s is in Joel Snyder, 'Territorial Photography', in Mitchell (ed.), *Landscape and Power*, pp. 175–201.
46. Hayes, 'Camera Africa', pp. 53–4.
47. Giorgio Miescher and Lorena Rizzo, 'Popular Pictorial Constructions of Kaoko in the Twentieth Century', in Miescher and Henrichsen (eds), *New Notes on Kaoko*, pp. 10–47, here pp. 28–9.

48. This increased prominence of women in the visual representation of Kaoko became particularly strong in the 1950s. Miescher and Rizzo, 'Popular Pictorial Constructions', p. 30.
49. Hayes, 'Camera Africa', p. 72, makes this point generally for Africans in a culturally undisturbed state.
50. Both an intra-Namibian and an international audience played a role in the post-war era. Silvester, Hayes and Hartmann, 'This Ideal Conquest', p. 16. For a more general discussion of the spaces where ethnographic photographs were consumed, see John Tagg, *The Burden of Representation: Essays on Photographies and Histories* (Basingstoke: Macmillan, 1988), p. 71.
51. See Landau, 'Empires of the Visual', p. 56, which describes a 'double alienation' of women as Africans and as women.
52. NAN A 340, Bernard Carp to Heinz Roth, 13 November 1951. Carp asks Roth to send him particular photographs, describing one in a rather symptomatic manner: 'Herero girl with Cori (enormous breast)'.
53. Tagg, based on Foucault, extensively discusses observation of the body as a form of institutional and state control and surveillance. John Tagg, *The Burden of Representation*, pp. 83–7. My point here is that the observation of female bodies and their visual representation have to be seen both as reflecting male colonial fantasies of female sexuality and within a context of colonial rule, control and supervision.
54. Interview with Heinz Roth, Windhoek, 18 March 2002.
55. Interviews with Alfred Nai-Khaib, Sesfontein, 21 December 2001; Emily Kazombaruru Kavari, Kaoko Otavi, 9 January 2002.
56. Silvester, Hayes and Hartmann, 'This Ideal Conquest', p. 16.
57. See Tony Emmett, *Popular Resistance and the Roots of Nationalism in Namibia, 1915–66* (Basel: PSP Publishing, 1999), pp. 250–6.
58. Hayes, 'Camera Africa', p. 61.
59. Hayes, 'Camera Africa, p. 70.
60. See Green, *Lords of the Last Frontier*, pp. 36–65.
61. The native commissioner C. H. L. Hahn wrote extensively on this issue in his regular reports to the secretary of South West Africa, e.g., NAN NAO 20, Hahn's monthly report February and March 1938, 30 March 1938.
62. From the beginning the council system caused problems for the administration. It was mainly the groups and headmen living on the region's southern and north-western margins who refused to attend meetings or to implement administrative requests. For example, NAN NAO 29 24/2 Sgt. du Buisson to Hahn, 2 July 1937; 24/4 Sgt. du Buisson to Hahn, 5 January 1938.
63. NAN SWAA 2513, NC Ondangua to CNC, Inspection Report: Kaokoveld Native Reserve, 10 October 1949. The monthly and annual reports on Kaoko contain information on increasing pressure on natural resources, droughts and famine and restrictions to mobility, trade and economic activities within the reserve. NAN SWAA 2513 & SWAA 1168.
64. Particularly the forced removals of inhabitants of southern Kaoko to the central areas; NAN NAO 29 24/1/3.
65. This was the case up to the late 1940s and early 1950s, when complaints were increasingly raised by the 'Ovatjimba' community in Kaoko Otavi, finally leading to the administration appointing their representatives to the headmen council. See NAN SWAA 2513, minutes of a headmen meeting at Opuwo, 16 April 1952 and NAO 51 3/8, NC Ondangua to CNC Windhoek, 3 August 1953.
66. Green describes him as one of the wealthiest men in Kaoko Otavi. Green, *Lords of the Last Frontier*, pp. 50–1.
67. Interview with Solomon Hartley and Rahimiz Hartley, Oruwandjai, 11 January 2002. The women in the photographs were identified by several people present at the interview, yet it was particularly Solomon Hartley's sister, Rahimiz Hartley, who recognised most people in the photographs.

68. See Martha Rosler, as quoted in Abigail Solomon-Godeau, 'Wer spricht so? Einige Fragen zur Dokumentarfotografie', in, Herta Wolf and Susanne Holschbach (eds), *Paradigma Fotografie: Fotokritik am Ende des fotografischen Zeitalters*, vol. 2: *Diskurse der Fotografie* (Frankfurt a.M.: Suhrkamp, 2003), pp. 51–74. English language original: Abigail Solomon Godeau, 'Who Is Speaking Thus? Some Questions about Documentary Photography', in *Photography at the Dock* (Minneapolis: University of Minnesota Press, 1991), pp. 86–102.
69. NAN LAN 36 80, report on Kaoko, January 1926, NAN NAO 45 45/1, Hahn to CNC, 22 December 1938.
70. Miescher and Rizzo, 'Popular Pictorial Constructions', p. 36.
71. NAN A. 340, Bernard Carp to Heinz Roth, 12 March 1951; Bernard Carp to the Secretary of South West Africa, 26 April 1951; Heidi and Eberhard von Koenen, *Das alte Kaokoland*, p. 13.
72. The celebration of cars in the conquest of wilderness, including cars getting stuck all the time, is narrated in Green, *Lords of the Last Frontier*. For the significance of driving in constructing control of space, see Henrichsen, 'Pilgrimages into Kaoko', p. 168.
73. See Hayes, 'Northern Exposures', p. 173.
74. Hayes, 'Northern Exposures', p. 179; Landau, 'Empires of the Visual', p. 147.
75. There is extensive archival documentation dealing with game and game hunting in Kaoko, e.g., NAN PTJ 1 4/R, Hahn to secretary of South West Africa, 17 May 1926; NAN LAN 36 80, report on Kaokoveld, January 1926; NAN NAO 31 24/13, Kaokoveld Game 1936–1945. See also William Beinart, 'Review: Empire, Hunting and Ecological Change in Southern and Central Africa', *Past and Present* 128 (1990), pp. 162–86.
76. See Henrichsen, 'Pilgrimages into Kaoko', p. 172. Von Koenen confirms that Bernard Carp did in fact stress the significance of companionship and the necessity of enough time and space for leisure activities along with the work involved during the journey. Heidi and Eberhard von Koenen, *Das alte Kaokoland*, p. 14.
77. We may conceptualise 'nakedness' as one form of 'clothing', i.e. the absence of clothes and relate images of naked 'white' settler men to those showing them in female disguise or in African dress. The visuals could thereby be interpreted as specific statements on gender norms and relations and on the hierarchies of 'white' and African 'nakedness'. See David Bate, 'Fotografie und der koloniale Blick', in Wolf and Holschbach, *Paradigma Fotografie*, vol. 2, pp. 115–32.
78. All interviews in 2001–2002 were done together with Giorgio Miescher; all were recorded on tape. In Kaoko Otavi and Sesfontein we worked with local residents and teachers, Joshua Tourob, Lucretia Kapetua, Florentia Kasaona and Salatiel Muharukua, who translated the interviews. In Windhoek the interviews were translated and transcribed by Jenny Claasen and Silvia Katjepunda. I am relying on these transcriptions and on notes taken during the interviews.
79. None of the men and women we interviewed had seen the Roth photographs before, nor had those who visited the exhibition in Sesfontein in 2001 and 2002.
80. The photographs were exhibited in one of the classrooms of the Elias Amxab secondary school in Sesfontein. The organisation and opening of the exhibition was supported by Joshua Tourob and the regional councillor and pastor Theodore Hendriks.
81. We only met one person in Sesfontein who identified himself in one of the Roth photographs.
82. The term is taken from Christopher Pinney, *Camera Indica: The Social Life of Indian Photographs* (Chicago: University of Chicago Press, 1997).
83. The interrelation of various forms of narrating the past is a prominent issue in historiography, mostly concerning the construction of written versus oral historiographies. Elizabeth Tonkin, 'Investigating Oral Tradition', *Journal of African History* 27 (1986), pp. 203–13; Isabel Hofmeyr, *'We Spend our Years as a Tale that Is Told': Oral Historical Narrative in a South African Chiefdom* (London, Portsmouth, Johannesburg: James Currey, Heinemann, University of the Witwatersrand Press, 1994); Luise White,

Stephan Miescher and David William Cohen, 'Voices, Words and African History', in Luise White, Stephan Miescher and David William Cohen (eds), *African Words, African Voices: Critical Practices in Oral History* (Bloomington: Indiana University Press, 2001), pp. 1–27. Visual sources have only recently been included in these debates. For a discussion see Mitchell, 'Imperial Landscape'; and Hayes and Bank, 'Introduction'.

84. For a critique of information obtained through interviews see Tamara Giles-Vernick, 'Lives, Histories and Sites of Recollection', in White, Miescher and Cohen (eds), *African Words, African Voices*, pp. 194–213.
85. C. H. L. Hahn, Heinrich Vedder and Louis Fourie, *The Native Tribes of South West Africa* (Cape Town: Cape Times, 1928).
86. Heinrich Vedder's work is quite popular in central Kaoko; people such as government anthropologist N. J. van Warmelo, often rely on Vedder and other authors to underline their arguments. On another occasion an interviewee showed us a photocopy of a drawing C. H. L. Hahn had done of Vita Tom in the late 1930s as part of an obituary notice. Interview with Nandu Tom Ndjai, Kaoko Otavi, 4 January 2002.
87. Interviews with Mbatambauka Rutjindo, Onjette, 10 January 2002; Kangurupe Koviti, Kaoko Otavi, 7 January 2002.
88. Interview with Uetjipuraije Hiatjivi, Onjette, 9 January 2002 and 7 May 2002.
89. For a brief summary and for oral traditions on life in southern Angola and the immigration to Kaoko, see Bollig and Mbunguha, '*When War Came the Cattle Slept–*'.
90. Tjongoha and his generation of political leaders in Kaoko Otavi do not figure by name in the archival documents on Kaoko in the NAN. In Heinrich Vedder, 'The Herero', in Hahn, Vedder and Fourie, *The Native Tribes of South West Africa*, pp. 153–211, he is mentioned as 'headman' and photographed, but not identified individually.
91. See Georg Hartmann, 'Meine Expedition 1900 ins nördliche Kaokofeld und 1901 ins Amboland. Mit besonderer Berücksichtigung der Zukunftsaufgaben in Deutsch-Südwestafrika', *Beiträge zur Kolonialpolitik und Kolonialwirtschaft* 4 (1902/03), pp. 399–430; Julius Kuntz, 'Die Owatjimba im nördlichen Kaokofeld (Deutsch-Südwestafrika)', *Petermanns Geographische Mitteilungen* 58 (1912), p. 206; Heinrich Vedder, 'The Herero'.
92. Interviews with Ngakurupe Koviti, Kaoko Otavi, 7 January 2002; David Humu, Kaoko Otavi, 12 January 2002.
93. The same photograph is reproduced in Miescher and Rizzo, 'Popular Pictorial Constructions', p. 21.
94. Comment by Salatiel Muharukua, Kaoko Otavi, 3 January 2002. A similar argument could be made about Uerimunga Adam Kasaona, one of the headmen in Sesfontein repeatedly photographed by Heinz Roth in 1951. When we showed the photographs of Kasaona in Sesfontein and surroundings in 2001/2002, memories of the man – including praise songs, organised visits to the grave, etc. – were revitalised and the photographs were enthusiastically circulated within the community.
95. Debates on women/gender and colonialism have increasingly stressed the need to differentiate within entities such as 'women' instead of reproducing rigid categorisations. For a brief overview see Ann-Marie Gallagher, Cathy Lubelska and Louise Ryan, 'Introduction', in Ann-Marie Gallagher, Cathy Lubelska and Louise Ryan (eds), *Re-Presenting the Past: Women and History* (Harlow: Longman, 2001), pp. 1–19; Jean Allman, Susan Geiger and Nakanyike Musisi, 'Women in African Colonial Histories: An Introduction', in Jean Allman, Susan Geiger and Nakanyike Musisi (eds), *Women in African Colonial Histories* (Bloomington: Indiana University Press, 2002), pp. 1–15. It is important to note here that most of the women we interviewed were young when men such as Vita Tom and Thomas Mutate established themselves in Kaoko. Their status as young women made them particularly vulnerable both to colonial rule and to pressure from the local male elite. For an elaborated discussion of gender and age, see Meredith McKittrick, 'Generational Struggle and Social Mobility in Western Ovambo Communities 1915–1954', in Hartmann, Silvester and Hayes, *The Colonising Camera*, pp. 241–62.

96. Interviews with Kainaa Menjengua Tjihero, Kaoko Otavi, 8 January 2002; Maririro Koviti Tjurura, Kaoko Otavi, 4 January 2002.
97. Our interviews suggest that the raids in the 1910s and 1920s affected the women in central Kaoko more than women living in the southern parts of Kaoko, such as the Sesfontein area.
98. There is a methodological and theoretical problem with the absence/presence dichotomy with regard to colonial discourses on women and gender. See Cherryl Walker, 'Women and Gender in Southern Africa to 1945: An Overview', in Cherryl Walker (ed.), *Women and Gender in Southern Africa to 1945* (Cape Town, London: David Philip, James Currey, 1990), pp. 1–32; Wendy Woodward, Patricia Hayes and Gary Minkley (eds), *Deep hiStories. Gender and Colonialism in Southern Africa* (Amsterdam: Rodopi, 2002), pp. xi–xvii.
99. For a broader and differentiating Namibian perspective see Gesine Krüger, '"The Men Should Marry": Koloniale Herrschaft, Geschlechterkonflikte und gesellschaftliche Rekonstruktion im Waterberg Reservat, Namibia', *Werkstatt Geschichte* 14 (1996), pp. 22–38; Patricia Hayes, 'The "Famine of the Dams": Gender, Labour and Politics in Colonial Ovamboland 1929–30', in Hartmann, Silvester and Hayes, *The Colonising Camera*, pp. 117–46.
100. Interviews with Kvairani Kavari, Kaoko Otavi, 3 January 2002 and 6 May 2002; Jairaeua Tjihoto, Kaoko Otavi, 6 May 2002.
101. Three photographs of the woman are kept in NAN, Collection of Photographs, nos 2983, 2984, 2985. Besides the portrait discussed here, one image shows her as part of a group of three people; the third is a profile portrait, with a slight physiognomic touch.
102. Interview with Uetjipuraije Hiatjivi, Onjette/Kaoko Otavi, 9 January 2002.
103. This point is made with some caution, because there was gender differentiation with regard to the issuing of passes; however there were some exceptions based on the reason for mobility – labour migration, medical treatment, etc. Some cases of individual women applying for passes and permits to leave Kaoko are archived. See NAN NAO 29 24/16, permits and passes Kaoko 1930s, therein e.g. Magistrate Outjo, 24 November 1937; NAN SWAA 2513, additional NC of SWA to Chief NC, 24 June 1939; NAN NAO 28, Kaokoveld General Vol. 2, on a case of female migration in 1935.
104. NAN 19, NC Owamboland, monthly report October, labour migration of men to farms in the Outjo district, 3 November 1933; SWAA 2513, Officer in Charge Opuwo, monthly report June, 5 June 1943.
105. NAN NAO 19, NC Owamboland, annual report 1932, n.d.; NAN NAO 28, Kaokoveld general, vol. 2, NC Owamboland to Sgt Cogill, 13 September 1932.
106. Interviews with Uetjipuraije Hiatjivi, Onjette/Kaoko Otavi, 9 January 2002; Salomon Hartley, Oruwanjai, 11 January 2002; Jarerua Tjihoto, Kaoko Otavi, 3 January 2002; Nandu Tom Ndjai, Kaoko Otavi, 4 January 2002.
107. Hayes, 'Northern Exposures', p. 178.
108. Interviews with Emily Kazombaruru Kavari, 9 January 2002; Jarerua Tjihoto, Kaoko Otavi, 3 January 2002.
109. Interviews with Kainaa Menjengua Tjihero, Kaoko Otavi, 8 January 2002; Nadu Tom Ndjai, Kaoko Otavi, 4 January 2002. There was no missionary presence in Kaoko up to the 1950s, when the Dutch Reformed Church began mission work. The Rhenish mission station in Sesfontein had been led continuously by local evangelists and was only occasionally visited by the missionaries from Outjo.

8 Decoration and Desire in the Watts Chapel, Compton: Narratives of Gender, Class and Colonialism

Elaine Cheasley Paterson

Perched on a hill in Compton, in the south-east English county of Surrey, sits the Watts Mortuary Chapel, whose exterior of vivid terracotta tiles and sculpted frieze complements the intricately gilded, silvered and painted gesso panels within (Figure 1). In 1895, the Scottish artist-craftworker Mary Seton Watts (1849–1938) volunteered to design and build the chapel for the new burial ground in Compton village. Motivated by the ideals of the Home Arts Movement, particularly national cultural improvement through craft revival, she established a guild of craftworkers to produce the terracotta and gesso decoration for the chapel. The domed roof, cruciform plan and rich surface decoration of the chapel's small vaulted interior reflect its Byzantine style. The decoration formed an integral part of the building's design and was intended to complete the structure. This article explores the crafted space of the Watts Mortuary Chapel in relation to its attendant sites of cultural production – the Guild's craft workshops, the craftworkers' hostel, the adjoining Picture Gallery and the Watts's home, Limnerslease, and sets these into a gendered context of colonialism and class.

The Home Arts Movement was started in Britain by women in the late nineteenth century. It was centrally organised through the London-based Home Arts and Industries Association (HAIA), founded in 1884 by Eglantyne Jebb, inspired by art critic and social philosopher John Ruskin and supported by William Morris and his followers. Indeed, the HAIA shared in the social and artistic ideals of the higher-profile and very public Arts and Crafts Movement by advocating the handmade, supporting rural regeneration and promoting artistic innovation. As with Arts and Crafts, a characteristic of the Home Arts Movement was the

Figure 1: Watts Mortuary Chapel, Compton, Surrey, 1895–1898. Photograph by the author, 2002.

involvement of women at all levels, whether as needy workers in craft industries, artistic designers, entrepreneurs or patrons.[1] Mary Seton Watts's craft collective was a branch of the Home Arts and Industries Association and later became the Compton Potters' Arts Guild (Figure 2). Following the social and educational reforms proposed by the Home Arts Movement, the Guild sought to produce and market beautiful objects crafted in the Arts and Crafts tradition of drawing on the past without simply imitating historical models; using local materials; forging links between industry and craft; and promoting art as a way of life. As the home art industry that produced the chapel, the Potters' Arts Guild blended the Victorian concepts of the feminised 'private sphere' of home with the masculine 'public sphere' of work and commerce.[2] Its layout and organisation also challenged an established hierarchy of art and craft, one grounded in assumptions based on the location and gender of the maker. As such, the chapel's origins in the Home Arts Movement made it a space intersected by differences of class and gender.

The Watts Chapel must be situated within the artistic context of nineteenth-century British design reform, with its search for a new, universal language of design appropriate to its historical moment. The particular design language developed by Mary Seton Watts came from her understanding of John Ruskin's writing on design reform and from her own extensive research into the symbolism of world cultures.[3] This distinctive language became the hallmark of her craft guild and was imprinted on the chapel, making it a site of symbolic exchange linking different cultures together. It is important to note the enormous impact of colonialism on Victorian life at the time the chapel was conceived and constructed (1895–1904) and how this particular phase of imperialism marked the creative output of this middle class Scottish woman, as she studied current theories of design reform and global art histories while practising and teaching art in England. This complicated history may be accessed in the built environment of the chapel itself.

The building is also defined by its history as a place of work, where women and men of different social classes collaborated. This past infuses the space with secular meanings unrelated to its function as a mortuary chapel. More recently, this history has been invoked as a point of interest for tourists, layering a narrative of tourist consumption upon a space devoted to the private ceremony of remembrance and mourning. This article is particularly concerned with how these layered narratives of gender, class and colonialism affect the reception and consumption of the chapel as a cultural product.

Figure 2: Photograph of Mary Seton Watts (far left) and her assistants working on the gesso panels for the interior of the Watts Mortuary Chapel, c.1902. Reproduced courtesy of the Watts Picture Gallery, Compton.

Spaces of social reform

In the late nineteenth century, the hierarchical and gendered divisions between art and craft meant that the latter was typically feminised, to be produced in and for the home, while the former was seen as masculine production, in and for the public professional sphere of the studio and gallery. Mary Seton Watts and her husband, the celebrated symbolist painter and Royal Academician, G. F. Watts (1817–1904), shared living, working and exhibition spaces with each other and with the craftworkers of the Potters' Arts Guild (Figure 2).[4] The original classes in terracotta and gesso work were held in the converted billiards room of Limnerslease, the couple's home. A kiln was built on their property in consultation with Arts and Crafts ceramist William de Morgan and, once the industry developed beyond the evening classes in her home, Mary Seton Watts built a pottery workshop down the hill from Limnerslease.[5] Gesso work continued to be produced in her home while, after 1903, the garden ornaments and 'great jars' of the Guild were decorated and thrown in the pottery workshop. Local newspapers highlighted this aspect of production, explaining that 'an additional interest is given to the work by the fact that Mrs Watts has trained the villagers – in classes held during several successive winters at her own house'.[6] Through this creative use of space, art and craft overlapped, as did production and display, redefining the gendered meanings of these spaces and blurring the boundaries between home and work. Thus, the actual layout of this home art industry contested divisions of work and home, art and craft, masculine and feminine, public and private.

To assist in the production of terracotta works, initially for the chapel and later for exhibition by the Potters' Arts Guild, Mary Seton Watts built living quarters for the Guild's craftworkers in 1903. This hostel was an extension of the Picture Gallery, intended to house her husband's artwork.[7] Both buildings were designed by Christopher Turnor, a local Arts and Crafts architect. The pottery and gesso workshops as well as the kiln were also among these buildings, while the chapel was within walking distance. Limnerslease was on a hill overlooking this compound of buildings all designed with a common purpose of bringing art and craft to the people of Compton. The close physical proximity of the craftworkers both to the site of their cultural production and to their middle-class patron was intentional. In this shared setting, art and craft were brought together on an equal footing in an effort to convey the 'morally uplifting' qualities of culture.

In his 1889 paper 'Home Arts and Industries', Arts and Crafts lecturer and Home Arts advocate Alfred Harris explained that the work of the Home Arts Movement was 'as a great social lever for bringing into closer sympathy and uniting by stronger bonds, wealth and poverty, culture and ignorance, refinement with coarseness'. Social reformers involved in the movement were 'active workers in a great but silent revolution which will help to weld together in a common sympathy the widely varied and far removed ranks in our great and complicated social system'.[8] Certainly, connecting the Compton workers' hostel and pottery building to the Picture Gallery was an effort to fulfil the Home Arts Movement's goal of welding the social classes together, whereby the working class might benefit from exposure to the perceived moral and cultural superiority of the middle class. Visitors to the gallery could not overlook the pottery workshop, with its many clay pots displayed on the grounds. The structured display of fine art within the gallery was contrasted to the workshop production of the pottery, although both were intended to function as vehicles for moral reform through cultural improvement.

The Home Arts Movement's mission of making art accessible to everyone was a primary reason for establishing the Picture Gallery in the Surrey countryside, as well as its well-known precedent at Whitechapel from 1881. Mary Seton Watts worked with Henrietta and Samuel Barnett in East London where the Whitechapel exhibition model was developed to create a working-class art public and promote urban renewal and social reclamation. The Barnetts were also leaders in the movement to build free libraries, to establish urban open spaces and to design and construct municipally subsidised housing in the poorer neighbourhoods of London.[9] This desire to reshape the interior and exterior landscapes of the urban poor was transplanted to the countryside by Mary Seton Watts and manifested in the design and layout of her craft workshop, Picture Gallery and chapel in Compton. In order to maximise the benefits of beautiful outdoor spaces for the rural workers of the Guild, the buildings were laid out following an Arts and Crafts model that sought to unite buildings and gardens with the local landscape. All the buildings were designed to reflect the vernacular traditions of Surrey and were surrounded by gardens that incorporated the existing woods and grasslands. This Arts and Crafts garden philosophy meant it was appropriate to 'use a mountain as a garden ornament provided that you own it yourself', a telling reflection of the economic and social class system that produced the movement.[10]

As she developed her Guild's line of terracotta garden wares, Mary Seton Watts became acquainted with prominent Arts and Crafts garden designers, including Gertrude Jekyll (1843–1932) with whom she collaborated to produce the 'Jekyll Bowl' for the Potters' Arts Guild. Gertrude Jekyll worked extensively with the architect Edwin Lutyens (1869–1944) and their treatment of both internal and external space was the hallmark of this successful partnership. The buildings and hedgerows, streets, heaths, villages and lanes of southwest Surrey engaged and affected the lives and work of the garden designer and the architect. Jekyll was also a follower of William Robinson, who advocated 'drawing on the wealth of the vast variety of temperate Empire plants' to create an 'enhanced naturalistic English system'.[11] As well as supplying and designing garden pots for Gertrude Jekyll, the Potters' Arts Guild held award-winning displays at both the Royal Botanical Society and Royal Horticultural Society, all of which demonstrated the excellence of the Guild's work and secured its place within the Arts and Crafts horticultural community.[12]

Mary Seton Watts's determination to establish skilled and independent employment for women (and men) through her Potters' Arts Guild was part of more general moves for professional training and status for women. The energy and ingenuity that distinguished successful women craftworkers and gardeners were equally applicable to political agitation. Mary Seton Watts not only collaborated with Gertrude Jekyll but also supplied garden pots to Lady Frances Wolseley's College for Lady Gardeners at Glynde in East Sussex. The school (begun c.1901) sought to perpetuate standards of professionalism for women gardeners. An early prospectus stated that it was 'run practically upon the lines of a Market Garden, so as to prove what an educational thinking Head can accomplish towards making land profitable, to show how much money can be made with a properly cultivated and well cropped garden'. Lady Wolseley located and secured head-gardener positions for which her women students would be considered.[13]

In the first decade of the twentieth century, communities of women meeting or working together in affiliations such as garden clubs and colleges or craft communes spawned a variety of suffrage activity. Through their participation in these philanthropic organisations, women (particularly middle-class women) became politicised and further organised reform societies to agitate for legislative change to improve conditions for women.[14] The feminism articulated by these women was a 'politics of everyday life', where social and political concerns were expressed in the concrete activities of their working lives. For instance, a meeting in 1912 of Frances Wolseley's women horticultural students at Gertrude Jekyll's house in Surrey was disrupted by the police on suspicion of subversive activities.[15] After 1904, in her widowhood Mary Seton Watts used the Picture Gallery to host meetings of the local branch of the women's suffrage movement – inserting women's political activism into the setting of male art production and display.[16]

By 1910, Seton Watts was president of the Godalming Women's Suffrage Society (which encompassed the Compton area), the local affiliate of the National Union of Women's Suffrage Societies.[17] The

Society held 'suffrage teas', where a small gathering of women would read and discuss papers, and 'drawing room meetings' in the homes of upper-class women in the Compton-Godalming area. As president of the Society, Seton Watts supported events to promote women's suffrage. Both she and Gertrude Jekyll are listed on a pamphlet in support of the Surrey demonstration and banner procession of 'Society and Industry in favour of Women's Suffrage' on 29 October 1910. Seton Watts was also involved in organising an exhibition of sweated industries in November 1911, which included 'six sweated women at work in the large hall' and was accompanied by an exhibition of arts and crafts by the local women's suffrage societies.[18] Her presidency allowed Mary Seton Watts publicly to declare her support for the highly political cause of women's suffrage.

Although her commitment to women's art education, employment and suffrage culminated in Seton Watts's presidency of the suffrage society, it had manifested itself earlier in her commitments to the Home Arts Movement and the women's dress reformmovement. She and her husband were both vice-presidents of the Healthy and Artistic Dress Union, founded in July 1890 with the goal of 'sound education' concerning women's dress and health.[19] The Union sought to reform fashionable dress based on past styles considered superior and more beautiful, particularly medieval and Greek models of dressing. An article published by the Union explained how to dress without the corset and sought to counter the belief that 'its disuse meant catching cold, great untidiness in appearance and in fact, general discomfort'. The author based her arguments on her own experiences of wearing a corset for three years and then 'abolishing them', with the consequence of being 'obliged to reform her clothing'.[20] Fashion historian Diana Crane suggests that clothing, as a form of symbolic communication, was enormously important in the nineteenth century as a means of conveying information about the wearer's social role, social standing and personal character. She claims that Victorian clothing was a form of social control that contributed to the maintenance of women in a dependant, subservient role. Yet clothing discourses often express social tensions and push widely accepted conceptions of social roles in new directions.[21] As such, clothing was the site of much debate and controversy in the nineteenth century. The Healthy and Artistic Dress Union wanted women to be healthy and to liberate them from restrictive clothing customs through artful dressing – a combination of social and aesthetic aims characteristic of Mary Seton Watts's activism.

An ornamented dwelling

The Watts Mortuary Chapel was consciously gendered feminine by its designer-maker. The language with which she defined the chapel's design drew on associations with women's dress and fashion as well as textile art, particularly embroidery. In this building cloaked in femininity, the sculpted and gesso decoration was an essential and integral part of the space and completed the structure. While the 'organic decoration' of the Watts Mortuary Chapel succeeded in 'uniting solemnity and splendour' in this sacred space, it also represented a carefully gendered design aesthetic.[22] Yet as a woman politically active in campaigns for women's suffrage and a proponent of education and work for women, Mary Seton Watts's craftwork and design invoke femininity as it might be defined outside the construct of the 'separate spheres' to become a tool for transgressing these categories.[23]

According to Seton Watts, the gesso panels lining the chapel interior were designed to 'clothe the walls'. As a 'home for the dead', the chapel envelops mourners, creating a 'domestic' environment suggestive of maternal comfort and love. On the building's exterior, the spandrel of the doorway was intended to represent an embroidered hanging or 'wall veil'. This decorative feature was formally titled the 'Garment of Praise', a biblical reference associated with comforting the bereaved.[24] It cloaks the entrance to the chapel with an intricate pattern representing the multifaceted spiritual imagination of its designer. Details include the symbol of the Rig Veda, an ancient collection of Hindu sacred verse, 'representing night and day as well as hospitality'.[25] The peacock, a bird sacred to Brahmins and buddhists and especially popular with members of the Aesthetic Movement, is also a prominent symbol in the chapel's terracotta work. Mary Seton Watts hoped this work would be her *rita* – her favourite Hindu word, meaning the realisation of truth through an ordered and purposeful pattern.[26] Believing religion was the 'earnest endeavour of every moment', she sought to express her own faith in the chapel's complex decorative scheme in terracotta and gesso.[27]

Many of the chapel's textile references come from *The Word in the Pattern*, Mary Seton Watts's key to its design, published in 1904. These associations also permeate other writing about the building, including her will, where she set aside money for the permanent preservation of the chapel and its surrounding area. The income generated from this lump sum was for the upkeep and repair of 'the fabric and decoration' of the chapel.[28] Historians continue to use this type of textile vocabulary to describe, for instance, the building's dome as a 'world fabric' divided into four sections, each with its own tree of life spreading all-embracing branches into the blue heaven, the whole 'woven as it were, into a mystical garment'.[29] Art historian Elizabeth Cumming suggests these terms of decoration denote a 'symbolic form of stitched vestment' made specifically for the building, an applied art form that enriches the structure. This symbolism becomes material if one considers, as

Cumming does, the manual dexterity needed to create the intricate patterning of the chapel as akin to stitchery.[30]

The organic decoration devised by Mary Seton Watts for the chapel involved a subtle and multilayered embodiment of private ideals within public art. For instance, the terracotta frieze wrapped around the exterior of the chapel represents four 'spirits': Hope, Truth, Love and Light. The southeast section is the *Spirit of Hope* (Figure 3) where Celtic interlace patterning weaves angels, birds and animals into the design. Hope is represented here by a peacock, with angels guarding the symbols of Comfort (a dove), Courage (a lion) and Patience (a spider). The design of each spirit's frieze is anchored with a symbolic bird: a peacock for Hope, an owl for Truth, a pelican for Love and an eagle for Light.[31] By 'stitching' these terracotta designs to the exterior of the chapel and clothing its interior with gesso panels, Mary Seton Watts drew attention away from her trespass into the field of architecture and the sphere of work, while extending the boundaries of her domestic, 'feminine' social role to include these activities.

The gilded, silvered and painted gesso panels form a stunning mural decoration for the small, vaulted interior of the Watts Mortuary Chapel. Daylight seeps through the lozenge-shaped leaded windows of yellow slab glass, adding to the jewel-like quality of this space.[32] Each gesso panel depicts angels facing inwards and outwards, holding medallions bound by Celtic cord and interlace knots (representing growth/decay,

Figure 3: *Spirit of Hope*, frieze on the southeast section of the Watts Mortuary Chapel. Terracotta, 1896–1898. Photograph by the author, 2001.

ebb/flow, life/death, joy/sorrow) above a tree of life and a golden girdle (Figure 4). Although elements of the chapel's decoration were exhibited by the Potters' Arts Guild, the physical nature of the gesso and terracotta work inevitably tied this craftwork to the structure itself. The chapel represents a move towards a more imaginative unity of art and architecture that makes the decoration integral to the building's history. Following Arts and Crafts ideals, its designer-maker valued all aspects of the building as contributing equally to the entire aesthetic and thus breaking down the hierarchy established between architecture and decoration.

In the crafted space of the chapel the sacred merged with the secular to serve ritual and commemorative as well as social, political and commercial purposes. One such purpose was to fulfil the Home Arts Movement's social mission of national cultural improvement. Indeed, Mary Seton Watts's belief in the redemptive power of art is demonstrated by her commitment to the Home Arts and Industries Association. By dedicating *The Word in the Pattern* to Eglantyne Jebb, Mary Seton Watts formally connected her chapel to the goals and accomplishments of the Home Arts. The Movement's 'gifts of culture and skill' were bestowed upon the rural working classes of Compton by a middle-class woman in this site of cross-class cultural exchange. Still, the chapel was a space intersected by differences of class and gender. Its creation was closely identified with an idealised way of life for the craftworkers as imagined by Home Arts reformers like Mary Seton Watts. The work on the chapel was decorative rather than structural but the building itself was a place of work necessitating organised managerial skills and a high level of artistic competence from its designer. Defying restrictive social norms, Mary Seton Watts took on the role of designer-maker and general contractor, supervising as many as seventy craftworkers during the completion of the chapel. In July 1898, a local newspaper reported that all the decorative work on the chapel was completed by the Compton Guild: for instance, 'Thomas Stedman of Compton carved the elaborate chestnut covering of the Chapel doors and the ironwork of the doors was executed by Clarence Sex of Compton'.[33] The result of this effort was a public space devoted to the private ceremony of remembrance and mourning. With its exterior of vivid terracotta tiles and rich gesso interior, the chapel provided 'an ornamented dwelling not for the everyday life, but for occasional use as a shared home for personal memories'.[34] The crafted space of the chapel blended its private intimate function as a home of comfort and memory with its previous role as a place of work, where women and men of different classes participated in the communal creation of a public building.

Figure 4: Interior decoration of the Watts Mortuary Chapel, 1901–1904. Gilded, silvered and painted gesso panels and terracotta with piping cord. Photograph by the author, 2001.

Designing a shared culture

Many nineteenth-century social reformers were committed to an ideal that shared aesthetic and moral experiences would lead to political, social, economic and cultural solidarity. A shared culture was meant to help transcend class divisions and to foster a unified nation.[35] In this view, 'national culture' is ideologically motivated by social currents within England and thus safely circumscribed within local boundaries.[36] Theorist Gayatri Spivak suggests that to accept this type of self-contained version of the West is to ignore its production by the imperialist project, understood as England's social mission. As a pervasive economic, social, political and cultural formation, imperialism had an impact on all levels of British domestic life.[37] It was discussed, debated and contested as an issue of the day, present in everyday activities and diverse forms of cultural production, including that of the Potters' Arts Guild.[38] The craftwork of the Guild must be understood as part of nineteenth-century design reform, led by critics like John Ruskin and W. R. Lethaby and its particular phase of the Arts and Crafts Movement. Yet the search for sources that would allow a new modern language of design to emerge, characteristic of both the larger design reform movement and the specific instance of the chapel, depended in part on an imperial horizon and as such must be grounded in the global history of colonialism.

Although raised at her grandparents' Highland estate near Inverness, Mary Seton Watts had been born in India, where her father was a member of the East India Company's civil service. She later became acquainted with her husband's west London Holland Park friends, including the Anglo-Indian Pattle and Prinsep families. The Pattle sisters had spent their formative years in India and, when visiting together, would reportedly speak Hindustani to each other. When he met Mary Seton Watts, G. F. Watts was the permanent guest of Thoby and Sara Prinsep (née Pattle), who had married in Calcutta in 1835. Thoby Prinsep was Chief Secretary to the Government of India when he retired from the civil service in 1843.[39] Sara Prinsep's sister, the photographer Julia Margaret Cameron (née Pattle), had also married a man involved in Indian politics and government. Her husband was appointed the first legal member of the Supreme Council of India, a position which meant the couple socially out-ranked almost everyone in British India.[40] In these social circles, Mary Seton Watts surrounded herself with friends fascinated by the politics, culture and religion of India. These friendships coupled with her childhood in Scotland and her father's position in the Indian civil service shaped her worldview.

The designer-maker was further marked by her extensive honeymoon in Europe, North Africa and Asia in 1886. The couple travelled to Malta and then on to Egypt, arriving in Cairo via the Suez Canal. They took a seventy-day trip down the Nile River, stopping in Karnak, Luxor and Aswan, eventually returning to Cairo. They continued to Greece, visiting Athens and navigating the islands to Turkey. Throughout the honeymoon, Mary Seton Watts kept a travel diary filled with sketches of architectural details and patterns from decorative work she saw, along with her thoughts on the cultural traditions of the people she observed (she mentions Berber peoples in particular). Interestingly, given her later work in Compton, Mary Seton Watts noted in both her diary and commonplace book that while in Istanbul she had met a European woman who had established an art embroidery home industry there to help Bulgarian and Armenian refugee women.[41]

Historian Catherine Hall suggests that travel generates narratives that are acutely concerned with self-realisation in the spaces of the other.[42] In her published account of this lengthy trip and her personal reflections on it in her diary, Mary Seton Watts related the couple's experiences in these 'spaces of the other' as offering a better understanding of themselves while also improving their aesthetic sensibilities, especially the ability to appreciate colour and form. She viewed her constantly changing surroundings from a purely aesthetic perspective as fodder for her own creative impulses. As her husband explained, 'when you have seen Greece and Egypt, you have got the keynote to all that is beautiful in art'.[43] Her family background, 'worldly' friendships and lengthy travels and experiences in foreign countries deeply affected how Mary Seton Watts made sense of the world, particularly in her design for the Watts Mortuary Chapel.

The essentialising impulse characteristic of the chapel's design reflects both her own imaginative self-fashioning and a fashioning of others in order to construct a meaningful narrative. Following Lethaby's argument that architecture should 'carry a story and convey a message', Mary Seton Watts sought to create a symbolism relevant to her own place and time. Her earlier gesso ceiling scheme at Limnerslease consisted of a series of panels depicting early Christian, Irish revival, Egyptian, Greek, Chinese and Buddhist symbols to illustrate her interest in world art.[44] Seton Watts's knowledge and interpretation of these symbols came from her study of ancient manuscripts and recent antiquarian scholarship as well as travel in many of these countries. A special focus of her studies and later of her chapel design, was Hinduism, the most prominent religion in India, and its Sanskrit language, based on translations by German-born British scholar Max Müller.[45] The resulting 'architectural orientalism' of the chapel, an appropriation of symbols from many cultures where the original meaning was either unknown or translated to suit the story conveyed in the building, was far from hostile to the colonised cultures it borrowed from, but does indicate how the chapel's designer was marked by her location and experiences.[46]

Though the couple did not travel as extensively after their honeymoon, visitors to Limnerslease and the terracotta workshops included Earl Grey and Cecil Rhodes, providing the Wattses with opportunities to meet prominent figures involved in developing and implementing British colonial policies. Throughout the 1890s, Earl Grey was administrator of Rhodesia and later director of the British South Africa Company, chartered in 1889 to administer Rhodesia. He subsequently became Governor General of Canada (1904–11).[47] British financier Cecil Rhodes became prime minister of the South African Cape Colony in 1890 but was forced to resign in 1896 after orchestrating an attempt to overthrow the Boer regime in the Transvaal, one of the events which led to the outbreak of the Anglo–Boer War of 1899–1902.[48] Mary Seton Watts confronted the harsh reality of British colonial expansion when two of her brothers were called to serve in South Africa with the Lovat Scouts during this war. While some might have regarded this as hardship, she remarked that the Scouts were a 'most interesting cargo of fine men' many of whom 'left good appointments to go and work so splendidly'.[49] Indeed, she spoke with 'high praise of the fitness of the British race for colonisation'. She elaborated on this belief in print, where she recounted a conversation with Rhodes on one of his visits to Compton and the chapel, during which she asked him 'to what he attributed this quality' in the British people. Her account of his response, that it was 'the village life and if I may say so the village church', allowed Mary Seton Watts to present a parallel between those best suited to carry out the project of colonisation (Rhodes's villagers) and those most suited to benefit from the social and cultural reforms of the Home Arts Movement – in both cases the rural working classes.[50] Rhodes had also made this link earlier, when he wrote to Seton Watts that the future of the British Empire would be secured by 'educating the youth to their responsibilities' and teaching them that 'work is paramount'.[51] In the context of her work at Compton, these comments may be seen to relate the Home Arts Movement's use of art to 'civilise the poor' and the goal of the Potters' Arts Guild, to educate and employ rural craftworkers in Compton, to England's larger colonial project.

This project can also be distinguished in Seton Watts's engagement in the Celtic revival. At a time when Scotland was being reinvented as a tourist attraction and, politically and economically, as an extension of England, Mary Seton Watts's privileging of Celtic ancestry expressed the patriotism of a Scottish woman. The cultural nationalism expressed in her design language was typical of many Arts and Crafts reformers. Yet, while it is possible to view Scotland as a colonised nation, the Seton family's Highland estate suggests they may not have been displaced and damaged Scots. Indeed, her interest in comparative religions and world cultures, from which she borrowed both inspiration and design, indicates how Mary Seton Watts might still have perceived herself as part of an imperial British nation.

Many of Mary Seton Watts's designs used Celtic symbols taken from carved stones and crosses or illuminated manuscripts held in museums and libraries.[52] For instance, she exhibited a 'remarkable Celtic bedhead panel' with the Potters' Arts Guild at the 1901 HAIA exhibition in London. Her design for this piece drew on Scottish oral tradition and folklore. The panel symbolised a sleep blessing used by fishermen from the West Coast of Scotland.[53] She knew the Scottish artist Margaret Macdonald and the Irish artist Phoebe Traquair (who lived and produced most of her art in Edinburgh) and was well aware of Scottish initiatives in art at this time. She praised Scottish entrepreneur James Morton for attempting to design Celtic-style rugs: 'how glad I am that you are going to *carry forward* the Celtic Art … it is *our own*'.[54] Even in her writing on the early work of the Potters' Arts Guild, her language was inflected by Celtic imagery: '[the Guild] was as a seed planted, which became a growing plant, a tree of life'.[55] Clearly, she aligned herself with the popular Celtic revival in her native Scotland, as well as in Ireland. As a Scot herself, Mary Seton Watts could 'legitimately' assert this heritage, a claim for belonging involving both propriety and property. Acting as a Scottish woman, Mary Seton Watts authenticated goods and promoted sales, consecrating the craft objects she produced and translating the romance of the Celtic fringe into material for visual display.[56]

The chapel design was informed by Seton Watts's many cultural interests and her readings in architecture, design, world cultures, comparative religions and science are all reflected in the decoration of this building. She was familiar with the writings of John Ruskin, Walter Crane and W. R. Lethaby. In *Architecture, Mysticism and Myth*, Lethaby explored spirituality and symbolism within world cultures, advancing the idea of an ahistorical symbolism as the basis of architecture. The approach appealed to Mary Seton Watts, who was a dedicated Christian but abhorred narrow doctrine. Instead, she picked broader aspects from Buddhist, Hindu and Jewish teachings to incorporate into her personal faith.[57] The chapel design echoed her study of world religions just as the space itself was meant as a sanctuary to people of all creeds.

The design of the chapel is essentially a form of cultural translation. However, in this instance, the translations are marked by the pervasive orientalism readily available as a discursive system.[58] In the process of translating the symbols and traditions of other cultures, many of which were experiencing the effects of British colonialism, Mary Seton Watts imposed her own meanings upon them in order to create her particular design language. The publication of her key to the chapel's decorative scheme conferred upon Seton Watts the power to narrate these traditions. Although she genuinely attempted to understand the original significance of the symbols she selected, her knowledge of the cultures producing them was inextricably bound up with Britain's dominance over many of these cultures. While the chapel project must be read within the wider context of British colonialism, it remains as much a contribution to contemporary debates in design reform, one grounded firmly in the Arts and Crafts ideals proposed by Ruskin and Lethaby.

Architecturally, the ground plan of the red brick and terracotta chapel building is a hybrid of neo-Romanesque and Byzantine circular cruciform design. Mary Seton Watts explained that many of the symbols in the chapel design were 'immeasurably older than any Celtic art and travelled here ... like the root-words of languages, from their birth-place in the East and the general plan of the chapel is one of these symbols'.[59] The initial impetus for the late nineteenth-century Byzantine revival came from accounts of travel to Italy, Greece and Turkey that contained descriptions of Early Christian and Byzantine buildings, and from specialist books on Byzantine and Early Christian architecture. Ruskin and Lethaby discussed Byzantine as an architecture whose undoubted Eastern character, far from sullying its interest, was a main ingredient of its success.[60] Certainly, Seton Watts's familiarity with the writings of these design reformers, her own travel to these countries and extensive study of their history of art and architecture made this particular style appropriate to her ambitious chapel project. The imagined multicultural identity and geographical range of the Byzantine Empire appealed to this designer well versed in and deeply motivated by her studies in comparative religions and world culture. The synthesis of cultures in the chapel design was an example of what Lethaby referred to as a 'microcosm of the world'[61] – a world characterised by the increased political and social interventions of late nineteenth-century British colonial expansion.

Finishing touches: the tourist-viewer

Mary Seton Watts's desire to translate rather than appropriate the art of other cultures in order to construct a universally meaningful design for her chapel is evident in an early article about the Potters' Arts Guild. In it she explained that her aim was not to copy the 'dead language of another time and people' but rather to 'get the knowledge of the true principles underlying all good art' and to use 'our simple, natural art to express the thought to meet the needs of our own place and time'.[62] Since the building's completion, the tourist narrative that has developed about the Watts Mortuary Chapel has made the space relevant to visitors of varied 'places and times'. Indeed, it is in this new layer of meaning that the chapel may finally achieve the relevance sought by its designer.

This tourist narrative is steeped in the history of the Guild as part of the Home Arts Movement and focuses on the local craftworkers and Mary Seton Watts as designer-maker, rather than on the religious symbolism and function of the building. If, as sociologist Pierre Bourdieu suggests, the capacity to *see* is a function of *knowledge*, then this narrative affects the reception of the chapel as a cultural product, since the selective history it presents 'educates' the tourist-viewer.[63] Perceptions of the chapel's meaning and purpose are also mediated by the class position and experiences of the viewers, who play an active and participatory role in creating the finished cultural product. Take, for example, a woman visitor in 2002 who was overheard exclaiming how the plain straw mats covering the stone benches inside the chapel were 'lovely and beautiful'. This viewer's specific 'cultural competence', or knowledge, shaped her understanding of the chapel in ways that diverged from the intentions of the building's designer-maker and made these mats a newly relevant part of the design. In this instance, tourist consumption of the chapel is its final stage of creation.

As a permanent presence in a particular setting, any discussion of the crafted space of the Watts Mortuary Chapel demands imaginative sensitivity to the vision of future time cherished by its makers.[64] Before the interior gesso work of the chapel was completed, a narrative of tourist consumption was layered onto this space devoted to private ceremony. Guides like E. A. Judges's 1901 *Some West Surrey Villages*, reported that, thanks to the 'untiring personal labours' of Mary Seton Watts and the Watts's joint generosity, Compton owned a mortuary chapel that was 'unique in the country'.[65] Another writer praised Mary Seton Watts's leadership of this project, believing the whole structure to be an 'admirable specimen of what can be done by the employment of good material fashioned by carefully trained hands, under the direction of a highly artistic mind'.[66]

These early accounts of the chapel layered secular concerns for the architectural history of the building and its origins in the Home Arts Movement onto the religious function of the space: 'the chapel is essentially an application of the principles of the Home Arts and Industries Association – a striking example of successful efforts to revive the taste for and skill in, those home arts and crafts which may be made to play so beneficent a part in our village life'.[67] The original role of the chapel as a place of work, rather than its subsequent role as a place of worship, became the focus of this writing geared towards attracting tourists to Compton. The sacred aspects of the chapel were also discussed in ways designed to appeal to a wide audience: 'though founded upon the great central truths of the Christian faith, [the chapel] does not express any accepted dogmas of religion, but enforces only the universal laws of justice, charity and love and is so broad and catholic in its teaching that it should conciliate even the most divergent ecclesiastical sects'.[68]

Upon visiting the Surrey Downs where the chapel is located, travel writers explain romantically that 'this little building, in brick and terracotta, which crowns a knoll within a stone's-throw of Limnerslease, is remarkable both in design and in execution'.[69] Others enthuse that it 'shines among the trees, with whose green foliage its red roof and wall strikingly contrast and looks like an oriental building that has somehow strayed to our country'.[70] These types of descriptive accounts are often followed by a remark about the craftworkers: 'so far as manual work is concerned, it is the work of those for whose service it is built'.[71] In these narratives, those who crafted the space and those who use it are linked for posterity and for the tourist consumer. This connection is furthered inside the chapel itself, where a wall panel by the entrance offers a short history of the space, focusing on the design and execution of the building (particularly the diverse nature of its symbolism), its connection to Mary Seton Watts and her husband, the benefits its construction offered the rural workers of Compton and its ties to the Home Arts Movement.

The sense of community and social concern evoked by this concise history of the chapel and in the subsequent writing, recently led to the restoration of the chapel and cemetery. In 2002, the project earned a Queen's Jubilee Heritage Award, which recognised the joint efforts of Compton Parish Council and Guildford Borough Council in the restoration.[72] Given its history in the Home Arts Movement as well as the social reforms and inclusive design language advocated by Mary Seton Watts, it is not surprising that renewed interest in the preservation and history of the Watts Mortuary Chapel coincides with the continued development of a popular community-based view of the world, where distance and isolation are dramatically reduced by electronic media. In this view, cultural differences, especially as manifested in local craft traditions, are often packaged and sold to Western consumers following international 'fair trade' practices, becoming (like the chapel) symbols of a globally shared culture. Just as the original narratives of gender, class and colonialism shaped the production and acceptance of the chapel space, these recent parallels give the building new currency with contemporary viewers and continue to shape the space through narratives of tourism and preservation to 'meet the needs of our own place and time'.

As a Scottish woman teaching and practising art in England, Mary Seton Watts's design language was a reworking of socially shared understandings of other cultures within the British Empire, including that of her native Scotland, in accordance with leading theories of design reform. Based on the ethic of social and cultural improvement promoted by the Home Arts Movement, she founded the Potters' Arts Guild and the Watts Mortuary Chapel, establishing a tenuous partnership between working- and middle-class cultures and creating a cultural setting where art and craft production were given equal priority. Within this setting, divisions between the public and private spaces of work and home were disrupted as craftwork was taught inside her home in order to produce a public building, and the private living space of the craftworkers was connected to the public viewing space of the Picture Gallery. Ultimately, Mary Seton Watts may be understood in terms of a structure of systemic differences that placed her as superior in the East–West divide of colonialism, while at the same time placing her as inferior in the gendered divides of nineteenth-century British art and society.[73] From this position, at once privileged and restricted, she effectively negotiated her way within and across the categories of art and craft, public and private, masculine and feminine to create the Watts Mortuary Chapel – a unique space constructed not only by those whose design and craftwork graces its walls but by those who continue to use and cherish it.

Notes

The Social Sciences and Humanities Research Council of Canada and the *Fonds Québécois pour la Formation de Chercheurs et l'Aide à la Recherche* generously funded the research for this article. I thank Janice Helland and Lynne Walker for their careful reading of the text and their helpful suggestions. In addition, I thank the two anonymous readers; their insightful comments were much appreciated.

1. See Janice Helland, 'Working Bodies, Celtic Textiles and the Donegal Industrial Fund, 1883–1890', *Textile* 2 (2004), pp. 134–55; Anne Anderson, 'Victorian High Society and Social Duty', *Journal of the History of Education* (2002), pp. 311–34; Tanya Harrod, '"For Love and Not for Money": Reviving "Peasant Art" in Britain 1880–1930', in David Crowley and Lou Taylor (eds), *The Lost Arts of Europe* (Haslemere: Haslemere Education Museum, 2000), pp. 13–24; Julian Holder, 'The Home Arts and Industries Association', *Sheffield Art Review* (1993), pp. 13–20.
2. Feminist writers continue to reveal the inconsistencies and limitations of the Victorian ideology of the 'separate spheres' as an understanding of social organisation. See for example, Amanda Vickery, 'Golden Age to Separate Spheres? A Review of the Categories and Chronology of English Women's History', *Historical Journal* 36 (1993), pp. 383–414; Joan Wallach Scott, 'Gender: A Useful Category of Historical Analysis', *American Historical Review* 91 (1986), pp. 1053–75.

3. Mary Seton Watts and her husband, G. F. Watts possessed a complete autographed set of John Ruskin's writings: Watts Archive, Compton, Surrey (WA). I thank Richard Jefferies, Curator of the Watts Gallery, for his expertise and generosity during my visits to the archive.
4. George Frederic Watts was an established painter in nineteenth-century Britain, most noted for his portraiture. See Wilfrid Blunt, *England's Michelangelo* (London: Hamish Hamilton, 1975). For detailed discussion of his marriage to Mary Seton Watts see Melanie Unwin, 'Significant Other: Art and Craft in the Career and Marriage of Mary Watts', *Journal of Design History* 17 (2004), pp. 237–50.
5. Mrs Steuart Erskine, 'Mrs G. F. Watts' Terracotta Industry', c.1903, pp. 152–8, an uncited published article in the archive's clippings book: WA.
6. *Surrey Times*, 9 July 1898, p. 7. Limnerslease was designed for the couple by the Arts and Crafts architect Ernest George in 1890–1.
7. 'Compton: An Interesting Birthday Ceremony', 23 February 1903, Newspaper Clipping Book, WA. The article describes G. F. Watts laying the cornerstone for the Gallery and hostel as part of his birthday celebrations.
8. Alfred Harris, 'Home Arts and Industries', in *Transactions of the National Association for the Advancement of Art and its Application to Industry: Edinburgh Meeting, 1889* (London: 1890), pp. 421–33, here p. 431.
9. Henrietta Octavia Barnett, *Canon Barnett – His Life, Work and Friends* (London: John Murray, 1918); Seth Koven, 'The Whitechapel Picture Exhibitions and the Politics of Seeing', in Daniel J. Sherman and Irit Rogoff (eds), *Museum Culture: Histories, Discourses, Spectacles* (Minneapolis: University of Minnesota Press, 1994), pp. 22–48; Gavin Budge, 'Poverty and the Picture Gallery: The Whitechapel Exhibitions and the Social Project of Ruskinian Aesthetics', *Visual Culture in Britain* 1 (2000), pp. 43–56.
10. Peter Davey, 'Arts and Crafts Gardens', *Architectural Review* 179 (1985), pp. 32–7, here p. 35. See Cecilia Lady Boston's account of Compton history for a description of the Norman-inspired Surrey vernacular, Cecilia, Lady Boston, *The History of Compton in Surrey* (1933; repr. Cambridge: Black Bear Press, 1987).
11. Jekyll's first book describes her early relationship to Lutyens and sets out her Robinsonian beliefs. Gertrude Jekyll, *Wood and Garden* (London: Longmans, Green, 1899). See also Gertrude Jekyll, *Old West Surrey* (London: Longmans, Green, 1904); Sally Festing, *Gertrude Jekyll* (New York: Viking, 1991).
12. The Potters' Arts Guild won gold and silver medals from both organisations. See 'Home Arts and Industries Association (HAIA)', *Art Journal* (1900); 'Art Handiwork and Manufacture', *Art Journal* (1906).
13. Wendy Hitchmough, *Arts and Crafts Gardens* (London: Pavilion Books, 1997), p. 196.
14. See Maria Luddy, *Women and Philanthropy in Nineteenth-Century Ireland* (New York: Cambridge University Press, 1995); Frank K. Prochaska, *Women and Philanthropy in Nineteenth-Century England* (Oxford: Clarendon Press, 1980).
15. Francis Jekyll, *Gertrude Jekyll a Memoir by Francis Jekyll with a Foreword by Sir Edwin Lutyens and an Introduction by Agnes Jekyll* (London: J. Cape, 1934), p. 174.
16. Hitchmough, *Arts and Crafts Gardens*, p. 196.
17. See Society letterhead, dated 21 January 1910, in the NUWSS correspondence archive 292/1 File 2, Women's Library, London (WL).
18. Guildford Women's Suffrage Society file, WL. Gertrude Jekyll supplied banners to the Guildford and Godalming branches of the Women's Suffrage Society and attended meetings at Mary Seton Watts's pottery workshop. Jekyll, *Gertrude Jekyll*, p. 174.
19. *AGLAIA: The Journal of the Healthy and Artistic Dress Union* 1 (July 1893). For more on the dress reform movement, including the Union as well as Rational and Aesthetic dress, see Stella Mary Newton, *Health, Art & Reason: Dress Reformers of the Nineteenth Century* (London: John Murray, 1974); Geoffrey Squire (ed.), *Simply Stunning: The Pre-Raphaelite Art of Dressing* (Cheltenham: Cheltenham Art Gallery and Museum, 1996).

20. E. M. W. Wheeler, 'How to Dress without a Corset', *AGLAIA*, n.d. See also, Valerie Steele, *The Corset: A Cultural History* (New Haven: Yale University Press, 2001).
21. Diana Crane, 'Clothing Behaviour as Non-Verbal Resistance: Marginal Women and Alternative Dress in the Nineteenth Century', *Fashion Theory: The Journal of Dress, Body and Culture* 3 (1999), pp. 241–68, here p. 242.
22. The term 'organic decoration' comes from Walter Crane's theory on decoration in buildings. His 'organic theory' defined decoration as essential to the completion of a structure. Walter Crane, 'Of the Decoration of Public Buildings', in *Art and Life and the Building and Decoration of Cities: Lectures by Members of the Arts and Crafts Society* (London: Victoria and Albert Museum, 1896), held at the National Art Library, Victoria and Albert Museum, London. Crane (1845–1915) was a leading figure in the Arts and Crafts Movement and a versatile and prolific painter, illustrator and designer of wallpaper, textiles and ceramics. He was a founding member of the Art Workers Guild.
23. Janice Helland, 'Frances Macdonald: The Self as Fin-de-Siècle Woman', *Woman's Art Journal* (1993), pp. 15–22.
24. 'To give them beauty for ashes, the oil of joy for mourning, *the garment of praise* for the spirit of heaviness' (Isaiah 61:3), in Mary Seton Watts, The Word in the Pattern (1904; repr. Compton: The Society for the Arts and Crafts Movement in Surrey, 2000), p. 14.
25. Seton Watts, *The Word in the Pattern*, p. 14.
26. See Ven. Jampa Choskyi, 'Symbolism of Animals in Buddhism', *Buddhist Himalaya* 1 (1988) unpaginated, <http://www.ccbs.ntu.edu.tw>; Hindu symbolism and language, <http://www.hindunet.org>.
27. Mary Seton Watts (MSW) Diary, 9 September 1894 and 3 February 1895: WA.
28. Last Will and Testament of Mary Seton Watts, 5 April 1924: Somerset House, London.
29. Julian Holder, 'Architecture, Mysticism and Myth and its Influence', in Sylvia Backemeyer and Theresa Gronberg (eds), *W. R. Lethaby, 1857–1931: Architecture, Design and Education* (London: Lund Humphries, 1984), pp. 56–63, here p. 62.
30. Elizabeth Cumming, 'Patterns of Life: The Art and Design of Phoebe Anna Traquair and Mary Seton Watts', in Bridget Elliott and Janice Helland (eds), *Women Artists and the Decorative Arts 1880–1935: The Gender of Ornament* (Aldershot: Ashgate, 2002), pp. 13–34.
31. Seton Watts, *The Word in the Pattern*, pp. 18–25. The eagle refers to St John's Biblical symbol and his ascension after death (see the symbols of the four evangelists page in Bernard Meehan, *The Book of Kells: An Illustrated Introduction to the Manuscript in Trinity College, Dublin* (London: Thames & Hudson, 1994), p. 41). For a description of the chapel design, see Veronica Franklin Gould, *The Watts Chapel* (Farnham: Arrow Press, n.d.); Veronica Franklin Gould, *Mary Seton Watts (1849–1938): Unsung Heroine of the Art Nouveau*, exhibition catalogue (Compton: V. F. Gould for the Watts Gallery, 1998).
32. The glass in the chapel is likely slab glass, a kind of thick irregular glass favoured by Arts and Crafts stained-glass artists like Christopher Whall, who was probably responsible for the chapel windows, judging from the leading pattern and use of glass. I thank Peter Cormack, curator of the William Morris Gallery, London, for this valuable assessment.
33. *Surrey Times*, 9 July 1898.
34. Cumming, 'Patterns of Life', p. 13.
35. Koven, 'Whitechapel Picture Exhibitions', pp. 22–48.
36. Gauri Viswanathan, 'Raymond Williams and British Colonialism: The Limits of Metropolitan Cultural Theory', in Dennis L. Dworkin and Leslie G. Roman (eds), *Views beyond the Border Country: Raymond Williams and Cultural Politics* (New York: Routledge, 1993), pp. 217–30.

37. Gayatri Spivak, 'Can the Subaltern Speak?', in Cary Nelson and Lawrence Grossberg (eds), *Marxism and the Interpretation of Culture* (Basingstoke: Macmillan Education, 1988), pp. 271–313.
38. At the time the Watts Chapel was built, approximately one-third of the world was dominated economically and culturally by Britain. See Reina Lewis, *Gendering Orientalism: Race, Femininity and Representation* (New York: Routledge, 1996); Catherine Hall (ed.), *Cultures of Empire: Colonizers in Britain and the Empire in the Nineteenth and Twentieth Centuries* (New York: Routledge, 2000).
39. Mary Seton Watts, *George Frederic Watts*, vol. 1: *The Annals of an Artist's Life* (London: Macmillan & Company, 1912), p. 124.
40. Elizabeth Boyd, 'The Pattle Sisters', unpublished manuscript (1976) in private collection, cited in Caroline Dakers, *The Holland Park Circle: Artists and Victorian Society* (New Haven: Yale University Press, 1999), p. 22.
41. Mrs Arthur Hanson organised embroidery work in Constantinople for Bulgarian and Armenian women in the area and arranged for a market in Vienna, Paris and London. Mary Seton Watts Commonplace Book and Diary, WA. The Turkish Compassionate Fund (*c*.1886) was a similar industry instituted by Baroness Burdett-Coutts (assisted by Lady Layard and Lady Charlotte Schreiber). *Lady's World*, November 1887, p. 39. I thank Dr Janice Helland for this reference to the Turkish Fund.
42. Hall, *Cultures of Empire*, p. 26. See also Simon Gikandi, *Maps of Englishness: Writing Identity in the Culture of Colonialism* (New York: Columbia University Press, 1996).
43. Seton Watts, *George Frederic Watts*, vol. 2, pp. 63–6.
44. The ceiling was completed in 1890–1. For detailed discussion of the panels and their symbolism see Veronica Franklin Gould, 'The Symbolic Bas-Relief Designs of Mary Watts', *Decorative Arts Society Journal* 21 (1997), pp. 9–21.
45. Max Müller (1823–1900) was a philologist and orientalist who lectured widely in Britain, in particular London and Glasgow. In her Commonplace Book, Mary Seton Watts transcribed Müller's 'Origin and Growth of Religion as Illustrated by the Religions of India', Hibbert Lectures, 1878. MSW Commonplace Book, WA.
46. See Mark Crinson, *Empire Building: Orientalism and Victorian Architecture* (New York: Routledge, 1996).
47. Seton Watts, *George Frederick Watts*, vol. 2, pp. 271–3. See also, R. Common, 'The Missing Banners of Lord Grey', *Embroidery Canada* (1981), pp. 5–7.
48. Seton Watts, *George Frederic Watts*, vol. 2, pp. 271–3; Sarah Millin, *Cecil Rhodes* (San Diego: Simon Publications, 2001).
49. Mary Seton Watts to James Morton, 15 March 1902. Morton Sundour Archive, Archive of Art and Design, Victoria and Albert Museum, London (AAD).
50. Seton Watts, *George Frederic Watts*, vol. 2, p. 269.
51. Cecil Rhodes to Mary Seton Watts, *c*.1898, regarding his visit to the Watts's home and the didactic role which he envisaged for his portrait by G. F. Watts. National Portrait Gallery Online, <http://www.npg.org.uk>.
52. In a letter she noted that her sources included: the seventh-century Irish manuscript *The Book of Durrow* (from the British Library, London); Lord Lindsay, *Sketches of the History of Christian Art*, 1847; Joseph Anderson, *Early Christian Monuments of Scotland*, Rhind lectures, 1892; John Stuart, *The Sculptured Stones of Scotland*, Spalding Club, 1867; the South Kensington handbook 'Celtic Arts' by Miss M. Stokes; and *The Antiphonary of Bangor* (London: F. F. Warren, 1893). Mary Seton Watts to James Morton, 15 March 1901, AAD. (Closer bibliographic specification of the items listed was not possible.)
53. *The Studio* 23 (1901), p. 83; E. W. Gregory, 'Home Arts and Industries', *The Artist* (1901), pp. 135–6.
54. Mary Seton Watts to James Morton, 15 March 1901. AAD. Emphases in original.
55. Mary Seton Watts to James Nicol, first manager of the Potters' Arts Guild, 17 December 1900. WA.

56. Janice Helland, 'Rural Women and Urban Extravagance in Late Nineteenth-Century Britain', *Rural History* 13 (2002), pp. 179–97.
57. Veronica Franklin Gould, 'Archibald Knox and Mary Seton Watts: Pioneers of "Modern Celtic Art" Garden Pottery', in Stephen A. Martin (ed.), *Archibald Knox* (London: Artmedia Press, 2001), pp. 76–84, here p. 81.
58. Gayatri Spivak, 'The Politics of Translation', in Michèle Barrett and Anne Phillips (eds), *Destabilizing Theory: Contemporary Feminist Debates* (Stanford: Stanford University Press, 1992), pp. 177–200, here pp. 178–83.
59. Seton Watts, *The Word in the Pattern*, p. 4. The circular centre of the cruciform building is 24 feet in diameter. See Lesley Gillilan, 'A Woman's Studies', *Guardian*, 'Space' section, 5 June 1998, p. 10.
60. For instance, W. R. Lethaby and H. Swainson's detailed first-hand analysis of Byzantine architecture, in particular the Hagia Sophia. William Richard Lethaby and Harold Swainson, *The Church of Sancta Sophis, Constantinople; A Study of Byzantine Building* (London: Macmillan, 1894). One of the most notable British Byzantine pioneers was the Scottish art historian and connoisseur Lord Lindsay, whose book was a reference for the chapel design. Alexander Crawford Lindsay, Earl of Crawford, *Sketches of the History of Christian Art* (London: J. Murray, 1847). Mary Seton Watts would have been familiar with Ruskin's discussion of Byzantine architecture in his *The Stones of Venice* (London: Smith, Elder & Co., 1851–3).
61. Holder, 'Architecture, Mysticism and Myth and its Influence', p. 61.
62. Mrs Steuart Erskine, 'Mrs G. F. Watts' Terracotta Industry', p. 157.
63. Pierre Bourdieu, *Distinction: A Social Critique of the Judgement of Taste*, tr. Richard Nice (Cambridge: Harvard University Press, 1984).
64. Clare A. P. Willsdon, *Mural Painting in Britain 1840–1940: Image and Meaning* (Oxford: Oxford University Press, 2000), p. viii. I thank Joseph McBrinn for bringing this source to my attention.
65. E. A. Judges, *Some West Surrey Villages* (Guildford: Surrey Times Printing and Publishing Co., 1901), pp. 136–8.
66. Hugh MacMillan, *The Life-Work of George Frederic Watts, RA* (New York: E. P. Dutton & Co., 1906), pp. 63–6. MacMillan died shortly before the book was published and the final manuscript was revised by George Frederic Watts and Mary Seton Watts. Apparently, except for a few alterations at their request, the book remains as he wrote it, suggesting the couple endorsed this version of the chapel's history.
67. Judges, *Some West Surrey Villages*, pp. 136–8.
68. MacMillan, *The Life-Work of George Frederic Watts*, pp. 63–6.
69. MacMillan, *The Life-Work of George Frederic Watts*, pp. 63–6.
70. Judges, *Some West Surrey Villages*, pp. 136–8.
71. Judges, *Some West Surrey Villages*, pp. 136–8.
72. The councils contributed more than £15,000, successfully prepared a Heritage Lottery Fund bid which brought in another £250,000 and provided professional expertise for the restoration. Guildford Borough Council, <http://www.guildford.gov.uk>.
73. Lewis, *Gendering Orientalism*, pp. 4–5.

9 Faces and Bodies: Gendered Modernity and Fashion Photography in Tehran

Alec H. Balasescu

This article discusses the production of fashion photography in Tehran, emphasising the modes of representation of bodies in public spaces. The empirical argument of this article is based on interviews with fashion designers and three photographers in Tehran, observations at two photographic sessions for fashion and observations on different visual regimes in this city. The research took place between 2002 and 2004.[1] The analysis of fashion photographic practices reveals the dynamic of norms regarding body-presence in Tehran's urban spaces. The argument here concerns the representation of mobility and the meanings that body mobility gains in relation to gender and the concept of modernity.

Driving or walking through Tehran, one cannot but notice the advertisements for 'e-cut' (Figure 1). E-cut, a ready-to-wear fashion brand for men, uses 'stars' to advertise its products. Mohammad Reza Golzar, the lead singer in the band Aryan, appears on the banners in two different poses: at the seashore, barefoot, dressed in an e-cut three-piece suit, petting a horse (only the head of the horse is visible, along with Mr Golzar from the chest up). The same model can also be seen shooting an arrow with a defiant attitude. In contrast with this, in and around Tehran there are no banners advertising women's fashion. Likewise, with a few exceptions that will be discussed in the text, there are no representations of women at all on Tehran's streets, parks or public spaces. At the moment, e-cut is the only brand that advertises fashion products on public hoardings.

Photography is a matter of concern in any public space, be it Muslim or not. Representing an object (the body) through photography means not only invoking the spectre of that object but also recreating its material presence, albeit a two-dimensional one. Approaching the

Figure 1: Advertising for e-cut brand, Tehran, 2003. Photo by Alec Balasescu.

practices of fashion photography and clothing display in Tehran's urban spaces, this article proposes a divorce from liberal Western notions of a visible subject for understanding the construction of civil society in a Muslim context. It shows how the relationship between women's mobility and body visibility is multi-layered and thus demands rethinking the concept of meaningful participation in the public sphere.

Since body visibility is a delicate issue and spatial segregation of the sexes is an important moral concern in the Islamic Republic of Iran, practices surrounding representations of bodies are predictably sensitive to these contexts. In the streets of Tehran, representations of women's bodies are subjected to the requirement of modesty, or *hijab*. This refers not only to photographs for billboards, but also to shop window mannequins that lack the upper half of their heads and facial features (as opposed to male or child mannequins, which are realistic in their representation) (Figures 2a and 2b). Contrary to women's bodies in movement, mannequins and photographs are fixed, identifiable, and thus more easily subjected to the dominant discourse. Photographic practices in Tehran's fashion world reveal a certain mode of imagining and representing (women's) bodies in relation to modern repertoires (like fashion) in the spatial regime of ideal public and private separation along the lines of gender. At a second degree of reading, this finely traced line, based on visual regimes and on modes of representations (and presence) of women's bodies in public, also constitutes a discursive separation between a modern West and a non-modern Iran. Nonetheless, this (imaged) separation is continuously rearranged, explored and renegotiated through practices of fashion photography.

In general, much of the critique of modernity has been concerned with the nature of the public sphere. Theoretical analyses of the dichotomy of the public and the private have come to emphasise the gendered social construction of spatiality that juxtaposes public and private with masculinity and femininity respectively.[2] Many scholars of colonialism have explored the political significance of this dichotomy, as well as its Eurocentric character. This in turn has contributed to the broadening debate on multiple modernities. Here I prefer the term 'multiple' to 'alternative' modernities, because the latter suggests that there is a singular, central modernity from which the others branch out.[3]

Without wishing to over-simplify, an implicit argument that traverses these approaches tends to associate 'public' with visibility. The legitimate public (and political) subjects are thus visible subjects. This kind of public sphere, privileging unmarked male subjects, is the basis of Western modernity. The significant absence of women (and other minorities) in public is central in the critique of the Habermasian concept of the public sphere. More to our point, photographic representations of

Figures 2a and 2b: Two fashion boutique-windows in Tehran, 2004. Note the difference between female (above) and male (below) mannequins. Photo by Alec Balasescu.

women in various contexts reveal the same discursive strategy of minimising the role of women or eliminating women's bodies altogether from the public sphere. Thus, in the history of advertising in Europe and United States, women usually appear in subordinated roles, especially if they are non-white. In medical representations of the body women were, until recently, altogether absent unless the reproductive system was in question. This underlines the naturalised inferior position in which women have been represented in Western modern public spheres and the social reproductive role they are assigned in public discourse (where images are discursive practices).[4]

In Eurocentric definitions of the public sphere, politically meaningful presence is therefore tied up with the question of visibility, an invisible body being automatically considered absent or politically meaningless. Speech, visibility and mobility are not only linked but also interchangeable. Research on the Muslim public sphere and Islamic modernities, however, calls into question the universality of this frame of analysis, pointing out both the importance of women's presence in the public sphere and the complicated relationship between visibility, mobility and political engagement. The presence of Muslim women in national and transnational public spheres is accompanied by, or follows the rules of, 'choreographies of ambivalence' that seem contradictory to Eurocentric modernity.[5] The dead end reached by the veil dispute in France (and the law against wearing the headscarf promulgated in 2003 is a dead end) is the expression of this incapacity to conceive of the modern political subject in terms other than those of Western liberalism.[6]

The article is organised in two main sections. The first part gives the necessary historical background on the dynamic of body regulation in Iran starting with the beginning of the twentieth century. It continues with a reconsideration of the conversation on gender and Orientalism that (re)calls into question the separation between public and private spaces. The second part of the essay analyses body mobility in Tehranian photographic practices and representations in different spatial contexts. In Iran gender segregation and its spatial inscription are part of a historical process. This segregation is reflected in fashion photographic practices, but it does not follow a rigid framework along the lines of public/private, secular/Muslim, modern/non-modern.

The modern body in Iran

'Clothing matters', as Emma Tarlo has shown in detail.[7] During the period of colonialism it became the instrument of modernisation policies, as well as a form of anti-colonial struggle and the affirmation of national identity. Iran, although not directly colonised, was no exception.

It is difficult to write about Iran without waking the ghosts of a variety of 'isms', from Orientalism to Modernism, passing through and obsessively lingering on Islamism. The popular perspective[8] on Iran is that after its period of modernisation under the Reza dynasty, the Islamic Revolution gave way to a regime that attempted to crush its previous social 'achievements'. This new regime marked its coming to power through laws derived from *shari'a*, many of them targeting women and women's attire: wearing the headscarf and/or *chador* in public spaces became compulsory. For many Western eyes this meant blocking their own vision, blinding them to the social dynamics and transformations taking place beyond this visible obstacle.[9]

Iran, like any other place, has a long-term dynamic that needs to be assessed to provide a background for contextualising later developments. The twentieth century was one of a sustained process of modernisation understood as Westernisation, and the Reza dynasty was its exponent. The Constitutional Revolution in 1904–6 and the formation of the first Iranian parliament were the signs of the new era to come for Iran. The commercial classes from the *bazaar* and the *shi'a* clergy were the main actors in this movement, which forced the Qajar Shah to ratify the first Constitution of Iran in 1906. The adoption of the Constitution created a new political landscape. The political class's desires to construct a modern society brought about a series of reforms designed to give a modern aspect to Iranian society: key to this aim were laws that targeted *men's* attire.

From the early 1920s to the mid-1930s, Iran was swept up by a series of cabinet decrees and parliamentary laws meant to regulate men's dress. The first law, in 1923, concerned the obligation for government employees to wear Iranian-made clothes during office hours. Five years later, after Reza Shah's coming to power, a cabinet bill stipulated that Iranian men should wear Western-style clothes. This law was part of the project of Iranian national identity construction. Uniform dress, in the Shah's opinion, was supposed to forge a feeling of national unity beyond the regional and tribal divides.[10] Other reforms in the same period concerned headgear for men; turbans were to be replaced with specific hats called *kolah-e Pahlavi* (Pahlavi's hats). These reforms were contested by large sectors of the population from different social strata. Intellectuals claimed the laws were unconstitutional, textile manufacturers felt their trade was threatened and clergymen saw their power contested in public space.

Around the same period, Reza Shah felt his power was sufficiently consolidated and began limiting the autonomy of the religious authorities in an attempt to enforce his own cabinet's power over the legislative apparatus. This tendency was displayed publicly through actions of the royal family meant to show how little control clergy had over public space. In 1928, during a visit to the religious shrines in Qom, Reza's wife appeared unveiled:

> One Ayatollah Bafqi, present at the Shrine, sent a message to the Queen: 'If you are not Muslim why did you come to the shrine? If you are then why are you not veiled?' When his message was ignored, Bafqi delivered a sermon denouncing the shah and inciting the crowd. In response, Reza Shah personally went to Qom, *entered the shrine in his boots*, horsewhipped Bafqi and had him arrested.[11]

One sees in this passage how the overt confrontation between the clergy and the new power was publicly displayed through dress and bodily attitudes. Not only had the queen appeared unveiled, but the Shah horsewhipped the Ayatollah and disregarded the religious codes by himself entering the shrine wearing boots.

Despite increased public discontent, Reza Shah continued his policies. After he visited Turkey in 1934 and met Kemal Atatürk, he became determined to accelerate his reforms towards modernisation and to generalise the wearing of Western attire. A July 1935 cabinet decree replaced the *kolah-e Pahlavi* with the full brim hat for all Persian working-class men and government clerks. This caused new and serious upheavals in the population. In the same month, a resistance movement lead by Sheikh Mohammed Taqi Bohlul found refuge in Gowharshad Mosque in Mashhad. The authorities responded with arms, and between 400 and 500 people were killed. Gradually, with the exception of religious authorities, urban men almost entirely abandoned head covering.[12]

Up to Reza's visit to Turkey and despite the appearance of fashions from Europe, women were not the focus of the shah's policies. Women of the upper classes or at the court were already wearing European hats and were participating in public gatherings. On 8 January 1936 at the graduation ceremony at the Normal Governmental School, Reza came with his wife and daughters unveiled and gave a speech about the necessity of women being unveiled. This gesture was preceded by a 1935 decree that forbade the veil in schools for both students and educators. In the same year women were required to appear uncovered when dealing with public administration.[13] It is interesting to note that Kemal Atatürk's policies in Turkey were driven by a clear secular agenda. He not only forbade Islamic veiling but also replaced the *shari'a* family code with the Swiss family code, translated and adopted word for word. Despite his concern for women's image in public, Atatürk failed to secure an equal position for women in Turkish society; theirs was a naturalised, nurturing place in the new nation, just as was that of their Western counterparts.[14] In Iran, Reza Shah attempted to give a modern appearance to the public space without reforming the family code too much. His was not an explicit secular project for nation building in Iran, since he was in a constant fight for legitimacy with the *shi'a* clerics.

After the 1936 speech at the graduation ceremony, Reza promulgated a law forbidding veil-wearing in public spaces, with disastrous effects for a large part of the population. For many women, this law meant confinement to their homes for the rest of their lives. At the same time, various new regulations of women's behaviour came into use under the guise of 'good manners' training that prescribed a highly codified 'Victorian' set of rules that secured 'veiling in the absence of the veil'. Women lost their bodily mobility even when and if their bodies were more visible in public.[15] The 'un-veiling law' was followed by sustained repression. Facing women's refusal to unveil (based on traditionally grounded beliefs and the association of the veil with chastity) police forcefully (and violently) unveiled women in the streets and searched private houses for veils.[16]

After Reza Shah's forced abdication, in September 1941, many women resumed veiling. Under the pressure of *ulama* (the religious authority), who had partially regained influence, Muhammad Reza, the new shah, abrogated the law concerning the veil. Nevertheless, the years of forced unveiling left a deep mark in the society: veiling habits became not only indicators of education and class difference, but also modalities for construction of those differences, through the limitations on behaviour and mobility that they imposed. For the entire period of forced unveiling, access to education was practically impossible for women coming from traditional social environments. For them, mobility in public was literally forbidden by law. The veil as object of official policy, or more precisely, its imposed absence, greatly contributed to the perpetuation of illiteracy among those women who were caught between the patriarchal pressure of the family and the modernising laws of the state.

Moral dress and the Islamic Revolution

It has been argued that the practices of modernisation put in place since the Westernising economic and cultural reforms of Reza Shah in the 1920s created persistent polarisations at the level of social dynamics, opposing the reformist liberal Westernised class to the conservative traditionalist classes. As Nikki Keddie puts it, 'Modernization creates not only a dual economy but also a dual society, in which the wealthier Westernized classes speak a different language from the traditional or popular classes and have a very different lifestyle and cultural values'.[17]

Developing this observation, this article argues that there is a continuous dynamic in terms of class distinction accompanying the aesthetic definition of Western style. The Islamic Revolution introduced new forms of social mobility, creating access to superior education and jobs for women from traditionalist classes. That is to say, although a divide based on lifestyle and cultural values exists in Iran today (especially in urban settings), Western style is appropriated and reworked by people in different class positions and with different political orientations. This divide is the expression of different modes of engagement with the modern repertoire in Iran, rather than a reflection of a society constituted out of modern and non-modern polarised populations.

Media and journalistic political discourses in the West have picked up and reproduced this dual image of Iranian society, rather than accounted for the complex social reality within the country. After the Islamic Revolution, political commentaries and documentaries have tended to equate Iranian disenfranchised classes with excessive Islamic religiosity, at the same time presenting an allegedly secular (in Western terms), Westernised and reformist young student population. However, it is important to emphasise that even during the wave of modernisation at the beginning of the twentieth century, the opposition to forced modernisation displayed on the body came from a variety of social actors, including pro-modernisation intellectuals.

The Islamic Revolution emerged from a long-term dynamic that reunited a variety of social classes in the struggle against the shah's despotic regime. The emerging educated classes, leftist intellectuals among them, linked their interests with those of the commercial class of the Bazaar (*bazaari*) acting under the leadership of the religious authorities.[18] The *ulama* were unhappy with the monarchic form of government and its modern overtones. One of the main sources of conflict concerned the regulation of land and legal procedures regarding contracts. While *shari'a* prohibited state intervention in land and property, the shah's government introduced agrarian land reform and also regulated urban property in the 1960s. Contracts were regulated according to public policies that were not in harmony with the *shari'a* (or with the private interests of well-to-do clergymen and *bazaari*).[19] Muhammad Reza Shah encouraged industrial modernisation with the help of foreign specialists. The employment of foreign experts meant that local universities, while offering higher education and training, could not ensure jobs to their new graduates. In this context, leftist ideas began to circulate among newly educated persons.[20]

The Islamic Revolution erupted in the late 1970s as civil unrest; the shah's policies were associated with westernisation, including dress regulations. Thus, after the first violent repression of the regime's opponents on 8 September 1978, wearing non-Western style clothing meant resistance against the shah. According to Patricia Baker,

> For over a year the word *kravati* (tie-wearer) had come to be the fashionable term for disparagement for any intellectual and smart, clean clothing was seen as *estekbar* (ostentation) and thus unfitting to devout Muslim men, in revolutionary circles. The *chador* was rapidly becoming an acknowledged symbol of rebellion against the established political order, although *it did not necessarily imply support for the establishment of an Islamic state*. Thus, after veiled women had been refused entry into university in 1977, it was symbolically donned as a sign of protest (against Pahlavi regime) by most female demonstrators in the following year.[21]

With the installation of the new government led by Ayatollah Khomeini, women working in government positions were required to wear a form of dress cover. In the spring of 1980 big demonstrations against head coverings swept Tehran. A period of unrest followed. On 13 March 1980, the Ayatollah announced publicly that women should consider it a moral duty to wear the *chador*, and on 5 July all women in public and employment were required to wear the headscarf. The restoration of *shari'a* law on 30 May 1981 established a punishment of imprisonment up to one year for all women, Muslim or not, who did not wear *hijab* in public.

For the period that followed, studies of women's dress in Iran are scarce; the subject is a delicate one. Notable is Fariba Adelkhah's *Revolution under the Veil*, which shows how the veiling policy empowered a large number of women, who were now able to attend schools and become educated without the pressure of the family restricting their mobility outside the home.[22] This increased social mobility among the lower classes, and contributed to the formation of a new middle class, attuned to Islamic sensibilities. This is the period of the 'normalisation' of the Islamic Revolution, characterised by the professionalisation of the Revolutionary class.

The establishment of *shari'a* in Iran also meant the regulation of conduct in public spaces, on which more below. Among these 'Islamic' regulations, those that refer to bodily attitudes and to photographic representations are most important for this essay. Besides the dress code for women, the representation of the uncovered female body in public is formally forbidden. Men's bodies also need to be covered, short trousers being considered inappropriate.

After the election of President Khatami in 1998, with widespread popular support from the young generation, the imposition of the dress code became more relaxed. Western media took up this subject and presented it as a sign of the liberalisation, if not secularisation, of Iranian society. Documentary films show the divide between the Westernised class and all others, and the recurrent theme is the attitude toward dress, veiling and, ultimately, consumption that is supposed to indicate the divorce of an Iranian upper middle class from Islamic 'traditional' values. In the overwhelming majority of journalistic accounts, this traditional/westernised divide has spatial expression as public/private space, where in private people (especially women of the upper classes) can behave 'freely' (read in a non-Islamic fashion), while in public they would fall under oppressive traditionalism. Talal Asad emphasises that Islamic societies are generally depicted as totalitarian systems that impose *shari'a* law upon their subjects. He shows how this position is in fact the outcome of a secularist intellectual position that does not take into account the historicity of secularism or the role of religion in the formation of the secular. Asad argues that *shari'a* is a legal form that is able to regulate only some aspects of social life. He contrasts this with the secular state's mechanisms of power that are pervasive in all aspects of life, be they public or private. 'The reach of institutional powers' in a modern secular state extends in harmony with the mode of subject formation in these states, and depends on the spatial organisation and the emphasis on visibility.[23]

This article strives to undo this binary while approaching fashion photography practices in terms of their relationship with the bodies, spaces, places and times of fashion in Tehran. While there is a clear difference between the Westernised population and the traditional one, their relationship can perhaps best be understood as a continuum and not a divide, mostly related to access to fashion objects and aesthetic preferences, and independent of political choice or personal ethical concerns. The distinction is therefore less related to 'different cultural values' than to different practices that shape distinct subjectivities within the same overarching Islamic context. Beyond these aesthetic choices, issues of male dominance, sexuality and segregation of gender in exterior spaces may remain common concerns among a greater part of the population and cut across Westernised/traditionalist separated categories. The Iranian socio-political landscape is characterised by a particular dynamic that distinguishes it from the surrounding Islamic world. This dynamic is very well depicted in the work of Michael Fischer, who emphatically affirms that Iranian society 'may yet prove to be a leader in an escape from what has been a fundamentalising direction of politics in the Islamic world where, in places other than Iran, Islamic welfare and fighting organizations have stepped into voids of the disintegration of state services, and [resulting in] the creation of "sacrifice zones" outside the enclaves of wealth and transnational trade'.[24] This article underlines the formation of a certain type of female political subjectivity, a constitutive part of this dynamic.

In my interviewees' accounts, the term 'modernity' appears both linked to a geographic space (the West) and to behaviour and body mobility. The two are not always coincident, that is, wearing modern clothes does not necessarily make you 'modern', and 'being modern in Iran' may have a completely different meaning to modernity in the West.[25]

Latent Orientalism and feminist critiques: Inside the modern Middle East

The question of visibility and its effect on the reorganisation of social and physical space is at the core of feminist critiques of Orientalism. The game of interior/exterior, of public and private, of political and civil, plays at the border that separates the two, where their significances are negotiated in terms of visibility.[26] The gendered attributes of public and private lie at the core of different understandings of the veil.[27] Many anthropologists have explored the implications of the new political categories that emerged along with the Enlightenment ideologies of separate spheres and their complicated intertwining.[28] The negotiation of the borders between public and private is a social practice that itself informs the structure of this dichotomy. It implies uses of spaces and objects that gradually become socially perceived as borders. One of the best examples of these objects is the women's veil. Although the veil is not central to this article, it is central to many feminist critiques of Orientalism. The dichotomies created through a representation of the East are not only political, but also gendered and sexual. Meyda Yeğenoğlu is one of the voices that points to Edward Said's lack of engagement with 'latent Orientalism'.[29] Described but not analysed in Said's book, 'latent Orientalism' refers not only to the gendered differences in the Orient and sexual fantasies revolving around Oriental women, but also to the way in which the difference West/Orient is represented in gendered terms.[30] Thus in Western colonial narratives, the veiled woman stands for the non-Western spaces that should open up to the gaze of the coloniser, and the difference 'West versus indigenous' is imagined and concentrated on the woman's body and/or its absence (covered by the veil). In this (colonial and post-colonial) discursive configuration, the presence of the veil is equated with the absence of women from the public (political) sphere, because women's bodies were not 'entirely visible' in this space. In other words, the veil meant a non-modern social space and indicated an otherness against which the Western self is constructed.[31] Moving towards Tehran, this article shows how women's body mobility and visibility are two categories found in interrelation. This dynamic calls into question this very type of separation between the modern West and its others.

In the past two decades, feminist studies of the Middle East have addressed and deconstructed the narrative that separates a modern

West and a non-modern (Muslim) Middle East. These critiques take two main approaches: first, the historical study of 'modernising the region' from women's perspective. During the colonial period, non-Western locations addressed and shaped the modern project, even if they were not directly part of the colonies. Some scholars of the Middle East addressed the way in which new political configurations and new forms of citizenship emerged during the nineteenth and twentieth centuries and women's role in this modernising project.[32]

A second way of approaching and blurring the dichotomy between a modern West and a non-modern other is through studying the recent women's movement and mobilisation of women in the Middle East. These movements may have secular or Islamic undertones, but they all crystallise around the idea of women's liberation and participation in the public sphere.[33] Women's movements in the Middle East directly relate to the modern construction of citizenship and participation, regardless of their (non)religious orientation.[34]

Both these approaches show how developments in women's political participation engage modern modes of subject formation in a specific context and configuration of power relations, defined by patriarchy, religious domination or secular projects. Authors underline the importance of the physical presence of women in different spaces of debate, be they public and literary, political or scientific. Bodily mobility accompanies and (in)forms this presence. All these critiques help us understand how modernity forms a repertoire of modes of subject formation, rather than a unique model that is adopted or rejected in 'non-Western' locations. Fashion practices in general are the expression of a particular mode of understanding oneself in relation to society, part of what one may call the modern subjectivity repertoire. This article presents the intersection of elements of this repertoire (especially fashion photography) with local specificities configuring a particular 'regime of modernity'[35] that emerges (in Iran) as a rhizomatic occurrence[36] rather than as genealogic branches from a central modern root situated in the West.

The ideal body of 'modern' photography

The second part of this article presents in ethnographic detail the processes of photographic production as I observed them on two occasions in Tehran. The comments of the people directly involved in the process, as well as descriptions of the studios and the surroundings, will contribute to the understanding of the material conditions of image creation in the Tehran fashion industry. Interviews were conducted in English if not otherwise specified, and were transcribed without corrections.

Many designers in Tehran have their creations worn by models (always amateurs, mainly friends or the designers themselves) and photographed. They arrange the pictures in catalogues or portfolios to be presented to their clients. I saw a number of portfolios, the most impressive being Parissa's. She had collected photos of her creations since she began designing twenty years earlier. Although the photos were not neatly arranged, I was able to see the transformation in her style. Both photographer and models were her friends. The pictures were taken in her own house or garden. One of the most interesting settings was an empty swimming pool, with autumn leaves spread all over the blue background (in fact the autumn collection is Parissa's favourite, precisely because of the colours).

Although I met three photographers who worked with fashion designers in Tehran, I would hesitate to speak of an established field of fashion photography in Iran. A young designer, Mehran, first took me to the workshop of the photographer with whom he works. Situated downtown, not far from Baharestan, the studio was in a modified fourth-floor apartment. Laya, the dynamic and well-coiffed photographer, invited me to have tea along with three other women in their twenties. I later found out that one of them acted as a model for Mehran's creations. None of the women wore headscarves or *manto* (the overall coat compulsory in public spaces that comes in a wide variety of fabrics, cuts and colours) inside the studio. They were sitting on a low bed in the middle room of the apartment, now converted into the office of the studio. On the desk there was a telephone, a set of *Aks*, the local photography publication, a calendar and fiscal receipts, along with other office supplies. The room to the left of the entrance was the laboratory, to which I did not have access. I was invited into the studio, the room at the right of the entrance. The space contained only a metallic shelf against the right-hand wall and a chair in the farthest left-hand corner. In the same corner hung big blue, red and yellow curtains used for backgrounds in taking pictures. The studio was equipped with two projectors, some tripods and an electric heater, which the host turned on.

During our talk, we mainly discussed the profession of photographer in Tehran. The lack of an appropriate space for a studio is what bothered Laya the most. Nevertheless, she showed me some of her work, mostly portraits; her passion was doing portraits, especially women's portraits. Laya confessed that because of the specificity of the public spaces in Tehran, not all of her work may be exhibited. Her collaboration with Mehran was limited to the collection he did as a student for his BA degree. That collection was later sent to Finland for the international fashion exhibition in 2002. At first glance, her photographs disturbed me, but I was not exactly sure why. Only later, while witnessing a photographic session (which I will describe in detail shortly), did I realise that the static position of the fashion models seemed odd. The bodies in the photographs suggested immobility in their poses, even the photographs of fashion creations had a quality reminiscent of old-fashioned wedding pictures. In contrast, fashion photographs in Europe are characterised by a certain mobility of the body, achieved through different techniques, from rapid shooting to image collage.[37] This is rarely seen in Tehran fashion photography.

In Tehran fashion photography, the body, and the female body in particular, is represented in an immobile position. In public spaces one can easily observe the immobility of women, and their restraint in movements and gestures. This was a characteristic that has seemed strange to my eyes since the beginning of my first sojourn in this city. Women on the street were generally very conscious of their body position, almost always looking straight ahead; eye contact was generally avoided. Hands were kept near the body, when they were not hidden by the *chador*. In her analysis of body movement in Tehran, Soheila Shahshahani explains how public and private spaces are differently marked through body postures and gestures.[38] She argues that while men's bodies, which are allowed a great liberty of movement, dominate the public, the private gives women more mobility. The author uses the example of dancing in private quarters to illustrate her case. Dance movement is the final expression of this domestic mobility, complementary to women's public immobility. Photographic representations follow this model, sometimes in unexpected ways. Explanations for this tendency may be found in the intersection between various twentieth-century political reforms and a specific gendering of space, as Shahshahani would argue. I found similar body immobility in fashion photographs for *Lotus* magazine (Figure 3), the publication of the Lotus fashion house whose first issue appeared in March 2003. Lotus, owned by Mrs Mahla Zamani, is the only women's fashion house with a public image in Iran. Besides designs for individual uses, it provides uniforms for a variety of governmental and private institutions.

Lotus fashion magazine compensates for the lack of other advertising for women's dress. In fact, although there are billboards all over Tehran advertising various products, clothing is almost never their focus. Officially, following *shari'a* moral rules, bodies are not to be shown in their entirety, especially women's bodies. Thus, advertising for commodities uses photos of the object itself, accompanied by bilingual texts (Farsi and English, an interesting detail in itself) and sometimes parts of the body, such as eyes or hands manipulating the commodity. Because of these regulations, *Lotus* has had a difficult birth. In order to be able to

Figure 3: Cover of Lotus fashion magazine. © Mahla Zamani, 2003, reproduced with permission.

publish this locally produced fashion magazine, Mahla Zamani needed to develop a strategy. The journal is registered for professional use – that is, *Lotus* is officially addressed to the people who are involved in the fashion industry. Nevertheless, according to Mahla's account, it is the first post-Revolution magazine showing the faces of Iranian models:

> We could not show the face of the person, the original person in the photo. And even now, I was thinking they may not accept it (my magazine) and this is the first magazine that comes out with the original faces of the models. Some years ago they were like invisible masks. Sometimes it was a painting instead of the face.[39]

Destined for public use, these photographs show models taking up static poses, standing and, more rarely, sitting. There is one notable exception to this rule: a moving woman's body is acceptable only when associated with home appliances, for example the advertisement for the LG vacuum cleaner (Figure 4). Although a public representation, this photograph depicts a domestic woman's body attending to home chores. In the configuration of patriarchal, religious and state power at play in public, this is, along with dance, another instance of unproblematic motion of a woman's body.[40]

The only fashion photographs I have seen with models giving the impression of movement were in private portfolios. As Nasser, a photographer, told me later on, posing in motion is a frequent motif in photographs taken for private designers. To designate difference in types of fashion photographs, Nasser used a term that immediately interested me: 'And I can take many kind of poses for girls, but it is forbidden to take *modern* pictures. Just you have to show the quality and the dresses' (emphasis added). This formulation suggests that 'the quality of dresses' is insufficient to ensure the modernity of a picture. In Nasser's opinion there is something that is missing in a non-modern picture, a constitutive part that adds to the form, colours, cut of the dress, in order to give it the modern quality. I immediately inquired about his meaning of 'modern pictures'; his response raised several key themes:

> Of course you have seen the *Elle* magazine, or *Vogue*, but we cannot do this here. When you see *Elle* or *Vogue*, or other fashion magazines, you see the model maybe moving, maybe in a special pose, lying or something like that. But here, no, we cannot do this. Just straight looking and it has to be simple.[41]

Thus, 'modern' is equated with bodies in movement, leaving tradition to the realm of the immobile, static and unfashionable. The modern woman's body is a dynamic one, the deeper characteristics of modernity inscribed upon it: acceleration of time, social flexibility and mobility, all expressed in fashion's rhythm and its capacity for transforming the body's expression or the body itself. In Tehran, restrictions regarding

Figure 4: Advertising for vacuum cleaner on a bus in northern Tehran – Tajrish Square, 2003. Photo by Alec Balasescu.

the pose of the body, coupled with the equation 'fashion equals modernity', led the photographers I interviewed to conclude that fashion is non-existent in Tehran. However, many stylists involved in fashion production have a different opinion. Fashion is constituted as a contested domain because of its immediate reference to modernity. For Nasser a modern body is simultaneously visible and mobile, following Western ideal types. For the stylists creating in the context of Tehran fashion production, the Western ideal type, while present, is only one reference among others contributing to the creation of a variety of aesthetic styles.

On 5 April 2003, I visited Nasser's studio, a three-storey red brick building near Hafte-tir Square. I was invited by Mahla, in order to witness the photographic session for the second issue of her fashion magazine. The studio had offices on each storey, providing a high-ceilinged photographic studio with a metallic bridge about ten metres high. The architectural plans were brought through a friend of the photographer from Germany. I arrived at the studio at around 3pm, after I helped with loading the dresses for the photographic session into Mahla's car (an old model Mini Morris). Three female models in their early twenties arrived, whose first gesture was to remove their veils and comb their hair. I was offered potato chips, which are very popular among young people in Tehran.

The first session was for school uniforms (Figure 5). Presenting children's fashion and school uniforms was a new idea for Mahla. The first issue of her journal did not have such a presentation. The three models she used for the children's photographic session were between six and nine years old, and their mothers accompanied them. At the ground level there was the hall for taking pictures, in the underground was another big hall, used by the models to prepare themselves for the session – there were no real dressing rooms, just a big hall, with a small table, chairs and a telephone in one corner, and a tap and sink against one of the walls. I later found out that this room was also used as a studio. I made light conversation with the models – one of them spoke Spanish, another German. We were on the ground floor. Three men prepared the studio. A polyester frame was set up to protect the photographer from the light of the professional photographic projectors.

During the photographic session I talked to Farshid, a photographer, the models and Mahla. The models were all university students; Mahla personally recruited them. She told me the story of one particular young woman whom she had seen while driving her car. Mahla made a U-turn and followed the young woman's car until it stopped. Mahla offered the job directly to the young woman who now came to the *Lotus* office accompanied by her mother. Over tea, Mahla explained her work and

Figure 5: Schoolgirls photography in Lotus Magazine. © Mahla Zamani, 2003, reproduced with permission.

showed them the dress she was currently producing and the first issue of *Lotus* magazine.

The models told me that there was no material gain in this work, but they did it as a hobby. One man was running from projector to projector modifying the light's intensity. Two others were talking about the photographic materials. The schoolgirls entered the studio, accompanied by their mothers. Mahla very carefully tied their shoes, talking gently with them. In the conversations I had, fashion, dress codes and modernity intertwined, bringing the contested social meanings of these terms to the surface. Farshid complained about having to do fashion photography, as he was a specialist in still photography. 'Fashion photography is new here. I do not like to do it'. Mahla answered promptly: 'He doesn't like it, because he doesn't like the headscarf'. The photographer replied: 'I don't like it but I have to do it. Each country has a tradition. Here we have to deal with this tradition'. Farshid perceived 'tradition' as an impediment to the development of fashion, as something that directly opposed fashion, and rendered useless Mahla's efforts to create a fashion magazine. His experience abroad, in Switzerland, where he would spend the summer, contrasted with his manner of working in Tehran:

> You are looking at fashion in Tehran?! This is my question to you: [amply gesturing towards the little girls wearing blue headscarves]. If you think this is fashion, I will say it is fashion! And these are the children of fashion.[42]

Leaving aside his ironic and caustic tone, Farshid's affirmation distils the meaning he attaches to the term fashion. For him (as for many others I interviewed) fashion was anything but the work he was engaged in at the moment of our meeting, even though he was photographing for a fashion magazine. His affirmation became even more interesting when he discussed the issue of body posture and pose. 'Fashion (in Switzerland) is different,' he continued. 'You can do everything you want! Here you cannot! I see women as men, no difference. So it should be no difference here, too'. The difference was both gendered and geographically marked. In Farshid's words, there was a 'here' where gender organised fashion photography and a 'there' where gender was erased. 'There' was modern (and fashion existed) while 'here' was not. This *difference* was deeply reflected in Tehran fashion practices, but the dynamic of these practices may also reflect shifts in the meaning of this difference. The restraint in women's body movements and postures and the limited tolerance in most public places towards experimental clothing are indicators of the difference between men and women in Tehran. Thus, while talking about fashion, Nasser told me, 'Young people like to be fashionable. You can see it everywhere, and there is no problem for the guys. But for women ... In the houses yes, in the parties, yes'.[43] Here one can find the same perceived and perpetual separation and juxtaposition men/women, public/private. 'In the houses, in the parties' are private locations open to 'modern bodies' and to the display of fashionable clothing.

I witnessed photographing for 'private portfolios' in the workshop of Shadi Parand, a designer who gained momentum after she was invited to exhibit her work at the Victoria and Albert Museum, London, in January 2004. A night of Iranian fashion animated the Statues' Hall of the museum, featuring Iranian designers from Tehran, Paris and London. When I talked with her after the show and after a series of articles on her creations published in Western European journals, Shadi started to build a portfolio using clients as models. The designer used the portfolio to show her clients and to promote herself in Western fashion journals. She also recruited a young woman, Safro, who had finished her studies in Iranian handicrafts, and who was both assistant and model. Safro initially was Shadi's client and became a model after she expressed interest in working in fashion design. Shadi herself took the photographs of her creations, and sometimes invited a male friend to help. At the time of my visit, using two digital cameras, Shadi and her friend took pictures of Safro and a client wearing the clothes she had ordered. While Safro displayed a relaxed bodily attitude, moving freely and posing for the cameras, the client was rigid in her posing. Shadi's friend's and my presence, both of us armed with cameras, obviously made her uncomfortable. Knowing that the photographs would be used only for private purposes did not change the client's body attitude. In a certain manner, our presence there already constituted a public, unlike Safro who was used to posing for an audience (Figure 6). Photographs of her wearing Shadi's creations were also used in Western European journals.

By this point, the rules followed by photographic representations and mobility in public should have become clearer. A geography of visibility/mobility is established, with multi-layered spaces presenting different degrees of acceptance of body exposure for women. Thus, private or semi-private spaces allow the circulation of images that freely combine mobility and visibility. The same mode of representation is used outside Iran. In Iran, it seems that the representations of women in public must integrate a certain immobility or strict attitude of the body. However, public representations of women may integrate body mobility when they show women performing in the domestic space.

The practice of fashion advertising in Tehran's urban spaces follows the same gender separation inscribed in the spatial regime. Easier to control, visual representations generally follow the dominant discourse

Gendered Modernity and Fashion Photography in Tehran 241

Figure 6: Safro posing for Shadi's portfolio, 2004. © Shadi Parand, reproduced with permission.

that allows visibility for men's bodies, while women's bodies are invisible or at best immobile when in public. In particular, the association of women's mobile bodies with fashion products is rendered invisible in the spaces that fall under official control. Fashion boutiques for women in Tehran do not have women models' images on the banners above the door, in contrast to men's fashion stores (Figures 7a and 7b).

In Tehran there is one important exception concerning the representation of women and women's bodies in public: film posters. The importance of the film industry to the bodily aesthetic, and the marriage of fashion and film, is not recent.[44] In spring 2003, to celebrate the long collaboration between fashion and film, the Parisian stores Printemps and Bon Marché both organised exhibitions presenting famous actors and their fashion choices, in film or in private life. In winter 2000, the Guggenheim Museum in New York organised an Armani retrospective. One special section was dedicated to stars and their Armani dresses, as they appeared on the silver screen. And the lifetime 'aesthetic marriage' between Yves Saint Laurent and Catherine Deneuve is widely known. In many cases film stars set the trend in fashion.

Tehran is no exception to this rule. Azade is one of the most famous costume and set designers in Iran (nominated twice for the Sixth Iranian Cinema Festival Award). At the same time, she is a keen observer of the aesthetic influences film has on the fashioning of the body in Tehran.

> For example, when I worked on the movie 'Haman, in '68' (1990), ... I tried to change a little the dress of women appearing on the street. I give to actresses appearing on the street to wear not only *mantos*, but two pieces dress or things like this.[45]

The film is set in contemporary Tehran and tells the story of a woman who tries to divorce her husband. He opposes the divorce because he is still in love with her (and because the *shari'a* laws benefit men and allow him to do so). At the time, two-piece dresses were not seen on the streets of Tehran. Azade used this artifice mainly to suggest the change of setting from public spaces to private houses.

> The film has been very popular, and it was the first movie after the revolution in which we could see women dressed differently. After this, I have seen how the designers from Tehran, in their small creation houses, started to change the clothing style: colours, cuts ...[46]

I can only rely on her account regarding this film as the generator of new style, but what is interesting in this case is not the 'originality' of the design, but rather the back-and-forth of aesthetic canons from the screen to everyday life. In 2004, some banners for popular movies in Tehran were showing the actors in their entirety, dressed in street clothes, walking

Figures 7a and 7b: Entrances fashion boutiques for women (above) and for men (below), Tehran, 2004. Photo by Alec Balasescu.

towards the viewer. Women occupied an important place in these posters; they often had lead roles in films with a contemporary setting.[47] One of the most recent examples is the movie *Ghogha*, which follows the story of a woman who escapes from prison in order to enquire into her dark past and to avenge her sister. The film touches current urban themes such as AIDS, class division and prostitution. The poster shows Ghogha, the heroine, dressed in a blue headscarf, a dark blue overcoat, jeans and dark glasses, walking towards the viewer followed by two young men, also dressed in a streetwise fashion (Figure 8). It is interesting to note that on this banner (and in the movie), the woman is the leader, the centre of the image, while in other posters women usually follow men. With the exception of film posters, no other banners at the time of my fieldwork in Tehran showed women's bodies engaged in movement in a publicly

Figure 8: Banner for the motion picture *Ghogha*, centre of Tehran, 2003. Photo by Alec Balasescu.

meaningful way. These posters constitute an ad hoc sort of advertising for women's dress, proposing, through the actresses' presence, different styles of the body in public. While this may not be a new phenomenon, I only noticed it during the summer of 2003. It must be remembered that in all of the cases, including movie posters, the women wear headscarves.

While body mobility and exposure is equated with Western-type modernity, in Tehran's public spaces women's bodies are ideally immobile and covered. Nonetheless, while one may find this ideal in most of the public photographic representation and in shop-window mannequins, women's fashion practices introduce new dimensions and meanings to the use of urban space in Tehran. Just as in the movie *Ghogha*, certain types of modern (mobile) women are making their presence known in the predominantly masculine urban public space of Tehran.

Conclusion

Social and historical analysis of twentieth-century Iran shows that dress reforms concerned and directly influenced the mobility and visibility of women's bodies. Afsaneh Najmabadi's analysis of the creation of the modern body in Iran explains how the unveiling practices were accompanied by physical education and new prescriptions in etiquette for women who appeared in public unveiled.[48] In her account of the modernisation of women in early twentieth-century Iran, the author shows how women were trained to 'veil' their verbal language as well as their body language in the absence of the veil. School curricula and etiquette books were the vehicles of this training. Body training and practices were part of modern subject formation. Modernisation meant the exit of (some) Iranian women from the homosocial space of domesticity into public (masculine) space. The early twentieth-century ideal modern Iranian woman was portrayed as an ungendered person, chaste and restrained in her bodily motions and expressions. Therefore, women's appropriation of a modern Iranian public space was accompanied by the creation of a new type of women's subjectivity, through new processes of subject formation that emphasised immobility and restraint. This essay has shown how the early twentieth-century modern asexual woman's body is now thought of and presented as non-modern in media discourses about Iran. This is the very body that the Islamic regime idealises in its representations. Fashion practices, from production to consumption and representation, offer the spaces for Iranian women and men to call into question and re-work this ideal Islamic republican body daily.

In Iran it may be said that Reza Shah's wave of modernisation allowed women's visibility in public. All the while, the configuration of power in social and cultural contexts allowed this visibility at the expense of mobility. Women from traditionalist classes entirely lost their mobility, while those from upper classes were trained to be immobile in their public appearance. In the period immediately following the Islamic Revolution the visibility of the previous period was reformed; from a certain perspective, it was taken away. However, mobility increased for women who had previously been deprived of the opportunity to be present in socially meaningful spaces. The new regime proposed a new type of modern body that echoed the previous one, while encouraging mobility at the expense of visibility. Spatially coded standards of mobility and exposure for women's bodies continue to be vigorously enacted and are visible in photographic representations in Tehran's public spaces and in fashion photography practices. New aesthetics emerging from the encounter between fashion (and aesthetic models of public presence and behaviour) and the Iranian modern regime, create a new understanding of the self in relation to other and to the politics of public presence. In contemporary Iran old standards are redefined, combining requirements of the Islamic Republic's regulations with new definitions of gender and mobility.

A deeper analysis reveals that the distinction between public and private is difficult to make according to regimes of visibility. While fashion photographs destined for private portfolios display mobile bodies, the portfolios themselves are, in a way, for public, albeit restrained, use. Representations of mobile women's bodies similarly appear sometimes in public (as in the case of vacuum cleaner advertising) when they are not associated with publicly meaningful actions. Women's bodies' visibility and mobility is ideally regulated in all public spaces in Tehran, but can be strictly controlled only in certain areas, such as fashion boutiques' advertising banners, that fall within the reach of administrative power. Women's fashion itself is a problematic category for the Islamic regime in Iran, since it promotes a type of body not exactly in conformity with the ideal of the Revolution. However, the social dynamic after the Islamic Revolution needs to be reassessed, in order to avoid the risk of perpetuating the stereotype of an elusive and *static* Islamic non-modern state and an oppositional modernised civil society. Interstitial spaces out of reach or harder to control are the spaces in which some Iranians are experimenting with a mobile type of body (and subjectivity). This body is the expression of the new type of subjectivity that combines state regulations with daily practices (like fashion). This subjectivity emerges at the intersection of desire, aesthetic choices, class position, religious convictions, state regulation, social practices and spatial configurations. It is not necessarily (nor simultaneously) Westernised, secular or contestatory towards the political regime, but it is inevitably modern.

Notes

This research was supported by funding from the Wenner-Gren Foundation for Anthropological Research and the French Institute of Research in Iran (IFRI). This essay is a re-worked chapter from the author's PhD thesis. The author is deeply indebted to all the following individuals for their comments and help, notably: William Maurer, Karen Leonard, Teresa Caldeira, Liisa Malkki, James Ferguson, Susan Ossman, Mahla Zamani, Shadi Parand, Maryam, Ghassideh and Houshang Golmakani, Nilüfer Göle, Soheila Shahshahani, Nader and Michael Tingay for editing. Without the dedicated work of Patricia Hayes and Marti Lybeck this article would not have attained its intellectual coherence and fluidity. All names of the interviewees have been changed out of respect for the personal desire for anonymity.

1. The research forms part of Alexandru Balasescu, 'Fashioning Subjects, Unveiling Modernity: The Co/motion of Aesthetics between Paris and Tehran', unpublished PhD thesis, University of California, Irvine, 2004.
2. Pierre Bourdieu, *Outline of a Theory of Practice*, tr. Richard Nice (Cambridge: Cambridge University Press, 1977); Jürgen Habermas, *The Structural Transformation of the Public Sphere*, trans. Thomas Burger (Cambridge, MA: MIT Press, 1989); Michelle Zimbalist Rosaldo and Louise Lamphere (eds), *Woman, Culture, and Society* (Stanford: Stanford University Press, 1974). For an overview of historical transformations of public space see Richard Sennett, *The Fall of the Public Man* (New York: W. W. Norton, 1994).
3. See Dipesh Chakrabarty, *Provincializing Europe: Postcolonial Thought and Historical Difference* (Princeton: Princeton University Press, 2000); James Ferguson, *Expectations of Modernity: Myths and Meanings of Urban Life on the Zambian Copperbelt* (Berkeley: University of California Press, 1999); John Comaroff and Jean Comaroff, *Of Revelation and Revolution*, vol. 2: *The Dialectics of Modernity on a South African Frontier* (Chicago: University of Chicago Press, 1997).
4. See William M. O'Barr, *Culture and the Ad: Exploring Otherness in the World of Advertising* (Boulder, CO: Westview Press, 1994); Paula A. Treichler, Lisa Cartwright and Constance Penley (eds), *The Visible Woman: Imaging Technologies, Gender, and Science* (New York: New York University Press, 1998).
5. Much has been written on transnational Islam. For a general overview see David Herbert, 'Religious Traditions in the Public Sphere: Herbert, MacIntyre and the Representation of Religious Minorities', in Wasef Abdelrahman Shadid and P. S. Van Koningsveld (eds), *Muslims in the Margin: Political Responses to the Presence of Islam in Western Europe* (Kampen: Kok Pharos Publishing House, 1996) pp. 66–79, and the entire volume. For Muslim women's transnational experience, see Fedwa Malti-Douglas, *Medicines of the Soul: Female Bodies and Sacred Geographies in a Transnational Islam* (Berkeley: University of California Press; 2001) and Victoria Bernal, 'Islam, Transnational Culture and Modernity in Rural Sudan', in Maria Grosz-Ngaté and Omari Kokole (eds), *Gendered Encounters: Challenging Cultural Boundaries and Social Hierarchies in Africa* (New York: Routledge, 1997). Lara Deeb makes the case for an 'enchanted modern' that allows women an active role in the construction of civil society following an Islamic role model, that of Imam Husayn's sister, Zaynab. Lara Deeb, '"Doing Good like Sayyida Zaynab": Lebanese Shi'i Women's Participation in the Public Sphere', in Armando Salvatore and Mark LeVine (eds), *Religion, Social Practice, and Contested Hegemonies: Reconstructing the Public Sphere in Muslim Majority Societies* (New York: Palgrave, 2005). See Nilüfer Göle, 'Snapshots of Islamic Modernities', *Daedalus* 129 (2000), pp. 91–117, Nilüfer Göle, 'The Gendered Nature of the Public Sphere', *Public Culture* 10 (1997), pp. 61–81; Nilüfer Göle, 'Islam in Public: New Visibilities and New Imaginaries', *Public Culture* 14 (2002), pp. 173–90.
6. See Norma Claire Moruzzi, 'A Problem with Headscarves: Contemporary Complexities of Political and Social Identity', *Political Theory* 22 (1994), pp. 653–72.
7. Emma Tarlo, *Clothing Matters: Dress and Identity in India* (Chicago: University of Chicago Press, 1996).

8. One example of this is the recent bestseller, Azar Nafisi, *Reading Lolita in Tehran: A Memoir in Books* (New York: Random House, 2004). See also 'Iran: le président Khatami annonce un processus réformiste irréversible pour la République islamique', *Le Monde*, 5 March 2004, http://www.lemonde.fr/cgi-bin/ACHATS/acheter.cgi?offre= ARCHIVES&type_item=ART_ARCH_30J&objet_id=852900, accessed 9 May 2004; Nicholas D. Kristof, 'Those Sexy Iranians', *New York Times*, 8 May 2004 p. A17.
9. Fariba Adelkhah, *La révolution sous le voile:Femmes islamiques d'Iran* (Paris: Editions Karthala, 1991); Elaine Sciolino, *Persian Mirrors: The Elusive Face of Iran* (New York: Free Press, 2000).
10. See Patricia L. Baker, 'Politics of Dress: The Dress Reform Laws of 1920/30s Iran', in Nancy Lindisfarne-Tapper and Bruce Ingham (eds), *Languages of Dress in the Middle East* (Richmond, Surrey: Curzon, 1997), pp. 178–92; Houshang Chehabi, 'Staging the Emperor's New Clothes: Dress Codes and Nation Building under Reza Shah', *Iranian Studies* 26 (1993), pp. 209–30.
11. Sami Zubaida, *Law and Power in the Islamic World* (London: I. B. Tauris, 2003), p. 187 (emphasis added).
12. Ehsan Yarshater (ed.), *Encyclopaedia Iranica*, vol. 5 (Costa Mesa, CA: Mazda, 1992), p. 809 (emphasis added).
13. Baker, 'Politics of Dress', p. 185.
14. Carol Delaney, 'Father State, Motherland, and the Birth of Modern Turkey', in Sylvia Yanagisako and Carol Delaney (eds), *Naturalizing Power: Essays in Feminist Cultural Analysis* (New York: Routledge, 1995), pp. 177–200.
15. See Afsaneh Najmabadi, 'Veiled Discourse – Unveiled Bodies', *Feminist Studies* 19 (1993), pp. 487–518.
16. Yarshater (ed.), *Encyclopaedia Iranica*, vol. 5, p. 809.
17. Nikki Keddie, 'Introduction', in Michael E. Bonine and Nikki Keddie (eds), *Modern Iran: The Dialectics of Continuity and Change* (Albany: SUNY Press, 1981), pp. 1–16.
18. See Michael M. J. Fischer, *Iran: From Religious Dispute to Revolution* (Madison: University of Wisconsin Press, 2003). Fischer provides an inspiring reflection on the type of civil society emerging in Iran in his introduction.
19. See also Zubaida, *Law and Power in the Islamic World*.
20. See Jean-Pierre Digard, Bernard Hourcade and Yann Richard, *L'Iran au XXe siècle* (Paris: Fayard, 1996).
21. Baker, 'Politics of Dress', p. 185 (emphasis added).
22. Fariba Adelkhah, *Being Modern in Iran* (London: Hurst & Co., 1999).
23. Talal Asad, 'The Idea of an Anthropology of Islam', *Occasional Papers Series*, Center for Contemporary Arab Studies (Washington, D.C.: Georgetown University, 1986).
24. Fischer, *Iran*, pp. xxv–xxvi.
25. See Adelkhah, *Being Modern in Iran*.
26. See Pamela Z. Karimi, 'Women's Portable Habitats', *ISIM Newsletter* 13 (December 2003), pp. 14–15.
27. See Lila Abu-Lughod, *Veiled Sentiments: Honor and Poetry in a Bedouin Society*, (Berkeley: University of California Press, 1986); FatimaMernissi, *Beyond the Veil: Male-Female Dynamics in Modern Muslim Society*, revised edn (Bloomington: Indiana University Press, 1987); Malek Chebel, *L'Esprit de sérail: Mythes et pratiques sexuels au Maghreb* (Paris: Editions Payot et Rivages, 1995).
28. Michelle Z. Rosaldo, 'The Use and Abuse of Anthropology: Reflections on Feminism and Cross-Cultural Misunderstanding', *Signs* 5 (1980), pp. 389–417.
29. Meyda Yeğenoğlu, *Colonial Fantasies: Towards a Feminist Reading of Orientalism* (Cambridge: Cambridge University Press, 1998).
30. Edward W. Said, *Orientalism* (New York: Pantheon Books, 1978).
31. See Nilüfer Göle, *The Forbidden Modern: Civilization and Veiling* (Ann Arbor, MI: University of Michigan Press, 1996); Nadje Al-Ali, *Secularism, Gender, and the State in the Middle East: The Egyptian Women's Movement* (Cambridge: Cambridge University Press, 2000); Peter van

Gendered Modernity and Fashion Photography in Tehran 249

der Veer, 'The Moral State: Religion, Nation, and Empire in Victorian Britain and British India', in Peter van der Veer and Hartmut Lehmann (eds), *Nation and Religion: Perspectives on Europe and Asia* (Princeton, NJ: Princeton University Press, 1999), pp. 15–43; Mahmut Mutman, 'Pictures from Afar: Shooting the Middle East', in Mahmut Mutman and Yeğenoğlu Meyda (eds), *Orientalism and Cultural Differences* (Santa Cruz, CA: Center for Cultural Studies, University of California, Santa Cruz, 1992) pp. 1–44.

32. Timothy Mitchell, *Colonising Egypt* (Berkeley: University of California Press, 1991) analyses the technologies of the formation of the modern body in its relation with architectural space. Nikki Keddie offers an overview of the modernising attempts during the Qajar period in nineteenth-century Iran. Nikki Keddie, *Qajar Iran and the Rise of Reza Khan 1796–1925* (Costa Mesa, CA: Mazda Publishers, 1999). The impact of modernisation on women's bodies in Turkey may be followed in Göle, *Forbidden Modern*, as well as the essays in Şirin Tekeli (ed.), *Women in Modern Turkish Society: A Reader* (London: Zed Books, 1995).

33. See, for an overview of debates on women's movements in the Middle East, Suad Joseph (ed.), *Gender and Citizenship in the Middle East* (Syracuse, NY: Syracuse University Press, 2000); Lila Abu-Lughod, 'Orientalism and Middle East Feminist Studies', *Feminist Studies* 27 (2001), pp. 101–13; Valentine M. Moghadam, *Modernizing Women: Gender and Social Change in the Middle East*, 2nd edn (Boulder, CO: Lynne Rienner Publishers, 2003). The particular case of Iran is analysed by Parvin Paidar, 'Feminism and Islam in Iran', in Deniz Kandiyoti (ed.), *Gendering the Middle East: Emerging Perspectives* (Syracuse, NY: Syracuse University Press, 1996), pp. 51–69.

34. See Anna Secor, 'The Veil and Urban Space in Istanbul: Women's Dress, Mobility and Islamic Knowledge', *Gender, Place and Culture* 9 (2002), pp. 5–22, and Deeb, 'Doing Good like Sayyida Zaynab'.

35. With thanks to Teresa Caldeira for suggesting the term.

36. Gilles Deleuze and Félix Guattari introduced this term to designate similar phenomena emerging in different geographical locations without a traceable common root: Gilles Deleuze and Félix Guattari, *A Thousand Plateaus: Capitalism and Schizophrenia* tr. Brian Massumi (London: Athlone Press, 1986).

37. Photography developed in Iran in the last 100 years, and it followed a sinuous path. Even in the peak period of the Pahlavi reign, after the oil boom, representations of women in photography followed the same logic of gender differentiation as their western counterparts. Mobile bodies are part of photographic rules of representation in the west, but men and women are represented differently (as discussed in the introduction). Generally speaking, in Western photographic representations women seem to be less in control of the space of the photography, an interpretation suggested by the convention of women gazing at the camera, despite the body mobility suggested by the image. Also, the non-Western other is always represented in an inferior posture, more so if a woman is in question, perpetuating the politics of stereotyping. See Catherine A. Lutz and Jane L. Collins, *Reading National Geographic* (Chicago: University of Chicago Press, 1993); Michel Frizot (ed.), *A New History of Photography* (Cologne: Könemann, 1998); Stuart Hall (ed.), *Representation: Cultural Representations and Signifying Practices* (London: Sage, 1997); Wendy Woodward, Patricia Hayes and Gary Minkley (eds), *Deep Histories: Gender and Colonialism in Southern Africa* (Amsterdam: Rodopi, 2002).

38. Soheila Shahshahani, *Body as Medium of Meaning* (Somerset, NJ: Transaction Publishers, 2005).

39. Author interview with Malila Zamani, Tehran, 3 March 2003.

40. After the release of the photographs of prisoner abuse in Abu Ghraib, six painted banners representing the horrid scenes appeared on a freeway in northern Tehran. One of them had at the centre the American woman soldier keeping an Iraqi prisoner on a leash. The representation is rather masculine-looking, the unisex shape of the military uniform and the short haircut contributing to this impression. It is notable that her head is uncovered, and the original photo is reproduced in detail. The soldier represents the militarised

Western woman, unquestionably present in a publicly meaningful way. The image conflates Western women with an evil presence that dominates a Muslim man. While represented in public, this type of woman (unveiled, mobile, authoritarian) is shown as a counter-ideal for Iranian women.
41. Author interview with Nasser, Tehran, June 2003.
42. This and quotations in the preceding paragraph from author's conversations with Farshid, Mahla, and the models, Tehran, 5 April 2003.
43. Author interview with Nasser, Tehran, June 2003.
44. The Iranian film industry is an important source of political and social commentary. Recently Iranian directors have been widely recognised on the international scene. However, the use of film (and literature) as a tool for social critique is not recent in Iran; social injustice during the Pahlavi regime and the post-Islamic Revolution society was in the focus of filmmakers. See Michael M. J. Fischer, *Mute Dreams, Blind Owls, and Dispersed Knowledges: Persian Poesis in the Transnational Circuitry* (Durham: Duke University Press, 2004).
45. Author interview with Azade, Tehran, March 2003.
46. Author interview with Azade, Tehran, March 2003.
47. See Hamid Naficy, 'Poetics and Politics of Veil, Voice and Vision in Iranian Post-revolutionary Cinema', in David A. Bailey and Gilane Tawadros (eds), *Veil: Veiling, Representation and Contemporary Art* (Cambridge, MA: MIT Press, 2003), pp. 137–159.
48. Najmabadi, 'Veiled Discourse – Unveiled Bodies'.

10 Arne Svenson's Queer Taxonomy

Elizabeth C. Birdsall

New York photographer Arne Svenson is, unabashedly and purposefully, an artist with an archivist's eye. While consistently working in series that are taxonomically influenced, his aesthetic in the mid-1990s bore strong similarities to clinical and institutional imagery, moving away from earlier narrative hints at *noir*-ish drama and towards pictures that recall those made at police precincts and in medical laboratories. While Svenson has since begun to reintroduce subtly nuanced narrative and almost sentimental drama into newer projects, such as the darkly humorous *Sock Monkey* series and his tenderly ominous portraits of forensic sculptures, this refreshed emotiveness was built on and has benefited from a period in the 1990s when the artist's best work closely resembled data-collection practices.

This period produced Svenson's most challenging work to date – a deceptively simple aesthetic project which, when analysed contextually, reveals substantive historical, political and social meanings. This project consists of over seventy meticulously printed sixteen by twenty-inch gelatine-silver photographs, each depicting a man standing alone against a white wall on a wood floor, arms by his side. These images lack the traditional portrait conventions that convey messages about their subjects' status and interior lives. Instead of employing props, dramatic poses and rhetorical lighting to distinguish individuals, each subject was photographed under identically spare and regimented physical conditions. This effectively reduces the visible differences between Svenson's models to their most basic physical characteristics. The stark uniformity with which these images were made indicates that, while the pictures portray individual people, the subjects have also been accumulated as a group. Rather than an array of fine-art portraits, then, the series is a systematised recording of data collected under carefully controlled circumstances.

While the pictures' clinical technique is reminiscent of institutional photography, their format (pristine large-scale prints, matted and framed) and technical virtuosity (sharp focus, fine tonal range) mark them as art objects. The aesthetic tension that this duality presents (are the pictures art made to look like evidence, or evidence made to look like art?) is underscored by the drab background and the repetitively posed models' neutral expressions, limiting cues about who the subjects are and what they share. It is difficult to deduce the group's logic from what is directly pictured in the images: one shows a man with short, dark hair in a three button suit, leaning at a barely perceptible angle (Figure 1); another depicts a robust man wearing his T-shirt tucked into denim shorts, hiking boots planted firmly on the floor, with a full, salt-and-pepper beard and long hair smoothly pulled back (Figure 2). Also included are a bespectacled gentleman wearing a houndstooth coat and polo shirt, right arm outstretched to hold the top of a knobby cane (Figure 3); an athletic, moustachioed man with close-cropped hair, sparely costumed in white long underwear and a simple bracelet (Figure 4); a wide-eyed man with spiky hair and a five o'clock shadow, sparely costumed in dark socks and business shoes, a white undershirt tucked into white boxers and a wristwatch (Figure 5); and a fair, faintly smiling man dressed in the garb of an Episcopal minister (Figure 6). Each model adheres to normative male visual stereotypes, but this is the only readily apparent shared attribute. Beyond this, inconsistencies break the patterns that otherwise suggest themselves. Most but not all appear to be young men of European descent. The majority look quite healthy, but some seem to be ailing. A few are in various states of undress and some are nude, but the bulk are clothed in street or business attire. Each subject looks squarely into the camera's lens with an unwavering gaze, giving the impression that they were photographed consensually. This lends the pictures a suggestion of collaboration that destabilises the authority of their institutional aesthetic.

Svenson's big, bold, stark accumulation of men is compelling and provocative. Even with the implied collaboration, the images' aesthetic suggests that the photographer was collecting evidence and exploiting the camera's claims to objectivity. Thus, despite the destabilising effect of the subjects' consensual gaze, the pictures bear an uncomfortable similarity to police mug shots. Their deliberate and uniform staging creates a sense of the subject as suspect, prompting the viewer to question the photographs' possible functions. The dissonance between the institutional, data-collection implications of the images in the context of the art gallery emphasises the degree to which their interpretation relies on factors outside the frame. For the images alone do not articulate the logic of their archival collection. We must look elsewhere to determine the shared attribute that justifies them as a group. This attribute is found in the work's title, *Faggots*. Svenson has collected, labelled and grouped his models according to their supposed sexual identity.

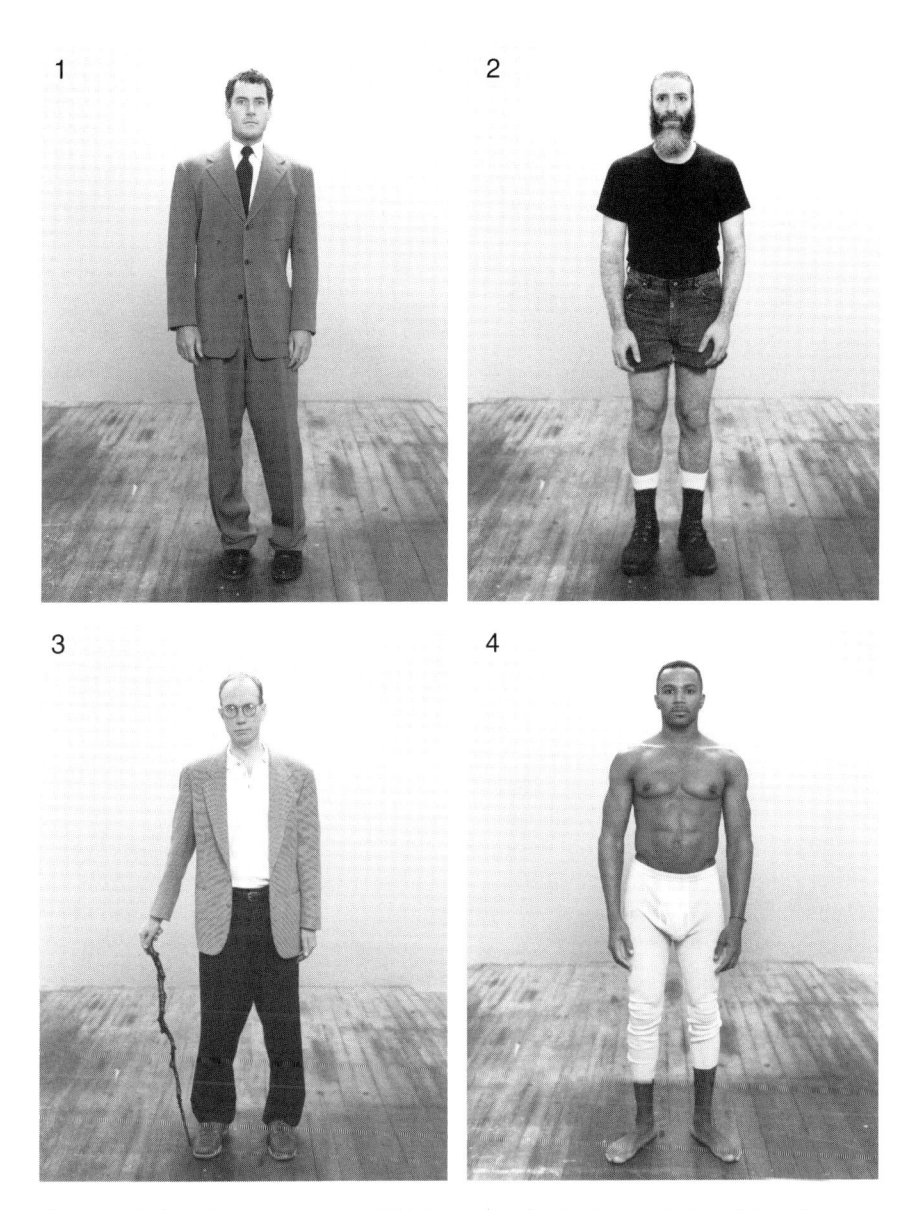

Figures 1–4: Arne Svenson, *Faggots*, 1994. Reproduced with the permission of Arne Svenson,

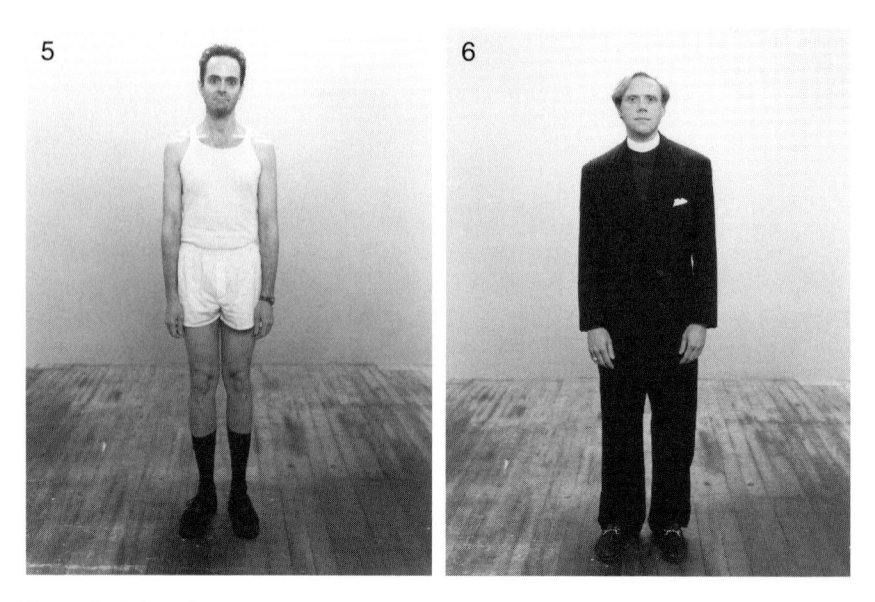

Figures 5–6: Arne Svenson, *Faggots*, 1994. Reproduced with the permission of Arne Svenson.

The title is an obvious and immediate challenge. The derogative social and cultural associations attached to the word 'faggot' further unsettle the work. Is its use ironic, literal or simply there for shock value? What is the purpose of an artwork that groups its subjects according to sexuality? The degree to which viewers can confidently establish a position from which to interpret the work's meanings and implications is contingent on the context in which they encounter it.

The work's 1994 public debut at New York University's Grey Art Gallery and Study Center offers a useful test case for analysing how its dissemination steers meaning and establishes viewing positions. The debut is the sole occasion where the series has been exhibited in its entirety and where the title has been prominently displayed. At this exhibit, the word 'FAGGOTS' was emblazoned in capital letters over the gallery entryway and an explanatory text was prominently placed just inside the gallery threshold. Combining Svenson's statement (the first two paragraphs) and curatorial comment, the panel declared:

> I want to look at men who some call 'faggots'. I want to see those signs and indications that you people who yell out the word 'faggot' see. I want to look at men who are staring back, the men called 'faggots' at who, as a boy, I wasn't supposed to look.
>
> I call up my friends and ask them to pose. They call up men – strangers to me – and they agree to pose. I photograph any man who will come to my studio. I ask every

one to stand on the same spot, holding their arms at their sides, eyes straight ahead. They choose what to wear or not to wear. Other than the pose, the only requirement that I have is that each man understands and acknowledges that this on-going series is called 'Faggots' and that, consequently, he may be labeled as such simply by virtue of inclusion.

[Statistically, 'faggot' is the word that is the most frequently used pejorative term for a male homosexual.]

Arne Svenson strives to photograph that which doesn't show. His oeuvre has been devoted to an investigation of the true nature of taxonomy. He endeavors to look for that indelible link which is not readily visible through markings or group membership. His photographs are never visually self-captioned; the title is the only evidence that holds them together.[1]

This text raises several questions. Does the artist suggest that there *are* visible 'signs and indications' for homosexuality, or is he contesting such assertions? It also suggests a tension between how artist and curator perceive the work – does the artist succeed in photographing 'that which doesn't show'? Does Svenson's statement or work indicate that he even attempts to? The text orients the viewer by explaining that the series was made by a gay man who is problematising 'faggot' as an essential quality and as a negative label. While Svenson's statements do not specifically enunciate this, the tone and content is enough to assure the viewer that the artist is working from an 'insider' position. The text establishes what the title and the images indicate more ambiguously: Svenson's series addresses issues of homosexual identity and identification, desire and the gaze. The combination of taxonomic and artistic practice in a project linked to personal identity suggests that complex historical and political relationships are embedded in these otherwise simple, straightforward images. This juxtaposition of form and content highlights the ambiguities that inhere in the conventions of science and culture, classification and identity, objects and subjects, art and photography.

Svenson embarked on the *Faggots* project in 1993, in a cultural climate that had been shaped by the politics and activism of the 1980s. By the early 1990s, the New York art scene and the city's gay population were emerging from several years of strife; both communities were at once newly strengthened and severely stressed. For the previous decade, members of these communities had fought against the intertwined issues of the AIDS crisis and attacks on freedom of artistic expression. These struggles had coalesced into the complicated fact that gay-themed art suddenly was more visible than before but also was increasingly subject to censorship.[2] For many, the overt intertwining of politics and art in the 1980s led to an evolution of aesthetic practices that were complex and sometimes contradictory, but ultimately positive, for they generated a new visibility and indeed an *effectiveness* of gay-themed art, much of it activist-oriented. In a discussion of the artistic practices associated with AIDS activism in the 1980s, James Meyer concluded that 'within postmodern political movements, representational practice has become flexible, self-critical, at least double: a representation that not only unveils, parodies, resists, but also informs, articulates – and above all contests'.[3] While Svenson's work is not directly associated with the activist art practice that Meyer refers to here, it is part of the larger project Meyer addresses. Svenson's work certainly can be said to parody, resist, inform, articulate and contest a social structure badly in need of revision.

When Svenson conceived of *Faggots*, the efforts of activists in addressing the AIDS crisis in particular and gay civil rights more generally had made enough headway for some to feel that there was an opportunity for reflection – contemplation, even. While the issues of AIDS and the suppression of gay-themed art remained and remain important, unfinished struggles, in the early 1990s there was a perceived opportunity to pause and reflect on what had been gained, lost and learned thus far. The approaching twenty-fifth anniversary of the Stonewall Riot, an important landmark for the gay civil-rights movement, provided an obvious touchstone for artists' and activists' reflections. Svenson's debut of *Faggots* intentionally coincided with this anniversary.

As a homosexual artist living and working in Manhattan since 1978, Svenson is an engaged participant in New York's art world and gay communities and it was through these avenues that he found men to participate in *Faggots*. The impetus for the series was born of his distressed response to a not-uncommon incident: seeing someone yelling the word 'faggot' at an anonymous passer-by.[4] On this particular occasion, in addition to being disturbed, Svenson was moved to ask himself what it was about that person that *visually* inspired such vitriol – and, perhaps more importantly, such confident labelling – from a stranger. There was nothing about the individual that, to Svenson, outwardly marked him as gay, but the epithet was hurled nonetheless. Svenson began to wonder: is homosexuality something that can be visually traced? Could he gather evidence? Would detectable similarities emerge from a collection of photographically assembled gay men? This line of questioning resulted in his word of mouth solicitation of models for the *Faggots* series ('I called up my friends …').[5]

In addition to the context of its conception and debut, Svenson's series should be considered against the background of twentieth-century evolutions in gay-themed art. The post-Stonewall years have seen the increasing visibility of works that directly reference homosexuality. The new prevalence of such imagery is a result not only of the socio-political changes of the 1970s and 1980s but also of the efforts of pioneering artists working in the decades leading up to Stonewall. Notably, beginning in the late 1950s and early 1960s Andy Warhol challenged repression by making visible images that had previously been private, highly censored, or so coded as to be unreadable by the uninitiated viewer. However, even in much of Warhol's work, particularly his 1964 *13 Most Wanted Men* and certainly in the work of other artists committed to picturing homosexuality before him (such as Paul Cadmus in the 1930s, 1940s and 1950s), 'homosexuality is alluded to rather than named, suggested rather than spoken'.[6] As Richard Meyer has shown, it is not just the representations of homosexuality that were vague in these works: the critical response to homosexual content generally skirted the issue as well, 'suggesting' but not 'naming' this subject matter.[7]

Though critics have traditionally glossed over this fact and artists themselves often coded their associations, some (particularly Warhol) were pioneers in bringing self-representations of gay bodies and gay desire into the sphere of visual culture, effecting a 'public face of queerness',[8] allowing overt representation of what previously had been underground or relegated to culture's outer margins. However, despite Warhol's trailblazing work and the subsequent prominence of gay artists making gay-themed imagery (such as Robert Mapplethorpe), photographic self-representation of homosexuals has been, when compared to heterosexual self-representation, both rare and repressed.[9] Thus any body of work that combats this inequity, including Svenson's, is part of the important project of minority self-representation. Additionally, and to my mind critically, Svenson's project does just the kind of declarative naming that earlier works avoided, producing a gay-themed art that is loudly and overtly out of the closet, not just suggesting, but shouting.

While the series' anti-homophobic intentions are deducible from the Grey Gallery wall text, the art-institutional presentation of the work and the exhibit's conjunction with the Stonewall anniversary celebrations, the degree to which this orientation is perceptible is debatable and was indeed in question from its first exhibition. Because the show was not reviewed, an assessment of the work's initial reception must rely on anecdotal evidence and the artist's recollections.[10] This suggests that, while many viewers found the exhibit unsettling, it was also viewed as compelling and the intended anti-homophobic frame was generally recognised. However, Svenson recalls two primary dissents. A few of the models were disappointed by the images, expecting their pictures to be more glamorous ('They wanted Mapplethorpe meets Avedon, but got something quite different', he recalled). On the other hand, some homosexual viewers bristled, one remarking that 'this is what homophobes do to us all the time; why are you perpetuating it?'

This second comment is in fact the crux of the work's double nature and points the way to how it can be understood as anti-homophobic in all of its incarnations: my reading here is that Svenson's work deploys what Michel Foucault has termed 'reverse discourse', a strategy of resistance whereby homosexuals disarm the repressive properties of the dominant culture and employ them in reconstructing a sense of self-empowered identity. As Foucault has shown, when homosexuality began to be both named and institutionally marginalised as a deviance in the nineteenth century, the very categories of 'social control' enabled a 'reverse discourse' wherein 'homosexuality began, in its own behalf, to demand that its legitimacy or "naturality" be acknowledged, often in the same vocabulary, using the same categories by which it was medically disqualified'.[11] In this way, and as Richard Meyer has pointed out, to 'utilize negative terms of homosexuality is not necessarily to endorse or accept those terms. It may also be to restage one's own outlaw status within a different register of representation and thereby to reopen the question of homosexuality for further inquiry'.[12] Cultural critics and art historians such as Meyer have found Foucault's theory of reverse discourse useful in showing how queer-positive writers and artists have worked with traditional modes of representation to subvert their prejudicial effects. The theory of reverse discourse is descriptive of how homosexuals, as both subjects and makers of images, have appropriated the tools of a heterosexist culture and turned them to liberating advantage. Taking my cue from Foucault and Meyer, I contend that Svenson's work appropriates the dominant culture's 'negative terms' in an anti-homophobic inquiry, utilising historically repressive language (the work's title) and photographic methods (its institutional aesthetic) to destabilise and deconstruct them.

A fundamental aspect of the resulting exploration of homosexual identity is the spectre of homosexual desire. A consideration of this issue will lead us to a thorough and contextual explanation of how Svenson's work deploys reverse discourse via its dissemination and aesthetic. The desire explored through *Faggots* is that of Svenson, his models and in some cases the viewers of the series. A remarkable difference between Svenson's series and much other gay-themed photographic work is that the former addresses desire while resisting overt erotics. Desire is referred to subtly, appearing as an implied part of sexuality, which we are cued to associate with the images by way of the title of the series. Thus desire presents itself in the title's simplicity, labelling the subjects according to sexuality and aligning them with an identity that is inextricable from desire. Nevertheless, the men stand alone, in neutral poses. The thing that most *obviously* marks a man as gay (another gay man, or, in the terms of psychoanalysis, an 'object choice') is missing. Furthermore, the models pose in a manner that disallows coquetry, obviating the tendency to sexually objectify them. This is not to say that the series *avoids* objectifying its subjects. After all, Svenson's aesthetic pointedly capitalises on the camera's ability to turn people into data and thus to objectify them. But this objectification is not sexual *per se*. True, some of the models are nude and many would fit into widely accepted notions of attractiveness, but the lack of a sexually suggestive pose – in fact, the lack of any true pose – mitigates the extent to which a viewer will associate the series explicitly with the erotic aspect of homosexuality. Rather, desire is a subtext of the series' intent and its functions: it is implicit, but not articulated. Its presence in the series is underscored by the fact that, while Svenson's project does not eroticise its subjects, his interests in the gay male body were not simply representational.

Svenson has remarked that the series allowed him to do the looking he was denied as a child. He referred to this in the Grey Art Gallery explanatory text and in a later interview during which he remarked that 'as a gay kid, you want to look at the object of your desire, but you're not allowed to. So I went back in time and stilled the object of my desire'. When viewed in light of this remark, the element of desire in *Faggots* brings to mind Roland Barthes's notion of a photograph's 'punctum', which he defined as 'a kind of subtle *beyond* – as if the image launched desire beyond what it permits us to see'.[13] Additionally, photographs are often thought of as 'capturing' the image of their subjects; Svenson's 'stilling' of men willingly identified as homosexual implies his subjects' consent in being viewed as 'objects of desire'. However, one might find it useful to consider that Svenson presumably allowed himself the freedom to do this kind of 'desiring' looking long before embarking on this project. Thus an exploration of the artist's *personal* desire is not central to the series. However, the work's commitment to picturing a *general* spectre of homosexual desire is one of its key elements and fundamental to its anti-homophobic use.

For example, the fact that Svenson was not just looking for himself but picturing (and demystifying) for others by assembling a kind of catalogue of desire suggests that the artist's 'roll call' of gay men could serve reparative and transformative purposes. Specifically, *Faggots* might serve as a venue for the kind of desiring looking Svenson felt was unavailable to him as a child. The subjects in the series might also serve as effective and affecting role models for gay male viewers, the series might show that 'faggot' was something they not only desired (the men they want to look at) but also something they desired to be (not just homosexual, but also student, lawyer, minister, museum director). The series provides examples of gay men gazing neutrally into the camera and hence into the eyes of the viewer, men attached to an epithet, which they invert and appropriate by appearing in the project as willing subjects. Work like this has the potential to allow a person to see himself. For 'before the acquisition of an affirming identity grounded in homosexual desire ... [how] do you explain about yourself to yourself, let alone to others, when you have absolutely no legitimate or legitimating model for your own most intensely personal feelings about other people and the world?'[14] *Faggots* presents such legitimating models and thus can aid in the acquisition of such affirming identity. It does so, however, with a bite: the title reminds the viewer that, as much as he may like what he is looking at, identifying with those models means opening himself up to the hostility of those who judge homosexual desire as deviant. Nevertheless, in this series the ugliness of the title and the ugliness of the photographic archive's history are appropriated and disarmed, resulting in representations of men that a viewer could both desire to be with and desire to be. The work's liberating properties – those of self-definition, presenting legitimating models of homosexuality, problematising the history of taxonomic photography and appropriating a label that had been a slur – are in turn tempered by the responsibilities that come with acknowledging the continued oppressiveness of a homohobic and heterosexist culture.

The series raises general questions about the ambiguity of identity, as well as about how identity is constructed and understood. Thus while *Faggots* is specifically gay-themed, it is, more broadly, an identity-politics project, even if only by virtue of the fact that personal lives (particularly those of the disenfranchised) are linked to politics whether they care to be or not. Despite his recurring interest in destabilising archives and taxonomies and the fact that his tendency towards seriality can be understood as a queer-inflected mode of resistance, Svenson's previous and subsequent work eschews overt politics. Thus the personal/political duality is not the very locus of Svenson's creative expression. In this sense the artist broke new ground with this series. Speaking of his decision to embark on an overtly political and personal project, Svenson remarked 'I'm not that brave, strident guy. But sometimes you don't have a choice. There was that sinking feeling when you have to do something'.

Because *Faggots* is Svenson's only direct engagement with this subject, he does not fit neatly into the genre of art whose overarching project is identity politics. Nor can he be aligned with those artists who insist that their personal identity is incidental to their work.[15] The genre that fits Svenson is that of taxonomically influenced art photography, a broad category that is populated by artists of myriad movements, backgrounds, sexualities and ethnicities. As such, Svenson's work can be related logically to projects as divergent as Bernd and Hilla Becher's documentation of vernacular architecture and Ed Ruscha's famed Conceptual piece *Thirty Four Parking Lots*.

In this sense, Svenson's work is part of the Modernist photographic continuum. Svenson employs an archivist's aesthetic in almost all of his work; it is particularly evident in his deconstructed botanical series from 1993, in an ongoing project documenting artefacts from Philadelphia's Mutter Museum of Pathology, in the aforementioned *Sock Monkeys*, in pictures of Las Vegas that span the last decade and in his collecting and re-formatting of negatives made by nineteenth-century police photographer Clara Sheldon Smith. He has remarked of this work, 'I hope to combine an archivist's eye with an artist's eye'. Thus the *Faggots* series fits neatly into his oeuvre in its approach (if not in its subject): it is an example of the artist's ongoing interest in exploring and destabilising archives and/or taxonomies.

Thus in the bulk of his work, Svenson is concerned with combining the practices of art making and of documenting – documenting places, objects, plants and artefacts. Despite its popularity, this is notoriously troubled territory for photographers: does art occur where taxonomy, aesthetics and creative enquiry converge? The consistent and growing interest in and production of work that hinges on this nexus would suggest that many feel the answer is emphatically affirmative.

From the nineteenth-century studies of British algae by Anna Atkins to Hiroshi Sugimoto's contemporary analysis of waxworks portraits, documentation of artefacts, locales and types has been a primary project of photographers. Historically, photographic archives and taxonomies have served scientific, historic, educational, preservationist, political and legal agendas. Over time, however, the modes and intents of the photographic archive have broadened, making room for the aforementioned art context. As Russell Roberts has observed:

> The use of serial or archival methods of recording has many links with early and late modernism ... The archival model established in the nineteenth century is configured in twentieth-century work in terms of formalist aesthetic and ideological critique, shifting from an ambiguous relationship to those histories, to one which is more aware of the political dimensions of taxonomic discourse.[16]

Thus Svenson and others working along taxonomic models are directly engaging with the history of archival photography while simultaneously bringing the taxonomic aesthetic into new territory. While earlier practitioners generally used their data to satisfy a specific scientific or documentary claim, photographic archivists working after 1950 (such as the Bechers, Ruscha, Sugimoto and Carrie Mae Weems) make Modernist or Conceptual art for the more varied purposes of gallery, museum or performance settings. Unlike their forbears, who confidently employed photography as an evidentiary medium, these artists make no claims that the data they collect is actual 'evidence' that 'proves' something. In fact, their use of archival aesthetics is frequently derived from an interest in troubling and questioning traditional uses of taxonomic practices. Additionally, work by earlier taxonomical photographers who did not have fine art aspirations has been folded into the fine-art context and enthusiastically embraced by museums, collectors and, most importantly, claimed by artists as inspiration or even source material – often for reasons that intentionally contravene the original purposes of these images.

The earliest major instance of this kind of appropriation was probably the surrealist celebration of the work of Eugene Atget, spearheaded by Man Ray in the 1920s. However, the most notable precedent for our purposes is undeniably August Sander, the German photographer who spent the first three decades of the twentieth century documenting German 'types' for his vast *Man of the Twentieth Century* project, the first volume of which was published as *Antlitz der Zeit* in 1929, before it was censored by the Nazis. Svenson's and Sander's projects are obviously linked because they both pose questions regarding what about a person can be revealed photographically. These queries both fix their subjects with an 'organising eye' that attempts to draw conclusions about 'representative types'.[17] However, a major difference between the two is that the notion that a person's 'essence' or character might be discovered in his or her physiognomy, widely held in the early twentieth century when Sander was working, has since fallen out of favour and Svenson is by no means trying to revive it. Instead of enforcing or producing stereotypes, Svenson refutes and destabilises them.

Faggots asks if there are characteristics inherent to sexuality that can be revealed photographically. While the anti-homophobic intent of his project might suggest a resolutely negative answer to this question, it does not necessarily do so. There is nothing in the series itself, or in his discussions of it, to indicate that Svenson has a clear opinion on the matter. Rather, the series acknowledges that the issue persists in the face of its ambiguities. For despite the fact that the practice of visually 'typing' others has been discredited, one must consider Walter Benjamin's assertion that 'One may come from the Right or the Left – he will have to get used to being viewed according to where he comes from'.[18] Justifiably or not, this notion, coupled with the idea that origins can be inferred from appearances, persists. The very existence of Svenson's project can be claimed as evidence of this. In fact, while acknowledging that the idea of sexuality's visibility has troubling consequences, *Faggots* can be read as suggesting that there also might be positive implications. For instance, as discussed above, if homosexuality could be seen, the desiring eye would know where to look. Regardless of its implications, the simple question of visibility resists an answer, suggesting perhaps that it is not outer trappings that signal sexuality or desire, but that homosexuality can still somehow be visually perceived.

The concept that there actually *is* something about homosexuality that might be pictured has been addressed, contested and problematised by many and has its origins, like the photographic archive, in the nineteenth century. In the nineteenth century what had been a practice (intercourse between men) became constructed as 'a species', an identity that was 'everywhere present' in the man who engaged in sex (or simply wanted to engage in sex) with other men.[19] This led to the building of a homosexual identity and eventually to visibility.

> By the 1880's, in the United States, sexually 'abnormal' individuals were beginning to perceive themselves and to be seen, as members of a group. The mutual association and new visibility of such persons in American cities and their naming by the medical profession, made their group existence manifest in a way that it had not been earlier.[20]

It is perhaps not a coincidence that the nineteenth century saw both the invention of a widely accessible new form of representation (photography) and of an entrenched cultural construction of distinct sexualities. In Foucault's discussion of this construction, he remarks that, in the nineteenth century, a man's homosexuality became perceived as 'written immodestly on his face and body because it was a secret that always gave itself away'.[21] This notion that the invisible *is* somehow written persists. The lout on the street yells 'faggot' at someone he perceives as gay, just as, inversely, a gay man makes eye contact with another across the proverbial crowded room – both somehow making connections that are cued (correctly or not) by something that seems to be, paradoxically, both invisible and apparent. Additionally, *Faggots* can be linked to earlier, less sexually specific, non-art-oriented ethno-photographic practices that sought to 'provide a symptom of the invisible, a means whereby that which cannot be seen can be interpreted through its visible manifestations'.[22] It is not just sexuality that has been photographically subject to this kind of classification: race, gender, mental health and criminality have been similarly scrutinised.

A sense of the sexually visible often results from cultural signifiers (particularly fashion) or some kind of eye contact, but it also occurs in the absence of these things.[23] Is it possible to name, visually, what about an individual prompts another to mark him as homosexual? Or does responsibility fall wholly on the observer? *Faggots* engages with this paradox, but cannot answer it. More usefully, the series prompts viewers to consider the issue and its problems, providing a forum for individual viewer contemplation and serving as a critique of repressive linguistic, pseudo-scientific and photographic practices.

By aesthetically referring to the discredited 'science' of phrenology, Svenson's series reminds us that even posing the question of sexuality's visibility is troubled. Svenson's persistence in paring down cultural signifiers and in neutralising his subjects' poses both mimics and mocks modes of taxonomic photography employed by outdated and dubious social and biological sciences in their attempt to specify visible signs for invisible qualities. Notions that a person's identity (be it professional, sexual, religious, moral or ethnic) can confidently be deduced from his or her facial features are disturbing for various and well-documented reasons; reluctance to give credence to these notions has repeatedly been justified by history. Generally, the troubling implication of such visibility is that it has often been recruited into the oppression of those who are thus labelled. With this problematic history in mind, it is useful to return to a more general discussion of contemporary fine art photography made with the archivist's eye and its implications for writing the theory of reverse discourse onto Svenson's work.

The popularity of artwork that follows taxonomic models poses several questions: what function(s) does art made with an archivist's eye serve? How and why can an archive be more at home in a fine art museum than in a natural history museum? As Svenson's work shows, it does so by employing the taxonomic model for inquiries that are not ultimately taxonomic in themselves. In Svenson's case, a taxonomic model is appropriated to reveal that sexuality cannot be measured purely scientifically and explores the ways in which sexuality and gender are culturally determined. In this sense, *Faggots* is a sociological project, heir to August Sander's *Antlitz der Zeit* but with a fine-art intention that distances it from the social sciences that it alludes to.

Artistic interest in taxonomy and the archive has connections both to the subjects documented (in Svenson's case, homosexual men) as well as broader associations with historical artistic, photographic and museum practices. With Svenson's project and others like it, the notion of photography as evidence is simultaneously underscored and contested. Challenging the long-standing claim that photography is an objective art presents a real tension between what can and cannot be seen in its images.

In further unpacking the meanings embedded in *Faggots* and the relevance of its use of an archival aesthetic, it is useful to consider some issues raised by Allan Sekula's essay, 'The Body and the Archive'.[24] Here, Sekula analyses how photography has been employed, since its invention, in archival and taxonomic projects to regulate, control and oppress 'dangerous classes', whether they were actually criminal or simply 'other'. Almost since its first days, critics have acknowledged the many conflicting functions of photographic representation, including the fact that its activities can be simultaneously conducive to both repression and liberation. Referring to photographic portraiture, Sekula defines this conflicted function as 'a double system: a system of representation capable of functioning both *honorifically* and *repressively*'.[25]

One of the positive aspects of photography's invention was that it created a vehicle for representation of classes and relationships previously unpictured as well as new opportunities for self-representation – a particularly democratising effect of the portrait's honorific functions.[26] However, while painted, sculpted, or photographed portraits of individuals can all function to honour the subject, only the photographic portrait lays a virtually unopposed claim to actual evidentiary status. This status readily lends the photographic image to medical, scientific or police uses through which representations become vulnerable to repressive functions. This is not to suggest that other media do not employ representation repressively. Rather, photography is widely accepted as evidence in a way that other media are not and is thus particularly employable in representing a disenfranchised group as naturally 'deviant' rather than constructed as deviant by a repressive society. Hence the very media that made it possible for populations other than those in power to picture themselves also facilitated their repression and control through the evidentiary archival image. Indeed, according to Sekula, 'in serving to introduce the panoptic principle into daily life, photography welded the honorific and repressive functions together'.[27] Such repressive uses have traditionally been used to picture a perceived 'deviance or social pathology' and thus to define a 'generalised look' of particular groups.[28] Sekula also proposes that 'every proper portrait has its lurking, objectifying inverse in the files of the police'.[29] Any photographic portrait can be used as evidence, either for or against the person depicted, regardless of intentions. Furthermore,

> the emergence of [the photograph as] a truth-apparatus ... cannot be adequately reduced to the optical model provided by the camera. The camera is integrated into a larger ensemble: a bureaucratic-clerical-statistical system of 'intelligence'. This system can be described as a sophisticated form of the archive. The central artifact of this system is not the camera but the filing cabinet.[30]

According to Sekula, then, the photograph is a device employed by a larger system whose modern project was to delimit, to repress and to regulate. While historic evidentiary photographic practices were not all part of repressive projects, they were generally connected to the categorisation of artefacts, animals or populations. While these subjects may be relatively innocuous items such as plants or butterflies, when people are involved the supposed objectivity of the photographic eye is increasingly troubled. Even if the photographic archive is not deployed by a controlling group such as the police, it frequently documents criminal or marginalised groups. This necessarily associates the marginal with the criminal and reveals an institutional opposition to difference, to that which has been canonised by those in power as 'normal' and acceptable.

Svenson, like the nineteenth-century police photographers discussed by Sekula, devised an 'aesthetically neutral standard of representation'.[31] The regimented manner in which he arranged his subjects has a number of similarities with methods employed by early photographic archivists of human subjects. These early archivists were not generally artists; they were scientists, sociologists and police officers. Despite his very different intentions and orientation, Svenson, like these early archivists in general and police photographers in particular, made representations by adhering to fixed principles of identical lens, lighting, pose and exposure for each subject.[32] By neutralising the presentation of its subjects, this system makes differences in basic appearance easier to spot. In Svenson's case, he denied his sitters their own pose and discouraged them (sometimes unsuccessfully) from wearing any type of garment that could be considered a 'giveaway' to their sexuality, such as gay pride regalia. As such, *Faggots* is creative documentation – a riff on taxonomy. But it is still linked inextricably to its repressive precedents and this needs to be explained and explored, because the nineteenth-century development of police photography, along with photography's contributions to a mania for the dubious practice of phrenology and the horrific applications of eugenics, leave a worrisome legacy whose practices are still employable for repressive ends. Svenson's 'typing' of gay men has ancestors that *promote* rather than contest repression, which is what makes his use of reverse discourse both possible and powerful.

Sekula's essay concedes that projects which adopt evidentiary methods similar to those used for repressive purposes *can* be executed in a manner that denies and/or contests their repressive precedents. However, even though he finds some documentary photographic and filmic examples successful in this attempted subversion, Sekula mentions primarily work that he thinks fails.[33] Thus he argues that it is difficult to overcome the archive's repressive history within more ambiguously framed practices such as art photography. Sekula offers this caution: 'For an artist or a critic to resurrect the methods of biosocial typology without once acknowledging the historical context and consequences of these procedures is naïve at best and cynical at worst'.[34]

It is my belief that Svenson acknowledges these contexts and consequences – that he in fact *employs* them in his anti-homophobic project.

By adopting modes similar to those developed in the nineteenth century for penal and sociological archives and taxonomies for an artistically oriented project that challenges oppression, Svenson turns repressive uses of photography inside out. *Faggots*' troubling precedents are thus a necessary part of his project, which serves as a contemporary subversion of traditional archival and taxonomic practices.

Likewise, a consideration of the title of the series is at least as instrumental in understanding the work as an act of reverse discourse as Svenson's use of a taxonomic model is. Svenson's use of the term 'faggot' highlights the degree to which the question of homosexuality's visibility – or lack thereof – is inextricably and uncomfortably linked to the problem of homophobia. Furthermore, a critical element of Svenson's project is that the sexuality of its subjects does not *need* to be visible, because it is given by the title: its subjects are linguistically marked. When Svenson's use of reverse discourse is recognised, the viewer can perceive this marking as a wilful act of self-definition. For Svenson, the slur 'faggot' was an instrumental element in the work's conception; he was resolute in his decision to use it as the title. Svenson felt that use of the academically canonised term 'queer' or the socially neutralised 'gay' would undermine the work's impact. Only the appropriation of a clearly derogatory term would suit.

In discussing the title's implications and uses, it is useful to note that Svenson is not the first gay artist to name a work *Faggots*. This position belongs to the author Larry Kramer, who in 1978 gave the same title to a fictional account of gay life in New York City.[35] Kramer's use of the word had a similar insider's edginess that smacked of reverse discourse rather than the homophobia usually associated with the term. Of course, while reverse discourse is ultimately empowering for its subjects, by definition it gets to its positive ends *through* adopting the trappings of the repressive modes it seeks to undermine. Only by acknowledging the damage of a word like 'faggot' and in fact by taking on some of that damage, can it be inverted. Like Kramer before him, Svenson was keenly aware that the term still had the power to shock both insider and outsider audiences productively.

Another notable similarity between Kramer's and Svenson's *Faggots* is that both works are committed to displaying the prevalence of homosexual men. Kramer's book begins with statistics – literally with the numbers of gay men living in the New York metropolitan area – Svenson's project too gets much of its impact from sheer accumulation. The soundtrack to both these arithmetic exercises is the semi-exhausted ennui of the gay-rights marching chant 'We're here, we're queer, get used to it'. While some gay men may return to the closet if the heterosexist global community continues its persecutions, homosexuality itself will still exist. The counting practice found in Kramer's and Svenson's projects can be read in both as a kind of beleaguered yet defiant emphasis of this fact.

An intrinsic and persistent problem for these works, which has been noted by their gay critics, is that both are vulnerable to being utilised by homophobes. As Reynolds Price notes in his introduction to Grove Press's 2000 edition of Kramer's *Faggots*, the authorities against whom Kramer worked in his later role as founder of Act-Up would not have found in *Faggots* an argument that changed their views about the dangerousness of homosexual sex.[36] Similarly, the homophobic viewer of Svenson's work, while possibly surprised out of a stereotyped notion of what gay men look like, is unlikely to find a way out of heterosexist beliefs through viewing the piece. In fact, such a viewer may feel justified in his position by the linguistic and aesthetic cues that Svenson employs to produce reverse discourse. This is all to say that an unfortunate standard of reverse discourse (like much discourse, for that matter, and particularly that related to identity politics) is that it often only serves those subjects who are already self-reflective enough to employ it. When such practices are noticed by unsympathetic observers, the repressed group's appropriation of the dominant culture's negative terms can actually serve to strengthen the confidence with which oppression is implemented. This brings us to recognise that the degree to which Svenson's use of reverse discourse is rhetorically established by *Faggots* is stubbornly contingent on individual viewer response as well as the manner in which the work is disseminated.

While the reverse discourse intention was established successfully in the Grey Art Gallery exhibit, the second venue to show images from *Faggots* made its anti-homophobic orientation more ambiguous. In 1997, six of the *Faggots* images were included in a large exhibition produced by the Museum of Modern Art at Oxford that travelled to four other locations throughout Europe. Entitled 'In Visible Light: Photography and Classification in Art, Science and the Everyday', the show included work by taxonomic photographers from the nineteenth century to the twentieth, from explorers and scientists such as Roger Fenton and Charles Darwin to contemporary artists such as Andres Serrano, Sherrie Levine and Hiroshi Sugimoto.

The catalogue published to accompany 'In Visible Light' includes four of Svenson's images, accompanied by the simple caption 'Arne Svenson *Faggots* 1994'. The same images (with the same caption) were the exclusive illustration for the exhibit's poster. Plastered all over London, these posters allowed the work to function in a new manner. In the Grey Art Gallery exhibit, one saw the title of the series before one saw the images themselves. Furthermore, the New York viewers had the explanatory text to help in their orientation to the work. On the poster and also in the Oxford exhibit, the viewer had to read the small print to know what was shared by the men in the photographs. From a distance, they are just men, but with the title, they are men with something in common and have been labelled accordingly. 'One might read all kinds of things into these faces; the captions, however, tell us what to see'.[37] As Thomas Sokolowski remarked in the Grey Art Gallery explanatory text, 'the title is the only evidence that holds them together'. These remarks, coupled with the ambiguity of the men's images in the Oxford poster, imply that, in this instance, the question of sexuality's visibility posed by the series does in fact have an answer and that it is in the negative. Svenson noted that the poster and the presentation of the prints in the Oxford show allowed the viewer to see images before reading the title: 'from [a distance], photographs of four guys, from close enough to read the caption, four gay guys. It's magic'.[38] How the viewer chooses to respond to the caption is, of course, her personal choice. That her response might contravene the artist's anti-homophobic perspective is the aforementioned inherent and menacing aspect of any employment of reverse discourse.

Numerous scholars have weighed in on the particular importance of the caption to understanding a photograph's meaning, to the reception of the message the image-maker intends to send.[39] According to this scholarship, each image has an 'original rhetorical function'[40] that is related to intent, and Svenson's is no exception. Photographs are not natural; their meaning is not readable in an 'intrinsic or universal' sense. That they are often perceived as such is as a result of the assumed transparency of the image: the erroneous assumption that a photograph is 'the re-presentation of nature itself ... an unmediated copy of the real world'.[41] But in actuality, 'every photographic image is a sign, above all, of someone's investment in the sending of a message'.[42] Thus a difficulty for incarnations of Svenson's work that include the title but not the explanatory text or the environment in which the Grey Art Gallery exhibit occurred is that its anti-homophobic message(s) are made ambiguous, only available via recognition of reverse discourse.

So, where messages sent by the Grey Art Gallery exhibit were fairly directed, the messages sent by the Oxford exhibit (and its subsequent inclusion in the international exhibits 'Geometry of the Face' and 'Pandemic: Facing AIDS') were less so, opening the work up to repressive interpretations. Abigail Solomon-Godeau has suggested that photographers with socially critical or reformist intentions have a responsibility to strictly regiment how their work is shown and disseminated so that their images are not employed for nefarious purposes.[43] Of course, we have established that this is possible in Svenson's work. We have also established that drawing conclusions about character or identity based on photographic appearances has potentially dangerous and disturbing consequences:

> history continues to teach us the difficulties of establishing correspondences between human appearance and other realities: appearance shifts day to day and minute by minute, from observing eye to observing eye. Nazi Germany itself provides enough examples ... which make it difficult to retain faith in our final ability to learn to read accurately ... uncaptioned or unannotated photographs.[44]

However, as we see in *Faggots*, the difficulty of reading 'accurately' (if by this we are meant to understand 'reading according to the photographer's intentions') persists even when a caption *is* provided. This is compounded by the fact that Svenson deliberately chooses not to direct his viewers as forcefully or specifically as Solomon-Godeau's criticism calls for. His adherence to the Modernist notion that an artwork should 'speak for itself' has contributed to Svenson's reluctance to engage in this kind of control; he has said that providing a theoretical grounding of his work is 'not [his] job'. However, Svenson's choice to eschew the sort of overt political rhetoric that critics such Solomon-Godeau promote is also consistent with the methods he deploys in making work which is indeed quite political and intentionally so. It is fundamental to the deployment of reverse discourse that the message sender (in this case, Svenson) *expects* its recipients to produce their own meanings. In this case, the possibility of homophobic responses is instrumental to the function of reverse discourse. It cannot be overemphasised that the employment of reverse discourse to contest and deconstruct repressive socio-political practices requires calling on those practices themselves. This is how and why reverse discourse is a subversive and effective mode of cultural critique.

In conclusion, Svenson employs reverse discourse to distance *Faggots* from its precedents and to invert the taxonomic model's repressive history by using this model to *contest* a repressive ideology (homophobia) rather than support one. Svenson's methods refer to modes that objectified and disempowered their subjects (such as nineteenth-century portraits of the insane) without exposing his collaborators/subjects to the same indignities. The fact that the men pictured in *Faggots* were photographed by their own choice rather than for monetary reward or through coercion goes a long way towards explaining how his images avoid this kind of objectification. However, this does not mean his subjects do not become objects. As I have discussed, they do become objects, quite literally (they become photographs) and figuratively as well. However, the objectification in these images works to *contest* their construction as deviant. Unlike many other photographed 'types', Svenson's subjects were conscious that they would be 'typed' and in fact exercised agency in agreeing to that typing.[45] They volunteered to be photographed and labelled, unlike the taxonomic subject upon whom photographic documentation and derogatory labelling is foisted.

Svenson's taxonomic approach can be read as an employment of aesthetics to comment on the repression of homosexuals in our culture. By presenting his subjects in a manner that has its basis in medical or police photography, Svenson challenges his viewer to acknowledge that homosexuality has been treated as deviant and in some cases criminal. Contemplating this (which is part of the experience of contemplating the body of work as a whole) can help articulate and contextualise the current tenuous position of gay civil rights in America.

Svenson has said that he photographs taxonomically in order to understand that which is otherwise opaque, that which refuses to yield its secrets. However, the exploration enacted through *Faggots* has only reinforced the opacity of Foucault's written secret. And this is perhaps its ultimate success. By exploring and critiquing a method of classification by practising it, Svenson addresses the mystery of sexuality's visibility by maintaining its ambiguity, employing 'reverse discourse' to contest homosexuality's association with deviance.

And lastly, to return to the issue of visibility – by playing with the fugitive notion of whether one can actually *see* sexuality, *Faggots* treads a delicate balance between its anti-homophobic intentions and functions and their opposites. Despite its inversion of repression by appropriation, the hatred of difference responsible for the series' title and the problematics of the photographic archive's tradition lurk within *Faggots*, helping the series to do its work through its employment of reverse discourse. One might assume that the images stake a claim to collective, gendered portraiture. But as we have seen, they actually trouble the notion of group identity and contest the idea that sexuality can be pictured photographically. The series accomplishes this by exposing the evidential claims of the camera as tenuous, even fraudulent. While employing an aesthetic that is associated with *staking* evidential claims, Svenson actually undermines the camera's claims to objectivity, pushing against the idea that gender and sexual identity can be pictured and displayed, that they can be confidently seen and photographically represented. So, rather than reinforcing the negative associations of homophobic language and the controlling functions of archival photography, Svenson's series opposes these repressive terms. By referencing these histories in an anti-homophobic context, Svenson challenges them, thereby contesting the notion of homosexuality as deviant.

Notes

1. This is the wall text as it appears in its archived copy, including brackets. There is no source listed for the statistical assertion. Arne Svenson and Thomas Sokolowski, wall text for *Faggots* exhibition, Summer 1994, Archives of The Grey Art Gallery and Study Center at New York University. This source will be referred to in the remainder of the notes as 'NYU text'.
2. Landmarks for these issues include the founding of the AIDS activist group ACT UP/New York in 1987 (ACT UP extensively utilises art in its activism), the 1990 closing of Robert Mapplethorpe's Cincinnati Contemporary Arts Center exhibit and the 1990 adoption by the National Endowment for the Arts of a 'decency clause' that led to the revocation of grants to three homosexual artists. See Richard Bolton (ed.), *Culture Wars: Documents from the Recent Controversies in the Arts* (New York: New Press, 1992) and Richard Meyer, *Outlaw Representation: Censorship and Homosexuality in Twentieth-Century American Art* (New York: Oxford University Press, 2002).
3. James Meyer, 'Aids and Postmodernism', *Arts Magazine* 66 (1992), pp. 62–8, here p. 68.
4. Author's interview with Arne Svenson, 23 October 2000. Unless otherwise indicated, biographical details, quotes from the artist and Svenson's opinions as stated in this paper derive from this interview.
5. NYU text.
6. Meyer, *Outlaw Representation*, p. 111.
7. Meyer, *Outlaw Representation*, p. 111.
8. Simon Watney, 'Queer Andy', in Jennifer Doyle, Jonathan Flatley and José Esteben Muñoz (eds), *Pop Out: Queer Warhol* (Durham: Duke University Press, 1996), pp. 20–30, here p. 21.
9. Jan Zita Grover, 'Dykes in Context: Some Problems in Minority Representation', in Richard Bolton (ed.), *The Contest of Meaning: Critical Histories of Photography* (Boston: MIT Press, 1989), pp. 162–96, here p. 174. For a source that delves into the photographic history of representing men's (not necessarily homosexual) affection for one another, see David Deitcher, *Dear Friends: American Photographs of Men Together, 1840–1918* (New York: Harry N. Abrams, 2001).
10. While it is surprising that not even the gay press took note, this is perhaps for two related reasons: in 1993, Svenson was just beginning to establish a critical reputation and because of the Stonewall anniversary the gay press was working in overdrive that summer. There may simply have been too much competition for an up-and-comer to be noticed through reviews at this time. However, the considerable growth of Svenson's reputation over the last decade has not seen increased critical attention to this particular body of work (except by me). For example, in its three subsequent exhibitions, images from the *Faggots* series have been included in three internationally exhibited group shows. However, reviews of these shows (the international touring exhibit, 'In Visible Light', curated by Russell Roberts for The Museum of Modern Art, Oxford and exhibited there from March–July 1997, the international touring exhibit 'Pandemic: Facing AIDS', curated by Nan Richardson and Lesley A. Martin and on view at various locations from July 2002 to December 2005 and 'Geometry of the Face' at the National Museum of Photography, Copenhagen, October 2003–July 2004) have also not referred to the work and only one of the three associated catalogues has discussed *Faggots* in print (though all three reproduced the images). In that catalogue, Mette Mortensen, 'Photography in the Public Arena', in Mette Mortensen, Christian Rud Anderson and Gertrude With (eds), *Geometry of the Face: Photographic Portraits* (Copenhagen: The National Museum of Photography, The Royal Library, 2003), pp. 11–39, esp. p. 26, uses an earlier, unpublished version of this paper as its reference. The other catalogues are: Russell Roberts and Chrissie Iles (eds), *In Visible Light: Photography and Classification in Art, Science and the Everyday* (Oxford: Museum of Modern Art, 1997); and Lesley Martin, (ed.), *Pandemic: Facing AIDS* (New York: Umbrage Editions/Moxie Firecracker Films, 2003).

11. Michel Foucault, *The History of Sexuality*, vol. 1: *An Introduction*, tr. Robert Hurley (New York: Pantheon Books, 1978), p. 101.
12. Meyer, *Outlaw Representation*, p. 8.
13. Roland Barthes, *Camera Lucida: Reflections on Photography*, tr. Richard Howard (New York: Farrar, Strauss & Giroux, 1981), p. 59.
14. Watney, 'Queer Andy', p. 24.
15. Many artists are justifiably wary that reference to sexuality, gender or race 'may displace any other information about [his/her] life and work' and so consciously avoid such associations. Quote from Meyer, *Outlaw Representation*, p. 280.
16. Russell Roberts, 'Taxonomy: Some Notes towards the Histories of Photography and Classification', in Roberts and Iles (eds), *In Visible Light*, pp. 9–53, here p. 51.
17. Anne Halley, 'August Sander', *The Massachusetts Review* 19 (1978), pp. 663–74, here p. 666.
18. Walter Benjamin, 'A Short History of Photography', in Alan Trachtenberg (ed.), *Classic Essays on Photography* (New Haven, CT: Leete's Island Books, 1980), pp. 199–216, here p. 211. Another translation of Benjamin's remarks makes this connection between origins and appearance even more explicit: 'Rightists or Leftists – we will have to get used to having our origins read in our faces'. Quoted in Anne Halley, 'August Sander', p. 668.
19. Foucault, *The History of Sexuality*, p. 43.
20. Jonathan Ned Katz, quoted in Meyer, *Outlaw Representation*, p. 286, note 14.
21. Foucault, *The History of Sexuality*, p. 43.
22. Michel Frizot, 'Body of Evidence: The Ethnophotography of Difference', in Michel Frizot (ed.), *A New History of Photography* (Cologne: Könemann, 1998), pp. 259–71, here p. 265.
23. While fashion is often a major cultural cue to sexual orientation, its codes are often unreadable to outsiders.
24. Allan Sekula, 'The Body and the Archive', in Bolton (ed.), *The Contest of Meaning: Critical Histories of Photography* (Boston: MIT Press, 1989), pp. 343–89.
25. Sekula, 'The Body and the Archive', p. 345.
26. For evidence of photography's use in the *privately* queer imagery of sub-cultural self-representation (an issue not addressed in the Sekula essay), see David Deitcher, *Dear Friends*.
27. Sekula, 'The Body and the Archive', p. 347.
28. Sekula, 'The Body and the Archive', p. 345.
29. Sekula, 'The Body and the Archive', p. 347.
30. Sekula, 'The Body and the Archive', p. 351.
31. Sekula, 'The Body and the Archive', p. 361.
32. For descriptions of nineteenth-century police photographic practices, see Frizot, 'Body of Evidence', p. 264; and Sekula, 'The Body and the Archive', p. 360.
33. See Sekula's remarks on Nancy Burson, Sekula, 'The Body and the Archive', p. 377.
34. Sekula, 'The Body and the Archive', p. 377.
35. Larry Kramer, *Faggots* (1978; repr. New York: Grove Press, 2000).
36. Reynolds Price, 'Larry Kramer's *Faggots*' in Kramer, *Faggots*, pp. xi–xvi, here p. xvi.
37. Halley, 'August Sander', p. 669.
38. Arne Svenson, 15 November 2000, e-mail to the author.
39. See especially Abigail Solomon-Godeau, 'Who Is Speaking Thus? Some Questions About Documentary Photography', in *Photography at the Dock: Essays on Photographic History, Institutions, and Practices* (Minneapolis: University of Minnesota Press, 1991), pp. 169–83; Allan Sekula, 'On the Invention of Photographic Meaning', in Victor Burgin (ed.), *Thinking Photography* (Basingstoke: Macmillan, 1982), pp. 84–109; Roland Barthes, 'The Rhetoric of the Image' (1964), in *Image Music Text*, tr. Stephen Heath (New York: Hill & Wang, 1977), pp. 32–51; Benjamin, 'A Short History of Photography', pp. 199–216.
40. Sekula, 'On the Invention of Photographic Meaning', p. 92.
41. Sekula, 'On the Invention of Photographic Meaning', p. 86.
42. Sekula, 'On the Invention of Photographic Meaning', p. 87.

43. Solomon-Godeau, 'Who Is Speaking Thus', p. 183.
44. Halley, 'August Sander', p. 666.
45. The social documentary work of Jacob Riis is a classic example of a disenfranchised group being photographed without consent and/or agency. For critiques of these practices, see Abigail Solomon-Godeau, 'Who Is Speaking Thus?'; and Martha Rosler, 'in, around, and afterthoughts (on documentary photography)', in Bolton (ed.), *The Contest of Meaning*, pp. 303–41.

11 The Temperance Temple and Architectural Representation in Late Nineteenth-Century Chicago

Paula Young Lee

The tall office building or skyscraper has long been interpreted as the physical expression of capitalist ambitions. Minimising ornamentation in order to maximise profitability, office buildings' exposed skeleton frames claimed 'truth to materials' along with the value of structural 'honesty'. Though their stark appearance was informed by economic concerns, other pressures helped shape the commercial style in late nineteenth-century Chicago.[1] For example, terms such as 'honesty' and 'truth' fold a moral position into practical decisions and point to cultural factors that were vitally important to the assessment of form but not driven by finances. Among other concerns, the severe style responded to an ideology of gender that maintained the separation of the spheres, for which reason it was largely imagined that the owners and tenants of such 'masculine' buildings must be men, even as the house, as the representative form of domestic life, was shaped by feminine desires and thus embodied women.[2] Yet one of the most technologically advanced tall office buildings of the late nineteenth-century period, the Woman's Christian Temperance Union Building (1891–1926), was sponsored by a group of civic-minded women (Figure 1). Located in the heart of the commercial district known as the Loop, the dramatic height of 'the Temple' reflected the financial demands of productivity and profit. To its Gilded Age audience, however, this same physical quality also dramatically conveyed the higher moral purpose of Frances Willard (1839–98) and the organisation she headed from 1879 until her death, the Woman's Christian Temperance Union (WCTU).

Figure 1: Daniel Burnham and John Root, 'Woman's Christian Temperance Union Building', Chicago (destroyed), in *Industrial Chicago* (Chicago: Godspeed Press, 1851).

The conflicting demands of religion, capitalism, propriety and patronage were directly negotiated in the realisation of this project, which remains the unique effort by American women to appropriate the social medium of architecture and attach it to a female-driven cause. To be sure, the Woman's Building designed by Sophia Hayden for the 1893 World's Columbian Exposition in Chicago might be volunteered as another example. However, that impermanent project was shaped by the utopian rubric offered by the White City, an urban fantasy that was later condemned by architectural critics for relying on borrowed Beaux-Arts formulas. By contrast, the WCTU Building was a free-standing commercial structure located in the very sector of Chicago that was struggling to 'invent' modern architecture as 'virile' and 'progressive' activity. As a working office building, it directly confronted the exigencies of offering rental space inside a bustling business district. Because it was an exception that did not set the rule, the Temple thus raises a number of questions related to the politics of architectural representation, including the aesthetics of American capitalism and the gendering of social space in the urban setting. Specifically, this article examines the critical reception of the building during a historical period when the Temperance movement was widely persuasive, rather than analysing the building as a case study of American women raising an office building, only to swiftly renounce their affiliation.

Within four decades of its completion, the Temperance Temple was destroyed. Viewed in isolation, it might appear that this tall office building fell because women were its patrons. Yet it joined a long litany of other commercial projects in Chicago that shared the same fate, including celebrated architectural monuments such as Burnham & Root's Montauk Block, William Le Baron Jenney's Home Insurance Building and Henry Hobson Richardson's Marshall Field Wholesale Store, all demolished after the 1929 crash.[3] Their patrons were men, yet to attribute their collapse to that fact seems both oversimplified and misguided. In other words, if gender is to be meaningful as an interpretive category within this history, it must be considered inside the complex currents informing architectural representation in late nineteenth-century Chicago, birthplace of a commercial style that briefly celebrated the Temple as one of its most accomplished examples. How did the temperance cause affect the building's critical reception? What role did women play in its development? Crucially, it was not women in general or even middle-class American women in particular that gave the building its identity, but the Woman's Christian Temperance Union, an activist association whose cause then enjoyed a high degree of visibility. It was the group's own membership that dubbed this edifice the 'Temperance Temple', steadily advancing the moral cause while leaving the name of women out of it. Even as this ambitious project thrust the temperance movement and the image of women into public view, it affirmed that the two were not synonymous. Taking its cues from the building itself, the following article explores the changing perceptions of the Temperance Temple at the turn of the century.

Patronising architecture

> 'Architects live in an environment consisting of clients, male and female, very exacting and often unreasonable'.[4]

Designed by the prestigious architectural partnership of Daniel Burnham & John Wellborn Root, the Woman's Christian Temperance Union Building was a commercial building as well as the home of the WCTU. Yet contrary to the belief held by most of its 200,000 members across the United States, the WCTU was not the building's sponsor, owner or even primary stockholder. As Michigan chapter president Mary Torrans Lathrap emphasised in 1893, 'the National WCTU has declined, from the first, organically to take responsibility for the erection of the building known as the Temple'.[5] The WCTU remained separate from the financing and daily operations of the building that bore its name. Instead, the motive force behind the project was Matilda Bradley Carse, president of the powerful Chicago chapter and the self-appointed trustee of funds donated to the Woman's Temperance Building Association (WTBA), the independent body that actually controlled the finances. Carse argued that the WCTU's membership participated in the Temple's development through her, but there is little indication that she acted on any opinion except her own. She admitted as much at the cornerstone ceremony, remarking with prideful embarrassment that she could not relate the Temple's history 'without the use of the personal pronoun': it was the story of 'I' not 'we'.[6] As a result, the WCTU had no direct control over the ambitious new edifice that had become the central headquarters for its city, state and national offices, as well as the new home of the Woman's Temperance Publication Association. Yet the Publication Association was not only legally separate from the WCTU, it was once again founded and directed by Carse, who was also the primary author of the 'Temperance Temple' columns for the *Union Signal*, the WCTU's official organ.

Did the Temple accurately represent the collective desires of the Union? Could Carse legitimately claim that she spoke for all? Because of its drama and lasting impact, the internal dissent over the 'Temple Question' has been the subject of several scholarly inquiries.[7] Studies by Rachel Bohlmann and Ruth Bordin have mapped out the internal challenges to Carse's authority, much of which swirled around finances. To be sure, given that the Chicago real-estate market was volatile, her decision to enter the fray was rightly questioned by the membership. From its very outset, the Temple's economic difficulties were wrapped up in external forces affecting Chicago construction as a whole: the new building confronted the overbuilt commercial real-estate market just as the local economy crashed in 1892 and it would reach its end in 1926, during that difficult interregnum bracketed by two world wars. But the Union's protracted struggles over the Temple's finances also reflected a specific set of concerns that centred on the politics of representation. These conflicts were expressed through the familiar vehicle of the dollar bill, for as a symbolic system 'money' requires that each unit be identical in appearance and equitable in value. Unless its numeric value is guaranteed by the government, a bill is just an engraved piece of paper, deprived of its power to act as a medium for exchange. As a social and cultural sign, however, money also reflects values that operate independently of this system. The possession of wealth might function as a sign of God's grace, but it also performed as a vector for sin, a marker of status and denominator of class. The means of its acquisition, like the mode of its spending, was also coded through gender. Though women could spend and earn wages, for example, the abstract production of capital might be understood to be a masculine activity. As a result of these incompatible readings, the capacity of a business building to represent a group of women was fraught with uncertainty and contradiction.

Even as sums and figures were tossed around, it was the WCTU's emotional investment in the building that lay in the balance. Among the membership, angry renunciations of the Temple flew back and forth, for although Carse had Willard's strong support, it was not Willard's project. Nonetheless, Carse never presumed to put herself in the iconic place of Willard, the 'beloved leader'. Instead, she offered an office building to embody the Union, arguing for the necessity of a permanent home to consolidate the movement's public image. Writing in support of the project, Willard noted, 'The white-ribboners are moving out of their tents and into their fortresses of brick, stone and mortar. We hope they will call their headquarters, "Temperance Temples"'.[8] For Willard, the symbolic benefits were clear. The unwilling vagabondage of the volunteer organisation would end with the construction of its building, which would provide a stable home and confirm the lasting role of the WCTU as a social institution. But Willard spoke in general terms, supporting the basic ideas rather than specific plans. When Carse took action, she placed the national headquarters inside a frankly commercial structure and located the building in the Loop, thrusting the Union inside an emergent capitalist space being shaped by masculine values. In this 'chauvinist' setting,[9] middle-class women were conspicuously out of place. Yet the WCTU's only other option was to be pushed out of urban centres and to be politically marginalised in the process. This was precisely why Carse had proposed an office building large enough to generate self-sustaining revenues. For women to survive inside a masculine arena, they had to accept a system of social order that directly aligned power to profits. Only by acknowledging these conditions could the WCTU fully enter this arena and claim its potential benefits.

In 1883, it had been the gendered segregation of urban space that had catalysed the Temple project. The Chicago branch of the WCTU had held its meetings downtown at the Young Men's Christian Association (YMCA) until its doors were closed to women. Having been forced to relocate and facing the same problem of gender discrimination at every turn, Carse determined that the WCTU would always be vulnerable to eviction until it controlled its own building. That a new building itself might be a profitable source of revenue seemed an ideal solution as well as a powerful symbol of the temperance movement. But her decision to stake such a claim could not have been easy. For women to sponsor a business building required them to venture outside the intimate spaces that they 'naturally' inhabited and to appropriate an art form that was inherently public because of its scale and collective character.

Aggressively inserted into the social landscape, commercial architecture in particular defined a 'masculine' set of operations, inextricable from the ruthless politics of the marketplace because of its elaborate infrastructure and complex financing. As a result, women could not invest in this kind of architecture without assuming a particular kind of risk. For any organisation, the decision to sponsor a business building represented a gamble. But as Sarah Burns has stated, 'women invaded male territory at the peril of becoming unnatural, unsexed, repellent, barren and offensive'.[10] Carse's bold entry into the business of real estate rendered her vulnerable to such epithets. Consistently, however, it was the WCTU's own membership that ventured these personal attacks. By using her as a scapegoat and declaring her renegade, the members of the Union could escape being cloaked in the negative stereotypes that undermined activist women by challenging their femininity.

In this regard, Carse's competence was her undoing. Not only had she offended the Union by declaring herself its agent without bothering to secure its consent, but her financial plan reflected her aggravating competence in business, which pitted her success in masculine affairs against the conventions of female respectability. Carse planned to sell shares to the membership at $100 per share. If each of the 10,000 local chapters of the WCTU purchased one share, capital of one million dollars could be raised, more than fully meeting the cost of building the Temple. But Carse expected that many of the unions would not participate because of fiscal decline or internal dissent, and adjusted her calculations accordingly. As a result, only half of the national membership needed to contribute in order to completely pay off the shares, which were established at $500,000. To set the project in motion, department-store mogul Marshall Field and other local businessmen had agreed to buy them up, thus providing the investment funds necessary to begin construction. This gesture was understood to be philanthropic because these shares would be sold back without interest once the WCTU had amassed sufficient donations from its national membership. The remainder of the building's cost, originally projected at $800,000, would be floated as bonds bearing a low, 5 per cent interest rate that would, according to the plan, be eventually recouped through rentals. The independent Woman's Temperance Building Association would handle all the financial affairs. Once the major debt was paid, the WCTU would gain the controlling share and the right to the titles.[11]

When first presented at the national meeting in 1887, the project generated frissons of enthusiasm, with the privilege of purchasing the first share of stock predictably given to Willard. Encouragement from outside the Union was also forthcoming: Field, a teetotaller and strong supporter of the temperance cause, granted Carse a 200-year perpetual lease at the corner of LaSalle Street and Monroe Avenue, a prime location in the Loop. In addition, Field had agreed to waive rental fees for the first eighteen months. Once the building was raised and ready to rent, the major part would serve as commercial office space, the 'large' rental income of which was projected to be 'at least' $200,000 a year. Carse optimistically calculated that the $800,000 base investment required to finance the construction would be entirely recouped in four years, after which point most of these revenues would become pure profit for the organisation.[12]

Supporters of this quintessentially American 'revenue church' quoted Luke 16:10: 'If therefore ye have not been faithful in the unrighteous mammon, who will commit to your trust the true riches?'[13] The murky verse reconciled fiscal responsibility – and, by extension, profitability – with Protestant values.[14] For Field and the other forty-five outside investors, the worthiness of the Temple's cause more than compensated for their own loss of revenue. True to the rhetorical strategies that tied financial success to God's grace, their immense personal fortunes would be put to work for the greater good represented by the merits of temperance. As Joseph Kirkland pointed out in 1892, only the 'little soul' saw wealth as its own reward; the 'truly great man' saw his riches as a 'glorious means for public benefaction'.[15] The argument was persuasive and widespread. Less grandiose in scale, a similar set of associations helped convince the national membership to contribute to the projected building. Carse's weekly column in the *Union Signal* reminded the women to drop a daily penny into mite boxes shaped like tiny Temples; once the member sent in her mite box full of copper coins, she received a colour lithograph of the building in return. The steady droplets of small change transformed the Temple into a piggy bank and each donation into a loving expression of faith in their Christian cause. 'Surely', Carse declared, the Temple 'is to be built of more precious things than silver or gold. It will truly be an offering worthy to lay at our Master's feet, for it will be odorous with the perfume of love and selfsacrifice'.[16]

Such evangelising rhetoric had astonishing power to reassign and even reverse meaning. Circulated in effigy among the WCTU's members and domesticated through miniaturisation, the building presented rightly-gotten gains as the quickest pathway to heaven. By its very presence in the Loop, the Temple acted as an efficient engine of conversion, capable of changing sinners into Christians as easily as it converted 'filthy lucre' into a blessing. Arguably, it is as an experimental site of cultural transformation that the building is best understood. A hybrid form that married technological innovation to a historicist mass, it offered a site of convergence that revised the terms of business as an uplifting and even spiritual practice. For this audience, such a place could be 'memorial in its character' yet serve as a 'fine office' without any sense of hypocrisy or contradiction.[17] In this cultural context, the production of wealth could be an act of Christian piety if conducted in the proper spirit. As explained by Lady Henry Somerset, leader of the WCTU in England, 'Just as in the old days the magnificent cathedrals were reared with the expression of the people's faith, so to-day the Temple is the expression of the faith of the temperance women'.[18] Whether it expressed their faith in God or faith in the stock market did not particularly matter. In late nineteenth-century Chicago, the practice of worshipping 'two idols in the same temple' presented no ideological or theological conflict. Instead, in the eyes of contemporary observers, the fact that the Temple combined religious 'sentiment' with 'cold business policy' was to be rightfully commended.

To Carse and her supporters, it seemed obvious to align religious values with financial profits, as both demanded equal amounts of devotion, piety and discipline from their followers. To soothe the soul, the twelve-storey Temple would feature a street-level sanctuary 'where the rum-cursed victims of the legalised liquor traffic could find a refuge'.[19] A 'holy place' at its foundation, the Temple's upper storeys would function as 'a humming hive of business', full of workers supporting a higher vision through the steady production of capital.[20] Widely repeated throughout the period, the metaphor of the hive promoted the image of natural riches bestowed on the Midwestern prairie. By implication, even insects recognised that such abundant resources were sinful to waste; to gather the cornucopia was a simple act of obedience. The bee collective was such a ubiquitous part of the cultural imagination that a glowing blue finial shaped like a hive would top off the Straus Building (today the landmark Britannica Center) on Michigan Avenue. Yet neither Carse nor any other commentator of the period mentioned that bees participate in a matriarchy: the hive is governed by a Queen and its workers are all female.[21] To have insisted on this notion would have transformed the Temple project into a feminist polemic and explicit social experiment. The banishment of 'woman' from the building's unofficial name might be understood as a tacit acknowledgment of the social challenges this 'humming hive' might pose, were it to enact the politics of gender rather than simply engage them.

With women as its agents, the Temple asserted the temperance cause. Its admixture of commercial and religious interests was consistent with other building projects of the period. It was only when practised by a young and determined widow that the application of a 'cold business policy' to one of these new secular cathedrals acquired a negative resonance. Yet Carse's strongest critics were other WCTU women. Though her sensible business decisions helped the building rise and remain standing, they also undermined the image of the nurturing, sentimental female invested in the Christian call for temperance.

Seeing the light

When newly completed in 1892, the Temple had no difficulties attracting lessees, which included four major banks and the unaffiliated Woman's Land Syndicate.[22] Though there were many new office buildings in the Loop, the Temple was especially attractive to potential clients because it was linked to the temperance movement. As Daniel Bluestone has noted, the skyscraper itself could 'vouch for the substance and good character of the company associated with the building either by name or by tenantry'.[23] A sober man was a reliable man; the image of moral conservatism was valuable to business. In the increasingly important realm of appearances, the WCTU's moral integrity would be imparted to the owner of any company lodged in the building, cast as a transformative agent capable of remaking vice into virtue by sustaining a spiritual atmosphere. As *Industrial Chicago* explained, 'great moral results follow from people's houses being pretty as well as healthy. It makes an educated man domestic; it makes him a lover of neatness and accuracy; it usually makes him gentle and amiable'.[24] It is architecture's purported capacity to 'make' a man into a civilised being that matters in this statement, for it directly assigns social responsibility to aesthetic properties. Were this power properly developed, the

WCTU's 'House Beautiful', as the Temperance Temple was sometimes described, could not only make businessmen into devoted lovers of 'neatness and accuracy'. It also had the potential to reform the fallen soul by virtue of its feminine qualities, especially its 'purity' and 'cleanliness'.[25]

How were 'purity' and 'cleanliness' perceived? What features made a house seem 'pretty'? Two rostrum paintings commissioned for Willard Hall, located on the ground floor of the Temple, afford some access to the aesthetic terms informing the interpretation of the building (Figure 2). Presumed destroyed and now known only through blurred monochrome reproductions, these paintings were part of a series of four panels showing female personifications of Temperance, Purity, Justice and Perseverance. Prepared by British artist Walter Crane, a member of the Arts and Crafts movement best known for his sumptuous book illustrations and socialist politics, the life-sized panels shared the sinuous lines and flattened surfaces characteristic of his work. No primary documents related to the commission of these paintings have emerged.[26] However, the female personifications of spring, summer, winter and autumn that appear in Crane's *Masque of the Four Seasons*, 1891 (private collection), resemble the quartet painted for the Temple, allowing something of the saturated green and gold palette of the leafy background to be deduced by comparison.[27] On the right, as described by the *Chicago Daily Tribune* in 1893, the 'beautiful' figure of Temperance held back the 'hound of evil indulgence', whose bloodshot eyes and slavering mouth 'typify the ravages of intemperance'.[28] Vicious and frightening, the dog represented the bestial condition in man released by his maddening thirsts. Temperance herself was veiled by the 'protective folds of her cloak', her bowed head and downcast eyes offering the 'very picture of restraint'. Averting her gaze, she offered herself as an object of scrutiny that tied virtuous womanhood to an introspective state of silence, letting her actions be more powerful than words. On the left, Purity, who was 'by far the most beautiful' of the four figures, the *Tribune* noted appreciatively, was shown holding up a crystal ball into which she peered intently. Why most beautiful? What made Purity the superior image of femininity? Both figures emphasised the importance of the female actor's decorum, identifying women with a pacifying nature signalled by the branches and leaves scattered at their feet. But they offered two different versions of the metaphor of sight: Temperance's demure gaze was fixed on the ugly task at hand, whereas Purity's uplifted eyes searched a bright but nebulous future. Released from the requirements of the mundane, her body pale and ethereal, Purity was 'most beautiful' because she incarnated an ideal state of being.

Figure 2: Walter Crane, 'Purity and Temperance', wall painting for Willard Hall, 1892 (lost, presumed destroyed), *Chicago Daily Tribune*, 8 January 1893, p. 12.

Given the painting's location inside this steel frame building, the 'entirely novel'[29] inclusion of Purity's glass globe was an interesting iconographic invention. With its ability to concentrate light, the clear orb transforms natural energy into a mystical, even supernatural force. From a formal standpoint, both Purity and Temperance bear obvious connections to early modern images of witches, such as Albrecht Dürer's engraving of the *Four Witches* (*c.* 1497, Metropolitan Museum of Art, New York). Though the work was certainly known by Crane, whose own oeuvre, like Dürer's, grounded itself in reproductive technologies that made art available to the masses, that resemblance is primarily noteworthy because it was never mentioned by period commentators. Though Dürer's nude figures were accessorised with a black beast and a crystal ball, both standard attributes of sorceresses, the reading conditions imposed by the Temple pre-empted their image from bearing a subversive pagan legacy. Instead, Purity's globe evoked the promise of a bright future held out before the dazzled (male, drunk) viewer, who by stumbling towards it would free himself from his destructive addiction. As a tool of the occult, a crystal ball revealed truths, but only to those gifted with inner vision. Held in Purity's allegorical hands, by contrast, the glass globe became a vehicle of moral change, a catalyst for the masses rather than a contemplative mirror. Inside this building, light's transformative powers were shown to be newly grasped by a woman, who would use its force to cleanse profit of any sordid associations.

Within this secular Temple, the theme was consistent with an emerging rhetoric of light and space associated with the technologically advanced skyscraper. Briefly the tallest building in the world, the Temple offered four desirable intangibles linked to the demands of capitalist space: greater volume, increased verticality, more light and ventilation and a prominent urban location. Following the symbolics of conspicuous consumption articulated by Chicago School economist Thorstein Veblen, these qualities all added up to greater social prestige for the client, whose units received more light and space in accordance with his financial resources.[30] Each of the Temple's offices presented itself as one of an identical series, a feature that would appeal to commercial clients by confirming the oft-stated linkage between this new, 'indigenous' architecture and the values of American democracy. The building's stumpy 'H' plan allowed each office to receive natural light from at least one pair of double-hung windows, thereby allowing maximal daylight and healthy ventilation to enter into each room. The corner offices would receive natural light from three separate windows, the loss of wall space being compensated for by the extra illumination. Two small bathrooms and two coatrooms served twenty-nine offices per floor. At the back of the Temple, there was an arcing embankment of eight elevators, crucial to any office building of more than four storeys and an unmistakable statement of its modernity, fronted by elegant iron grilles and flanked on each side by artificially lit stairwells (Figure 3). Because they articulated public space, such ornamental flourishes were not irrelevant: as both Bluestone and Willis have demonstrated, they were a useful and consistent feature of other tall office buildings rising in the Loop. Offering a combination of technology and grace that confirmed mastery over these brutish new materials, the wrought ironwork sustained a level of artistry that also helped raise rental values.

An H-shaped, double-loaded corridor allowed access to offices, each of which had its own built-in vault located at the furthest point from the window. Because all the offices were internally connected, it was possible to pass through every office unit without exiting to the hallway. The detail suggests that entire floors were rented by a single client, a possibility further supported by the ninth-floor plan dated 23 July 1891, which indicates that the dividing walls were removed from the interior of the left pavilion. The resulting 'great room' would have resembled the sort earlier created on the celebrated ninth floor of the nearby Phenix Building, 1885–7, also located in the Loop and designed by Root.

Figure 3: First Floor Elevator Screens from 'Woman's Temperance Temple Building [sic]', (architects Burnham & Root, 1890–92), manufactured by the Winslow Brothers. Photographs: Winslow Brothers. Published in Winslow Brothers Company, *Ornamental Iron: Reproductions from Photographs of Ornamental Iron and Art Metal Work in Place* (Chicago: Winslow Brothers, 1894), Plate 51.

Serving as headquarters for the Phenix Insurance Company, the open floor was capable of 'accommodating hundreds of clerical workers' who remained constantly available for view, promoting the idea of the one-body corporate collective through the dramatic extension of interior space made possible by engineering (Figure 4).[31]

Inside such technologically-enhanced spaces, 'space' and 'light' became marketable assets, rendered visible in this photograph because of the slow exposure required for the albumin silver process. Natural light enters the perspectival box of space as a qualitative substance, flooding the office through the window bays and bouncing off the high, slick ceiling. The brightness suffusing the interior emphasised the room's homogenous character, yielding a powerful visual statement regarding the benefits of the modern workspace. The ability to see was essential to productivity, just as the open plan facilitated circulation and efficiency. Together, light and space served as the primary vehicles effectuating the capitalist transformation of labour into profit. As Willis has argued, the need for natural light was one of the most powerful forces shaping the architectural 'vernacular of capitalism' during this period. Though florescent and incandescent lighting had long been available, they were costly and weak sources of illumination. Happily, innovations in steel-frame construction were not only making it possible to build higher buildings; they were also releasing the wall from its load-bearing functions, permitting the expansion of windows without compromising structural safety. The amount of natural light penetrating these stretched panes informed the 'economic depth' of office spaces, Willis noted, setting a ratio that remained stable well into the twentieth century.[32] What changed instead was the symbolic and actual value of height. The introduction of passenger elevators had freed clients and employees from the obligation of huffing up stairs. As a result, the *piano nobile* – the traditional seat of the aristocracy one storey up from the ground floor – began to lose its prestige. Offices on upper storeys received direct sunlight, the quality of which was more intense than the filtered light corrupted by dust kicked up from the streets. Formerly scorned and associated with gasping poverty, rooms that were higher up began to glow with desirable purity.

The elegance, luminosity and amplitude concentrated in the Temperance Temple were marketable assets, advantageously associated with a religious cause. In this setting, however, 'light' must also be understood as a cultural agent as well as a marketable commodity. Combined with the basilica-like simplicity of the interior, natural luminescence scrubbed away darkness, helping to create a 'clean' environment where quiet, repetitive work could operate as a bourgeois expression of virtue. Similarly exploited in the Temple and combined with the rhetoric of temperance, the sun itself could become the

Figure 4. John Root, Phenix Building, Chicago, ninth floor, photograph. Courtesy of the Western Union Telegraphy Company Records, Archives Center, National Museum of American History, Behring Center, Smithsonian Institution, Washington, DC.

instrument of salvation, facilitating the Protestant ethic of work that earned one's place in a man-made heaven.

From bank to beauty

> 'Ethics and aesthetics are alike out of the question to men working, working, working'.[33]

The lessons of God's grace and good citizenship were taught by the Temple, the sheer size of which testified to the benefits of sobriety. Its message was clear: a life of temperance contributed to wealth, even as drinking dribbled away money. 'The additional sums which might be saved to American labouring classes, if there were no spirits or beer in the world', Kirkland declared in 1892, 'would transfer to their ownership all the most valuable property in the country, railways, mines and manufactures, in a single generation'.[34] In less than a decade, a group of crusading women had shown Kirkland's claim to be true: there was no 'healthier' purchase in Chicago than that of property and no quicker way to attain heaven on earth than to build it yourself.

Because the Temple demonstrated the power of sobriety to line the virtuous wallet, it posed a subtle threat to social order for the same reason. If the working class as a whole claimed temperance as its model, a social hierarchy based primarily on income would surely collapse, the redistribution of wealth forcing a corresponding redistribution of political power and influence. The Temple's existence demonstrated that destabilising possibility, for the women whose cause it represented were largely disenfranchised from the cash economy and as such were classless citizens.[35] Nonetheless, with these wives and daughters at its base, the temperance movement had appropriated a patch of 'the most valuable property' in the city, confirming Kirkland's prediction. The repeated, albeit erroneous claim that the Temple was entirely financed by 'contributions raised in small sums in all parts of the country'[36] was part of the building's symbolic resonance, since the immensity of the sum raised in this grassroots fashion confirmed the power of women to effect social change. The WCTU's success implied that other politically marginalised and economically weak citizens, such as immigrants or itinerants, could likewise someday claim the city centres for themselves, redefining its socio-political geography. If drunks could go dry as a result of God's grace and temperance, so too might the working class gain the upper hand through the same transformative influences.

According to the rhetoric, the Temple had converted coins into masonry, each stone representing an invisible supporter inside that female collective. The end result, a manifestly commercial building, thus stood as the abstract embodiment of hundreds of Christian women. Yet did the building expressly evoke a female form or a feminine image? And if it did, whose body did it nominate: a middle-class, married white-ribboner or a working-class woman toiling in the business district? Since its historical origins, architecture has submitted to anthropomorphic projection, ranging from the literalism of female caryatid columns to the recapitulation of Christ's crucified body in the cross-shaped plan of the cathedral.[37] So, for example, when Chicago School architect Louis Sullivan gazed on Richardson's Marshall Field's Wholesale Store, he saw the proud figure of 'a man that walks on two legs instead of four ... a real man, a manly man; a virile force' standing there.[38] The long-standing analogy between human bodies and buildings was only strengthened by Chicago's mixture of pragmatism and piety. Because the WCTU building was called 'Temple', Willard observed, visitors would also be reminded of 'the temple of the Holy Ghost' that is the mortal body.[39] In other words, the 'house of the soul' was a material thing, akin to the 'House Beautiful' being raised by the reformist spirit of women. As the man-made envelope animated by the collective desires of the membership, Willard concluded, the Temple's stones would be invested with the 'highest significance possible'.[40]

To this audience, it mattered that the Temple's success transpired through the hearts and hands of middle-class American women. What is less clear is how, if at all, the building represented them. For Sullivan, for example, '*every building you see is the image of a man whom you do not see* [emphasis in original]':[41] in his opinion, a work of architecture was the 'offspring' of its (male) architect and more specifically, the representation of his mind.[42] For some critics, hence, the Temple's impressive mass did not evoke its female patrons but embodied the 'high sense' of its architect, John Root; in the building, they saw a 'great man' standing like a tower 'in the city of God'.[43] The process of negotiation informing the Temple's design thus requires some discussion, for it cannot be assumed that the WCTU wanted its Temple to embody a female image or even a 'feminine force' (thereby countering Sullivan's insistence on 'virile force') by offering itself as a commercial building.

Did the WCTU have any input into the process? How did the architect interpret the commission? Though the project had Willard's approval, the Temple was Carse's dream and her mission to build it had the urgency of a holy calling:

> Daily the plan unfolded and grew; it became my thought by day and my dream by night. I became conscious, as conscious as if a voice from heaven had announced it, that I was to undertake the erection of such a building ... I told her [Willard] of the pattern the Lord had given me of a new Temple for the twentieth century. That

I had heard His voice saying to the temperance women of the nation, 'The set time has come, "arise and build"'.[44]

With Willard's support, Carse met with the architect Root, to whom she offered a description of the project. 'Now go home', she instructed him and 'pray that God will inspire you with a plan such as I saw in my vision'.[45]

Unmoved by Carse's fervour, Root envisioned the Temple as a frankly commercial building, phlegmatically pointing out: 'that's what it is'. The first version of 1887 was 'a square tall office building, nothing more', without any clearly indicated religious, spiritual or domestic references (Figure 5). As architectural historian Donald Hoffman has suggested, it resembled a bank, specifically the Society for Savings Building, 1887–90, which Root had recently completed in Cleveland, Ohio (Figure 6). Both eleven-storey masonry buildings sprang from a flaring, ground-level arcade that was supported by squat, muscular columns. These columns supported five bays on each face that terminated in blunted ogive arches. Each corner was capped with a slim turret and the massive block of the whole expressed the forbidding sensibility of a fortress reminiscent of the Palazzo Vecchio in Florence. Root explained that the style evoked a 'time when the [princely] dwelling was also a fortified castle' and combined the refinements of 'wealth' with an appropriately warlike attitude.[46] Though his explanation seems strained, he certainly knew that the merchant-princes of the Renaissance had fostered art as a civic good that effaced the taint of materialism. The theme of fortification was also consistent with the crusading mission of the WCTU, which had adopted a militant position in its war against drink. A simplified elevation was quickly redrawn for the *Union Signal*, which added it to its arsenal of imagery promoting the Temple. Yet this boxy version pleased neither client nor architect, though poet-editor Harriet Monroe praised its tower as one of the best her brother-in-law ever designed.[47] Part of the problem might have been its emphasis on defence, offering thick walls that anticipated attack and prevented unlawful entrance. However, the WCTU's goal of 'home protection' was not accomplished by barring the gates against the rabble, but by strengthening the will against temptation. In principle, as a refuge for sinners, the Temple welcomed errant souls shuffling towards sobriety. By offering 'nothing more' than the utilitarian basics required for a commercial building, this version of the Temple fulfilled its practical charge but failed to accommodate its reformist programme.

Ultimately, it was neither God nor Carse but Root's charismatic design partner, Daniel Burnham, who provided the inspiration for the crucial changes. Disappointed by the preliminary project, Burnham suggested

Figure 5: John Root, 'Woman's Temple', watercolor wash and line drawing, published in *Inland Architect and News Record* 12 (December 1888). Photography ©Art Institute of Chicago.

Figure 6: John Root, 'Society for Savings Building', Cleveland, Ohio, 1887–1890. Photo Credit: The Western Reserve Historical Society, Cleveland, Ohio.

that his partner was 'not yet interested' in the Temple and pushed Root to 'put [his] soul into it'.[48] As described by Monroe, Root's drafting-room colleagues argued that the multi-storied Temple should express his client's 'higher hopes' and not just the need to turn a profit. He was encouraged to give the whole mass a more 'spiritual' expression and a roof was suggested to alleviate its harsh, 'commercial' lines. The final design was, in many critics' opinions, Root's masterpiece – an undulating office building capped by a 'beautiful roof' and surmounted by a 'slender upward-pointing flèche' finished by a statue of a young praying woman.[49] Because of a lack of funds, neither flèche nor statue was built, without discernible injury to the overall appeal of the building. Instead, this masterful blend of technology and good taste was routinely considered one of Burnham & Root's most 'beautiful' buildings.[50] For Root's contemporary Henry Van Brunt, for example, the Temple's skylines were 'beyond all praise'. In his opinion,

> The serious and noble quality of the building is due to the underlying Romanesque sentiment, which, though not expressed technically, has to my mind clearly served to eliminate the luxury and gaiety which distinguished its prototypes, the royal chateaux of France.[51]

Simultaneously opulent and restrained, the Temple's form invoked a suitably rich heritage while avoiding the patina of immoral excess. Saturated in deep red, the flaring piers of the rusticated, rectangular base provided a sturdy foundation, setting off a lobby lit by skylights and anchored by a bank at each corner. In the building's mid-section, smooth walls were rounded out into turrets and rolled back into bays, its mass regularly broken by deeply punched windows. At the top storey, its surface broke out into a flourish of embroidery-like ornamentation, complemented by slim brickwork bands underlining the upper-level fenestration. Though it was the tallest building in Chicago at the time of its completion, its overall effect was not of anthropomorphic verticality. Instead, the building continued to prioritise the horizontal line, its pronounced curves softening the overall mass and strengthening its connection to the sweeping contours of the prairie.

In the opinion of the anonymous editors of *Industrial Chicago*, the Temple was a work of true 'architecture'. Although it conceded to the demand for height increasingly expected of commercial projects, it maintained an 'exterior beauty' lacking in other tall office buildings. By contrast, the review bemoaned, the stark, vertical slab of the nearby Monadnock Block, also by Burnham & Root, was merely expressive of 'engineering', having sacrificed elegance to maximise profitability. 'Massiveness is not magnificence', *Industrial Chicago* admonished. 'It is not beauty. It is only the ground work, out of which and on which the beautiful may be wrought by talent aided by wealth'.[52] The American business spirit had ushered in the 'age of bigness', connecting great size to success in society and industry, but there was also a sense that overwhelming mass alone was somehow insufficient. The aspiration to build skywards had formerly been represented by the spire of the cathedral, the upward strain of which represented the soul's 'alienation' from the sagging flesh.[53] By the mid-nineteenth century, as architectural historian Thomas A. P. van Leeuwen has observed, architectural height and the expression of verticality remained markers of spiritual values, but they were increasingly fed into a 'quasi-religious' rationale invoked to justify the new commercial cathedrals.[54] Consequently, neither a flèche pointing towards heaven nor a praying woman surmounting the whole was needed to convey the Temple's religious aspirations. They were directly communicated through its massing and great height, coded as beautiful and not just big because its distinctive resemblance to a chateau connected it to the imagery of civic leadership.

Crucially, however, admiring assessments of its form would later become cause for scholarly amusement, a 'quaint' symptom of an aesthetic conservatism that preferred the Temple's placating veneer of historicism.[55] From a historiographic standpoint, it has been frequently noted that the impact of Sigfried Giedion's canonical *Space, Time and Architecture* (1947) was such that transitional buildings including the Temple, which retained sculptural ornament and an elaborate roof to top off its striking height, appeared hopelessly contrary to the sleek and striving principles of modernism.[56] Much as Crane's allegorical renderings of Purity and Temperance had rejected nudity in order to answer to American standards of decorum, the sober French-Renaissance cloak wrapped around the Temple's steel frame had softened its sharp edges, thereby rendering its appearance pleasing to a late-nineteenth century audience. Yet by being thus touched by 'real beauty', it engaged the vagaries of fashion and was exposed to ridicule once stylistic trends shifted.[57] By contrast, the Monadnock Block and other plain buildings in the 'commercial style' were neither beautiful nor artistic, *Industrial Chicago* admitted, but they would never 'go out of fashion' for precisely the same reason.[58] Capitalist imperatives would force a revision of cultural sensibilities: just as architectural verticality was becoming increasingly associated with the rising stock market, so too was 'beauty' no longer seen to lodge in refined silhouettes but in brutal mass exulting in rawness. By the 1890s in Chicago, buildings that made 'thrifty' use of their land, combined with a laudable sort of 'greed', had already begun to achieve a sort of 'stately beauty' by virtue of their stark sensibilities.[59]

The claim to beauty was not transparent. According to Friedrich Nietzsche, writing in 1887, to designate 'beauty' was to offer a particular kind of judgement, one which endows that person or thing with a kind of distracting 'magic'. He minced no words. 'To experience a thing as beautiful means: to experience it necessarily wrongly'.[60] In his reading, beauty was a temporal value that prevented a thing from being seen as itself. From a historical perspective, the changing critical assessments of the Temple's physical appearance cannot be extricated from the temperance cause that it represented. In a literal sense, the Temple stood for temperance: wherefore this 'sky-high menace to the liquor fiend' could not be attacked without challenging the validity of the cause.[61] As Lady Somerset observed, 'when those adverse to your work wish to cast a slur and doubt upon it, the argument that is made use of now is just this: The Temple is a failure. If the Temple is a failure, the WCTU's work is not all that it has been represented to us'.[62] Such observations follow a false logic, for the artistic merits of a building bear no necessary connection to the ethical standards of its owners. Nonetheless, her remarks register the temporary exemption of the building from the usual terms of architectural criticism, for words attacking the building were perceived as weapons raised against women. Instead, the Temple briefly enjoyed a nearly unassailable status as a direct extension of the temperance cause, the nobility of which was expressed through the building's 'real beauty'.[63]

With its pure lines, sober aspect, fair distribution and solid structure, affirming Purity, Temperance, Justice and Perseverance, the building was consequently elevated above the others of its commercial kind in form and expressivity. Although officially named the 'WCTU Building', its titular designation as 'temple' and not 'headquarters' (which 'has a sound perhaps too military', Willard commented[64]) helped secure the desired reading. 'I am [pleased] that the business name of the great building of our WCTU is to be "The Temple", short, expressive, beautiful', wrote Mary Dye of Chicago.[65] There was a widespread cultural investment in sustaining that charge, for in beauty, there was power. Endowed with a supernatural force through the legitimating power of beauty, the Temple was assigned a quasi-magical authority that signalled its fictional exemption from the primordial convulsions of industry. For if a 'pretty' house could 'domesticate' a man, making him 'neat' and 'amiable', as *Industrial Chicago* had concluded, how much more effective would a 'beautiful' building be in sobering up an entire community?

Two temples, one home

As a 'beautiful' building that was 'orderly and sane', the Temple was set apart on the rhetorical plane from other commercial buildings in the Loop. There could be 'no danger of mistake or confusion', Mary Dye stated confidently. 'There is – will be – but one Temple in Chicago'.[66] Nonetheless, there was more than one secular Temple in Chicago's business district. The Temperance Temple stood in stark contrast to the nearby Masonic Temple, 1892, also designed by Burnham & Root (Figure 7). The Masonic Temple surpassed the Temperance Temple by seven storeys, taking away its short-lived notoriety as the tallest building in the city. As Walter Crane recalled of his 1892 visit to Chicago, 'one building was stated to have reached the height of twenty-two storeys – but *one* only'[67] and that was enough. The Masonic Temple's exorbitant height, Crane thought, marked the limits of the financial risk that insurers were willing to take; economic forces would rightfully impose 'natural' limits on the growth of these frighteningly tall buildings.[68] 'Monotonous' in appearance and 'extreme' in height, the Masonic Temple was a 'perpendicular tyranny of pilasters' that expressed nothing more than 'the apotheosis of the elevator in the modern social system', Van Brunt complained.[69] Yet if the Masonic Temple was disparaged for its 'plainness and uniformity of design', its hard-edged severity was also deemed appropriate to a society of men, wherefore its austere appearance was characteristic of Masonic temples in general.[70] Rising side by side, the 'Two Temples' were frequently paired in the papers, serving as

Figure 7: Daniel Burnham and John Root, Masonic Temple, Chicago, 1892. From *Unrivaled Chicago: Containing an Historical Narrative of the Great City's Development, and Descriptions of Points of Interest ... with Biographical Sketches of Representative Men in their Several Lines* (Chicago: Rand McNally, 1896).

twinned markers shaping the urban landscape according to a distinctly American syncopation.

Casting the philanthropic goals of female reformers on the one hand and the mysterious rituals of the masons on the other, the two Temples offered a tidy juxtaposition between public and private spheres passed through representative works of commercial architecture. Because they were both conspicuously identified with a same-sex group, the two Temples were also susceptible to gendered interpretation, which placed feminine virtue on one side and masculine ambition on the other. That juxtaposition rehearsed structuralist binaries of curved/straight, soft/hard, warm/cold, horizontal/vertical, spiritual/material, beautiful/ugly and so on, contrasts that are arguably discernible in this architectural pair. Yet it should also be evident that neither building's merits could be reduced to a single factor, even one as compelling and as seemingly obvious as gender. Instead, as Nietzsche had argued, what is specifically relevant in the contrast between beauty and ugliness is that their meaning derives from 'the most fundamental values of preservation'.[71] In sum, to understand what a society calls beautiful is to understand what it considers worth protecting.

As Nietzsche had stressed, neither beauty nor ugliness is an inherent attribute. Instead, both are relative to changing conditions of self-preservation, ranging from biological reproduction to economic survival. That which is considered beautiful preserves those values, whereas ugliness defies those conditions and even attacks them. As a result, a building once admired for its 'lovely', 'handsome' and otherwise pleasing appearance could later attract derision, because the temperance cause it represented had lost its moral imperative. On its own, the form did not dictate cultural readings: the strikingly different critical receptions of the two Temples in the 1890s and their reversals of aesthetic standing over time, show that equally distinctive factors such as exceptional height, historicising details and designation as 'temple' did not assure a positive reception. Both tall office buildings stood out sharply from the urban landscape, but not because they were exceptionally beautiful or ugly. Instead, they received critical attention precisely because they were experimental works of architecture susceptible to a wide range of interpretive possibilities. Not only were they both monuments to modern technology, but, as Joanna Merwood has recently argued, they were also models of social collectivity, vertical 'cities within cities' that fostered social progress through a rich concoction of art, business and religious values.[72] Proposed as vehicles for social change, the very range and sophistication of their programmes complicated their reception. Instead, these new commercial structures affirmed that performance – a high ratio of space to rents – secured survival in a capitalist economy. As a result, the appearance (not necessarily the reality) of high functionality became the basis of a new style, from which the need for visual pleasure was first minimised and then slowly eliminated.

The search for an indigenous architectural style was one of the most pressing design problems of the nineteenth century, linked to the politics of national identity coupled with romanticist readings of history.[73] In the American Midwest, a raucous combination of religious sentiment, land speculation and personal ambition had informed the immediate demand for commercial workspace. Quickly built in response, pragmatically oriented, free from tradition and unencumbered by deep obligations to precedent, these new elevator buildings eventually resolved into the 'Chicago Style', routinely identified as the first works of American architecture, both in style and in typology. According to Willis, the formal development of the 'tall office building' was strongly influenced by local building regulations such as lot size, height requirements and zoning restrictions. In keeping with the contextualised reading of buildings, one might add that natural phenomena such as climate, terrain and geography also imposed physical constraints affecting expressive possibilities. Nonetheless, though external factors may have strongly determined the plan and overall configuration of commercial buildings, it still leaves the question of how their vertical mass would be articulated. What architectural style? Whose visual values?

A great deal was at stake in the answers. In the American setting, the emerging aesthetics of capitalism were annexed to building technologies, linked to financial priorities and a willingness to experiment. Yet, following Bluestone, it might also be argued that the question of style also responded to cultural concerns, including the desire to see money serve the cause of moral improvement. As a social art, architecture was the most visible sign of a patron's concern for the public good, fostering universities, museums, libraries, hospitals and other civic institutions. As Helen Horowitz has demonstrated, cultural philanthropy in Chicago was valuable to social standing as well as personal reputation and was widespread and encouraged.[74] But it was a privileged position available only to the wealthy elite, which assumed the attitude of a benevolent paternalism investing in the welfare of the larger community. Rendered in palatial and neo-classical styles chiefly borrowed from Italy and France, Chicago's civic monuments sustained a vision of an idealised and homogenous history that removed itself from the sordid business of everyday life, in order to better commemorate the values of a 'modern' civilisation. By contrast, its tall office buildings partook of an unpredictable and confusing present, full of foreign elements and muscular hands that traversed between slaughterhouse and stock market.[75] Correspondingly, historians of the World's Columbian Exposition, noting the contrast between the academic conservatism of the Court of Honor (known as the 'White City' both for its uniform colour and the social composition of its visitors) and the colourful vulgarity of Little Egypt and the Ferris Wheel in the Exposition's Midway, have repeatedly drawn parallels between this divided fantasy and the stylistic struggles transpiring a few miles north at the lakefront and the Loop. In both settings, the fight over architectural style was partly a struggle over the representation of class, specifically a class structure defined by wealth, not family, and thus intrinsically volatile.

For Chicago's commercial buildings to have refused the niceties of architectural style was, on a certain level, to resist that genial dictatorship along with the monuments that sustained its claims to social superiority. In this sense, the Temple's red French-Renaissance wrapping must be understood as a compromise, which neither invoked the eternalising rhetoric of classicism nor succumbed to the pragmatism of an unadorned slab. Acting in the public good, the lofty goal of moral improvement was the WCTU's stated mission. Yet its arduous task was to be accomplished by women who would 'do everything' – the organisation's famous motto – including all of the actual work. In this sense it is interesting that Van Brunt had emphasised that the building resembled the residences of kings but had refused 'luxury and gaiety' in its appearance.[76] In other words, it was a civic monument that was all business: the keepers of the castle were also the servants doing the cleaning.

As Willard described, the Temple was the symbol of a 'new era of woman's work' and as such, she acknowledged that its membership and client base were not parvenus or *nouveaux riches*, but an expanding middle class. By the end of the nineteenth century, Chicago's clerical pools regularly included working-class women, such as the single female working in the Great Room of Root's Phenix Building (Figure 4).[77] Located in the lower right-hand corner of the photograph, she is identifiable by the mutton-chop pouf of her sleeves, noticeably different in silhouette from the starched shirts and vests worn by her male co-workers. Evocatively, her face is a blur: she is a woman on the move, caught in the very moment of social transition from working-class marginality to white-collar respectability. Crucially, though such women may have held similar jobs in the Temple, they did not represent its veritable work. According to Willard, such female clerks were doing men's work, i.e. performing as the anonymous extensions of male-owned business interests which bore none of the 'feminine' markers of 'compassion, spirituality, aesthetics and cooperation'.[78] Instead, the 'new women's work' was defined by the work of the WCTU, which mobilised respectable, middle-class women to 'save' their own 'home, children and land' by pushing them out into the 'dirty' streets, 'devilish' saloons and other 'dangerous' spaces that trapped drunkards, louts and fallen women into lives of poverty and despair. The urban landscape was to be 'cleansed' by dint of the WCTU's virtuous presence, casting femininity itself as a purifying agent and womanhood as its vehicle.[79]

As Willard had famously pronounced, the whole world should become 'homelike' and the 'House Beautiful' that was the Temple would be the site and symbol of this goal. As an activist and thinking individual, Willard supported reformist calls for cooperative housekeeping and socialised domestic work. But the Temple was not an explicitly feminist project, at least not in the sense explored at length by Dolores Hayden. Though Utopian in its ethos, the Temple was not a residence and it did not experiment with new systems of household labour and childcare, domestic work traditionally performed by women.[80] The 'house' in question was the house of the soul, a mortal dwelling threatened by weak morals and the destructive influence of drink. The 'home' itself was not a place but an idea sustaining normative Christian values, emphasising marriage, parenthood and the respect of the community. On the larger plane, 'home protection' was the objective and the crusade for temperance was the means. In the Victorian ideology of the period, the WCTU's defence of house and home was a mission worth supporting. Thus, to borrow Nietzsche's formulation, it was a thing of beauty. Offering itself as a model of decorous femininity, suffused by faith in a better future, the Temple's fenestrated lightness and formal restraint were meant to transform business itself into something pure, home-like and well-tempered, accomplishing the worthy task through its uplifting sensibilities.

From broken hearts to orphan building

As the eyes of the world turned to Chicago, host of the World's Columbian Exposition in 1893, Mrs Henry imagined the conversation of astonished visitors to the city:

> 'What is *that* storied pile?'
>
> 'That? It is the Temperance Temple ...'
>
> 'The women were heart-broken because of drink – this is the result! ...'
>
> 'The women had an eye to business; the rental must be immense!'

'There must have been a level head and integrity under all of *that*'.

'That was Matilda B. Carse'.

'Who's she?'

'Oh, a WCTU woman'.[81]

Step by step, the massive pile reduced to one: the cornerstone at its foundation was 'a WCTU woman' and for Mrs Henry, that woman was Carse. However, the formulation was flawed from the start. Though bristling with pride with what the WCTU had accomplished, her remarks also revealed a central schism between two visions of female activism and sought to resolve the gap between broken hearts and hard heads by advancing one representative for one group and one building. But in and around the landmark Temple, women's social roles were dramatically changing, and so were their assumptions and possibilities. Otherwise stated, 'the woman' of the 'Woman's Christian Temperance Union' had become 'women' along the way: by the end of the nineteenth century, it did not consist of a single uniform body, but a disparate collection of many.

As a commercial project set in the public sphere, the Temple project was an 'architecture of representation'[82] that forced the WCTU to confront its increasingly pluralistic and politically variegated composition. The fissures were already there; the stress of such a large undertaking merely thrust them into the open. In other words, the 'Temple Question' was not about the expense of a building – the need for a central headquarters was clear – but about the values held by its national membership and its unresolved self-image. The project posed the question directly, by asking the WCTU to stand behind a daring elevator building that would command the world's attention and to make a series of decisions that probed the Union's reformist identity and its commitment to its mission. With the establishment of the Temple, the shape and tone of the cause would be given public expression. For the sake of their homes and families, thousands of women would be crusading for temperance. But what good was it to accept the task? How could wives and mothers get drunks and politicians to listen? For Willard, moral force was the answer. Her visionary 'House Beautiful' prompted them to save a threatened domestic sphere by expanding its circumference, thereby assigning women the power to change the world because of and not in spite of, their compassion, virtue and aestheticism. The option Carse offered was less inspiring, but more realistic. The success of the Temperance Temple demonstrated that the business world would accommodate women as long as they accepted its terms, which meant foregoing the 'feminine' attributes that Willard had cherished. Rather than domesticating business and aligning it with female sensibilities, Carse accepted a power structure based on capital and sought to make women part of it.

Two charismatic women held out different choices: one concentrating on the dirty task at hand and accepting its familiar proximity, the other gazing at a shining future that offered an inspiring impossibility. Temperance or Purity? Business or beauty? As economic necessity drove increasing numbers of women to enter the workplace, the promise of a home-like world seemed increasingly hollow and naive. In the face of massive social change, the Temple's vision of cooperation began to falter. In February 1898, Willard died. Within six months, the WCTU voted to disaffiliate itself from a building that had never belonged to it in the first place.

Though frayed nerves and injured egos played a role in the administrative collapse of the project, it was not the volatile interplay of emotions that pushed the WCTU to reject one of the 'loveliest' big buildings in Chicago.[83] Rather, the WCTU made it clear that it could not see itself in it. Its uncomfortable relationship to the building and, by extension, to Carse, illuminated the cultural difficulties women faced when projecting themselves outside a middle-class, Christian framework of home and family. As a business building, the Temple already engaged a masculine rhetoric. For Carse, it was more practical to insert women inside this narrative, rather than attempting to rewrite it. Yet by renouncing the mantle of moral superiority, she made women vulnerable to attacks as unsexed, monstrous harridans. Indeed, the decisive implosion of the building in the frenzied interim between the two world wars seemed to prefigure the subsequent collapse of the WCTU's public image into little more than 'a cheap joke ... equated with cartoons of Carry Nation wielding her axe or with elderly spinsters finding an outlet for subconscious hostility against males'.[84] Not only would the reality of women working undo Willard's vision of new women's work, but the movement's once-admirable beauty would dissipate into caricature, reduced by changing social mores to a collection of bored and frustrated relics.

In its unembellished essence, the Temple was 'nothing more' than a commercial office building just as Root had first understood it to be, chiefly obligated to produce rents and remain profitable by offering space and light as bankable commodities. But as filtered through words and willed by the community, the form exuded grace and nobility, evoking the residences of French royalty whose wealth was far removed from the kind of 'work' required by modern urban industry. As the temperance movement lost its force, fading into anachronism, so too did the Temple begin to appear curious rather than daring, a lonely moralist among increasingly powerful materialists. Correspondingly, the Temperance Temple went from being 'perhaps the handsomest big building in Chicago'[85] to an amusing historical footnote, undergoing a dramatic reversal of critical fortune that mirrored its physical fate. In 1926, having become the property of the Field Museum, the building was destroyed. A bank was built in its place.

Notes

1. See, for example, Carol Willis, *Form Follows Finance: Skyscrapers and Skylines in New York and Chicago* (Princeton: Princeton Architectural Press, 1995). On the rise of the 'commercial style', see Carl Condit, *The Chicago School of Architecture: A History of Commercial and Public Building in the Chicago Area, 1875–1925* (Chicago: University of Chicago Press, 1964); William H. Jordy, 'Chicago and the "Commercial Style"', in *Progressive and Academic Ideals at the Turn of the Century* (Oxford: Oxford University Press, 1972), vol. 4: *American Buildings and their Architects*, pp. 1–82.
2. Daniel Bluestone, *Constructing Chicago* (New Haven: Yale University Press, 1991). On the relationship between women and domestic architecture, see Dolores Hayden, *The Grand Domestic Revolution: A History of Feminist Designs for American Homes, Neighborhoods, and Cities* (Cambridge, MA: MIT Press, 1981); Gwendolyn Wright, *Moralism and the Model Home: Domestic Architecture and Cultural Conflict in Chicago, 1873–1913* (Chicago: University of Chicago Press, 1980).
3. David Lowe, *Lost Chicago* (New York: Watson-Guptill, 2000).
4. William Le Baron Jenney to the Chicago Architectural Sketch Club, January 1889, in *Industrial Chicago*, revised ed. vol. 2 (Chicago: Goodspeed Press, 1891), p. 609.
5. 'Report on the Temple Question', *Union Signal*, 2 November 1893, p. 15. Details on Lathrap, one of the WCTU's original founders, are found in Carol Mattingly, *Well-Tempered Women: Nineteenth-Century Temperance Rhetoric* (Carbondale, IL: Southern Illinois University Press, 1998), pp. 47–50.
6. Matilda B. Carse, 'Inception of Plan and Present Status of "The Temple"', *Union Signal*, 6 November 1890, p. 3.
7. See Rachel E. Bohlmann, 'Our "House Beautiful": The Woman's Temple and the WCTU Effort to Establish Place and Identity in Downtown Chicago, 1887–1898', *Journal of Women's History* 11 (1999), pp. 110–34; Ruth Bordin, *Woman and Temperance: The Quest for Power and Liberty, 1873–1900* (Philadelphia: Temple University Press, 1981), pp. 140–48; Mary Earhart, *Frances Willard: From Prayers to Politics* (Chicago: University of Chicago Press, 1944), pp. 367–88.
8. Frances Willard, 'Temperance Temples', *Union Signal*, 3 May 1888, p. 7.
9. Louis H. Sullivan, *Kindergarten Chats and Other Writings* (New York: George Wittenborn, 1968), pp. 20–24.
10. Sarah Burns, *Inventing the Modern Artist: Art and Culture in Gilded Age America* (New Haven: Yale University Press, 1996), p. 169. The attempts by urban planners to regulate social space are explored by Elizabeth Wilson, *The Sphinx in the City: Urban Life, the Control of Disorder, and Women* (Los Angeles: University of California Press, 1992).
11. Earhart, *Frances Willard*, p. 348.
12. Matilda B. Carse, 'Temperance Temple Items', *Union Signal*, 19 December 1889, p. 4. The projected rental income was later cut in half; the revised numbers appear in Matilda B. Carse, 'To the Rescue of the Temple', 1 January 1898, Sophia Smith Collection, Archives of Smith College, Northampton, Massachusetts.

13. Harriet B. Kells, 'Temperance Temple Items', *Union Signal*, April 1892–May 1893. On the rise of the 'revenue church', see Thomas A. P. van Leeuwen, *The Skyward Trend of Thought: The Metaphysics of the American Skyscraper* (Cambridge: MIT Press, 1988), pp. 58–60.
14. See Max Weber, *The Protestant Ethic and the Spirit of Capitalism*, tr. Talcott Parsons (1930: repr. London: Routledge, 1992).
15. Joseph Kirkland, *The Story of Chicago* (Chicago: Dibble Publishing Company, 1892), p. 440.
16. Carse, 'Temperance Temple Items', *Union Signal*, 10 October 1889, p. 4.
17. Matilda B. Carse, 'The Temperance Temple', quoted in Donald Hoffman, *The Architecture of John Wellborn Root* (Baltimore: Johns Hopkins University Press, 1973), p. 193.
18. Lady Henry Somerset, quoted in Carse, 'Inception of Plan', *Union Signal*, 6 November 1890, p. 3.
19. Carse, 'The Temperance Temple' and 'History of the Temple Enterprise', quoted in Hoffman, *The Architecture of John Wellborn Root*, p. 193.
20. Carse, 'Inception of Plan and Present Status of the Temple', 6 November 1890, p. 3. The fullest account of nineteenth-century Chicago's exploitation of nature is William Cronon, *Nature's Metropolis: Chicago and the Great West* (New York: W.W. Norton, 1991).
21. On bee society as a political analogy, see Jeffrey Merrick, 'Royal Bees: The Gender Politics of the Beehive in Early Modern Europe', *Studies in Eighteenth-Century Culture* 18 (1988), pp. 7–37.
22. Bohlmann, 'Our "House Beautiful"', p. 119. As she indicates, the only stipulations placed on clients were that they neither be connected to the liquor trade nor sell alcohol or tobacco on the premises.
23. Bluestone, *Constructing Chicago*, p. 123.
24. *Industrial Chicago*, vol. 2, p. 493.
25. See comments cited in Bohlmann, 'Our "House Beautiful"', pp. 114–15.
26. Crane briefly mentions the Temple commission in Walter Crane, *An Artist's Reminiscences* (London: Methuen & Co., 1907), p. 405, but the details do not support Isobel Spencer's claim that he received the commission through architect William Pretyman, his host in Chicago. See Isobel Spencer, *Walter Crane* (London: Studio Vista, 1975), p. 172.
27. According to Morna O'Neill, who is completing a dissertation on Crane at Yale University, the *Masque of the Four Seasons* was exhibited in 1891 at the Fine Arts Society and in 1910 at the British-Japan Exhibition, where it was listed as 'property of the artist'. It was put up for auction at Sotheby's, 22 November 1988, lot number 71.
28. 'In Their New Home', *Chicago Daily Tribune*, 8 January 1893, p. 12. All subsequent quotations in this paragraph come from this source. Crane's two life-size panels (measuring 5$^{1}/_{2}$ feet by 6$^{1}/_{2}$ feet) are both lost and are presumed destroyed. The only photographic reproductions of these paintings appear in Otto von Schleinitz, *Walter Crane* (Bielefeld and Leipzig: Velhagen & Klasing, 1902), pp. 84–5; 111, but the quality is extremely poor. I am obliged to Morna O'Neill for the reference.
29. 'In Their New Home', *Chicago Daily Tribune*, 8 January 1893, p. 12.
30. Thorstein Veblen, *The Theory of the Leisure Class: An Economic Study of Institutions* (New York: Macmillan, 1899).
31. Hoffman, *The Architecture of John Wellborn Root*, p. 55. A copy of the first floor plan appears in Lowe, *Lost Chicago*, p. 143, which identified the source as the Chicago Historical Society (CHS). However, no plan or photograph could be located at the CHS and it is currently presumed lost.
32. Willis, *Form Follows Finance*, pp. 24–33.
33. Kirkland, *The Story of Chicago*, p. 437.
34. Kirkland, *The Story of Chicago*, p. 354. Kirkland estimated that the losses to Chicago's economy due to drinking alone, without factoring indirect costs provoked by sickness or

injury, were between twenty and thirty million dollars a year. Similar conclusions appear in 'Economics and Intemperance', *Union Signal*, 27 March 1890, p. 8.

35. On the classing of the WCTU's membership according to the husband's or father's professions, see Bordin, *Woman and Temperance*, Appendix, pp. 163–75. As she explains, they had limited means through inheritances and allowances, but 'no [outside] income' and no way of making money.
36. William H. Birkmire, *Skeleton Construction in Buildings* (New York: John Wiley & Sons, 1894), p. 4; Lowe, *Lost Chicago*, p. 143.
37. See Joseph Rykwert, *On Adam's House in Paradise: The Idea of the Primitive Hut in Architectural History* (New York and Chicago: Museum of Modern Art and Graham Foundation for Advanced Studies in the Fine Arts, 1972); and Françoise Choay, 'La ville et le domaine bâti comme corps dans les textes des architectes-théoriciens de la première Renaissance italienne', *Nouvelle revue de psychanalyse* 9 (1974), pp. 239–52.
38. Sullivan, *Kindergarten Chats*, p. 29.
39. Willard, 'Temperance Temples', p. 7.
40. Willard, 'Temperance Temples', p. 7.
41. Sullivan, *Kindergarten Chats*, p. 24. Emphasis added.
42. Sullivan, *Kindergarten Chats*, p. 24. For Sullivan, the resemblance was not mimetic, i.e. roof equals 'head' and 'foundation' equals feet. Rather, architecture was *a priori* a 'masculine' activity, as it was a work of the intellect requiring 'logic' and 'clarity'. Thus any building designed by an architect incarnated his state of mind, representing his creativity rather than reiterating his body.
43. Henry Van Brunt (paraphrasing Henry Wadsworth Longfellow), 'John Wellborn Root', *Inland Architect and News Record* (1891), quoted in Harriet Monroe, *John Wellborn Root, A Study of His Life and Work* (1896; repr. Park Forest, IL: Prairie School Press, 1966), p. 281.
44. Carse, 'Inception of Plan,' p. 3. She was quoting Nehemiah 2:20: 'The God of Heaven will give us success; therefore we, his servants, will arise and build'.
45. Carse, 'Temperance Temple Items', *Union Signal*, 29 January 1891, p. 3.
46. John Root, quoted by Matilda B. Carse, *The Temperance Temple, Report of the President of the Woman's Temperance Building Association, Delivered at the Annual Convention of the National W. C. T. U., Nashville, Tenn., November, 1887*, pamphlet, quoted in Bohlmann, 'Our "House Beautiful"', pp. 112–13. Bohlmann mistakenly attaches his remarks to the second version of the project that emerged in 1890. However, Root was describing the first version of 1887.
47. Monroe, *John Wellborn Root*, p. 143; also Carse, 'Inception of Plan and Present Status of "The Temple"', p. 3. The preliminary drawing was exhibited at the Third Annual Banquet of the Chicago Architectural Sketch Club, selected by a committee that included Root, Sullivan and William Le Baron Jenney.
48. Monroe, *John Wellborn Root*, p. 124–5.
49. Monroe, *John Wellborn Root*, p. 125; and John Root, paraphrased by Carse, 'Temperance Temple Items', *Union Signal*, 29 January 1891, p. 3.
50. *Industrial Chicago*, vol. 1 (Chicago: Goodspeed Publishing Co, 1889), p. 269.
51. Van Brunt, 'John Wellborn Root' (1891), quoted in Monroe, *John Wellborn Root*, p. 279.
52. *Industrial Chicago*, vol. 1, p. 269.
53. Frederick Baumann, 'Thoughts on Architecture', read to the American Institute of Architects, Washington, D.C., 1890, reprinted in *Industrial Chicago*, vol. 2, p. 585.
54. Van Leeuwen, *The Skyward Trend of Thought*, pp. 56–78.
55. Jordy, *Progressive and Academic Ideals*, pp. 72 and 379, note 44, commenting on *Industrial Chicago*, vol. 1, pp. 69–70; also 'John Wellborn Root', *American Society of the French Legion of Honor* (1952), pp. 139–52, here p. 148, which declares the Temple 'interesting as an early example of a steel-framed building' but 'less noteworthy in its design'.
56. See summary in van Leeuwen, *The Skyward Trend of Thought*, p. 59.
57. William Archer (1900), quoted in Jordy, *Progressive and Academic Ideals*, p. 45.

58. *Industrial Chicago*, vol. 1, p. 66. Similar comments appear throughout Thomas Tallmadge, *Architecture in Old Chicago* (Chicago: University of Chicago Press, 1941).
59. Kirkland, *The Story of Chicago*, p. 448.
60. Friedrich Nietzsche, *The Will to Power*, tr. Walter Kaufmann and R. J. Hollingdale (New York: Vintage Books, 1967), p. 424, entry 804 (Spring–Fall 1887).
61. Rev. T. N. Barkdall, quoted in Kells, 'Temperance Temple Items', *Union Signal*, 5 April 1892, p. 4.
62. Lady Henry Somerset, quoted in Carse, 'Inception of Plan', p. 3.
63. *Industrial Chicago*, vol. 2, p. 493.
64. Willard, 'Temperance Temples', p. 7.
65. Mary Dye, quoted in Monroe, *John Wellborn Root*, p. 124.
66. Mary Dye, quoted in Monroe, *John Wellborn Root*, p. 124.
67. Crane, *An Artist's Reminiscences*, p. 378. Emphasis in the original.
68. Crane, *An Artist's Reminiscences*, p. 378. See chapter 9, 'Bohemia – Italy – Visit to America, 1890–92'.
69. Van Brunt, 'John Wellborn Root', quoted in Monroe, *John Wellborn Root*, pp. 279–80.
70. 'A City Under One Roof – the Masonic Temple', *Scientific American* 70 (1894), p. 81, quoted by Joanna Merwood, 'The Lobby Becomes the Street: Chicago's Masonic Temple, 1892'. Paper presented at the annual meeting of the Society of Architectural Historians, April 2004. Quoted with the author's permission.
71. Nietzsche, *The Will to Power*, p. 425.
72. Merwood, 'The Lobby Becomes the Street'.
73. For a summary of the problem of style in the nineteenth century, see Heinrich Hübsch, *In What Style Shall We Build? The German Debate on Architectural Style*, tr. Wolfgang Hermann (1828; tr. Santa Monica, CA: Getty Center for the History of Art and the Humanities, 1992).
74. On cultural philanthropy in Chicago, see Helen Horowitz, *Culture and the City: Cultural Philanthropy in Chicago from the 1880s to 1917* (Lexington: University Press of Kentucky, 1976).
75. On slaughterhouses and urban space, see 'The Slaughterhouse and the City', *Food & History* 3 (2005), special issue, ed. Paula Young Lee; and Paula Young Lee (ed.), *Animal Slaughter and Modern Sensibilities* (Lebanon, NH: University Press of New England, forthcoming).
76. Van Brunt, 'John Wellborn Root', quoted in Monroe, *John Wellborn Root*, p. 279.
77. US Census Office, *Statistics of the Population of the United States, 1870* (Washington, DC: GPO, 1883), quoted in Bluestone, *Constructing Chicago*, p. 109.
78. Frances Willard, 'Three Children', 1887, quoted in Alison Parker, *Purifying America: Women, Cultural Reform, and Pro-Censorship Activism, 1873–1933* (Urbana and Chicago: University of Illinois Press, 1997), p. 170.
79. Carse, 'Temperance Temple', quoted in Hoffman, *The Architecture of John Wellborn Root*, p. 193.
80. Hayden, *The Grand Domestic Revolution*, pp. 114–31.
81. 'The Watch-Tower', comments by Mrs S. M. I. Henry, *Union Signal*, 6 November 1890, p. 6. All emphases in original.
82. Henri Lefebvre, *The Production of Space*, tr. Donald Nicholson-Smith (Oxford and Cambridge, MA: Blackwell, 1991).
83. Tallmadge, *Architecture in Old Chicago*, p. 203 Cambridge, MA; *Industrial Chicago*, vol. 1, p. 70.
84. Bordin, *Woman and Temperance*, pp. xvii and 155. As Alison Parker has similarly noted, historians of the Progressive Era have thus tended to cast the WCTU as a 'conservative and backward-looking organization' that was hardly worth noting. See Parker, *Purifying America*, pp. 8 and 233, note 24.
85. Birkmire, *Skeleton Construction in Buildings*, p. 4.

12 There's Something about Mary Wigman: The Woman Dancer as Subject in German Expressionist Art

Susan Laikin Funkenstein

As the most celebrated expressionist dancer in Weimar Germany (1918–33), Mary Wigman (1886–1973) presented a new model of female liberation. Unlike numerous popular, ballet and avant-garde dancers before her, whose sexuality or exoticism was instrumental in their appeal, Wigman performed socially constructed characters to explore expressivity and spirituality. And, whereas numerous women dancers have been objectified on stage – often, paradoxically, strategically constructing themselves as objects – Wigman denied objectification by obscuring her body and staring back at her audience.

Because of her innovations, talent and celebrity, a range of visual artists pursued the dancer and portrayed her in their works. Attracted to the emotionalism and modernist structures of her choreographies, the Expressionists Emil Nolde and Ernst Ludwig Kirchner knew the dancer well and depicted her often. As male artists depicting a strong female subject, their art tackled a dynamic permeating the history of art: the gaze. Although first theorised by Laura Mulvey as a strict binary, subsequent scholarship has complicated the notion of the gaze. Far from being monolithic, a range of gazes encompass varied peoples' experiences in looking and being looked at, because of class, ethnicity, sexual orientation and historical conditions that change over time. Men and women can objectify male pinups and male movie stars; mother and child can gaze upon each other with mutual admiration; filmmakers can create powerful male and female characters in ways that construct points of identification for a wide range of viewers.[1] Though the roots of these theories often lie in psychoanalytic theory, I would argue that these structures are instead based in historically bound social constructions of hierarchies (as are psychoanalytic practices, for that matter) and thus are changeable under the influence of strong individuals and sweeping cultural forces.

Wigman's group and solo performances of the 1920s resonate with these expanded formulations of the gaze by challenging the seemingly fixed and essentialising dynamics of spectatorship. She facilitated an environment of mutual respect between the female group dancers and herself as leader, and asserted a strong female subject on stage that provided points of identification for her female (and male) audiences. Moreover, Wigman's resistance to traditional gender roles through the characters she created on stage can be analysed as a consciously creative instance of gender performativity as articulated in the 1990s by Judith Butler. Through repeating physical gestures on stage and in rehearsals, Wigman and her dancers repetitively inscribed their cultural roles onto their bodies. In the process, the roles of the dancers were continuously constructed and fundamentally freed from the constrictions of essentialised identities.[2] Though Wigman created this dynamic on stage, it does not necessarily follow that the artists who imaged her would have portrayed her as she presented herself. After all, many were senior male artists a generation older than Wigman who had a long history of objectifying women in their artwork.

Wigman's particular predicament raises the following questions: If the artists had subscribed to the male (subject)/female (object) binaries in much of their oeuvre, what would happen if the female subject refused to be objectified? Would artists continue to sexualise her, manipulating the images to suit their own fantasies? Or, could a new corpus of images arise in which the subject–object relationships evident at times in the history of art no longer exist – one that instead embraces a more expansive understanding of the dynamics of power and more mutual respect?

In the case of Wigman, the answer to the last question is yes. Nolde and Kirchner created a new artistic language for themselves that in myriad ways embraced Wigman as a subject. Most notably, their works can be interpreted as a negotiation between their own artistic concerns and the theories and practices embedded in Wigman's work. They rendered her body as a site of her artistic pursuits, including her expression of spirituality, her theories of the 'Form in Space', and her fostering of a women's community. Both artists understood the nuances of her work and ideas and conveyed them in their artwork. More specifically, Nolde's vibrantly hued watercolours of Wigman suggest his ideal of the solitary, expressive Germanic artist, captured by the dominance of her physical presence in the composition and her forcefully emotive gestures. In contrast, Kirchner focused on the relationships between individuals and the constructions of hierarchies and communities in Wigman's group choreography *Dance of Death*, emphases that paralleled Wigman's own explorations of abstract dance, spatial relationships on stage and group dynamics. Because of her maturity (she turned forty in 1926), her eschewing of conventional femininity and her self-promotion as a spiritual leader, Wigman fundamentally challenged the notion that women's identity derived from their objectification. More than that, she influenced two senior male artists, both with long histories of objectifying women, to have them depict her choreographies on *her* own terms. In other words, there was 'something about Mary', but unlike the film alluded to in this article's title, in which male ownership of the character played by Cameron Diaz was integral to the fantasy of objectification, respect and kindred artistic ideals between Wigman and the artists fostered the constitution of a woman as subject.[3] By repositioning women, Nolde, Kirchner and Wigman provided a model for future artists and subjects seeking to challenge traditional power dynamics.

Wigman as subject

When Wigman emerged on the national dance scene, she quickly became a sensation. Recognised for her talents during her student years with Emile Jacques-Dalcroze in Hellerau in 1910–12 and with Rudolf von Laban in Ascona during World War I, she learned from them styles, principles and dynamics that would be central in her work and self-assertion as a woman. Both instructors emphasised improvisation, which she later employed as a working method, and like Laban, she prioritised movement by performing to silence or percussion. Laban's work with movement choirs, in which a group engages with and follows the lead of an individual dancer, was pivotal in her own teachings and group choreographies. Opened in Dresden in 1919, her dance school focused on young women's self-actualisation in a dance community and quickly became a locus for young women interested in dance. Wigman's approach was in stark contrast to other well-known modern dance schools in Germany, such as Isadora and Elizabeth Duncan's school in Berlin, which emphasised women's maternal functions and the teaching of small children. In Dresden, educated young women joined a female-centred dance community – no men performed in Wigman's group choreographies until 1930 – that focused around Wigman's strong personality. As a result of Wigman's guidance, many of the dancers who began their careers as her pupils, such as Yvonne Georgi, Hanya Holm, Gret Palucca and Vera Skoronel, became leading Weimar-era dancers. Through her teachings, students and choreographies, Wigman served as a central figure in German Expressionist dance in ways that valued creative and active women.

The critical recognition of Wigman's school and teachings was augmented by her fame in the popular press, which portrayed her and her dancing as the embodiment of the liberating possibilities of physical expression for women. Women's magazines frequently portrayed women dancers as having attained positions of power as creative forces and working women; the first issue of *Uhu*, for example, argued that the physical liberation of women was fundamentally tied to women's social and political freedoms.[4] Understood by many female readers as quintessence of women's emancipation, Wigman appeared so frequently in such magazines that a regular reader would have known of her most recent performances and dance studio activities. For example, her assistant Berthe Trümpy welcomed the readers of Uhuinto their women's dance community, as she described the rehearsals of the Wigman studio in a colloquial voice and presented Wigman's artistic dances as integral to collegial interactions between athletic and creative women.[5] A photograph of the tenth anniversary celebration of Wigman's school circulated widely; it appeared, for example, in one of the largest weekly glossy papers, the *Berliner Illustrirte Zeitung*. Here, former Wigman students who themselves had become famous dancers surround their mentor and pose in their glamorous dresses; the sheer force of their combined celebrity power demonstrates the potent self-actualisation Wigman fostered through dance.[6] Embodying the aspirations of its readers, Wigman's work provided an intellectual weight to women's political and social efforts not found in other forms of popular culture.

Wigman's emancipatory model paralleled broader political and economic developments of the Weimar Republic; her leadership was but one of the many ways in which Weimar women appeared to enjoy social and political liberation. During World War I, many women worked in the factories while men served at the front; though many aspects of women's lives and outlooks returned to their pre-war status after 1918, they did learn something about self-reliance while men were in combat. First granted suffrage with the 1919 Weimar Constitution, only months before Wigman opened her school, women comprised nearly 10 per cent of the Reichstag and between 5 and 10 per cent of state legislatures following the first election.[7] The percentages of women in elected office never exceeded that first vote and the euphoria quickly evaporated, as many men and women voted for parties that favoured traditional family structures out of fear that women's maternal functions would change, birth rates would decline even further and a collapse of the patriarchal system would ensue.[8] In employment, the number of employed women saw no dramatic statistical change, but the percentage of women in certain economic sectors shifted markedly from agriculture and the home and towards factories and the service economy, especially to positions such as shop assistants and secretaries.[9]

These changes in politics and employment created a sense of social and cultural instability. The roles women were to play in the public sphere and in family life were increasingly unclear; traditional male and female identities appeared to be in flux. This impermanence enabled women to explore new territories in leisure, lifestyle and entertainment, including dance. Nowhere was this more evident than in the New Woman, an idealised media symbol of female emancipation. Promoted by advertisers, the New Woman was a flapper in her twenties who embodied women's freedom of movement, worked for a secretary's wage, socialised in Berlin's cafes, smoked, drank and engaged in pre-marital sex. The New Woman might spend her wages on urban entertainment, clothes and even dance, purchasing tickets to dance performances, registering for dance classes and buying the latest in dance fashions. More than a mere media ideal, however, the New Woman image captured some of the realities experienced by historical Weimar women, who negotiated with the realities of societal constraints and personal responsibilities but nonetheless aspired to the independence and flexibility idealised in the New Woman icon. It was precisely these historical women who took classes from Wigman and her colleagues, promoted dance as a cultural form through their purchasing power and created social conditions that allowed for women such as Wigman to become cultural forces in their own right.[10]

Wigman personified this emancipated woman and was part of a broader culture of other early twentieth-century women dancers who asserted themselves as subjects on stage. Presenting herself in a variety of guises, Wigman – like Loïe Fuller two decades before her – challenged early twentieth-century stereotypes of feminine appearance by covering up her body. Instead of the orientalising costumes and gestures of Sent M'Ahesa or Ruth St Denis, the youthful, simple attitude of child star Niddy Impekoven, or the unerotic, Grecian-inspired forms of Duncan, Wigman wore billowy, often non-European inspired costumes that concealed her womanly form. What these dancers did share with Wigman, however, was their strong female agency, including their determination to pursue their art and their savvy self-promotion. All were able to work and thrive in the early twentieth century because the flux in socially prescribed gender roles provided them with the space to grow. Moreover, the life of the middle-class dancer became economically feasible, as urban women supported them by attending their dance concerts and by training in their studios. Wigman was part of a long lineage of strong women, but the economic, cultural and social circumstances now existed to make independent careers of women dancers such as Wigman truly viable.

One of the ways Wigman distinguished herself was in her choreographic style. Her performances of primal characters, such as witches and demons, associated the dancer with tempestuous spirits rather than with conventionally feminine women. For example, Wigman's solo dance cycle *Ekstatische Tänze* (*Ecstatic Dances*, 1917/1919), which included individual choreographies such as *The Nun*, *Idolatry* and *Temple Dance*, staged diverse religious epiphanies as experienced by figures with vacillating gender identities.[11] Trümpy remarked upon these gender shifts and interpreted the character in *The Nun* as a 'she', but the figure in *Götzendienst* (*Idolatry*) (Figure 1) as one that transformed from a 'he' to an 'it'.[12] One contemporary reviewer wrote, 'Some have characterised Wigman's art as masculine. "Impersonal" is more apt'.[13] This fundamental instability of gendered identification means that Wigman could momentarily take on personality qualities rather than firmly established roles; the critic's vagueness, furthermore, also suggests his or her confusion in defining Wigman's gender and at a particular historical moment in which such understandings were highly politicised. Wigman's gender flux allowed viewers to identify with and desire her in complex ways, as her characters could be interpreted as feminine, masculine or asexual – and often more than one simultaneously. As with Butler's theorisation of gender performativity, in which essentialised gender does not exist but is rather momentarily worn and infinitely changeable, Wigman's choreography challenged the notion that that a performing body necessitated a preconceived, biologically determined meaning.

In *Idolatry*, Wigman also denied the gaze. Dance historian Susan Manning first explored this feminist repositioning of the gaze in Wigman's work and my analysis of these power dynamics, as well as the choreographer's usage of modernist space and the dynamics of the group, is indebted to her scholarship. My approach diverges from Manning's, however, in my art historical emphasis on artistic renderings. With a straw costume that gathered around her neck and fell loosely to her thigh, her head covered by a stocking and her torso almost entirely obscured, a viewer could not have identified the dancer's gender, let alone understood the dancing body as a sexual object. In other choreographies, Wigman reversed the gaze. in *Hexentanz II* (*Witch Dance II*, 1926), she wore a mask that concealed her face yet stared through it at the audience, refusing to be looked at and yet gazing at those whose positioning, physically as well as historically, would have sought to objectify her. The instability of Wigman's performed genders made it nearly impossible to construct a stable power binary and to ascertain

Figure 1: Hugo Erfurth, Mary Wigman in *Idolatry* (*Götzendienst*), 1917. Reproduction courtesy of Stiftung Akademie der Künste, Berlin. [©2005 Artists Rights Society (ARS); New York/VG Bild-Kung Bonn]

which side Wigman should occupy – and for what duration. More than merely reversing the gaze, she demonstrated the unsustainability of the gaze itself as a power structure.

In addition to destabilising gender roles, Wigman's choreographies affirmed a powerful emotional and spiritual individual. Aptly described as the 'subjective desire for expression in an objective, intensified form', in Expressionist dances, the articulation of the inner self (*das Ich*) through emotional states was of utmost importance.[14] As a *Tieftänzerin* (a dancer that seldom leaps and jumps), Wigman evoked such feelings through her movements by dancing firmly on the ground with a heavier, solemn, sombre, earthbound style.[15] This emotionalism correlated to a spirituality that was articulated through a state of religious absorption. In *Idolatry*, the way her straw costume rose with the force of her spinning body signified the soaring of her own rapture. In *Witch Dance II*, Wigman raised her arms in the air and stomped her feet repeatedly against the floor as if she were a demonic force. Moreover, the forcefulness of her dancing aligned Wigman with a history of religious worship of strong women, such as cults of the Virgin Mary and relics of women saints, in which women could potently heal and transform the worshipper physically, behaviourally and spiritually. Through her active role in conveying spirituality and her self-portrayal as a religious leader through dance, Wigman presented herself as a subject.

Beyond the expression of the inner self, choreographers, including Wigman, were preoccupied with the modernist arrangement of dance forms. Wigman's efforts suggest how a woman could theorise about cultural forms associated with the body; because Cartesian theories of the Enlightenment (theories maintained well into the twentieth century) associated the feminine with nature and the masculine with culture, Wigman's exultation of the female body as culture innovatively reconfigured a conceptual binary of centuries-long standing.[16] Rejecting traditional narrative structures and considering music independent of or secondary to physical movement, modernist dancers such as Wigman concerned themselves with the structural composition and formal characteristics of bodies in motion. In Wigman, Laban and Bauhaus master Oskar Schlemmer's choreographies, dancers' movements correlated with and modified the physical space of the stage, even as those movements distinguished themselves as emotional, primitivist, marionette-like or axial. Beyond performing these principles, the choreographers theorised about these spatial relationships, Wigman terming the spatial configurations *Gestalt im Raum* (Form in Space) and Schlemmer articulating his version as *Figur im Raum* (Figure in Space).[17] Contemporaneous dance critics such as Fritz Böhme similarly recognised Wigman's and Laban's choreographic emphases on space and distinguished them from other dance forms that prioritised time. Lauding Wigman and Laban's work as based on 'necessary form', meaning that it focused on the most basic elements needed to delineate space, Böhme envisaged it as a culmination of absolute (modernist) dance.[18] Wigman's group choreographies such as *Totentanz* (*Dance of Death*) created an even more complex dynamic on stage, with spatial and physical juxtapositions of multiple dancers and of Wigman as leader in relation to the group. Rather than sustain the intellectualism/male and nature/female binary, Wigman's theorisation of modernist dance asserted a woman's presence in a discourse associated with men. In numerous ways, then, Wigman used dance to create a subject positioning for herself as a woman, an act that Emil Nolde and Ernst Ludwig Kirchner noticed, negotiated with, accepted and, on rare occasion, rejected.

Wigman, Nolde and the Germanic

At a time of the internationalisation of German culture, in which Americanised 'Girl' kick lines and jazz music dominated Berlin stages and French Impressionism influenced Berlin Secession painting, Nolde infused his art forms with a notion of Germanness. Both a reaction to and an independent development from these cultural forces, his explorations of Germanness brought together Expressionism, primitivism and essentialism with compositional priorities of colour and space. Many of these qualities are evident in his watercolours of Wigman, a dancer he knew well as a friend and respected colleague and whose dancing he attentively watched. The images suggest that Nolde envisaged in Wigman what his critics believed he himself embodied: the lone, deeply expressive, Germanic artist. The Nolde imagery promotes Wigman as more Germanic than was evident in her early 1920s choreographies, but for Nolde and his supporters the Germanic artist was held in high esteem and envisaged as the quintessence of authority and authenticity. Throughout these images Wigman remains compositionally dominant, respectfully clothed and individualistically expressive.

Most of the Nolde watercolours of Wigman depict a similar dramatic tension. With raised arms, enlarged hands and powerful gestures, the figure of Wigman reveals the emotionalism of Expressionist dance.[19] In most works, Nolde obscures Wigman's face or abstracts it to evoke a general mood; in none of them does she wear a mask, though her body is generally well concealed. Similar to his landscapes, the compositions are dominated by intense colours such as blues, purples, reds and greens, which allude to the moods and psychic states of the artist and dancer. The figure of Wigman twists and turns in these watercolours, pointing legs or feet in one direction and the arms, torso and head in another, as if exploring ways to relate the body to its surrounding space for maximum expressive effect. Nolde frequently places her body off-centre in his compositions, as if the unconventional figural placement in the watercolour parallels the unconventional dancing taking place within it.

For example, in *Tänzerin (Mary Wigman)* [*Female Dancer (Mary Wigman)*], Nolde portrays Wigman through her compositional dominance and nuanced expressivity (Figure 2). Dynamic juxtapositions of vivid yellows and reds throughout the watercolour, which themselves create jarring tensions of excitement and passion, accentuate the drama

Figure 2: Emil Nolde, *Female Dancer (Mary Wigman)*, early 1920s. Reproduction courtesy of Nolde-Stiftung Seebüll. © Nolde-Stiftung Seebüll.

of the body. The shape of a reversed letter K, the figure of Wigman lunges towards the left and bends her head down towards her arm, which diagonally juts towards the upper left corner, while her bent revealed leg implies a contrast with a ballet body's rigidity. As if putting into practice Wigman's concept of the Form in Space, Nolde positioned her just off-centre in the two-dimensional composition to heighten the effects of the performed tension. The raised arm and lunge suggest optimism, progress and forcefulness, whereas the downcast head implies pessimism, regression and weakness; these combined straight and bent positions denote the mixed moods and complex psychological states of a figure that is simultaneously introverted and extroverted, reaching out and turning inwards. The bold and largely abstract washes of colour highlight the dancer's overall dramatic form and correlate her abstract dancing to the abstraction of his art. Through these nuances of tension, expression and drama, Wigman is fashioned by Nolde into the solitary Germanic artist.

This portrayal of the dancer as a Germanic subject is unusual in Nolde's dance oeuvre. As with Kirchner, Nolde depicted dance scenes throughout his career, from working-class dance clubs to Asian and African performers; all utilise the erotic, exotic and sexual in order to objectify the female body. For example, Nolde's Berlin cabaret dancers from the early 1910s lift their skirts above their knees and twist their torsos to emphasise their fetishised legs, while his Burmese and Javanese dancers, completed during his extended voyage in South Asia in 1913–14, are bare-breasted and clothed in tightly fitting wraps that highlight the body's curves. Nudity and eroticism do not have to be correlated with one another – the nudity could stand for the artist's interest in the rather asexual nudist colonies of the time – but that is not the case in Nolde's images of dance in the cabarets and in the South Seas. In the inextricable linking of primitivism and eroticism in the South Sea dance renderings, the darkness of the skin and non-European style of movement function as signs of difference from the Germanic. Expressed through bare-breasted dancing and frenetic movement, the ecstasy of dance in several of Nolde's paintings, including *Candle Dancers* (1912) and *Dancing Girls* (1925), correlates with early Christianity and non-European religious rituals, as if such epiphanies are visually understood only through blatant eroticism. Lessened in the 1920s, this notion of the essentialised dancing body nonetheless remained in Nolde's work. A series of Spanish gypsy dancers from 1921, for example, depict the cultural attributes of the dance as a biological essence, with castanets rendered the same colour as the performers' skin, thus barely distinguishable from the body.[20]

All these dance images are part of Nolde's explorations of the primitive. Mark Antliff and Patricia Leighten interpret the primitive in modern art in terms of a socially constructed essentialised binary relationship between the 'civilised' self and the 'primitive' other. In particular, the 'primitive' figure is defined as such due to her temporal (e.g. from ancient times), gendered (female), economic (working or lower class) and racial (non-European) difference from the European individual.[21] Wigman's dancing both reinforces and contests this notion of the primitive; for example, her straw costume in *Idolatry* evokes the simplicity and materiality of non-European and ancient cultures, but Wigman's use of the straw to obscure her body does not allow for the presentation of a clearly gendered 'other'. Similarly, Nolde's watercolours of Wigman distinguish themselves as 'primitive' through religious rapture and simplified forms, but those 'primitive' forms correlate neither to the eroticism nor to the essentialism so prevalent in the rest of Nolde's primitivist dance imagery. Instead of constructing the other, the watercolours constitute Nolde's artistic self.

In contrast to Nolde's objectification of other dancers, he could image Wigman as a subject because they knew each other well and had developed a solid friendship. Moreover, their artistic visions were similar enough that her dancing could mesh with his work. They first met when she was a Dalcroze student. Wigman's friends and roommates from Hellerau, Ada Bruhn and Erna Hoffmann, participated in social circles that further connected Wigman to Nolde.[22] It was Nolde who suggested to Wigman that she study with Laban, to which Wigman responded positively; soon thereafter, Nolde received several letters from both dancers expressing enthusiasm for each other's talents. For example, Wigman wrote to the Noldes 'I send heartfelt greetings to you and your husband from Mr Laban. Upon your suggestion last year I visited Laban and I do not regret it'. That same week, Laban expressed to the Noldes, 'I have found a row of valuable people to work with me, among them Miss Wiegmann, whom you had told me about'.[23] Not only did Nolde see enormous potential in the young dancer, he was also seminal in Wigman's pursuit of an innovative dance education, one that would be of enormous importance in her development as a dancer, choreographer and woman.

Wigman's friendship with the Noldes continued through the 1920s and their correspondence reveals the respectful, trusting and emotionally open relationship they shared. The dancer described Nolde as 'a taciturn man' and wrote of their friendship as one that thrived through his artistic process: 'he would reach for the pencil, draw a fleeting line on the paper and that was all that was needed to establish contact'.[24] When travelling to Berlin each year, Wigman notified the Noldes in advance and then visited them at their apartment and atelier at Tauentzienstrasse 8, on the same street as the fashionable department store Kaufhaus des Westens, in one of the busiest sections of the capital. When the Noldes moved in 1929 to a larger apartment on Bayernallee, Wigman continued to visit them there.[25] On numerous occasions, she gave or reserved tickets for them to her performances.[26] Wigman remembered the Noldes' frequent attendance at her concerts: 'The managers knew about him and were aware of what was expected from them. They reserved three seats: one for him, one for his tubes and pots of paints and one for his wife, who stood guard lest he should be disturbed'.[27] The letters further reveal her long, hectic and intense hours of work and touring; her dedication to dance, her company and teaching; and her stresses in juggling the diverse needs of her career.[28] As Wigman's reminiscences make clear, however, despite their mutual respect, their friendship took place on his terms, at his home and through his art – even when she was, quite literally, the star of the show. This power imbalance, a result in part of their nineteen-year age difference, nonetheless did not seem to hinder their admiration for one another, his engagement with her choreographies or his ability to depict Wigman as a subject.

Their friendship formed a basis for Nolde's images of Wigman, and as similar artistic selves, he depicted her in ways that fulfilled his own ideas about the role of the ideal artist. More specifically, Nolde constructed Wigman as the ideal he envisaged for himself: the Germanic creative spirit. In order to understand how Nolde portrayed Wigman in this vein, we must first explore how Nolde and his critics promoted Nolde as Germanic. Championed by Nolde and several of his critics, including art and architecture theorist Adolf Behne and Nolde biographer and Hamburg Museum of Arts and Crafts director Max Sauerlandt, the ideal Germanic artist's Expressionist style could not have developed without a fundamental bond with the German land. In Nolde's case, his Germanness derived from his roots in the landscape of Schleswig-Holstein, the flat farm and watery terrain that had been the northernmost territory of Germany before World War I. For Behne, the artist embodied an 'authentic' artist of the land, with 'elemental wildness' and a 'naked, elementary human essence', no matter where he might currently reside, because of his fundamental blood link to the natural world.[29] According to this argument, the Germanic land produced a self-sufficient and independent-minded artistic individual in Nolde, a trailblazer who did not slavishly follow trends and was, in Sauerlandt's words, 'proud of his far-away solitude'.[30] Free to create works stemming from his own experiences, feelings and psyche, Nolde rejected styles promoted by dominant cultural institutions. Nolde's fervent denunciation of Impressionism, a French-influenced and French-identified style enormously popular at the Berlin Secession, in favour of a more intuitive and emotionally revealing form of Expressionism, is an example in artistic terms of such independent thinking. Importantly, it also suggests how Nolde and Sauerlandt conceived of Expressionism as a fundamentally German style.[31]

These arguments for a Germanic, nationalist art might seem extreme in retrospect, but they were part of a much larger discourse in the Weimar era, some of which decried abstraction as cosmopolitanism in the arts, other strands of which, as with Nolde, positively correlated specific forms of modern art, such as Expressionism, with Germanness. In retrospect, Germanness is often defined vis-à-vis a Nazi aesthetic solidified around 1937, the year of the Degenerate Art exhibition, but 1920s cultural leaders explored Germanness in ways that did not necessarily lead to the Third Reich.[32] Nolde's and Wigman's lives and creative work were intertwined with Germanness, national identity and political action in the Weimar and Nazi eras and the complexity of the situation suggests how challenging it was (and is) to understand their roles of resistance and compliance. For example, both spoke out frequently after World War II against the Third Reich and painted themselves as victims of the regime, but both were at times complicit, Nolde joining the Nazi Party and Wigman choreographing commissions for the Third Reich's Cultural Ministry in 1934, 1935 and 1936, including the 1936 Berlin Olympics. As the Third Reich's policies and aesthetic priorities changed, so too did Nolde's and Wigman's places within the Nazi cultural landscape, as Nolde continued to work in an Expressionist vein and was thus forbidden to paint, while Wigman's dances coincided more with Nazi priorities, in part because of both changes in her choreographies and continuities in body culture.[33] Nolde and Wigman both made pivotal choices during the Third Reich that contributed to and negotiated with the broader Nazi agenda in the arts, but it is important to recognise the complexity of the situation when the aesthetic criteria and administration continued to change, not to mention when lives and welfares were at stake. In a larger sense, Nolde's and Wigman's situations demonstrate how culturally bound and ever-changing such ideals of national identity are and that such definitions are both self-generated and imposed from outside.

Indeed, the artist's usage of Expressionist style, colour and composition, a usage deemed by Nolde's 1920s supporters as Germanic, is evident in his watercolour of Wigman, *Tänzerin (mit violettem Schleier)* [*Female Dancer (with Violet Veil)*] (Figure 3). The height of the page, the figure of Wigman dominates the space of the composition as she did on stage. Alone in the composition, she embodies the solitary expressive artist. By draping her in a long dress that reveals her arms, hands and shoulders, Nolde highlights those of her body parts deemed the most emotionally communicative. Her disproportionately massive forearms and hands extend above her head and connote their enormity of expression and her step forward in the picture plane suggests the dynamism of her controlled movement and her rapprochement with a viewer. At the same time, Nolde cuts off this rapprochement by obscuring her face with long dark hair and green and red stripes, thereby complicating the viewer's emotional empathy with her. Nolde's Wigman comes towards us, even reaches out to us as she emerges from the mysterious and melancholic colours of dark blues and purples, but the colours pull her back into the composition. Like many of Wigman's choreographed works in which she wore a mask, the watercolour suggests her strategies for revealing herself emotionally. Nolde's depiction treats Wigman as a subject in three ways: by obscuring her face, the watercolour reinforces Wigman's denial of the gaze; in creating a push–pull tension of colour, the work acknowledges her choreography's complexity; and through this coding of the Germanic, Nolde promotes Wigman as an authentic and independent artistic voice.

Figure 3: Emil Nolde, *Female Dancer (With Violet Veil)*, early 1920s. Reproduction courtesy of Nolde-Stiftung Seebüll. © Nolde-Stiftung Seebüll.

Though Nolde and Wigman both posited the dancer as a subject, the reasoning behind it in terms of nationality differed markedly. Wigman had to grapple directly with Germanness as a political reality during the Third Reich, but she was rarely defined in those terms in the early 1920s; instead, she and critic Rudolf von Delius analysed her work in more vague and internationalist terms. Writing in 1925, von Delius described Wigman as freely sampling from numerous cultures. In this context, national identity had little to do with one's chosen dancing style, as Wigman could utilise other cultures' styles, such as archaic, Asian, French and Spanish, to demonstrate her flexibility as a choreographer.[34] For von Delius, this international influence served as a positive sign of her cosmopolitanism and worldliness, even of her ambassadorial role.[35] When alluding to German history and themes, she did so indirectly. Her witch-like, nun-like, temple-bound, non-European-inspired characters seemed reminiscent of those seen in German Romanticism and German Expressionism, as did her overall emphasis on spirituality and emotionalism. Whereas Nolde's critics envisaged these qualities as fundamentally German, Wigman's critics of the early and mid-1920s did not ascribe them to one nationality. And unlike Nolde, Wigman's creativity was not linked to the German land. Only after 1930 and in particular after the ascent of the Third Reich, were Wigman's dances more consistently referred to as German.[36] Rather, her choreographies could be interpreted as nationalistic when it suited someone else's artistic or political purposes – a dynamic visible in Nolde's watercolours of Wigman as well.

Wigman's liberal sampling of cultural styles did mesh with Nolde's Expressionism, however, when it came to non-European sources. Not antithetical to his Germanness, such figural styles contributed to the creative power of both their works. The 'primitiveness' of Nolde's ancient, South Seas, Egyptian and European sources, according to Sauerlandt, enabled the artist to express his inner emotions more directly, the 'mystical power of invention'. That directness of feeling was also precisely what made him German.[37] Moreover, the non-European sources provided an antithesis to the refinement of French art, a national style that Nolde interpreted as too intellectualised. Wigman might not have shared Nolde's voracious anti-French sentiment, but she did employ styles, costumes and characters associated with Asia and Africa. Her angular gestures, stomps and twirls suggested African dance forms as well as whirling dervishes, while her costumes of Chinese brocades and African-inspired masks related her European body to non-European ritual. Moreover, her witch-like and spiritual characters evoked pagan religiosities, ones associated with polytheism and pre-Christian Europe. In these instances, Wigman performed primitivism, wearing it (literally) like a costume, which she could then take on and off from dance to dance. As in Judith Butler's theory of the performance of gender, Wigman's performance of ethnicity highlighted its very constructedness and malleability. Typical of many artists and intellectuals of the early twentieth century who believed that the trappings of European industrialised society hampered the clear articulation of spirituality or religiosity, Wigman and Nolde both turned to non-European forms out of a belief that they more directly expressed inner feeling.[38]

Indeed, Nolde and Wigman's shared emphasis on the expressive power of non-European forms is evident in Nolde's *Tanzszene (Zwei grüne Figuren)* [*Dance Scene (Two Green Figures)*] in which Wigman is portrayed dancing to the percussive accompaniment of her then-student, Gret Palucca (Figure 4). We see a woman dancer who, as Nolde admiringly writes in his autobiography several decades later, eschews traditional – read French – ballet practice: the long skirt, the curve of the body in three-quarter profile, the tilt of the head down towards her shoulder, the expressivity of the leg lift and of the arms over the head all contradict the technically refined and rigid positioning of ballet and demonstrate the possibilities of gesture in expressing emotion.[39] Moreover, the acid greens, oranges and yellows of the watercolour, as with other Nolde watercolours, heighten a viewer's emotional reaction to the scene. Both the body positioning and the colour contrast with Edgar Degas's art of the ballet, in which corseted young ballerinas

Figure 4: Emil Nolde, *Dance Scene (Two Green Figures)*, early 1920s. Reproduction courtesy of Nolde-Stiftung Seebüll. © Nolde-Stiftung Seebüll.

rehearse their arabesques with rigid torsos and straightened legs. Even the brilliantly coloured Degas pastels do not reach the acidity and intensity of Nolde's colours and thus would not elicit the same response in a viewer. While both are figurative, Degas's attention to costume and scenic detail is far different from Nolde's more abstract work, in which modelling is non-existent and the figures are created by bold washes of colour. By the 1920s Degas's work was firmly associated with French Impressionism and would have served as yet another example of French Impressionist influence on the Berlin Secession and the German art world.[40] In Nolde's watercolour, the percussive instrument played by the Palucca figure also negates ballet practice, for it punctuates the silence with occasional rhythms and does not dictate the dance's steps. Furthermore, Palucca's positioning by Nolde, sitting with her knees angularly bent to the sides and her arms held in triangle forms, resembles the Balinese and Javanese sculptures Nolde saw in his South Seas voyage almost a decade earlier, and suggests their mutual belief that non-European forms convey expression more directly than 'civilised' European ones. Here, Nolde utilised forms aligned with early twentieth-century primitivism then interpreted to heighten the dance's drama. But by disassociating primitivism from eroticism and sexuality, Nolde revealed new possibilities for representation in which primitive forms did not objectify the women represented.

Though the connection was infrequently made during the 1920s, dance was at the nexus of Nolde's notion of Germanness. Nolde's choice of dance subjects, such as Wigman, defined by their emotionalism, was in harmony with the qualities required to create an expression-filled German art; French ballet, with its rigid postures and technical refinement, is not found in his oeuvre. Whether South Asian, early Christian or antique pagan subjects, Nolde's dancers, like the South Seas images, convey a direct expression of an inner life, one released from the ties of civilisation. Nolde selects moments in Wigman's solo dances that fulfil this ideal of the solitary artist, rarely depicting her group choreographies, which were of great interest to Kirchner. His choices of dance moments and movements and cropping of scenes to heighten both her dominance and her solitariness on stage emphasised her role as the ideal German artist.

Wigman, Kirchner and the group

Like Nolde, Ernst Ludwig Kirchner knew Wigman, but instead of the former's emphasis on the solitary Germanic artist, Kirchner rendered the formalist structures of group dynamics and the roles of individuals within them. His sketches, created during his travels to Dresden in

January 1926 while watching Wigman and her group rehearse *Dance of Death*, capture his initial impressions and his engagement with the group's movements and the relationships between the individual dancers.[41] Though abstracted, these sketches often closely follow the notions of individuality, leadership and community promoted by Wigman's choreographies and depict the women dancers as subjects in their own right. Months later, Kirchner used several of these sketches as preliminary studies for prints and paintings. Because of Wigman's undisputed leadership, maturity and artistic vision shared with the artist, Kirchner consistently depicted Wigman in ways that coincided with her notions of modernism, androgyny and individuality. On the other hand, Kirchner's renderings of the group in prints and paintings grapple far more with the depiction of dance's three-dimensional spatiality in two-dimensional media.

Kirchner's negotiations with Wigman's choreography are distinct in his oeuvre, one recognised for its frequent and blatant objectification of women. During his affiliation with the Expressionist group *Die Brücke* (The Bridge, active 1905–13), Kirchner and his colleagues, who were in their early twenties, sought a bohemian alternative to the constraints of bourgeois Wilhelmine culture. They lived and depicted a life of unabashed eroticism. With scenes of nude women passively reclining and lounging around the atelier as if waiting for sex or squatting on the shores of watery ponds as men with erect penises leap near them, the works correlate the female body to primitivism and sexual liberation. Also sexually titillating, his dancers kick their legs high and reveal their undergarments to male audiences that gaze up at the women's bodies. This combination of nudity as eroticism and liberation abated somewhat in the 1920s but never vanished, evidenced by Nina Hard's nude dancing for Kirchner in the Alpine forests.[42] Within this context, Kirchner's frequent portrayal of Wigman herself as fully clothed, active, expressive and creative, signals a new and different response to and treatment of women.

Wigman's subject positioning in Kirchner's sketches is in no small part because of her personality and artistic vision. *Dance of Death*, her all-female group choreography, portrayed the strength of women as androgynous, individualised figures embroiled in emotional and physical struggles between life and death (Figure 5). The choreography featured eight dancers. One, a tormenter or beast, wearing monochromatic drapery with a squared mask, in Wigman's words, 'acts in a greedy, gruesomely lustful manner, cracking an invisible whip over the dark obscurity of being'. A second, a tormented martyr, was an 'alien body' performed by Wigman in a striped costume and a frowning mask, 'a plaything of irrational happenings' that 'could more readily yield to

Figure 5: August Scherl, *Mary Wigman and Group: Death Dance II*, 1926. Reproduction courtesy of Stiftung Akademie der Künste, Berlin. [© Scherl SV Bilderdienst, Munich]

unchained demonic powers'. Lastly, six figures in loose-fitting fabrics and masks, 'lemurs with their soulless lives', danced between the two soloists and often converged on Wigman.[43] The dancers' faces and bodies – and thus their femininities – were obfuscated by their costumes in favour of a universal expression of angst, pain and death.

Wigman described the beginning of *Dance of Death*: '"The graves open up and the dead arise ...". But then I envisioned movement: eerie, demoniacal, meaningful. Forces and counterforces, released in a spatial field of tensions, did not yet create the image of a realm of the dead'.[44] Wigman dominated the dance and emphasised her torment, her spatial relationship with and physical proximity to the floor suggestive of death and martyred sacrifice; her mask, unchangingly sad, implied that her anguish remained a permanent condition. As in other choreographies of this period, such as *Scenes from a Dance Drama* (1924), the group oriented itself around Wigman, bending, leaning, crouching and following her, but Wigman's leadership and the women dancers' individualism were not mutually exclusive. Instead, Wigman's position enabled the women to function as part of the group and at the same time 'they made the impression of variations on a theme, gaining independence in different phrases, only to melt into a many-headed body in its tense grouping'.[45] Within the modernist spatial field of the stage, *Dance of Death* created a dance community through spirituality, individuality and androgyny, three characteristics that together constituted Wigman as a female subject.

Seemingly recognising Wigman's principles and her possibilities for a new kind of female subject, Kirchner emulated them in his own work but made numerous artistic choices of his own along the way, and often employed colour, line and figural positioning to differentiate Wigman from the group. Kirchner's modernist preoccupations with line and composition on a two-dimensional surface parallel Wigman's concept of the Form in Space. Both artist and dancer concerned themselves with the complex formal and ever-changing spatial arrangements between the dancers. Often, Kirchner highlighted the individuality of the dancers, using slight variations in gestures or movements or striking colour contrasts to differentiate them. In one sketch, two dancers in yellow bend one leg and raise their arms to their chests; the variations between them – one lifts the bent leg while the other plants the foot on the floor – suggest that Kirchner watched a rehearsal in which the details have yet to be mastered, that each dancer expressed her individuality through nuanced details and that Kirchner himself varied the figures to suit his artistic priorities. Moreover, the dancers in yellow perform in front of others in blue and green, creating hierarchies within the group and compositional depth, as warm colours appear to jump forward and cool colours tend to recede. The bright colours also suggest the energy of the dance. At other moments, Kirchner portrayed the dynamics of Wigman's leadership. All of the figures in one sketch crouch close to the ground in a circle as Wigman looms over them, like a resurrected phoenix in a cycle of death and life. Fourteen pages later in the sketchbook, the group performs their reverence for their leader by bowing to the floor behind Wigman.[46] Though all of these images are relatively similar to the choreography, as documented by written descriptions and photographs, Kirchner made them his own through his sketchier style and vibrant Expressionist colour. And as these images suggest, Kirchner rendered Wigman as a subject because the group's structure portrayed her unquestionably and consistently as the authority figure. Through the movements and spatial configurations of Wigman and her ensemble, we as viewers, Kirchner included, are led to participate in that reverence.

Other sketches portray Wigman's authority as a spiritual leader. For example, two figures, one androgynous and purple, the other shapely and pink, kick up their legs and raise their arms in the direction of a green abstracted mass symbolising Wigman (Figure 6). Several other Kirchner sketches of these rehearsals portray Wigman in green; this particular abstracted mass can be understood as a spirit to which the

Figure 6: Ernst Ludwig Kirchner, page from Sketchbook 127, p. 33, 1926. Reproduction courtesy of the Kirchner Museum Davos. © Ingeborg and Dr Wolfgang Henze-Ketterer, Wichtrach/Bern.

dancers pray and which in turn leans towards them. Despite their differences in form and colour, the group dancers are united around their reverence for the Wigman spirit figure. Not a distant spirit, Kirchner's Wigman acknowledges and interacts with them in a way that fosters their own dance. Such a depiction of Wigman paralleled the dance criticism of the time, which identified the potency of her spiritual leadership. Rudolf von Delius, whose book *Mary Wigman* (1925) Kirchner owned, describes Wigman's spirituality as an internal essence given material form and recognises that her expressivity was not linked to one specific gender, but to spiritual and natural forces: 'Who was that? A man, a woman? I was not sure. But certainly a demon ... an element such as fire or wind'.[47] Within her group and Kirchner's sketches, Wigman's power derived from her blurring of gendered identifications and assumption of roles traditionally ascribed to men in leadership and spirituality.

Kirchner could envisage Wigman as a subject in the sketches in part because he knew her personally and was enormously impressed with her work. In his travel diaries, Kirchner frequently expressed his depressed condition and inconsolable sadness, but upon seeing Wigman's dances his mood lightened immediately. He writes:

> I feel that there are parallels [with my work], which are expressed in her dancing in the movement of the volumes, in which the solitary movement is strengthened through repetition. It is immeasurably fascinating and exciting to make drawings of these physical movements. I will paint large pictures from them. Yes, what we had suspected has become reality: there is the new art. M[ary] W[igman] instinctively took much from modern pictures and the creation of a modern concept of beauty operates just as much in her dancing as in my pictures.[48]

For Kirchner, Wigman's influence lay in their shared artistic principles. Interpreting her dancing through his own artistic challenges, Kirchner explored ways of capturing her movement in his drawings, but praised her choreographies on their own terms. Unlike numerous depictions of women dancers in which the male artist uses her gender or exoticism to contrast his male self from the female performing other, Kirchner seems to envision Wigman as a similar artistic self. Wigman's memory of Kirchner similarly alludes to an equal relationship of two subjects. She writes that 'each morning the painter Ernst Ludwig Kirchner was there, drawing, sketching, painting as a silent partner. While we both worked, we hardly ever spoke to one another. But I could always sense his presence, which made itself felt in a strangely inspiring way'.[49] As part of the process of formation of the dance, Kirchner's artistic presence contributed actively to *Dance of Death* and provided a kindred spirit and a spectatorial position against which she could work. Instead of a traditional subject–object relationship between artist and dancer, they fostered and respected each other's creative outputs as equals.

Beyond the influences of physical presence, Kirchner's art and Wigman's dances share modernist principles. Though the definition of modernism (and its relevance for individual artists) has changed over time, generally speaking modernist art is primarily concerned with the pictorial laws of composition and materiality, ranging from Clive Bell's emphasis on 'significant form' to Clement Greenberg's preoccupation with the flatness of the canvas. And while Greenberg and others vehemently argued for an abstract art disassociated from contemporary life, Thomas Crow has clarified how modernist art's engagement with mass culture was shocking precisely because it disrupted cultural hierarchies.[50] Crow's more expansive understanding of modernism can be extended to elucidate the place of Kirchner's Wigman imagery within modernism as a negotiation between the internal pictorial laws of form and composition and the culture of performance outside of the picture frame.

Similarly, Wigman's 'absolute dances' were not entirely abstract; her raised arms, arabesques and turns employed and modified the space of the stage with shapes and structures that created symbolic meaning, emotional states and tension between the members of the group. As a 'struggle in space around space', for von Delius the dances suggested moods instead of clear narratives, moods that were aided by the secondary elements of lighting and costuming.[51] For example, the dancers' frequent movements of collapse in *Dance of Death* produced diagonals and verticals within the stage's space and implied cycles of life and death.[52] Whereas Wigman's choreographies stressed the energy of movement through space, Kirchner's images evoke Wigman's dynamism in ways appropriate to a drawing or painting's static two-dimensional form. Both artistic forms emphasise process – one that she developed physically in space and another that Kirchner rendered as an initial impression on paper and then reinterpreted in later prints and paintings. Kirchner himself noted the importance of movement in Wigman's work and declared her choreographies to embody 'calm fantasy and fluid movement'.[53] As a like-minded artist, Kirchner employed a style that Wigman would have agreed upon stylistically and, similar to her choreographies, the sketches emphasise spatial configurations over gendered identifications. This very erasure of femininity was central to Wigman's self-presentation; Kirchner's sketches substantiate her assertions.

When Kirchner depicted Wigman's rehearsals in prints and a painting, however, he both reinforced and contradicted the notion of female subject status found in the preliminary sketches. Here Kirchner de-emphasised movement and prioritised the two-dimensionality of the paper or canvas. In minimising the complexity of her group's spatial dynamics by emphasising rows and linearity, Kirchner favoured the pictorial cohesion of the painting. In *Tanzgruppe* [*Dance Group*] (1926) four blocky, broad-shouldered individuals lean slightly in a straight row in the background, while downstage Wigman dances alone with her legs crossed and her arms over her head (Figure 7). Patterns in the floor reinforce the horizontal movement of the group. The dancers' androgyny coincides with Wigman's assertions, but their dynamics have been greatly reduced to static and linear relationships across the horizontal axis. Moreover, *Dance Group* shares some overall compositional similarities with what might be its preliminary sketch. In a similar sketch from the preceding sketch book page (see Figure 9), the figures are reversed, as if Kirchner created the woodcut's matrix to resemble the sketch's composition instead of the live rehearsals – a process coinciding with the Greenbergian modernist notion of art begetting art rather than art engaging with life.

Figure 7: Ernst Ludwig Kirchner, *Dance Group*, 1926. Reproduction courtesy of Galerie Henze & Ketterer AG. © Ingeborg and Dr. Wolfgang Henze-Ketterer, Wichtrach/Bern.

This emphasis on the flatness of the art work expressed through a linear group dynamic is also evident in Kirchner's painting (*Totentanzder Mary Wigman* [*Mary Wigman's Death Dance*], 1926) (Figure 8). On the far left the Wigman figure crouches, raises her arms above her head and glances upward in ways that suggest her emotional pain; on the

Figure 8: Ernst Ludwig Kirchner, *Mary Wigman's Death Dance*, 1926. Reproduction courtesy of Galerie Henze & Ketterer AG. © Ingeborg and Dr. Wolfgang Henze-Ketterer, Wichtrach/Bern.

opposite side of the canvas, the tormentor/beast figure reinforces her threat to Wigman by leaning towards her. Between them dance six women who appear remarkably similar to one another in their poses, costumes and womanliness, and who bend toward their leader in a row. Unlike the sketches, which capture the immediacy of dance and the group dynamics fostered by androgyny and individualism, the painting *Mary Wigman's Death Dance* obfuscates the differences between the women and emphasises their (as well as the beast's) curvy femininity. The arrangement of static elements within the painting seems of greater importance than a faithful portrayal of the structure of the dance. For example, the group angles left towards the figure of Wigman, the chevron-striped floor points from her to her tormentor on the right, who in turn reaches left towards the Wigman figure and past the group. All create a sense of balance in the painted composition as well as a cycle of physical and psychic connections that emphasise the drama in the foreground. In a Wigman choreography, this interchange between leader and group would have been subtle, shifting and three-dimensional, but in the painting the individuals in the group are less differentiated, assigned an obviously feminine appearance and stretched in a linear configuration along a strict horizontal, left-right axis to correlate with the canvas's rectangular shape. Wigman and Kirchner agreed in principle on modernist theories with their priorities of pictorial and spatial cohesion, but Kirchner's application of such style in his painting ended up removing the very spatial qualities Wigman emphasised in her choreography.

Beyond their similar aesthetic emphases, Kirchner's interest in Wigman and her *Dance of Death* may have also resided in her group's performance of community. According to Susan Manning, Wigman's group dances of the early and mid-1920s displayed a constructed, utopian and idealised community or *Gemeinschaft*.[54] Wigman served as a charismatic leader to her female dancers on stage; her dancers followed her not blindly or uniformly but in ways that for von Delius expressed the dancers' individualism and innermost personal feelings.[55] Evoking emotions through forms and movement, they performed non-narrative dances that suggested their own states of mind as part of a universal human condition. Moreover, in these all-female ensembles the sexual relations, tensions and narratives that had so dominated ballet seemed to vanish.[56] Instead, Wigman's young women performed as individuals and as subjects in their own right, under the gaze of no one.

Kirchner does not resist the utopian *Gemeinschaft* danced before him and if anything renders the group dancers as the androgynous ideal represented by Wigman herself. In one sketch in lavender crayon, five dancers stand close together and lean their shoulders and heads slightly toward the right. Slight variations between them express the dancers' individualism. Because of their blocky forms, their genders are ambiguously defined and by extension so too are their sociocultural functions as women. When the scene is expanded to include a depiction of Wigman (Figure 9), in a sketch that may have been a basis for the aforementioned woodcut *Dance Group* and painting *Mary Wigman's Death Dance* (Figures 7 and 8), the tormented martyr performs on the left side with her arms and legs crossed; the androgynous group leans towards her and though details of their bodies are omitted in favour of overall movement and linear structure, they do not appear as a uniform mass. Indeed, this performed community paralleled Kirchner and *Die Brücke's* creation of a close-knit *Gemeinschaft* in their Dresden studios, in which they artistically collaborated and lived communally.[57] Hardly as intense as his earlier period in Germany, Kirchner continued to seek an artistic community in 1920s Switzerland with younger artists in the region and depicted the ideals of the cultural community in his painting *Modern Bohemia* (1924). The communities were obviously different, most evidently in a paradigm shift of the testosterone-filled young male artist milieu to the all-female community based on individuality and female leadership, but the notion that artistry and artistic forms could represent utopia was one that Kirchner and Wigman shared.

Figure 9: Ernst Ludwig Kirchner, page from Sketchbook 133, p. 37, 1926. Reproduction courtesy of the Kirchner Museum Davos. © Ingeborg and Dr. Wolfgang Henze-Ketterer, Wichtrach/Bern.

On other occasions, Kirchner's dramatic changes from sketch to print questioned the subject positioning of the dancers by modifying the premises of the community. In one sketch, the group dance is represented as a series of semi-abstract curves, each one vaguely representing the heads, shoulders and backs of the dancers as they move in a relatively geometric and linear formation. Another sketch of the same moment portrays the group in more detail, including legs and body positioning, but does not identify the dancers in terms of gender.[58] Whereas these earlier sketches depict dancing bodies as modernist abstractions of geometric relations, the later woodcut *Gegentanz* ([*Oppositional Dance*], 1926) portrays nine nude women lunging and leaning in rows (Figure 10). Wigman's group never performed nude; the choreographer had expressed discomfort with nude dancing a decade earlier during her studies with Laban, when many of his female students danced nude and conducted sexual affairs with their much-admired teacher, both of which Wigman insisted she did not do.[59] And yet, given Kirchner's history of representing women, the nudity here is

Figure 10: Ernst Ludwig Kirchner, *Oppositional Dance*, 1926. Reproduction courtesy of Galerie Henze & Ketterer AG. © Ingeborg and Dr. Wolfgang Henze-Ketterer, Wichtrach/Bern.

problematic: are the women eroticised or not? Certainly Kirchner's rendering could be interpreted as sexual, but it need not be. One could interpret these bodies as uneroticised because they actively and creatively perform rather than lounge passively, and their nudity allows Kirchner to emphasise the formalist structure of their bodies rather than the simpler shapes of their billowy costumes. The women's short, cropped hair also suggests that these are fashionable, emancipated women of the 1920s and not traditionally feminine nudes; that sign of social emancipation links them to the physical liberations of dance and the possibilities for liberation outside traditional patriarchal structures. More specifically, early twentieth-century German dance was frequently associated with German nudist culture in which individuals danced nude in nature; in this context, dance was frequently a sexual and a part of a broader interest in healthy living and communing with nature and the sun. Kirchner personally would have been very aware of the nudist movements from his early work with *Die Brücke*. He took up residence in the Swiss resort of Davos during World War I, to a significant degree because of the proclaimed curative powers of its air and nature.[60] Liberating the body through nudity was a cornerstone of the nudist movement – in this print the nudity reveals the women's muscles and strength. If there is eroticism in *Oppositional Dance*, it is of women who are physically powerful and socially emancipated. The nudity might not have been to Wigman's taste, but the implications of liberation from social constraints may well have been ones upon which Kirchner and Wigman could have agreed.

Conclusion

Nolde and Kirchner's depictions of Wigman, as we have seen, are noteworthy in their emphasis on the dancer as a subject. By removing sexuality from the equation, Wigman posited herself as a distinctive type of woman performer. In fact, by grappling with the same modernist questions as male artists and male dancers, Wigman took dance, a traditionally female-dominated cultural form often deemed inferior because of its associations with corporeality and popular culture, and placed it on an equal footing with 'high art'. Clearly regarded as a kindred spirit by both Nolde and Kirchner, Wigman served not as an exotic other but performed primitivism to present herself as a similar artistic self. For both artists, however, resistance to Wigman's subject status existed. Nolde's work highlighted aspects of Wigman that coincided with his notion of the Germanic, whether or not she would have agreed with the nationalistic designation; Kirchner's depictions of the group dancers flatten the choreography's spatial concerns into a two-dimensional, axial visual form, contrary to the dynamic Wigman fostered. Despite her assertions to the contrary, the visual artists had the final say and at times their own visions – of identity, artistry or sexuality – dominated.

And yet, Wigman succeeded in influencing the visual culture that imaged her. Not only did she provide herself as a model outside a subject–object binary, she did so in ways that demonstrated the nuances of her creative enterprise with her complex investigations of expression, group dynamics and modernism. Her own assertions of self were strong enough to influence strong-willed senior male artists, but she also chose colleagues with whom she shared artistic principles and priorities. Some of their particular beliefs may have differed, but overall their artistry meshed. Because of these shared creative experiences, Wigman maintained symbiotic relationships. Indeed, it is precisely in this notion of a symbiotic relationship that the subject–object dichotomy dissolves; even with some differences, the fundamental respect shared by all parties for one another renders objectification unfeasible. Wigman's example illuminates that it is possible to assert oneself as distinctive without correlating difference with otherness, to insist on one's own status as a subject and for that power to be heard, understood and appreciated.

Notes

This research was made possible through a grant from the Provost's Fund at the University of Wisconsin-Parkside and I am most grateful to the institution for its support. I would like to thank Manfred Reuther, Director, Stiftung Ada und Emil Nolde, Seebüll, Germany (SAEN) and Roland Scotti, Curator, Kirchner Museum, Davos, Switzerland (KMD) for their assistance during my research visits; Susan Manning, for her help with my queries about Mary Wigman; and Jennifer Jordan, for her insights on this article. Unless otherwise noted, all translations are by the author.

1. Laura Mulvey, 'Visual Pleasure and Narrative Cinema', in Constance Penley (ed.), *Feminism and Film Theory* (New York: Routledge, 1988), pp. 57–68; Richard Dyer, 'Don't Look Now: The Male Pin-Up', in Mandy Merck (ed.), *The Sexual Subject: A Screen Reader in Sexuality* (New York and London: Routledge, 1992), pp. 265–76; E. Ann Kaplan (ed.), *Feminism and Film* (Oxford: Oxford University Press, 2000); Teresa de Lauretis, 'Rethinking Women's Cinema: Aesthetics and Feminist Theory', in *Technologies of Gender: Essays on Theory, Film and Fiction* (Bloomington: Indiana University Press, 1987), pp. 127–48.
2. Judith Butler, *Gender Trouble: Feminism and the Subversion of Identity* (New York: Routledge, 1990).
3. *There's Something About Mary*, Bobby and Peter Farrelly (directors), starring Cameron Diaz and Ben Stiller. USA, Twentieth Century Fox, 1998.
4. Eugen Höllander, 'Körper-Moden. Der Wandel im Schönheitsgeschmack', *Uhu* 1 (October 1924), pp. 18–24.
5. Berthe Trümpy, 'Tänzerinnen unter sich', *Uhu* 5 (January 1929), pp. 54–60. Marie Wiegmann later changed her name to Mary Wigman.
6. *Berliner Illustrirte Zeitung*, November 1929, press clipping collection Mary Wigman Archiv, Stiftung Akademie der Künste Berlin (MWA).
7. Renate Bridenthal and Claudia Koonz, 'Beyond *Kinder, Küche, Kirche*: Weimar Women in Politics and Work', in Renate Bridenthal, Atina Grossmann and Marion Kaplan (eds), *When Biology Became Destiny: Women in Weimar and Nazi Germany* (New York: Monthly Review Press, 1984), pp. 33–65, here pp. 35, 57 n. 9.
8. Bridenthal and Koonz, 'Beyond *Kinder, Küche, Kirche*', p. 37; Atina Grossmann, 'Abortion and Economic Crisis: The 1931 Campaign Against Paragraph 218', in Bridenthal, Grossmann and Kaplan (eds), *When Biology Became Destiny*, pp. 66–86.
9. Bridenthal and Koonz, 'Beyond *Kinder, Küche, Kirche*', pp. 44–5.
10. On the New Woman, see Siegfried Kracauer, 'The Little Shopgirls go to the Movies', in *The Mass Ornament: Weimar Essays*, tr., ed. and with an introduction by Thomas Y. Levin (Cambridge, MA: Harvard University Press, 1995), pp. 291–304; Patrice Petro, *Joyless Streets: Women and Melodramatic Representation in Weimar Germany* (Princeton: Princeton University Press, 1989), pp. 39–78; Katharina von Ankum (ed.), *Women in the Metropolis: Gender and Modernity in Weimar Culture* (Berkeley: University of California Press, 1997).
11. I use the past tense to describe Wigman's dances to emphasise that these are temporal works performed at specific historical moments. The dances could be reconstructed from photographs and written records, but Wigman's power as a dancer, as an influence on her dancers and in the dance world in the 1920s, is impossible to replicate.
12. Susan Manning, *Ecstasy and the Demon: Feminism and Nationalism in the Dances of Mary Wigman* (Berkeley: University of California Press, 1993), pp. 63–8.
13. Anonymous reviewer, *Zürcher Post*, in 'Mary Wigman: Kritiken der schweizer Presse', *Konzertdirektion Kantorowitz*, 1919, 6, MWA; in Manning, *Ecstasy and the Demon*, p. 67.
14. Rosalia Chladek, in Helmut Scheier, 'What Has Dance Theatre to Do with Ausdruckstanz', *Ballett International* (January 1987), p. 14, in Dianne Howe, *Individuality and Expression: The Aesthetics of the New German Dance, 1908–1936* (New York: Peter Lang, 1996), p. 1.

15. Howe, *Individuality and Expression*, p. 137.
16. On the nature/culture debate, see Sherry Ortner, 'Is Female to Male as Nature Is to Culture?' in Michelle Zimbalist Rosaldo and Louise Lamphere (eds), *Woman, Culture, and Society* (Stanford: Stanford University Press, 1974), pp. 67–87.
17. Manning translated *Gestalt im Raum* as 'Configuration of energy in space'. Manning, *Ecstasy and the Demon*, p. 41.
18. Fritz Böhme, *Tanzkunst* (Dessau: C. Dünnhaupt, 1926), pp. 162, 23–53, in Manning, *Ecstasy and the Demon*, p. 20.
19. According to the SAEN, Mary Wigman is the subject of twelve Nolde watercolours. Nolde neither dated nor titled his watercolours, but their style resembles that of other works by the artist from the early 1920s. My own analysis suggests that most of the watercolours are easy to connect to Wigman and I discuss here only the ones that to me clearly portray her. I am grateful to Manfred Reuther, Director, SAEN, for providing me with information about these works.
20. For an overview of Nolde's dance imagery, see Manfred Reuther, 'Emil Nolde: Der Tanz in Leben und Kunst', in Karin Adelsbach and Andrea Firmenich (eds), *Tanz in der Moderne: Von Matisse bis Schlemmer* (Cologne: Wienand Verlag, 1996), pp. 98–105. Reuther's essay and its accompanying colour plates (numbers 107–25) include several Nolde depictions of dancers from the Berlin cabarets, the South Seas and Southern Spain. Similarly reproduced in these pages are *Candle Dancers*, *Dancing Girls* and all of the Wigman depictions I discuss at length; moreover, all are in colour.
21. Mark Antliff and Patricia Leighten, 'Primitive', in Robert S. Nelson and Richard Shiff (eds), *Critical Terms for Art History*, 2nd edn (Chicago: University of Chicago Press, 2003), pp. 217–33.
22. Hedwig Müller, *Mary Wigman: Leben und Werk der grooßen Tänzerin* (Berlin: Quadriga Verlag, 1986), pp. 25–6.
23. Mary Wiegmann to Ada Nolde, 15 September 1913; Rudolf von Laban to Ada and Emil Nolde, 18 September 1913. See also Mary Wiegmann to Ada Nolde, 12 January 1913 and Rudolf von Laban to Ada and Emil Nolde, 23 September 1913. Collection SAEN.
24. Mary Wigman, 'Reminiscences', in Mary Wigman, *The Mary Wigman Book: Her Writings*, ed. and tr. Walter Sorell (Middletown, CT: Wesleyan University Press, 1975), pp. 25–70, here p. 55.
25. In the following letters from Wigman to Ada Nolde, the dancer discusses visiting the Noldes in Berlin: 12 January 1913; 15 September 1913; 27 September 1919; 17 December 1923; 7 November 1929; 24 November 1929; and 26 November 1929. Collection SAEN.
26. For example, Wigman wrote to Ada Nolde on 27 September 1919, notifying her that she will be performing in Berlin; three days later, on 30 September, Wigman sent an envelope with two tickets, which were not used. Four years later, Wigman's letter of 17 December 1923 informed Ada Nolde that the dancer had reserved tickets for the couple. Letters from 4 and 7 November 1929, also discuss reserving and picking up tickets and correspondence from 24 November 1929, asked if the Noldes would be interested in seeing a repeat performance. Collection SAEN.
27. Wigman, 'Reminiscences', p. 55.
28. Mary Wigman to Ada Nolde, 4 and 24 November 1929. Collection SAEN.
29. Adolf Behne, 'Emil Nolde Ausstellung des Werkes in Dresden', (Berlin: Kosmos-Verlag, 1927), n.p. Press clipping, SAEN.
30. Max Sauerlandt, *Emil Nolde* (Munich: Kurt Wolff Verlag, 1921), p. 10.
31. The Berlin Secession rejected Nolde's painting *Pfingsten* in 1910. Thereafter Nolde angrily chastised the Secession for what he saw as their emphasis on a French-identified Impressionist style. For more on Nolde's relationship with the Berlin Secession and his arguments against French Impressionism, see Nolde, letter 14 January 1920, in Sauerlandt, *Emil Nolde*, p. 77; Peter Paret, *The Berlin Secession: Modernism and its Enemies in Imperial Germany* (Cambridge, MA: Harvard University Press, 1980), pp. 210–16; Hans Fehr, *Emil Nolde: Ein Buch der Freundschaft* (Cologne: M. DuMont Schauberg, 1957), pp. 130–41.

32. For a broader look at anti-Semitism, modernism and German identity in the German art world, see Peter Paret, *German Encounters with Modernism, 1840–1945* (Cambridge: Cambridge University Press, 2001); Hans Belting, *The Germans and their Art: A Troublesome Relationship*, tr. Scott Kleager (New Haven: Yale University Press, 1998); Stephanie Barron (ed.), *Degenerate Art: The Fate of the Avant-Garde in Nazi Germany* (Los Angeles: Los Angeles County Museum of Art and New York: Harry N. Abrams, 1991).
33. Nolde, for example, promoted himself from the 1910s through the mid-1930s as the quintessential German artist and joined the Nazi Party. He joined the local Nordschleswig (Danish) branch of the Nazi Party (NSDAPN) first in 1920 and then affiliated himself with another Nazi-associated Nordschleswig organization (NSAN) in 1934. By the time the Nazis had developed their own art policy, however, Nolde's art had been removed from German museums and included in the Degenerate Art exhibition. For her part, Wigman modified her teaching in ways that meshed with National Socialist ideology, her school never closed and she continued to earn money as a choreographer and teacher throughout World War II. See Thomas Knubben, '"Mein Leid, meine Qual, meine Verachtung": Emil Nolde im Dritten Reich', in Tilman Osterwold and Thomas Knubben (eds), *Emil Nolde: Ungemalte Bilder* (Ostfildern-Ruit: Hatje Cantz Verlag, 1999), pp. 137–49, esp. 144; Paret, *German Encounters with Modernism 1840–1945*, p. 127; Hedwig Müller and Patricia Stockemann, '*Jeder Mensch ist ein Tänzer ...' Ausdruckstanz in Deutschland zwischen 1900 und 1945* (Gießen: Anabas Verlag, 1993), pp. 107–219; Susan A. Manning, 'Modern Dance in the Third Reich: Six Positions and a Coda', in Susan Leigh Foster (ed.), *Choreographing History* (Bloomington: Indiana University Press, 1995), pp. 165–76; Manning, *Ecstasy and the Demon*, pp. 167–220.
34. Rudolf von Delius, *Mary Wigman* (Dresden: Carl Reissner Verlag, 1925), pp. 19–20.
35. von Delius, *Mary Wigman*, pp. 55–6.
36. See, for example, Arthur Michel, 'The Development of the New German Dance', in Virginia Stewart (ed.), *Modern Dance* (New York: E. Weyhe, 1935), pp. 3–17.
37. Sauerlandt, *Emil Nolde*, p. 55.
38. See Carl Einstein, *Negerplastik* (Leipzig: Verlag der weissen Bücher, 1915).
39. For the related diary entry, see Emil Nolde, *Jahre der Kämpfe 1902–1914* (Cologne: M. DuMont Schauberg, 1967), p. 218.
40. On Degas and the ballet, see Jill deVonyar and Richard Kendall, *Degas and the Dance* (New York: Abrams, 2002).
41. Kirchner's Wigman visits, one of his stops during his travels in Germany from December 1925 to March 1926, were arranged at the artist's request by Will Grohmann, the Dresden-based art and dance critic who produced Wigman's first public performances in Dresden in 1919 and wrote two monographs on Kirchner in 1925 and 1926. For Kirchner and Wigman alike, Grohmann was a valued colleague. See letters from Kirchner to Grohmann, 8 July 1925, 11 December 1925, 9 April 1926, Will Grohmann Archiv, Staatsgalerie Stuttgart (WGA), typescript in KMD. See also Wigman, 'Reminiscences', pp. 55, 58–9.
42. On Kirchner's dance imagery, see Susan Funkenstein, 'Communities forMen: Ernst Ludwig Kirchner's Images of Berlin Nightlife', unpublished MA thesis (University of Chicago, 1994); Gabriele Lohberg (ed.), *Ernst Ludwig Kirchner: Der Tanz* (Davos: Kirchner Museum Davos, 1993); Andrea Firmenich, 'Vom "Cake-Walk" zum "Farbentanz": Das Tanzmotiv bei Ernst Ludwig Kirchner', in Adelsbach and Firmenich, *Tanz in der Moderne*, pp. 44–51; Colin Rhodes, 'The Body and the Dance: Kirchner's Swiss Work as Expressionism', in Shulamith Behr, David Fanning and Douglas Jarman (eds), *Expressionism Reassessed* (Manchester: Manchester University Press, 1993), pp. 133–46; Thomas Röske, *Ernst Ludwig Kirchner: Tanz zwischen den Frauen* (Frankfurt: Insel Verlag, 1993).
43. Mary Wigman, 'Dance of Death', in *The Mary Wigman Book*, pp. 97–8, 101.
44. Wigman, 'Dance of Death', p. 97.
45. Wigman, 'Dance of Death', p. 100; Susan Manning, *Ecstasy and the Demon*, pp. 122–27.

46. Sketchbook 131, pp. 21r, 35r. Collection KMD.
47. Von Delius, *Mary Wigman*, pp. 7–8. According to Lohberg, Grohmann's wife sent Kirchner's common-law wife Erna Kirchner a copy of the book in 1926, but Lohberg does not substantiate that claim. Lohberg (ed.), *Der Tanz*, p. 51.
48. Ernst Ludwig Kirchner, diary entry 16 January 1926 and after, in Lothar Griesebach (ed.), *E. L. Kirchners Davoser Tagebuch* (Cologne: Verlag M. DuMont Schauberg, 1968), p. 115, tr. in Rhodes, 'The Body and the Dance', p. 140. Kirchner's dates in his diaries are often imprecise because he wrote parts of them months later. After returning to Davos, Kirchner thanked Grohmann for his help in meeting the dancer and wrote of his enthusiasm for painting her. Letter 9 April 1926, original in WGA, typescript in KMD.
49. Wigman, 'Dance of Death', p. 99.
50. Clive Bell, 'The Debt to Cézanne', in Francis Frascina and Charles Harrison (eds), *Modern Art and Modernism: A Critical Anthology* (New York: Harper and Row, 1982), pp. 75–8; Clement Greenberg, 'Modernist Painting', *Modern Art and Modernism*, pp. 5–10; Thomas Crow, *Modern Art in the Common Culture* (New Haven: Yale University Press, 1996).
51. von Delius, *Mary Wigman*, p. 44.
52. Howe, *Individuality and Expression*, p. 122.
53. Sketchbook 157, p. 17v. Collection KMD. Page reprinted in Gerd Presler, *Ernst Ludwig Kirchner: Die Skizzenbücher: 'Ekstase des ersten Sehens': Monographie und Werkverzeichnis* (Karlsruhe: Engelhardt & Bauer, 1996), p. 351.
54. Manning, *Ecstasy and the Demon*, pp. 86–8.
55. von Delius, *Mary Wigman*, pp. 22–3.
56. Manning, *Ecstasy and the Demon*, p. 97.
57. See especially Jill Lloyd, *German Expressionism: Primitivism and Modernity* (New Haven: Yale University Press, 1991), pp. 21–49.
58. Sketchbook 131, page 33r; Sketchbook 130, page 38. Collection KMD. Presler, *Ernst Ludwig Kirchner*, p. 324, identifies these images as Wigman group studies.
59. Manning, *Ecstasy and the Demon*, p. 57–8.
60. On nudist movements, see Lloyd, *German Expressionism: Primitivism and Modernity*, pp. 102–29; Karl Toepfer, *Empire of Ecstasy: Nudity and Movement in German Body Culture, 1910–1935* (Berkeley: University of California Press, 1997). On the nude as a subject in art, see Lynda Nead, *The Female Nude: Art, Obscenity and Sexuality* (London: Routledge, 1992).

Index

Academy of Natural Sciences (Philadelphia), 122, 123
Adelkhah, Fariba, 228
Aesthetic Movement, 203
African photographs (Hellman's), 75; and anonymity, 89–90; and colonialism, 77–8, 83; contemporary impact of, 105; and documenting of poverty, 86–7, 105; as form of record-keeping, 105; gender dimension, 77, 86, 99, 102, 105; and identity, 78; as illustrations, 83–4; and image-text relationship, 78, 79, 83–5, 102, 105–6; and juxtaposition of images, 95–8; and memory-making, 78; and pictorial turn, 77; political/economic context, 93; public/private presentations of research, 94–104; and re-imaging of history, 77; as research tool, 75, 77, 78; and researcher/researched interaction, 90–2; and segregationist campaigning against slums, 88–9; and slum/township mobility, 95–9; stereotypes, 78, 86; and urban social anthropology, 79–93; and use of physical features, 83; and visions of tribal subjectivity, 81; and visual celebration of white South African modernity, 79–93
African women, 4–5
Agassiz, Louis, 114
Agnew, D. Hayes, 127
Aimer, Catherine, 125
Allen, Harrison, 121, 122–3, 124
American Anthropometric Society, 121
American Civil War, 113–14, 129
American Philosophical Society, 122
The American Race (Brinton), 123
Amherst College, 128
Amouroux, Henri, 151, 154, 156
anthropology, 114–16, 123, 165
Anthropometric Manual (Galton), 128
anthropometry, and Muybridge project *see* University of Pennsylvania project; and Penn athletics, 124–30; scientific interest in, 120–4
Armstrong, Nancy, 66
Arts and Crafts Movement, 196, 199, 200, 201, 205, 207, 210, 211, 283
Aryan (music group), 219
Asad, Talal, 229
Association for the Advancement of Physical Education, 128
Atatürk, Kemal, 225
Atget, Eugene, 262
Atkins, Anna, 261
Awards for Virtue (Argentina), 49–50, *see also* Virtue Ceremony (Argentina)
Azade, 242

Baer, Ulrich, 141, 144
Bailey, Ben, 119
Baker, Lee, 123
Baker, Patricia, 227
The Bantu-speaking Tribes of South Africa (Schapera), 82–3
Barnett, Samuel, 200
Barthes, Roland, 8, 91, 106, 144, 154, 259
Beard, Charles, 129
Bederman, Gail, 119

Beecher, Henry Ward, 129
Behne, Adolf, 320
Beneficent Society (Argentina), 4; activities of, 51–2; creation of, 49–50; maternalist virtues, 52, 62–3, 70; relationship with state, 50–1, 60–1
Benjamin, Walter, 6, 262
Bergen-Belsen, 26–32, 37–9, 40
Berger, John, 106
Berger, Martin, 119
Berliner Illustrirte Zeitung, 311
Berri, Claude, 150
Bluestone, Daniel, 283
Boas, Franz, 124
Bohlmann, Rachel, 278
Bohlul, Sheikh Mohammed Taqi, 225
Böhme, Fritz, 315
Bordin, Ruth, 278
Boston Globe, 40
Bourdieu, Pierre, 212
Bourke-White, Margaret, 25
Bowdoin College (USA), 127
Brasillach, Robert, 142
Brassens, Georges, 150
Braun, Marta, 118
Braun, Martin, 110
Brinton, Daniel G., 123–4
Broca, Paul, 114
Brossat, Alain, 147, 154
Burgin, Victor, 90
Burnham, Daniel, 278, 292, 294
Burns, Sarah, 280
Butler, Judith, 313, 323

Cadmus, Paul, 257
Cameron, Julia Margaret, 207
Capa, Robert, 5, 148, 154, 157
Carnegie Commission of Investigation into Poor White Problem (1932), 93
Carp, Bernard, 164, 168–9, 178, 180, 181
Carse, Matilda Bradley, 278–83, 291–2, 302–3
Cartier-Bresson, Henri, 148
Chaix, Marie, 146
Chambre Claire (Barthes), 154

Charcot, Jean-Martin, 144, 145
Chicago Daily Tribune, 283
Chicago School, 283
Cline, Albert, 125
Clinton, Hillary Rodham, 6–7
College for Lady Gardeners (Glynde, Sussex), 201
colonialism, 12, 77–8, 83, 164, 166–8, 179–82, 221
concentration camps, 9; and attempts at normalisation, 28–9; background, 20–4; before-and-after photographs, 30–2; and dehumanisation of internees, 25–6; filmic evidence, 22–3, 24–41; gender dimension, 21, 22–3, 27–9, 31–2, 39–42; illness/mortality in, 27; liberation of, 23–4; perpetrators of, 21, 22, 23, 38–42; photographers attitudes toward freed inmates, 23, 24–32; and question of visuality, 42–3; reality of, 20; reference to Harrods in, 27–9, 32; representations of victims, 21, 23, 24, 32–8; scepticism concerning, 20; setting up of, 23; transportation to, 23
Connelly, Robert, 130
Connerton, Paul, 61
Copello, Monsignor Santiago Luis, 55
Cortesi, Nuncio Felipe, 55
Crane, Diana, 202
Crane, Walter, 283, 286, 295, 297
Crow, Thomas, 330
Cumming, Elizabeth, 203

Damman, Carl, 114
darshan, 6
Darwin, Charles, 122, 268
De Morgan, William, 199
Dean, Carolyn, 152
Death Mills (film), 38–9, 40
Degas, Edgar, 324–5
Delacroix, Eugène, 142
Delaney, Michelle, 109
Delius, Rudolf von, 322–3, 329
Dercum, Francis Xavier, 120–1, 129
Dermer, Rachelle A., 130

Desforges, Régine, 157
Deutschland Erwache, 38
Die Todesmühlen (film, 1946), 34–7, 40
documenting, 8–11
Dorrego de Unzué, Inés, 53
Duncan, Elizabeth, 310
Duncan, Isadora, 310
Dye, Mary, 296–7

Eakins, Thomas, 109, 119, 120
Edwards, Elizabeth, 106
Epler, Blanche, 110, 119
ethnography, 123–4
Ethnological Gallery of the Races of Men (Damman), 114
experimenting, 13–14

Faggots (Svenson), 5, 13; and AIDS crisis, 255–6; and ambiguity of identity, 260–1; as anti-homophobic, 257–8, 262, 267; archival aesthetic, 261–6; arrangement of models, 252; and art making/documentation, 261, 266; comparison with Kramer's faggots, 267–8; cultural climate/context of, 255–6; historical background, 256–7; and homosexual identity/desire, 258–60, 263; initial reception of, 257; meaning of title, 254, 267; as part of Modernist photographic continuum, 261; poster for, 268–9; and reverse discourse, 268–71; and sexual visibility, 262–4, 271; as sociological project, 264; text accompanying, 254–5, 268–9
Faries, Randolph, 125–6
Farshid, 237, 239
Fenton, Roger, 268
Field, Marshall, 281, 291
Fiesta de la Virtud see Virtue Ceremony (Argentina)
film, 8–9; and documentation of Nazi crimes, 24, 25–9, 32–41; and gender distinction, 33–5, 39–41; morality/decency in, 33–4; objectification in, 35–7; potency of, 32–3; and testimonial evidence, 37–8
Fleck, Egon, 26
Foucault, Michel, 258
Franke, Victor, 166
Freedberg, David, 2
Freud, Sigmund, 144, 146
Fride, Bernard, 156
Frietta, Monsignor José, 55
Fuller, Loïe, 312

Galton, Francis, 128, 129
Gellhorn, Martha, 26
gender, as cross-cultural issue, 6; and homosocial enjoyment, 181–2; and intrusiveness of the camera, 175–80; and male mobility, 185–7; maternal discourse, 52, 63, 65; movement/instability of, 313–14; performativity of, 309, 323; as political vehicle, 159; and racialising of male models, 113, 119–20, 121–2, 123, 124–30; role games, 63; and role of women, 185; visual dimension, 2–3, 4–5; and working-class models, 125
Georgi, Yvonne, 310
Ghogha (film), 244, 245
Giedion, Sigfried, 295
Gillmann, Charlotte Perkins, 130
Gliddon, George R., 116
Godalming Women's Suffrage Society, 201–2
The Golden City (MacMillan), 79–81, 84–5
Golzar, Mohammad Reza, 219
Grande histoire des Français sous l'Occupation (Amouroux), 151
Green, Lawrence, 169, 181
Greenberg, Clement, 330, 331
Grey, Earl, 209
Grier, Thomas, 126
Grossmann, Atina, 21
Gunning, Tom, 109

Habermas, Jürgen, 221
Hahn, C.H.L., 1650

Hall, Catherine, 208
Hall, Harry, 181
Harris, Alfred, 199
Hartmann, Georg, 166
Harvard, 127, 128
Hayden, Dolores, 301
Hayden, Sophia, 276
Healthy and Artistic Dress Union, 202
Hellmann, Ellen, 10, 75–106, *see also* African photographs (Hellman's)
Hewitt, Leah, 142
Higginson, Thomas Wentworth, 129
Himmler, Heinrich, 22
Hiroshima mon amour (film), 145, 150, 157
Hitchcock, Edward, 128
Hoffman, Donald, 292
Holm, Hanya, 310
Holocaust, 21, 42–3, 140, 141, 145, 146, 148, 156
Home Arts and Industries Association (HAIA), 196, 212
Home Arts Movement, 12, 196–7, 199–200, 205, 209, 212, 213, 214
Hooton, Ernest A., 114
Horowitz, Helen, 299
Hrdlička, Aleš, 114, 123, 124
Hunt, Nancy Rose, 7

image, history made by, 2; interaction with, 2; power of, 1–2
image-text relationship, 78, 79, 83–5, 102, 105–6
Industrial Chicago journal, 283, 294, 295, 296
Intercollegiate Athletic Sports Association (USA), 126
International Hygiene Exhibition (Dresden, 1911), 128
International Museum of Photography, George Eastman House (Rochester, New York), 110
Iran, body visibility in, 221, 223, 229, 230, 240, 242, 245–6; dress reform in, 245; dual image of, 227; establishment of *shari'a* in, 228–9, 242; fashion photography in, 219, 221, 231–3, 235, 237, 239–40, 242, 244–5; film in, 242, 244; gender issues in, 229; headscarf/veil-wearing in, 225–6, 228, 230; Islamic Revolution in, 226–30; and male dress, 224, 225, 228; meaning of modernity in, 229–30; modern body in, 223–6; modernisation/westernisation of, 224, 227, 245–6; moral dress in, 226–30; public/private dichotomy in, 221, 223, 240, 246; religious authority in, 224–5

Jacques-Dalcroze, Emile, 310
Jebb, Eglantyne, 196
Jekyll, Gertrude, 200–1, 202
Journal of the Ethnological Society, 115
Judges, E.A., 212
Justo, Agustin P., 59

Kaoko, 15; analysis of, 166; colonial photography in, 164, 166–8; expeditions to, 164, 168–9; and gender, 175–80, 182, 183–7; historiography of, 164–6; and the internal gaze, 180–3; leadership/administration of, 167–8; migrations from/to, 168; military intervention, 167; and Namibian history, 187–9; native representations, 167–8, 174–80; nature/landscape representations, 167–8, 170–4; photographer of, 168–9; and settler ambitions, 180; and tribal politics, 178–9; use, circulation, archiving of images from, 169–70; and white/colonial power relations, 179–82
Keddie, Nikki, 226
Khatami, President, 228
Khomeini, Ayatollah, 228
Kirchner, Ernst Ludwig, 14, 308, 309–10; and the *Dance of Death*, 326–9, 330, 331, 333; emphasis on flatness,

332–4; and individuality of dancers, 328; modernism of, 330, 331, 333–4; and nudity/sexuality, 326, 335–7; relationship with Wigman, 325–37; subject positioning of Wigman, 326–30, 335, 337; and utopian *Gemeinschaft*, 334
Kirkland, Joseph, 281, 290
Koch, Ilse, 42
Koenen, Eberhard von, 180, 183
Kramer, Joseph, 38, 39
Kramer, Larry, 267–8
Kuhn, Annette, 31
Kuntz, Julius, 166
Kushlis, Joseph, 33

La Bicyclette Bleue (film), 157
La Garçonne (Dean), 152
Laban, Rudolf von, 310, 315
Lamas, Carlos Saavedra, 55
Lamprey, J.H., 114–16
Lathrap, Mary Torrans, 278
Laya, 232–3
Le Garrec, Evelyne, 146
Le syndrôme de Vichy (Rousso), 145
Le Vieil homme et l'enfant (film), 150
Leidy, Joseph, 121, 122
Les Camps de la Mort (film), 37
Lethaby, W.R., 207, 210
Levi, Primo, 26
Levine, Sherrie, 268
Lewis, Tony, 159
Limnerslease (Compton, Surrey), 196, 199, 208
Lords of the Last Frontier (Green), 169
Loring Brace, C., 114
Lott, Eric, 120
Lotus fashion house (Iran), 233
Lotus fashion magazine, 233–5
Lutyens, Edward, 200

Macdonald, Margaret, 210
Macmaster, Neil, 159
MacMillan, Allister, 79, 81
Madeira, Percy C., 125

Magnum, 148
M'Ahesa, Sent, 312
Malherbe, E.G., 93, 95
Man of the Twentieth Century (Sander), 262, 264
Manning, Charles, 167
Manning, Susan, 313, 334
Manzi, Homero, 59
Mapplethorpe, Robert, 257
Margueritte, Victor, 152
Marshall, William, 114
Mary Wigman (Delius), 329
Masque of the Four Seasons (Crane), 283
Mdantsane township, 1
Mehran, 232
Meigs, J. Aitken, 123
Memory of the Camps (film), 35, 37–8, 39
Merwood, Joanna, 298
Meyer, James, 256
Meyer, Richard, 257, 258
Miller, Lee, 147
Mitchell, S. Weir, 129–30
Mitchell, W.J.T., 2, 3
Mohr, Jean, 106
Morolong, Daniel, 1, 15–16
Morris, William, 196
Morton, James, 210
Morton, Samuel, 113–14, 122, 123
Mountain Club (Cape Town), 169
Movietone News, 38, 39–40
Müller, Max, 208
Mulvey, Laura, 308
Mutate, Thomas, 184
Muybridge, Edweard, 6, 10–11, 13, 109, 110, 112, 118, 124, 125, 126, 130, *see also* University of Pennsylvania project
Mydans, Carl, 148

Najmabadi, Afsaneh, 245
Namibia, 164–5, 187–9, *see also* Kaoko
Nasser, 235, 237, 239–40
National Archives of Namibia, 169

National Museum of American History (NMAH), 109–10
National Union of Women's Suffrage Societies, 201
The Native Tribes of South West Africa (Vedder), 184
Nazi Concentration Camps (1945), 37
neurasthenia, 129–30
New Woman, 312
New York Athletic Club, 127
Newman, Kathleen, 60
Nietzsche, Friedrich, 295–6, 298
Nolde, Emil, 14, 308, 309–10; dance images, 317–18; and eroticism/primitivism link, 318; Expressionist style, 320; and Germanness, 320–3; imagery of, 316; and non-European cultural influences, 323–4; relationship with Wigman, 316–25; and the Third Reich, 320–1; use of colour/movement, 316–17, 324–5
Nott, J.C., 116

Omi, Michael, 113
On Photography (Sontag), 146
Ophuls, Marcel, 150
Orientalism, 223, 224, 230–1
Ousby, Ian, 151, 154
Ovahimba, 165

Palucca, Gret, 310, 324
Papon, Maurice, 140, 158
Parand, Shadi, 240
Parissa, 232
Pennell, Robert, 126–7
Pepper, William, 109, 121, 123
Perón, Juan Domingo, 50, 61
photography, 7; and ambiguity/slipperiness of visual language/signifiers, 106; colonial, 12, 166–8; and discrimination, 10; ethnographic, 79, 81–3; evidentiary/repressive nature of, 11; Iranian fashion, 219, 221, 231–3, 235, 237, 239–40, 242, 244–5; landscape, 171–4; and memory, 147; multiplicity of discourses in, 70; and myth of sexualised collaboration, 148–54; and photographer/subject interaction, 90–2; and physical anthropology, 114–16; and power relations, 116; in public space, 219; and race, 10–11; representational space, 62, 69; and respectability, 10; retribution, 151–2; social biographies of, 169–70; social/hierarchical placement of people in, 63, 65, 66, 68; and spatial organisation, 90; subject/photographer interaction, 175–80; taxonomic, 13; and value systems, 9–10; and victimhood, 145–6, 148; and viewer distance, 159
A Phrenologist among the Todas (Marshall), 114
Pollard, Miranda, 150
Pollock, Griselda, 14–15, 90
Posel, Deborah, 95
Potters' Arts Guild (Compton, Surrey), 197, 199, 200–1, 205, 209, 210, 211
power, 4
Premios a la Virtud see Awards for Virtue (Argentina)
Premios a la Virtud (play), 68–9
Price, Reynolds, 268
Prinsep, Sara, 207
Prinsep, Thoby, 207
Problems of Urban Bantu Youth (Hellmann), 93–4
public/private sphere, and absence of women, 221; Eurocentric definitions, 221, 223; Iranian dichotomy, 221, 223, 240, 246; and photography, 219

race, 4; and gendering of male models, 113, 119–20, 121–2, 123, 124–30
Races and Peoples (Brinton), 123–4
Ray, Man, 262
Regarding the Pain of Others (Sontag), 146
Regnault, Felix-Louis, 124
Regulations for Intercollegiate Athletic Sports (USA), 127

Reiss, Steven A., 129
Revolution under the Veil (Adelkhah), 228
Reza Shah, 4, 245
Reza Shah, Muhammad, 226, 227
Rezah Shah, 224–6
Rhodes, Cecil, 209
Ringelheim, Joan, 21
Rivadavia, Bernardino, 49, 55, 62
Roberts, Mary Louise, 152
Roberts, Russell, 261
Robinson, William, 201
Rodriguez Larreta, Carmen Maria del Pilar de, 52
Rony, Fatimah Tobing, 124, 141
Rooiyard: A Sociological Study of an Urban Native Slum Yard (Hellmann), 75–8, 82, 83–4, 89–93, 94, 97, 105
Roosevelt, Theodore, 129
Root, John Wellborn, 278, 291–4, 303
Rosas, Juan Manuel de, 50
Rose, Gillian, 62, 86, 90, 106
Roth, Heinz, 5, 164, 165, 166, 168–89, *see also* Kaoko
Rousso, Henry, 145–6
Royal Botanical Society, 201
Royal Horticultural Society, 201

Safro, 240
Said, Edward, 30
St Denis, Ruth, 312
Sander, August, 262, 264
Sargent, Dudley Allen, 127, 128
Sartre, Jean-Paul, 142
Sauerlandt, Max, 320
Schapera, Isaac, 83
Schlemmer, Oskar, 315
Schwartz, Margit, 30–2
Science journal, 124
Sekula, Allan, 112, 264–6
Serrano, Andres, 268
Seton Watts, Mary, 12; and building of craft workshop/living quarters, 199, 200; as designer of Watts Chapel, 196, 202–6; desire to translate rather than appropriate art, 211–12; effect of travel on, 207–8; and Hindu/Celtic symbolism, 207–11; influences on, 197–8; interest in women's suffrage, 201–2; and setting up of Potters' Arts Guild, 200–1; and training of local villagers, 199
Sex, Clarence, 205
Shahshahani, Soheila, 233
Skoronel, Vera, 310
Smith, Clara Sheldon, 261
Sock Monkeys (Svenson), 251, 261
Sokolowksi, Thomas, 269
Solomon-Godeau, Abigail, 113, 269–70
Somerset, Lady Henry, 282
Sontag, Susan, 36, 144, 146, 147
Spectral Evidence: The Photography of Tauma (Baer), 144
Spitzka, Edward Charles, 121
Spivak, Gayatri, 207
Stanford, Leland, 109
Stedman, Thomas, 205
Stonewall Riot, 256–7
Sugimoto, Hiroshi, 261, 268
Sullivan, Louis, 291
Supreme Headquarters, Allied Expeditionary Forces (SHAEF), 24, 30
Svenson, Arne, 13; aesthetics, 251; clinical technique, 251–2; comparison with Kramer, 267–8; data-collection mode, 251–2, 261–2; *Faggots* series, 252–71; and historical context/consequences, 266–7; taxonomic model, 251, 261–2, 264–5, 267, 271; and use of neutral standard of representation, 266; and use of reverse discourse, 258, 268–71
Szarkowski, John, 113

13 Most Wanted Men (Warhol), 257
Tagg, John, 112
Tanner, Peter, 25
Tarlo, Emma, 223
Tehran, 15
Temperance Temple *see* Woman's Christian Temperance Union Building (Chicago)

Tenenbaum, Edward, 26
Third Reich, 320–1
Tjongoha (aka Hinunu), 185
'To Hell with Slums' (pamphlet), 87–8
Tom, Vita, 167
tondues, 2, 5, 11; background, 139–43; and collaboration as passive/feminised compromise, 140, 142–3; exclusions from, 149; as fetishised objects, 151–2; and gender-equity of perpetrators, 156, 157–8; and head-shaving, 151, 152, 154; interviewing of, 147; and male punishment, 151, 152; moral aspects, 148; nature/status of, 139, 144; and politics of memory, 140–1, 147, 159; and post-war retribution, 147; and psychoanalytic theories of visuality, 144–6, 148; reproduction, contextualisation, captioning of, 139–40; sexualised nature of, 141–3, 148–54; stereotype of, 149–50, 151, 159; and *tontes* rituals, 156–7; and trauma visualised as silent woman, 143–8; and Vichy regime, 140, 141, 142; violence within, 147; and voyeurism/memory, 148, 154–8
Touvier, Paul, 140
trafficking, 11–13
Transvaal Museum, 169
Traquair, Phoebe, 210
Trey, Bernard, 166
Trümpy, Berthe, 311
Turnor, Christopher, 199

Union Signal journal, 281
United Nations Relief and Rehabilitation Administration (UNRRA), 27
University of Pennsylvania project, anthropometric grid, 113–20; background, 109, 113–16; complexity/scope, 109–10, 112, 130; historiography concerning, 112–13; racialising/gendering of male models, 113, 119–20, 121–2, 123, 124–30; scientists' interest in, 120–4

Uriburu, José F., 57, 59
US Farm Security Administration, 87

Van Brunt, Henry, 294
Van Leeuwen, Thomas A.P., 295
Van Warmelo, N.J., 82–3, 165, 166
Veblen, Thorstein, 283
Vedder, Heinrich, 166, 184
Vichy regime, 5, 11, 140–1, 142, 143, 144, 145–6, 156
Virgili, Fabrice, 146, 147, 149, 152, 156
Virtue Ceremony (Argentina), 9–10, 50; centrality of women in, 53; choice of lower-class women for prizes, 55, 57, 63, 70; and construction of virtuous bodies, 61–2; effect of socio-political changes on, 57, 59–61; importance of, 52; and ladies as mothers of the nation, 62–3, 70; location of, 53–4, 67; and marginality of prize winners, 63, 65; media coverage, 53, 66–7; and the modern woman, 65–6; play concerning, 68–9; and popular-sector women as virtuous women, 63, 65–7; public visibility of, 70; and representation of women, 59–60; ritual of, 61–2, 67, 69–70; and social role of women, 52; and uniting of rich/poor, 53; visitors/attendees of, 53–5
Virtuous Poor (Argentina), 15
visibility, 3–4, 11, 15
vision, 6–7
visuality, 4, 11, 42–3

Warhol, Andy, 257
Watts Chapel, 12; art/architecture relationship, 205; background, 196–8; and Celtic symbolism, 209–10; and female employment, 201; gendered nature of, 203; organic decoration of, 204; orientalism of, 208–9, 211; as ornamented dwelling, 202–6; and pottery/gesso workshops, 199; sacred/secular merging in, 205;

synthesis of cultures in, 208–11; textile references in, 203–4; tourist-viewer aspects, 211–14; and uniting of buildings, gardens, local landscape, 200–1

Watts, G.F., 199, 207

Weimar Republic, 14, 308, 311–12, 320

Welt im Film: KZ, 40

Welt im Film 34 No.5, 34

Western Civilization and the Natives of South Africa (Schapera), 83

Whitechapel (London), 200

Wigman, Mary, 5, 14; choreographic style, 313–15; and *Dance of Death*, 326–8, 333–4; as emancipated woman, 311–13; emotionalism/forcefulness of dance, 314–15; and the gaze, 313–14, 334; and gender dentity, 313–14; and Germanness, 320, 322–3; influence on artists, 309–10; and Kirchner, 325–37; as modern dancer/teacher, 3101–11; and modernist arrangement of dance forms, 313, 315–16, 330; and Nolde, 316–25; and non-European cultural influences, 323–4; spirituality of, 329; as subject, 310–16, 329–30, 337; and subject/object binary, 308–10; and the Third Reich, 320–1, 322, 323; and utopian *Gemeinschaft*, 334

Wildlife Protection Association, 169

Willard, Frances, 275, 279, 291, 300–1, 303

Willis, Carol, 288, 299

Winant, Howard, 113

Windhoek Scientific Society, 169

Wolseley, Frances, 201

Woman's Building (Columbian Exposition Chicago, 1893), 276

Woman's Christian Temperance Union Building (Chicago), 14, 275; administrative collapse of, 303; and claim to beauty, 295–6; as commercial project, 302; compared with Masonic Temple, 297–8; design of, 276–7, 278, 291–2, 294–5; destruction of, 277, 304; and domestication of business, 302–3; economic position, 278–9, 280–1; feminine association, 291; and gendered segregation of urban space, 280; hive analogy, 282–3; interior architecture, 2868; letting of, 283–4; motivation for, 278; and new era of women's work, 300–1; Purity/Temperance personification, 284–6, 296; and religious values, 282; and rhetoric of light, 2868; support for, 279, 281–2; as threat to social order, 290

Woman's Land Syndicate, 283

Woman's Temperance Building Association (WTBA), 278, 281

Women's Christian Temperance Union (WCTU), 275, 302–3

Women's Civil Rights, Law on (1924, Argentina), 59–60

women's social movements, 51

Women's Temperance Movement, 14

Woods, Dennis, 169, 181

The Word in the Pattern (Seton Watts), 203, 205, 211

World War Two, 5, 139–41, 147, 148, 168, 320

World's Columbian Exposition (Chicago, 1893), 276, 300, 301–2

Yale, 127–8

Yeğenoğlu, Mayda, 230

Young Men's Christian Association (YMCA), 280

Zamani, Mrs Mahla, 233, 235, 237, 239

Zealy, Joseph T., 114